The Complete World of Soccer

THE COMPLETE WORLD OF SOCCER

by Joe Marcus

Ward Ritchie Press
Pasadena, California

A book of this magnitude can never be written without the help of many people. Among those I especially want to thank are Professor Julio Mazzei, Pelé's personal trainer and adviser; Gerry Beatty, himself a walking encyclopedia of soccer: Phil Fox, a long-time referee and a devoted soccer follower and, of course, all the great and not-so-great players of the past who gave their all to make soccer the world's most popular sport.

Picture Credits:
Author/*New York Post* 5, 6, 7, 8, 11, 12, 13, 17, 19, 20, 37, 40;
Julian Baum 2, 3, 4, 9, 10, 14, 16, 38;
Los Angeles Aztecs 18;
James Ruebsamen 21, 22, 23, 24, 25, 26, 27, 28, 29, 30, 31, 32, 33, 34, 35, 36, 39;
Dirk Young 1, 15

Cover photo by Julian Baum

Special thanks to the Los Angeles Aztecs
organization for their help in obtaining photographs
for this book.

First edition

Library of Congress Catalog Card Number: 77-76598
ISBN: 0-378-04066-9

PRINTED IN THE UNITED STATES OF AMERICA

Dedicated to my dear parents, who got me started in the world's most popular sport.

Contents

Preface

The game, or, as some say, the religion, of soccer is played by more athletes throughout the world than any other team sport. And although historians admit that they are unable to pin down its exact beginnings, it is a game that has been around for over a thousand years. Just where and when did the sport start? Who got Europe into the soccer arena, and who followed the growth of the game to South America, to the United States, to Africa, Asia, and the Caribbean?

I undertook this book with the idea of covering the game from *A* to *Z*, and that meant looking at soccer from many different angles. Unless a fan understands the rules of the game, for example, which with only slight variations are the same everywhere, he cannot share the enjoyment of the millions of soccer fans throughout the world. Consequently, in this book we will discuss the different requirements for a goalie, a fullback, a midfielder, a forward, and even the hectic duties of the referee. We will also explore team formations, from the early patterns to today's style of play.

There are many major tournaments in the soccer world that make baseball's World Series look insignificant by comparison, and we will look at some of the great soccer events such as the World Cup, the Copa America, the Olympic soccer competition, and the World Club Championship. We will look at the great soccer players — Pelé, Eusebio, Bobby Moore, Alfredo di Stefano, Sir Stanley Matthews, and Ferenc Puskas — and examine their achievements.

In my research I uncovered a number of facts about soccer that were so amazing that at first I did not believe that they were true. But as I continued my efforts to cover every aspect of the sport, I began to feel that there wasn't a person in the world who wouldn't be amazed at some of soccer's happenings. For example, after Brazil was defeated in the 1966 World Cup, the people of that nation were so disappointed that several committed suicide. That same year, England won the World Cup championship, and for the first time since World War II factories closed and there was a general 48-hour celebration. It is my hope that in reading this book, you too will be able to develop a real understanding of soccer — a sport that has no equal.

Foreword

I feel fortunate to be part of the great American Soccer Revolution. Playing the game now has certain rewards that never were evident before, and recognition is finally coming to Americans taking part in the world's greatest sport. To see Joe Marcus publish this book gives me a great feeling because when I started my high school soccer career I remember looking forward to Joe's reporting of top international games as well as small local games. Throughout his newspaper career, Joe has fought to see the game receive the coverage that it deserves. Sure, now we are playing in large stadiums before thousands of fans, but it wasn't that long ago that a crowd of 1,000 fans was considered large, and in bad weather the players sometimes even outnumbered the fans. But no matter where the game was being played and how many fans were on hand, one could count on seeing Joe, be they high school, college, amateur, or semiprofessional games, or matches involving American youngsters, like me, just starting out in the sport.

Joe Marcus has devoted much of his time to soccer. He was a player as soon as he could walk. He coached many teams, including the powerful North Shore Midgets on Long Island, where he doubled as the club's president. He was selected as the manager of the United States team that competed in the 1973 Maccabiah Games in Israel. In 15 years, Joe never missed covering an international game in the New York area, and his reports went deeply into detail about how the game was won or lost.

Joe has a deep feeling about the Americanization of soccer, and although many of his fellow reporters and columnists said that it couldn't be done, Joe fought hard to see the idea finally become a reality. The research he undertook in compiling this book is an outstanding example of his devotion to the game — almost matching the amount of time he puts into coaching. In a few years his son Arthur will be making a determined bid to win a goalie position with one of the big teams in this country, and if he is anything like his father, there is no doubt in my mind that one day I might well have the honor of turning over my spot to him.

In the middle of the 1976 season, I went to Joe's house, and I couldn't believe the files he had put together or the subjects covered in this book. I told him that I felt he was undertaking something too big, but he replied, "America has long needed a book of this magnitude, and if I can't do it so that it benefits everyone in soccer, then it's not worth the effort."

As I left his house I thought to myself, "This country needs more men so dedicated to the sport."

When the United States Soccer Federation gets around to honoring newspapermen by admitting them to the Soccer Hall of Fame, I will consider it a great honor to nominate for induction Joe Marcus.

Shep Messing

The Complete World of Soccer

I. History, Developments, and Championships

CHAPTER 1

When and Where

When, where and how did soccer, or association football as it is called in most of the world, originate and eventually become the world's most popular sport? If you ask that question about other major sports like baseball, basketball, and hockey, you will have little trouble getting an accurate answer. But ascertaining the true beginnings of the game that is played in more nations than the United Nations has members, has defied experts from many nations.

The *Federation Internationale de Football Association* (FIFA), soccer's worldwide governing body, has spent a great deal of time and money researching the development of the game. Over the past 30 years, it has set up various committees, examined numerous drawings, examined findings from archaeological projects, and read countless reports from people claiming to have discovered where the game actually began. Yet FIFA still has seen no concrete evidence that establishes without a doubt where the game was first played. Most of the national associations have also undertaken projects to try to discover the beginnings of the sport, and whenever they find new evidence, they pass it on to FIFA with the hope that the new information will help solve the puzzle.

HISTORY OF SOCCER

Some historians claim that a very simple form of soccer was played in the days of the cavemen. After defeating an enemy, proponents of this theory suggest, the victors would cut off his head and take turns kicking the head around the caves. Although to many this might seem plausible, there is absolutely no evidence to back it up, and we must eliminate it as a possibility.

There are reports that in China, during the Han Dynasty some 2,200 years ago, the game of soccer was played by the Chinese warriors and was called Tsu Chu, which means kick-ball. All the warriors, it is said, were required to engage in the sport to maintain physical fitness. There are only very sketchy reports to back up the claim, however, and it has never been clear what type of ball was used or what the rules of the game actually were.

Another possible source of soccer is Japan, where a sport called Kemari was played between 75 and 100 A.D. After examining some of the claims, however, here too, FIFA was unable to verify that the game was anything more than another form of the game played in China during the Han Dynasty, although it might have been altered in the 250 years that had elapsed.

Indochina's claim to having invented soccer has been accepted by many but almost completely discounted by those who have spent years futilely trying to establish its authentic beginnings. First of all, as the game was reported in Indochina, it was not a sport but a funerary rite for a dead chieftain. The "ball" was actually a sacrificial bull's head and was kicked over the dead chieftain's body as a tribute to him, by a person who had been selected in advance.

Historians have also turned their attention to Italy and claims that the Roman sport Harpastum was really the start of soccer in A.D. 200. The game was reported to resemble modern soccer in a number of ways. For example, the ball was advanced by kicking only and if a player touched the ball with his hands, his team would lose control of the ball and the nonviolating team would get the next kick. It was also necessary for the ball to cross a goal line for a team to score, and some reports have mentioned that the score counted only if the ball passed over a certain portion of the goal line. Although FIFA has never put its stamp of approval on the claim that soccer originated in Rome, the powerful Italian Football Association has carried the theory a step further, claiming that the Romans not only started the game but were responsible for bringing soccer to Britain. Supposedly, in A.D. 200 the town of Chester, which was founded by the Romans, hosted the first soccer game ever played in England. The belief that Chester is where soccer was first introduced into England is so strong that on every Shrove Tuesday a soccer game is played there, as well as in Derby, a town that also was founded by the Romans.

Little is known about the game's development, until the 12th century, when Henry II imposed a ban on the game because he was worried that the growth of the sport was interfering with archery practice. The ban was not officially lifted until 1605, by James I. From the 14th century come reports about an Oxford student who was killed by Irish students in a soccer game played on High Street. English researchers have uncovered reports that people were so eager to play the sport regardless of weather conditions that one of the most popular soccer fields became the River Trent when it was frozen. In 1638 eight men attempting to play a winter match on the frozen river were drowned when the ice collapsed. The same researchers have pointed out that Oliver Cromwell was a football player while at Cambridge and that the children of some of the leading dignitaries of the time engaged in the sport.

Over the next 200 years, soccer became the most popular game in universities and in public schools. Leagues were established among the different universities, and in 1848 representatives of several universities met at Trinity College in Cambridge and established in writing the first formal set of rules governing the sport. These rules were, however, ignored by other universities and by the private clubs that were emerging, because there was a split between those who felt that no players except the goalie should use their hands and others who favored what today is known as rugby. In 1862 a meeting was called between the two factions, and a futile attempt was made to resolve the problem. Several meetings were held, but it became evident that no solution would be reached. A special meeting was called the following year, and those who felt that players should not use their hands formed the Football Association (FA), officially separating themselves from the clubs that eventually organized the Rugby Association. Even though there were parties on both sides of the fence who felt that in time the differences could be ironed out, most backers of the Football Association were determined to exclude any player who was not willing to comply fully with the rules the soccer-oriented members had set down. Almost immediately the members of the Football Association found that the vast majority of clubs in Great Britain were solidly behind them. Eleven club representatives, including several from Scotland and Wales, signed the final agreement, and with the official formation of the association came an immediate drafting of rules for the "regulation of the game of football."

Seven years after the formation of the Football Association, an international match was arranged between England and Scotland. No official title was given to the match, and the result was recorded as a deadlock, with no winner ever determined. The next year the celebrated FA Cup was begun. Now, instead of being limited to only a few clubs or teams, organized competition was open to every member team in Great Britain. Later, however, when the Welsh, Irish, and Scottish associations became strong enough to run their own cup tournaments, only clubs in England proper were allowed to compete for the FA championship. The honor of being the first team to win the cup went to the Wanderers, who defeated the Royal Engineers with a score of 7-0 on a goal by M. P. Betts.

Although there was no official English Football League until 1888, the clubs that had agreed to the terms that the Football Association had set down in 1863 held round-robin competition among themselves. The year after the FA Cup was started, the first official England–Scotland game took place. The match was played at the West of Scotland Cricket Ground in Patrick, and the final score was 0-0. The popularity of the England–Scotland full international test prompted Wales to field a full international squad, which played its first game in 1876 in Glasgow against Scotland. When the game was over, Scotland had won, 4-0. It was six more years before the Irish felt ready for international competition. Unfortunately, after only a few minutes of their first game, held in Belfast, they realized that they still had a long way to go. They lost the match, 13-0.

As international soccer matches started to become popular, several crucial improvements in the game and its equipment also took place. In 1874 Sam Widdowson of Nottingham Forest introduced and registered the first pair of shinguards worn in competition. The following year a regular crossbar of wood was used to join the two goalposts together, replacing the tape on top of the posts, which up till then had served that function. Three years later, in 1878, the referees were given whistles. Now, they no longer had to scream at the top of their lungs when they wanted to stop a play or charge a foul. J. A. Brodie of Liverpool is credited with having invented the first set of goalnets in 1890, thus ending countless arguments from players about whether shots were placed through the goal area legitimately. Until 1876 there was no record of a professional player, but in that year Scotsman J.J. Lang joined the Sheffield Wednesday team and admitted that he was to receive money for playing. Many say that this event changed the gentlemanly nature of the game that had existed up till then. Soon many players began to ask their clubs to pay them. Two years later, in 1878, the first night soccer game was played. Floodlights were utilized at the grounds in Sheffield as two local clubs played a special challenge match. So uncertain were officials of both clubs about the outcome of the game that they agreed the match would not be recorded as an official game, but it was the beginning of the numerous exhibition floodlight games played in many areas in England and Scotland. The controversy continues today, however. Many fans and players around the world still say that soccer should be played only in daylight. It appears, however, that they are waging a losing battle because night games generally draw larger crowds.

The first English Football Association Cup was held during the 1871-72 season and 15 clubs entered, but at the last minute two teams decided to scratch themselves from the competition. In 1874 the first Scottish Cup championship was held, with Queen's Park defeating Clydesdale by a score of 2-0 to win the championship. Four years later the first Welsh Cup was held, and Wrexham edged past the Druids, 1-0, to win the crown. It wasn't until 1881, however, that the first Irish Cup was contested, and the winner of that match was Moyola Park, which defeated Cliftonville with a score of 7-0 to capture the title.

It was a long time before the English, Irish, Scots, and Welsh national associations were joined by other formal national organizations. The first new member to join the quartet was Denmark, which formed its own national association in 1889—six years before Belgium and Switzerland, home of FIFA, decided to go along with the idea. In 1900 Malta formed an official national organization, while powerful Hungary joined a year later. After the turn of the century, more national organizations were set up. Italy's was organized in 1905, Czechoslovakia's in 1906, Finland's in 1908, and Holland's in 1904. Germany had a national association by 1904 but after World War II, when the country was divided, the West Germans didn't form their own association until 1950. Two years later the East Germans followed suit.

FIFA

By the turn of the century it also became evident that international soccer needed a ruling body. Led by Chile, several organizations in South America had already held meetings to organize the base of international football in South America, but an international meeting was called in 1904 and FIFA was formed. Every national association was invited to join, and although some associations balked at having to relinquish their power to a higher body, the various national associations soon began to fall into line. Four years later FIFA was so powerful that the International Olympic Committee (IOC) had to consult it about running the 1908 Olympic soccer program. The competition was supervised by a full staff from the FIFA office, and FIFA carefully scrutinized the eligibility of all players involved in the championship game, in addition to appointing the game officials. Great Britain defeated Denmark, 2-0, for the championship. Holland, which had joined FIFA in 1904, defeated Sweden, 2-1, in the battle for the bronze medal. The IOC had little to do with the soccer phase of the Olympic Games and although there were many who complained

5

about it, this arrangement was adopted and has been followed in all the Olympic Games since. To this day, if FIFA is not satisfied with the plans for conducting the Olympic Soccer competition, it can withhold permission for the competing nations to participate until the International Olympic Committee changes the format.

FIFA is without a doubt the strongest worldwide ruling body in sports. Until 1930, when the World Cup was first established, it was kept busy arranging international matches and mediating disputes between factions in various national federations. Even today, when a national association is unable to solve a problem and a lawsuit seems imminent, FIFA will step in and make a final judgment. Its large staff of lawyers and office workers keeps a detailed list of all national officials and also keeps track of suspended players. FIFA prohibits a suspended player or a club banned from playing in its own nation from playing in another nation. Likewise, other clubs in the world are banned from playing against members of a suspended league and from signing players who are no longer in the good graces of their own national association and of FIFA. Failure to comply with a suspension notice can cause FIFA to suspend the offending team itself. Player suspensions have been argued in the courts, and FIFA regulations can create situations like that in 1967 when there were two major soccer leagues in the United States and Canada.

With rare exception FIFA is also responsible for all the rules of the game. If a FIFA member wants to play with a variation in the rules, it must first apply to FIFA, as the North American Soccer League did in 1972, when it adopted the controversial offside rule and its system for determining point totals for standings (see chapters 4 and 25).

FIFA's offside rule has caused more disputes and protests than any other regulation. Because the rules adopted in 1866 had stipulated that a player be considered offside* if he received the ball in the other team's half of the field and did not have at least three opponents between himself and the goal, when it was established, FIFA went along with that accepted rule. The English seemed content, as did the Scots, Welsh, and Irish. However, from its inception FIFA had been besieged by requests from other nations—among them Holland, Sweden, and Chile—to change the rule.

FIFA was not ready at first to make the change but discussed changing the rule in a meeting with English delegates. When the English steadfastly refused to even experiment with a new rule, FIFA an-

---

*When an offside violation is made, the rules call for a player of the opposing team to take an indirect free kick from the place where the infringement occurred. Players making offside violations are not penalized unless the referee feels that they are interfering with the play or are trying to gain an unfair advantage.

nounced that as far as it was concerned, the rule stood as it was and that no national association should even experiment with changing it. When English teams began to experience slow games, smaller crowds, and more stoppages in play, however, the English Football Association went to FIFA and asked for and received permission to try a new offside rule in which a player would be considered to be offside if he had fewer than two opponents between himself and the opposing goal at the time he received the ball. FIFA sent a large delegation of officials, its entire rules committee, and invited representatives from several member nations to watch the experiment in action. It cautioned, however, that it expected the regular rules to be enforced everywhere else until it made a final judgment on the new rule. The English Football Association set a time and date for a test game to try the new rule. The experimental game was an exhibition match between a team of professionals and a squad of amateurs at Arsenal Stadium in London. The game was played in two parts, the first half contested under the old three-man offside rule and the second half played under the new two-man offside regulations. In an effort to appease the traditionalists, who were dead set against the new rule in the three-man offside phase of the game, the offside area was extended from the other team's penalty area to the midfield strip. It is amazing that the new offside rule was approved after only 45 minutes—half a game.

On June 15, 1925, the new rule was adopted by the English Football Association, and two months later FIFA accepted it as the international offside rule. That season there was an almost overnight change from low-scoring games to games with scores that resembled those of American football. For example, on the first match day after the English Football Association approved the change, Aston Villa defeated Burnley, 10-0, and Tottenham Hotspur scored five goals (something it had been unable to do in its previous three games), winding up in a 5-5 deadlock with Huddersfield, which also came up with five goals.

Almost immediately, many writers were openly critical of the change. They complained that the game had lost its finesse and that scoring a goal, once considered a work of art requiring completely balanced teamwork, had lost its meaning. The Football League totals for the first season under the new rule showed that the goal production total had jumped dramatically. FIFA kept close records of scores around the world, and found the same increase in goal scoring evident worldwide. Had this one change completely revolutionized the game? Those in FIFA who supported the rule change predicted that the defense would quickly adapt to the new rule, which so obviously favored the forwards. It took only a short time for them to be proven right, as the offside trap, in which the fullbacks walk meekly upfield while the opposing team is attacking, became a tactical maneuver of every top club. The man many consider responsible for the development of the offside trap, Irish star William McCracken, also devised the third-man-back system of play. In this strategy, the two fullbacks are joined by the center halfback, who becomes known as the sweeper, the man who wanders behind the fullbacks, responsible for covering the loose or free man on the attack. The sweeper back was quickly adopted by clubs around the world, and the scores started to drop drastically. A poll of fans attending games in England was taken by a leading newspaper, and the great majority of those questioned said that they felt the two-man offside rule was an improvement.

So FIFA had survived its biggest rules test to the date. But almost immediately, in the late 1920s and early 1930s, other problems started to arise, the biggest one concerning regulation of the size of the field. FIFA quickly ruled that it was up to the national associations to set up and maintain a minimum and maximum distance and that it would not interfere. Consequently, even today one can find fields of vastly different dimensions. FIFA did, however, set up a committee to examine the area of a field for international matches, a phase of the game that it alone controls.

Once again the English Football Association was called in for consultation and after a two-day meeting, FIFA sent out a mandate to all its member associations, saying that from then on all international matches had to be played on a field measuring between 110 and 120 yards in length and between 70 and 80 yards in width. Unless previous approval was obtained from FIFA, failure to comply with these standards could nullify the outcome of a match and cause the violating promoters or national associations to pay a fine and face possible suspension. The outcry was great, as many stadiums around the world were found not to measure up to this standard. In England, for example, there were stadiums with fields limited to 100 yards in length, and these had been the scene of international matches for several years. FIFA turned a deaf ear to the pleas of those who wanted special permission, and there was much bitterness between members of the English Football Association and FIFA, but the uproar died down, and construction on several new stadiums was instituted instead.

CHAPTER 2

European Growth

With the creation of FIFA, the world's soccer attention focused on Europe. Although associations in various European nations weren't formed until well after the formation of FIFA, league play* was commonplace in many of the nations.

The organizing of FIFA also ended some of the disagreements among nations concerning the arrangement of international games and assigning game officials. Before FIFA there was no governing body to regulate the assignment of referees, and often a team visiting a foreign land would leave convinced that it had been cheated by a call made by a local official who naturally favored the home team in most cases. FIFA ruled that in all international matches, unless both nations involved in the game agreed otherwise, a referee from a neutral country would officiate the match. FIFA supplied a list of sanctioned referees, and if the countries couldn't agree on an official, they were required to ask FIFA to make the selection for them.

EARLY INTERCONTINENTAL COMPETITION

Although England boycotted the first three World Cups, held in 1930, 1934, and 1938, between 1900 and 1975 it participated in more inter-

*In most nations there are two distinct competitions. One is league plays in which clubs belonging to a specific league play set games against each other. Two points are awarded for a win, one for a tie, and none for a loss, and the team with the most points at the end of the season wins the league championship. In Cup competition, teams from all the leagues can enter. Matchups are determined by chance, and a team is eliminated after one defeat.

national matches than any other nation. Because of the difficulty of travel between nations, however, especially between Europe and South America, most of the English international games before World War II were held against other European nations. Scotland, Wales, and Northern Ireland also took part in many full international games. Other nations, like Austria, Hungary, and Denmark, also started to schedule international matches, prompting players throughout Europe to seek an International Cap, which is an honor given to a player named to play for his nation in a full international game.*

England

After competing for 30 years in international matches only against teams like Wales, Scotland, and Ireland, England ventured into its first international soccer test in 1908 in Vienna against Austria, which was regarded by many at the time as second only to England. The English demolished the Austrians in that first game, 6-1, with team member Windridge and substitute Hilsdon each scoring two goals to lead the assault. A rematch was arranged because the Austrians felt that they would do better. They proved wrong; the English tore them apart again, 11-1, as Woodward made four goals and Bradshaw added three more. Two days later the English found themselves in Budapest to match skills against the Hungarian National Team. With Hilsdon scoring four goals, they recorded an easy 7-0 victory. They wound up their four-game tour in Prague, facing the Bohemian National Team and won, 4-0, with Hilsdon scoring twice and Windridge and Rutherford each adding single tallies.

The following year they played their regular matches against Scotland, Wales, and Ireland and played three matches in four days, two against Hungary and one against Austria. They defeated the Hungarians, 4-2 and 8-2, and ripped the Austrians, 8-1. It was 12 years before an English National Team again ventured into the international arena in a match against a team from outside Great Britain, but in 1921 in Brussels the English defeated Belgium, 2-0. The following year they met Belgium on their home ground at Arsenal and won an easy 6-1 victory. That same year they also played a match against France and won, 4-1, and a 4-2 victory over Sweden in Stockholm was followed two days later by another victory against the same team, this time by a 3-1 score as Moore scored twice. But the English received their first major shock in international play as Belgium tied them, 2-2, in Antwerp in 1923. England remained unbeaten in

---

*In a full international match, all international rules are observed, while in a friendly international match, rules concerning time out, substitutions, etc. can be arranged.

matches with teams from outside Great Britain until meeting Spain in 1929 in Madrid and coming home a 4–3 loser. Two years later the English got their chance for revenge, however, and beat the Spanish, 7–1, at Arsenal as Smith, Johnson, and Crooks each scored twice.

England has faced 46 nations in international competition, including, of course, matches in such prestigious tournaments as the European Nations Cup and the World Cup, which England first competed for in 1950.

Although it had fielded a full international team since 1872 to compete against Ireland, England, and Wales, it wasn't until 1929 that Scotland played against a team from outside Great Britain. But on June 1 of that year, the Scottish team met the German team in Berlin and came away with a 1–1 tie, considered a fine showing at the time. Three days later the Scots were in Amsterdam for a match against Holland, and goals by Fleming and Rankin carried them to a 2–0 victory, as goalie McClaren was credited with 12 saves.

Wales
Wales' first international squad took the field in 1876 and lost, 4–0, to Scotland, and until 1933 it played international games only against the Scots, English, and Irish. But on May 25, 1933, in Paris, the Welsh went up against a high-ranked French team and drew a 1–1 score as Griffiths scored for them. But it was six years before they again played a team from outside Great Britain in another international game and again the opponent was France. The game was played on May 20 in Paris and Wales lost, 2–1.

Northern Ireland
Northern Ireland, which was separated from the Republic of Ireland, was the Irish representative after the break in the annual Home International Championship between 1939 and 1946 because of World War II. When one examines the history of Irish soccer, it's interesting to note that it was not until Northern Ireland took the field in Lisbon on January 15, 1957, that the Irish ever faced a club from outside Great Britain in international soccer. The game ended up a 1–1 tie, with Bingham scoring the lone goal for the Irish.

BRITISH HOME INTERNATIONAL CHAMPIONSHIPS

Because they lacked a full schedule of international contests, the four teams from Great Britain—England, Wales, Scotland, and Ireland, which eventually played under the name of Northern Ireland—created the annual Home Championship. From the time it was established in 1883, the English have been the dominant force in the four-nation tournament. As of 1976, England had won the championship 30 times and shared the title 20 times; Scotland, which defeated England, 2-1, in 1976, had won the title 23 times and shared the crown 17 times; Wales had taken the crown seven times and shared the championship five times; and the Irish had won the crown only once but shared it five times.

In 1976 England had a chance to even its all-time record against Scotland, but after losing, 2-1, the team found itself with 35 wins as opposed to 37 defeats and 22 ties. As of 1976, England had come up against Wales 88 times and had posted 58 wins, 11 defeats, and 19 ties. Against Ireland, the English had won 64 times, with six defeats and 13 ties. In 89 games, through the 1976 Home International Championship, Scotland had defeated Wales 54 times, with 15 defeats and 20 deadlocks. The Scots had beaten the Irish 57 times, losing only 13 and tying 11 other games. In matches with Ireland, Wales had recorded 39 wins, 26 defeats, and 18 draws.

European soccer competition has been influenced by fads, and the country or club that comes up with a unique formation is the one who usually can dominate the scene. It is unfair and misleading about what makes one national game more interesting than another, but each country has a distinctive style of playing. England and Germany probably were among the most successful teams over the past 30 years, because they utilized a third back once the offside pattern rule was changed from the original three-man rule to the two-man rule. For years the English have used the long ball down the wing on attack and the bump-and-run on defense; and the Polish team of the postwar years was the most disciplined, with every man fitting into the total plan of short passes and feedback plays. The Hungarians and the Austrians have focused their game around the center half, while the Soviets are a fast-striking team when the opportunity presents itself. After being eliminated from the 1974 World Cup competition, the Italians, once noted for their boring style of defensive soccer called *catenaccio,* in which as many as six players were on defense, changed to a formation resembling a 4-3-3 (see chapter 20) but retained the option of using a fifth defender if needed. The revolutionary change in total play took place with the Dutch, who almost won the 1974 World Cup. The men from the Netherlands utilized what is called total football—for offense they had 10 men on the attack; when they fell back on defense, all 10 field players joined the goalie.

Each country takes its best players and tries to build its national team around them. Except for Spain and Portugal, the style of soccer in Europe features long kicks with minimal passing and dribbling. English teams build up the attack rapidly, while Dutch teams move slowly until the opportunity presents itself for a breakaway attack. In Greece and Turkey, the defenders are sometimes like hatchet men, preventing opposing forwards from scoring in any manner they can, but when the style works and the teams win, there are few complaints.

NATIONAL CUP TEAMS

With the international soccer scene in Europe limited to a few World Cup qualifying matches, several amateur Olympic Game trials, and a hit-or-miss international series between several nations, the pre-World War II scene was dominated by club competition in every European nation. Even before some of the nations had formal national associations of their own, leagues were contested on a full-schedule basis, and many of the nations also had cup competitions.

England

Except for the years during World War I and World War II, the English have yearly played a full-league schedule and a Football Association Cup, besides other competitions like a London Cup and a Northern County Cup. The first league title was decided in 1889, with Preston North East capturing the crown. In 1892 so many clubs were trying to get into the Football League that the league was broken into a First Division and a Second Division, and was further expanded during the 1958-59 campaign into a Third and a Fourth Division.

Promotion and demotion have always been a regular feature of league competition. At the end of each season, the three lowest finishers in the First Division are relegated to the Second Division and are replaced by the highest three finishers in the Second Division. The three lowest clubs in the Second Division are dropped into the Third Division, and the Third Division's top three are moved up to the Second Division. The top four finishers in the Fourth Division advance to the Third Division and the lowest three or four teams in the Fourth Division are placed out of the Football League unless they are voted to remain. There are only a few cases in history, however, where a club finishing low in the Fourth Division has not been allowed to stay.

When it captured the 1975-76 First Division title, Liverpool surpassed the records of all other clubs in winning the prestigious top-league prize. Its victory gave the team nine First Division titles as opposed to the eight of Arsenal, Liverpool's closest competitor. The Football Association Cup, which is open to every league team regardless of which division it plays in, has been contested since the 1871-72 season. Throughout the years, Aston Villa has led the pack, with seven championships.

In 1960 the Football League voted to establish its own Football League Cup. Although many teams have refused to take part in the drawn-out competition, the play has often been exciting. Since the championship is decided before the league season ends and before the FA Cup is decided, many teams have complained that there are too many distractions for the competition to be really worthwhile. Aston Villa won the first League Cup over Rotherdham on a two-game aggregate score of 3-2. The competition remained a two-game, total goal series, in which the combined scores of the teams from two matches determine the winner, until it was changed during the 1966-67 campaign to a single championship game with overtime in the event of a deadlock. In the history of the competition, only Aston Villa has been able to capture the title twice, although many other prestigious clubs in England have at one time won the title. But to most fans the Football League Cup runs a poor third behind the FA Cup and the regular league championship.

Scotland

Throughout the years, Scottish soccer has been dominated by two bitter Glasgow rivals—the Rangers and Celtic—and every time the two teams meet, there is certain to be plenty of action not only on the field but in the stands. The first Scottish League Championship started in 1890, and since its inception, the Rangers have won the title 34 times and shared it once while Celtic has captured it 29 times. Celtic holds a 25-21 advantage over the Rangers in the Scottish Football Association Cup, which was first played in 1874. Queen's Park won the Cup the first three times it was contested, and until the start of the 1921-22 campaign and the development of a Second Division, it was open strictly to First Division clubs. In 1945 the Scottish League Cup was established, and the Rangers won the title in 1976, drawing even with Celtic, each with eight crowns.

Linfield has long been the dominant force in Irish soccer. It has won the league's title 30 times as opposed to runner-up Glentoran's 16 championships. Linfield has also won the Irish Cup 31 times and the City Cup 14 times, surpassing all of its rivals.

Wales

The biggest competition in Wales is the annual battle for the Welsh Cup. Over the years it has been a nip-and-tuck battle between Cardiff City and Wrexham, with the latter winning the Cup 20 times as of 1975-76, once more than Cardiff City.

14

But Great Britain is not the only center of soccer activity; national associations exist throughout Europe, and sometimes before an association could even be formally inducted into FIFA, a particular nation would have had several years of league play under its belt. Before World War II, such competitions as the European Nations Cup, the Cup-Winners' Cup, and the Fairs Cup were just ideas. They were not implemented until the 1950s, and until they were, supporters of a club could not prove that their team was better than another. But with the rising number of competitions after World War II, it was possible to establish team rankings.

Austria
In Austria, where several teams have been successful at various times, the overall champion has to be the great Rapid Vienna team, which as of 1975, had won 25 league championships. But Rapid was also forced to share some of its glory with its arch rival FK Austria, which captured the Austrian Cup 14 times—six times more than Rapid was able to achieve the honor.

Belgium
The top club in Belgium has been Anderlecht, with 16 league championships since the league was first organized in 1896. But it is followed closely by Standard Liège, whose record of three Belgium Cup titles is only one short of the total accumulated by Anderlecht since that competition was started in 1954.

Bulgaria
Bulgarian soccer is regarded by many as one of the roughest games in Europe, with referees that allow almost anything to go unpunished. Since the league was first organized in 1925, CSKA Sofia, formerly known as CDNA, has won the league crown 17 times, besides dominating the Cup (begun in 1946) with 10 titles.

Czechoslovakia
Three clubs from Prague have taken turns dominating the Czechoslovakian soccer season. Although a national association was formed in Czechoslovakia as far back as 1906, formal league play was not held until 20 years later. During the time of nonleague play, most games were between teams of players who came down to the field and chose sides. Since the league was established, however, Sparta Prague has won the championship 13 times—once more than its arch enemy Slavia Prague—while Dukla Prague, previously known as UDA, has taken the crown eight times. In the mid-1950s, Dukla emerged as the

most powerful club, also competing in the United States in the now-defunct International Soccer League. One player, Rudy Kucera, was the mainstay of the Dukla team, but in one of the club's league games in Czechoslovakia, he attempted to head a ball and suffered a brain concussion, which forced him to retire from action at the age of 22. Dukla and Slovan Bratislava each have won the National Cup four times, making them the two most successful clubs in the competition.

Denmark

The Danish Soccer Federation was formed in 1889, 24 years before the beginning of league competition. Although soccer in Denmark is just starting to develop to where there are several full-time pros, the history of amateur soccer in Denmark is rich in tradition and success. Twice Denmark has captured the coveted silver medal in Olympic soccer competition, winning the medal in 1908 and retaining the honor four years later. While Danish teams have found it difficult to compete on an equal basis with the more developed pros from the rest of Europe, especially in World Cup and European Nations Cup elimination series, the amateur program has remained successful, as Denmark finished third in the 1960 Olympic Games. Through the efforts of officials from such clubs as KB Copenhagen and the national association president Vilhelm Skousen, however, the need for improvement in the professional ranks has been made clear to every club, and every fan has been asked to help support the professional drive in some way. In league competition the title has been won 15 times by KB Copenhagen while in Cup play, which started in 1955, the most successful team has been Aarhus FG, with five Cup crowns to its credit.

Finland

Despite constant appeals from several of its leading players, and from fans, Finland is one of the few nations in the world whose soccer program is totally amateur. None of the nation's 35,500 registered players in 1976 receives any money. If a player in Finland is sought by a professional club in another nation, the national association actually urges him to leave Finland rather than risk a scandal in which he could be accused of taking money under the table. Although Finnish competition is strictly for amateurs, there are, nonetheless, bitter battles fought between the various clubs on every match day, and fans come to the games with picnics, prepared to enjoy themselves. Since the league was officially formed in 1949, the two most successful clubs have been Turun Palloseura and Kuopion Palloseura, each with four league titles to its credit as of 1976. In Cup competition, which did not begin until 1955, Valkeakosken leads the title race with five championships.

France

France became a member of FIFA at the organization's charter meeting in 1904, even though a formal national federation was not organized until 1919. The two men credited with getting FIFA off the ground, however, Jules Rimet, the founder of the World Cup, and Henri Delaunay, for whom the European Nations Cup now is named, were responsible for keeping French soccer in tow even without an official title. Until 1918 no formal competition was held. A handful of registered clubs simply made their own schedule and played as they felt. But in 1918 the French Cup was started. Olympique Marseilles, with eight titles, tops the list in this competition. In league play since 1933, when the league was formally standardized, the top club has been St. Etienne, with eight championship trophies. In 1974 and 1975, St. Etienne was also able to pull off the coveted double — winning both the league and Cup crowns.

East Germany

If there is one man who deserves credit for the tremendous growth and success of East German soccer, it is George Buschner. Under his guidance, East German soccer emerged from obscurity to develop one of the strongest teams in Europe, if not the world. At the end of World War II, there were only about 5,000 players and 500 clubs. But by 1976, East Germany, whose formal national association was founded in only 1952, had over 480,000 players, 26,000 teams, and 4,800 clubs. East German performance in the 1974 World Cup was a personal triumph for Buschner, who coached the team. In the first meeting ever between the two Germanys, East Germany defeated West Germany, 1-0. Also in 1974, FC Magdeburg gave the East Germans their first major championship, when they won the 1974 Cup-Winners' Cup. In league play, which started in 1950, ASK Vorwaerts has won the title six times, topping that honors list, while Carl Zeiss Jena, previously known as Motor Jena, has won the Cup four times since it was instituted in 1949.

West Germany

West Germany formed its own national association in 1950, dissolving the single German Federation that had operated from 1904 to 1945, but its records include some teams now located in East Germany. There is no doubt, however, that the West Germans, who won the World Cup in 1974 — two years after they had captured the European Nations Cup — are among the strongest players in international soccer. In 1976 Bayern-Münich won its third consecutive European Cup, while Borussia Mönchengladbach has captured both the Cup-Winners' Cup and the Union European Football Association's (UEFA) championship title. In league championships, IFC Nuremberg is in first place, with nine titles as of 1976. Bayern-Münich is in second place, having won the Cup championship five times since 1935, when it was first instituted and included teams now playing in the East German Federation.

Greece

Some of the hottest soccer matches have occurred in Greece, where Olympiakos and Panathinaikos have been the dominant clubs. Since the league was started in 1928, Olympiakos has won the loop title 21 times, while Panathinaikos has 11 titles to its credit. In Cup competition, begun in 1932, Olympiakos has 16 championships, more than twice the number of its closest competitor, AEK Athens.

Hungary

Hungarian soccer, once regarded by many as among the best in Europe, declined after the Soviet takeover of the nation in the late 1950s. Many of its leading players were thwarted in their efforts to develop their game; many others away on tour at the time were able to defect. The Hungarian Football Association was founded in 1901, the same year that the first organized league play took place. Since the formation of the league, Ferencvaros, formerly known as FTC, and MTK-VM, a combination of the Hungaria Bastay and Voros Lobogo clubs, have been the most successful teams, with the former winning the loop title 22 times and the latter taking the crown 18 times. In recent years, however, the big two have been joined by Újpest Dozsa, which, beginning in 1970, swept five straight championships. In Cup competition, which began in 1910 but was not played on an annual basis, Ferencvaros again is first, with 12 wins. The association has stressed amateur play, and the Hungarians won the Olympic soccer competition in 1952, 1964, and 1968, placing second in 1972. On a professional level, there is no one currently who can even come close to matching such past great players as Ferenc Puskas and Sandor Koscis, who electrified Hungarian crowds whenever they played for the Hungarian National Team. These two players also won titles while playing abroad for other teams, but when they wore Hungary's uniform in the international arena, their skill on the field made all Hungary come alive.

Ireland (Eire)

In the Republic of Ireland, soccer takes a back seat to hurling and curling, but there has been some good competition over the years nonetheless. The first league championship was decided in 1922, and since then the Shamrock Rovers have been the most successful club, winning the loop crown 10 times as of 1976. The Shelbourne team, their closest competitor, has won the title seven times. In Irish Cup play, also started in 1922, the Shamrock Rovers have monopolized the field, winning the crown 20 times. Their closest competitor, Drumcondra, has won only five titles.

Italy

Italy is one of the real hotbeds of soccer. Every game there in the Major A Division could well be considered a war. Battles between teams from Milan, such as Inter-Milan and AC Milan, fill the stadiums, and when the two Roman representatives, Roma and Lazio, square off, past records mean nothing. The same is true for the games between Juventus and Torino, both from Turin. Seven years before the Italian National Federation was formally founded in 1905, league play was already in high gear. Although the Cup was started in 1922, play was suspended for a period of 26 years, but Italian soccer was the most respected game before World War II. After the war ended, Torino made its mark in international play by defeating many top European teams. After winning the postwar title between 1946 and 1948, Torino's entire team, including its great star Valentino Mazzola, was killed in a plane crash in 1949. All of Italy went into mourning, and the league voted to declare Torino the league champion that season because the team was ahead in the standings at the time of the crash. As of 1976, Juventus was the leading team, however, with 17 league titles and five Cup crowns.

In addition to winning the World Cup in 1934 and retaining the crown four years later, Italy captured the Olympic gold medal in 1936 and won the European Nations competition in 1968. AC Milan won the World Club championship in 1969, five years after its bitter enemy Inter-Milan took the same title. Over the past few years, however, Italian soccer's defensive tactics have started to fail them. Conflicts among various clubs have caused friction in selecting the Italian National Team. Since the team was eliminated from the 1976 European Nations Cup, however, a concentrated effort has been made to end these conflicts and start restoring Italy to its once-esteemed position.

The Netherlands

The Netherlands, which presented the game of total soccer to the world and finished second to West Germany in the finals of the 1974 World Cup, also has a rich soccer tradition. The Dutch Football Federation was founded in 1904, but league play has been a way of life for players since 1898, a year before the Cup competition got underway. The two most powerful and successful clubs have been Ajax of Amsterdam and Feyenoord, but their unwillingness to allow their players to play on the same team for years prevented the Dutch from having a truly representative national team. For the 1974 World Cup, however, the two clubs agreed to bury the hatchet, and the unexpected support they received from their fans was very encouraging to the leaders of the national team. In league competition Ajax has won the title 17 times, five times more than Feyenoord, and has also had the upper hand in Cup titles, with seven crowns to Feyenoord's five. Ajax won the World Club championship in 1972, two years after Feyenoord had done the same. Ajax swept the European Cup in 1971, 1972, and 1973, after Feyenoord won the same crown in 1970. Feyenoord was the 1974 winner of the UEFA Cup.

The biggest fear of Dutch fans, and of club officials, however, is that top players will desert to other countries, where they receive much more money. Johann Cruyff, voted the Most Valuable Player in the 1974 World Cup, went to Barcelona, while Real Madrid lured Johann Neeskens away. The blow of having top players leave is softened somewhat when men like Cruyff and Neeskens return for appearances with the Dutch national team. But until the clubs are able to provide the salaries that the top players and managers in the Netherlands feel they deserve, there appears no solution to the desertion problem.

Poland
Poland, whose national federation was founded in 1923, has been unique in using only players that it terms "amateurs." As a result, Poland was able to win the Olympic title in 1972. Two years later, with all the same players except Wlodzimierz Lubanski, who had been injured, the Poles won the bronze medal in the World Cup. The team then was totally reorganized to play in the 1976 Olympic Games in Montreal. Formal league play began in Poland in 1921. As of 1976, Ruch Chorzów has won the crown 11 times, once more than Gornik Zabrze. Cup competition started in 1951, and Gornik Zabrze has won six crowns, two more than Legial of Warsaw has taken. Recently the backers of the national team constructed a 100,000-seat stadium, as the Polish team went all out to attract foreign full international opponents for at least five matches a year. With their third-place finish in the 1974 World Cup, the Poles displayed a disciplined style of playing, with men moving around almost as if they were on a checkerboard. The Poles also have been known to call out numbers that designate specific plays, much as some of the teams in American basketball do.

Portugal

In talking about Portuguese soccer, just mention Benfica and Sporting Lisbon to fans, and they will agree that without a doubt if these two clubs were merged, they would cause trouble for any team in the world. Benfica is the team that the poor man roots for, while the upper class generally favors Sporting Lisbon. In 1914 the National Federation was formed in Portugal, and even through many political conflicts, the group has been able to survive several attempts by the ruling government to take over its powers. The first formal league play was instituted in 1935, and since that time Benfica has won the crown 21 times, seven times more than Sporting Lisbon. Cup play started in 1939, and as of 1976, Benfica, riding the tide of such players as Eusebio and Antonio Simoes, has been the most successful team, winning the crown 15 times to Sporting Lisbon's eight times. Benfica has won the European Cup twice and finished third once, while Sporting Lisbon took the Cup-Winners' Cup in 1965.

One has to wonder what the record would be like if in the late 1950s Sporting had gotten Eusebio from Mozambique instead of Benfica. Portuguese soccer is one of the most appealing games in Europe, but the leaders of the national team have failed to get the various clubs to settle their differences and release their players for the national team competition. This, along with the clubs' reluctance to allow the national team adequate practice time, has cost Portugal dearly in international competition.

Spain

It is impossible not to mention Real Madrid in any discussion of Spanish soccer. Few, if any, teams in the history of world soccer have been able to match the power, determination, and skill displayed by Real Madrid, which, beginning in 1956 — the days of the great di Stefano, Rial, Gento, and Puskas — dominated the European Cup by winning the title five years straight. The formal league schedule didn't get underway until 1929, but 27 years earlier the Spanish Cup was already being contested. In league competition, Real Madrid has won the title 17 times, while Barcelona has taken the honor nine times. The surprise of Spanish soccer, however, is that in Cup competition Atletico Bilboa holds 22 titles over Barcelona's 17, while Real Madrid has only 13 Cup championships to its credit. So powerful are most of the clubs in Spain that in addition to Real Madrid's six European Cups, one World Club title, and one challenge championship against Benfica, Barcelona has won one European Nations Cup (in 1964), one European Cup, and three Fairs Cup titles; Atletico Bilboa has won one

European Cup and one Cup-Winners' Cup; Valencia has taken two Fairs Cup crowns; and Zaragoza has taken one Fairs title (in 1964).

Sweden
Sweden, which won the Olympic title in 1948 and was the runner-up to Brazil in the 1958 World Cup, began its league schedule in 1896. Cup play began in 1941, and Oergryte IS Göteborg currently holds the edge with 11 titles to Malmö FF's eight championships.

Switzerland
The greatest honor accomplished by a Swiss National Team was finishing as the runner-up in the 1924 Olympic Games. In club competition the Grasshoppers have been dominant, winning the league title, which was begun in 1898, 16 times and taking the Cup, started in 1926, 13 times.

Soviet Union
There are over four million registered soccer players in the Soviet Union, and the national association, founded in 1934, is at the mercy of the Ministry of Sports. So extreme are the weather conditions that teams in the central region must stop playing in October, only one month after the clubs competing from the northern area end their competition. Probably the greatest player in the history of Soviet soccer has been goalie Lev Yachin. Many consider him to be one of the greatest goalies of all time. It was Yachin's play in the 1960 European Nations Cup that gave the Soviets the championship. As a coach, Yachin has helped build the youth movement, which places top junior players in special training camps to learn under the careful guidance of established soccer stars.

Both the league and Cup competition in the Soviet Union were begun in 1936. In league play, Dynamo Moscow has been the most successful team, winning the crown 10 times, once more than its close competitor Spartak Moscow. In the annual Cup play, however, Spartak leads with nine titles to Torpedo Moscow's five.

Turkey
In 1923 the *Federation Turque de Football* was formed, and soccer in Turkey was formally organized. The game had been played haphazardly in that nation for 12 years before the national association was formed, but in spite of the formation of the national association, it wasn't until 1960 that league play took on some semblance of regularity. Since then, Fenerbance, with seven league crowns in the 16-team league, has been the dominant force. Cup competition was started in 1963,

and Fenerbance's arch rival Galatasaray leads in that category with five titles. Turkish play resembles a mixture of English and French soccer, and although Turkey has on occasion upset nations like Switzerland and Iran, the nation still seems to lack the soccer skill of many other European nations. Salaries are low and clubs have often been forced to sell some of their leading players abroad in an effort to remain solvent. In the early 1970s, a concentrated effort to organize the youth program was begun. It is hoped that this program will pay off in the 1980s.

Yugoslavia

The Yugoslavian Football Federation was started in 1919, but formal league play did not start until five years later. Red Star Belgrade has been the top team; it has taken the loop crown 11 times, and it also leads with nine titles in the Cup, which was begun in 1947. In the international arena, the Yugoslavians, who got into the 1974 World Cup by topping Spain, 1-0, in a special playoff, won the 1960 Olympic crown after finishing second the previous three times. That same year, they placed second in the European Nations Cup. In 1967 Dynamo Zagreb gave Yugoslavia its only big European club crown as it won the Fairs Cup.

Marshal Tito praised the development of Junior soccer in Yugoslavia, and clinics and camps for promising youthful players have been set up throughout the country. There are many who feel that Yugoslavia could be a major power in European soccer in years to come, but, obviously, it will face a stiff challenge from the many other nations who are competing in the world's most popular sport.

Clearly, then, Europe is the cradle of soccer and must still be highly respected — even by firm South American soccer fanatics.

CHAPTER 3

South American Growth

For a long time Uruguayans maintained that South American soccer began in their nation with a group of emigrants from England. But after a great deal of research, it has been found that although someone from England did indeed bring soccer to South America, it was not to Uruguay but to Brazil.

HISTORY

The man credited with bringing soccer to South America was Charles Miller. Born in England, he arrived in Brazil as a child in 1898, carrying two soccer balls with him. Miller had played the game in England, and when his parents decided to move to Brazil, he insisted on bringing along his prized soccer balls. According to reliable sources, Miller had few friends in Brazil with whom he could play soccer, and he often could be found in vacant lots practicing alone until finally he met others who had been exposed to the game while they were in Europe. From those humble beginnings, soccer developed further in Brazil as crews from foreign ships would play matches against opposing merchant seamen when they came to Brazilian ports.

Although Brazil was the first nation to play soccer in South America, the caliber of playing there was not terribly high, and the sport was not an instant success. In Uruguay, however, the game of soccer soon developed more extensively. Uruguay was a nation where if people accepted anything, they followed through on a grand scale. The often physical play of the merchant seamen excited the handful of spectators who turned out to see the sailors play. Word of the sport spread, and soon balls were imported, and the children in many leading Uruguayan cities started playing the game. From Uruguay the game spread to Argentina, where the style of play that developed was much different from that in either Uruguay or Brazil. The Argentinians liked to hit their opponents then almost as much as they do today. Soccer spread to Chile and Peru as well, and as the game developed throughout the continent, it eventually became evident that a governing body was needed to oversee the leagues that were springing up in various nations (which had already formed national associations). In 1916 the South American Football Confederation was formed, with member nations Brazil, Uruguay, Chile, and Argentina taking part in the initial organizing sessions.

Uruguay

Uruguay is a nation that has often pushed its weight around, looking for special consideration in international tournaments. It was because of that kind of pressure and, some say, even threats that Uruguay was able to hold the initial World Cup there in 1930. The style of play in Uruguay is considered a combination of the brilliant ball-control tactics of Brazil and the roughness that marks play in Argentina, and throughout the years, Uruguay has had many fine teams, such as Penarol, Cerro of Montevideo, and Nacional. In the battle for national supremacy, the league championship has become more important than a strong national team over the past 10 years. This has added to the financial woes of the teams, and along with the many disputes among the leading clubs, has caused the caliber of soccer in Uruguay to decrease steadily. The leading Uruguayan players have left their nation to play either in Europe or in any of several other South American countries.

Brazil

Brazil features two strong leagues—the São Paulo League and the Rio League. For many years the style of play of the two loops was almost completely opposite. The São Paulo League featured the brilliant ball-control tactics of a club like Santos, while long runs downfield were characteristic of Bangu, which led the Rio League.

On April 14, 1941, the Brazilian government passed Law No. 3199, which set up the CBD Federation—the body that regulates the Brazilian National Team as well as league and Cup play in Brazil. The federation has the final say on all matters dealing with selecting foreign teams for tours and regulating the selection of players for the Brazilian National Team. It was hoped that the battling clubs from opposing leagues would settle their differences and concentrate instead on building a strong national team. Although such cooperation did not develop overnight, by the late 1960s it was evident that the message, then almost 20 years old, had finally gotten through.

Teams like the great Santos club and Vasco de Gama have been dominant throughout the years, but other clubs, like Palmeiras, Botafoga, Cruzeiro, the Corinthians, and Gremio of Pôrto Alegre have all become strong contenders in the early 1970s. The flash style of play, utilized by many of the Brazilian forwards to get around defenders inside the penalty area, has prevented Brazil from developing strong goalies. Because the passes inside the penalty area are low rather than the high cross type, goalies in Brazil have suffered from lack of experience and have often fallen victim to headers off crosses* made by European opponents. The Brazilians are notable in soccer for having developed dribbling moves.

Argentina
Although the soccer stars of many South American nations have left their countries for European contracts, in Argentina that is not the case. Teams like Independiente, River Plate, Bôca Juniors, and Estudiantes are able year after year to retain their strongest players because of the extremely strong players association in Argentina. The Players Union was formed in 1945 and over the years has maintained high standards for Argentinian players. In 1971 the players felt that the clubs were not meeting the union's demands and went on a three-week strike that almost ruined some of the smaller clubs financially.

In 1973 the Argentinian government passed Law No. 20,160 entitled "The Statute of the Professional Football Player," which clearly defined the terms of the working agreement. The statute covers such financial terms as a monthly salary, bonuses for points won in official matches in league play, bonuses for friendly matches won or tied, and bonuses for qualification in both national and international competition. Another major provision in the law is that no soccer player belonging to the union can get less than the minimum national wage guaranteed to employees in other fields of employment. Other provisions regulate what happens if a member of the players union receives a better offer from another club. The player must get the club making the better offer to send a telegram to that effect, and his club then must either match that offer or give the player at least 60 percent of the salary they pay their highest-paid player. If the club refuses to

---

*A header off a cross is a maneuver in which the ball is passed toward the net and an attacking player flicks it into the goal with his head.

make either of these concessions, the player is then free to transfer, provided the club making the better offer pays the player's club an indemnity equivalent to three times the annual salary offered to the player. When a player is transferred to another club, he receives 10 percent of the transfer fee his club received from the purchasing team.

It is the best league contract in the world, but it has led to many disputes. Some of the richer clubs have been accused of raiding the poorer clubs for their better young players. It is for this reason that Independiente, Estudiantes, Bôca Juniors, River Plate, and the wealthy Racing Club have been able to dominate the rosters of the Argentinian National Team. Under the law, if the player does not sign a contract at the beginning of the season, his club can force him to sign a one-year contract at the current salary of workers in general; but at the end of the season, the player is free to choose where he will go and for whom he will play. The club also has the option of paying the player a salary 60 percent of that of the best-paid player on the team. The player must accept this offer, but after one year, he still is free to negotiate with any club he desires.

Most workers in Argentina get an annual complementary salary that is like a Christmas bonus. The players, however, have demanded and been guaranteed this salary in their contracts. Under the agreement worked out, the player receives as a bonus $\frac{1}{12}$ of his annual wage, no matter how well or poorly he has played. The law also declares the players eligible for a pension and guarantees their rest days, holidays, and injury recovery time without the loss of wages. In addition, no club can suspend a player for more than 60 days for any reason. The *Asociación del Futbol Argentino,* the ruling body of soccer in the country can, however, order further suspensions for disciplinary reasons. The Argentinian agreement has given players the freedom that they have been seeking for 20 years, and many European players unions are now studying it to see if they could benefit from a similar agreement.

If the clubs offer their top players good salaries to induce them to stay in Argentina, why doesn't Argentina dominate the South American soccer scene instead of Brazil? That question is even more puzzling when one looks at the annual South American club championship series and sees that the Argentinians are the most successful nation in that tournament. The reason, it appears, is that the rough body contact often allowed in the Argentinian Football League is not condoned by international officials, and whereas a player in Argentina is able to get away with rough activity in a league game, he is quickly ejected if he tries the same tactics in an international match. In addition, although Argentinian soccer is similar to the type of game played in

Brazil, the Argentinians have not been able to master the ball control of the Brazilians and Uruguayans.

Many times in the past 20 years, the Argentinian federation has had to appeal to the top clubs to forget their differences and release their top players from league competition to play on the national team. Even when the clubs have complied, in many of the practice sessions for the national team, open fights have broken out between players from opposing teams. No matter how many fines, suspensions, and warnings are issued, it is clear that a player in Argentina has far more loyalty to his own team than to his national team. With the 1978 World Cup set for Argentina, it is hoped that the pressure of the fans will force the clubs to solve the problem so that the Argentinians can make a good run for the title.

When a European visiting the United States was asked how Argentina would fare on the World Cup scene, however, he shrugged his shoulders and said, "It depends how long they can control their tempers. If they play like they have in past international games, then there is no chance that they will win the title. Too many of their stars will have been ejected from the games before the championship finale is ever decided. It's a shame, too, because if they play a clean game, then they do have the men who could bring them the title." It appears, then, that it is going to take a lot of self-control and hard work from everyone associated with the Argentinian National Team to get that nation in the running for the title.

The caliber of soccer played in Chile and Peru is slightly below that of Uruguay, Argentina, and Brazil, although teams from both nations have on occasion come through with major victories. According to Ramon Mifflin, the former captain of the Peruvian National Team, the style of play in both countries resembles Brazil's, with fast play, forwards who rush with give-and-go passes, the willingness to take chances that soccer nations such as England would frown on, and the desire for a bit of showmanship.

Both Peru and Chile started their soccer programs on a league basis after the programs of the big three of South American soccer were well established. But since the end of World War II, both countries have achieved a certain amount of success, and many of their leading players have been sought not only by other South American nations but also by European teams.

Chile
Some people have maintained that if Chile had ever played its return match against the Soviet Union in Chile, it would have been eliminated

from the 1974 World Cup competition. To those who claim this, the Chilean Federation has a pat answer: Chile tied the Soviets in the USSR, so no one can say that it wouldn't have won the return game in Chile.

Among the top teams in Chile are the crowd-pleasing Colo-Colo club, Union Española, and Palestino, Over the years, these three teams have constantly battled closely for the national championship. They have also been selected many times to represent their nation in international competition both on a club level and as the nucleus of the Chilean National Team. A decline in club soccer standards became evident after the overthrow of the Allende government; but in early 1976, many clubs were ordered to keep their star players and not allow them to be transferred to other nations. The Chileans hope to regain some of the status they formerly enjoyed, as in 1973 when Colo-Colo placed second in the South American club championship (called the *Copa Libertadores*). Chilean football is expected to be fully back to normal soon in light of several fine performances during 1975 and 1976 by Chilean youth teams. Top coaches from Brazil have come in to help the Chileans develop their junior program, and, as a result, the influence of Brazilian soccer is expected to become apparent in the systematic play to be utilized by the Chileans in the future.

Peru
Peru, like Chile, emulated Brazilian soccer but altered its style to include a little more physical contact, although not of the extreme type used by the Argentinians. In spite of the fact that many of its top players leave for foreign teams when they gain some measure of success, Peru has been able year after year to put together an above-average national team, as evidenced by its performances in the 1970 World Cup in Mexico and the 1975 South American National Team championship, which it won.

"In Peru, when we start playing soccer at an early age," said Ramon Mifflin,

we try to duplicate the moves of many of the Brazilian players. Of course, Pelé is the biggest hero in Peru even though he's from Brazil. Many top scouts from top teams in Uruguay and Brazil come to see our junior games, and I know that if a player is really good, they try to get him at an early age. I can honestly say, however, that since 1974 the salaries of players in Peru have gone up, and if I had been offered the type of money some of the players in Peru now get, I would not have gone to Santos in 1973. Coaching clinics are also a big part for the children, while the parents are given instructions on how to form teams, how to referee games, and how to help train their boys to make them fit for the running style that we use so much in Peru. I have no fear that these many programs will help my country catch up with Brazil and Argentina in a few more years. We have already shown our ability in international games, but on a club level we are still a few years away from the other two nations. This will also change. That I am sure of.

The two leading teams in Peru are Alianza of Lima, which since the late 1940s has won the national title eight times more than any other team, and Alfonso Ugarte of Puno, now considered one of the best teams in South America soccer competition.

Bolivia

There was not much enthusiasm when the Bolivian Football Federation celebrated its 50th anniversary in 1975. Attendance was down at almost all league games, and the lack of support for the national team was evident when the major stadium in La Paz was three-quarters vacant for an international exhibition match against Ecuador. Even the best players in the country receive only low wages, and the complete failure of the national team to make good showings in prestige events has caused a decline not only on the international level but also on the club level. Any player with even the slightest hope of success is long gone by the time he is ready to develop his talent. In international competition the Bolivian National Team has been one of the biggest jokes of sports fans in that nation.

The first time Bolivia appeared in the World Cup was in the tournament inaugural, held in 1930 in Uruguay, and the Bolivians dropped 4-0 decisions to both Brazil and Yugoslavia. Their next effort in the World Cup was in 1950, and in their one game they were demolished, 8-0, by Uruguay. Although there were strong supporters in Bolivia who pumped money into a fund for the development of top young players, nothing seemed to work. The Bolivians attempted to make the 1974 World Cup, but in their qualifying round against Argentina and Paraguay, they finished last. After losing, 4-0 and 1-0, to the Argentinians, they were beaten, 2-1 and 4-0, by Paraguay, which is not a strong soccer nation.

A seminar was held in La Paz in 1975 in which leading sports figures throughout the nation came forth with ideas on how to build up Bolivian soccer. But as is often the case with meetings held between delegations from several of the bigger clubs, nothing concrete was worked out; and by the beginning of 1976, the government was ready to take steps in earnest to help the program. Only if the Bolivian clubs can come up with better wages and if the national federation can convince its players to remain for a training session of at least a few months instead of rushing overseas, can the Bolivians even hold the slightest hope that they eventually will be able to match Peru, Chile, and even Colombia in international competition.

The two leading clubs in the country are the Guabira, which hails from the plains of Santa Cruz de la Sierra, and Bolivar of La Paz. Several large manufacturers have been spending money in an effort to help the smaller teams develop. As a result in 1975, for the first time since 1963, when they shocked Uruguay by winning the South American title in a tournament in which many of the opposing nations did not use their main stars, the Bolivians did manage to make some improvement, when they edged Chile, 2-1, in one of the qualifying games for the South American championship. That was, however, their only moment of glory, because after that win they lost, 4-0, to the Chileans in the return game and lost with 1-0 and 3-1 decisions to Peru.

Colombia

A nation that is on the rise in the soccer world is Colombia. Colombia not only offers its players sample contracts, but the government provides solid financial backing for renovation of stadiums and club facilities, and provides work with the clubs for members of the players' families. Colombia is currently enjoying the fruits of a junior development program in soccer that was started in the mid-1960s. Its clubs play an entertaining style of soccer that resembles Brazil's, except that the defenders always make sure that at least two of them are somewhere between the midfield line and their own goal line.

The Colombian position in the soccer arena is now regarded as close to that of Peru and Chile, and Colombia is expected to surpass both its neighbors by the mid-1980s. Every member of the national team was not only born and raised in Colombia but has been playing on a club level in his own nation since turning professional. It is a nation where league play is exciting, referees tolerate little or no nonsense, and the national federation not only threatens bans and stiff fines for infractions of the rules but carries out its threats, making a player think twice before striking an opponent or a referee. Defensive style is the key word in the success of most of Colombia's top teams, among them Independiente Santa Fe, Millonarios, Nacional and Deportive Cali, and unlike many other nations in South America, there has been a strong feeling of solidarity among the numerous Colombian clubs in helping with the national team. The clubs have been very cooperative about releasing players for national team practice, even if a player is important to his team for a league match, and in return, the Colombian Football Federation has authorized the leagues to postpone important games if a team finds itself without three or more players.

31

The Colombians, whose only appearance in the World Cup was in 1962, have been strengthening their national team slowly but surely, and the results are now evident. In the qualifying round for the 1974 World Cup, the Colombians won one game and tied their other three contests. (They recorded a 1-0 triumph and a tie with Uruguay; and two ties with Paraguay.) In 1975 the entire nation exploded with joy, when in the semifinals of the South American Nations Cup, the Colombians took a 3-0 win over Uruguay in the opening game in Bogotá and then lost, only 1-0, to the Uruguayans in Montevideo. The Colombians placed second to Peru in the South American Championship that year. National soccer spirit is high in Colombia and the government intends to keep it that way, going all out to get as many new recruits as possible for the junior clinics it runs.

Paraguay

Paraguay has not been too successful in developing its soccer teams, and, although its junior program is believed to be the hope for the future, in 1976 Paraguay withdrew at the last moment from its pre-Olympic Games schedule. Although there were financial reasons for the withdrawal, another major factor was the fear on the part of some soccer officials of suffering further embarrassments in amateur competition. The withdrawal drew stern criticism from much of the nation's press, but many officials said that they would make a sincere bid to gain a spot in the 1980 Olympic Games, hoping that by then the financial crisis plaguing many of the top teams in the league will be solved with sponsorship. For a time many of the clubs were holding lotteries in the cities where they live to help defray the cost of fielding teams. Naturally, with such financial burdens looming ahead, the top players have been quick to leave.

Paraguay needs a strong boost in the near future to start developing solidly. The top clubs in the nation have been unable to hold their own against teams from many of the other South American nations in *Copa* (Cup) games and even friendly exhibition matches. The Paraguayan style of play is not bad, but the teams try to duplicate the styles of the Brazilians and the Argentinians and don't have the manpower to field a team of stars. Often they have to use players who should still be in the juvenile program or on the reserve teams in their starting lineup. Teams such as Olimpia, Sportivo Lugueño of Luque, and Asunción, which has won the title more than any other club in the nation's 50-year soccer history, have been making a sincere attempt to improve the players on their rosters, often giving the top players not more money but material goods such as cars and even homes. This has slowed the exodus of top players somewhat, but until the Paraguayan League betters conditions for all its members, the migration is going to continue. It appears that Paraguay is now attempting to get better coaches on a regional level and have these coaches work with the man who heads the national team.

Ecuador

Ecuadorian soccer has been dominated by the Liga Deportiva Universiaria club of Quito, Emelec of Quito, and Deportivo of Cuenca. Of the approximately 30 clubs playing in the two divisions of the Ecuadorian League, Emelec is the one that has been selected most often to represent its nation abroad in international tournaments, like the one held in New York in 1974 with teams from Ecuador, Colombia, and Chile.

Like some of the other lesser-known soccer teams in South America, many Ecuadorian teams fail to recognize that imitating the Brazilian style of soccer is fruitless. The Ecuadorian National Team is also faced with the problems that confront other South American national teams. The three leading teams are not willing to cooperate in releasing key players for practice sessions. In the mid-1960s the Ecuadorian National Team actually played a match against Uruguay with no practice sessions under its belt. When Ecuador was beaten, 7-0, critics screamed, and several attempts were made to rectify the situation. But again it was only a short time before the various clubs refused to cooperate with one another. In 1975 the government, tired of the pettiness, mandated cooperation; but it soon became evident that enforcing the law was easier said than done. Key players from one of the clubs suddenly became "ill" and couldn't appear at the national team's practice sessions, although they had recovered sufficiently later in the day to train with their regular team. Obviously, more drastic moves were called for, and the national federation and government officials decided to reprimand the players who had been "ill." Not only were the players fined, but, under a hastily passed law, they were considered "too ill" to appear in their club's next two matches.

The Ecuadorians did manage to field a team in the 1975 *Copa Sudamericana* (South American Cup) but faired poorly, tying Paraguay in Guayaquil, 2-2, but then losing, 1-0 and 3-1, to Colombia before dropping a game against Paraguay, 3-1, in Asuncion. Complete understanding of the problems by both the government and the Ecuadorian Football Federation may provide a partial solution, but unless the rival teams settle some of their difficulties, which range from battling over the schedule to accusations of raiding the junior ranks to out-and-out battles on the playing field, the outlook for soccer in Ecuador will continue to be dim for years to come.

Venezuela

Ironically, in Venezuela, where the sport gained great popularity as foreigners came to work in the oil fields and spread the game to the youngsters of the nation, soccer is probably farther away from complete development than anywhere else in the South American scene. In 1956, before his overthrow, dictator Jiminez set up certain rules for developing soccer, which he ordered carried out by the national association. For a year, the rules helped produce some top juniors, and although they never attained the success that had been anticipated, they were still able to walk off the field at the end of a losing match with their heads held high. But since 1960, the sport has suffered an almost total regression, and the crisis has been so severe that at the last minute the Venezuelans decided to pull out of the qualifying round of the 1974 World Cup competition. They drew the ire of the entire South American Federation but maintained that they could not field a team truly representative of their nation's best. It seems that as in Ecuador, the Venezuelan clubs were at odds with one another and didn't want to "waste their time," as one of them said, getting a team ready that would be slaughtered in international competition. They preferred instead to keep their own squads together for the league season and any other international club tournaments that were coming up. For some reason FIFA went along with their withdrawal and didn't even fine them.

In 1975 the Venezuelans entered the South American championship and it was without a doubt one of the worst performances any national team has ever given. True, they were placed in the same bracket as Brazil and Argentina, and their chances of winning were virtually nil, but not even the most skeptical fan in the nation expected what happened. In their opening game, played in Caracas, they lost a 4-0 decision to Brazil in a game in which the Brazilians used their best players for less than half the time. Then they hosted Argentina in Caracas, and the Argentinians, using many of their lesser-known players, still managed to win, 5-1. Then they went to Rosario, and the Argentinians pounded in 11 goals and blanked the Venezuelans. Their final game was against Brazil in Belo Horizonte, and the Brazilians won, 6-0, again using their stars for only a brief first-half appearance.

Is there any real hope for Venezuela? Probably not, unless the entire development program is placed in the hands of competent instructors from abroad, who will work exclusively with Venezuelan youth. There are some fine clubs in the National League of Venezuela, such as Deportive Portuguesa and Deportive Galicia; but although they have dominated the league scene year after year, neither of them has been able to fare well against their bigger and better-developed neighbors.

Of all the South American nations, Venezuela's soccer situation is the bleakest. It will take at least 15 years to see the fruits of the junior program develop to where the country will be able to field a national team that can at least walk off the field in defeat with some honor.

Despite the problems of Ecuador, Paraguay, and Venezuela, the South American soccer structure, from full international tournaments down to the youth and the amateur levels is basically strong; and in a continent often beset by revolution, such stability is perhaps remarkable. But as a European reporter covering the 1950 World Cup in Brazil said, "In Europe there is great feeling in soccer, but it can never match the expressions of the fans in South America. In South America it is not a sport but a real religion worshipped by all."

CHAPTER 4

On Home Grounds

Even before the Boston Tea Party, Americans would venture onto the public field and laugh at the British soldiers who were kicking around a soccer ball during their breaks. Although the Spanish in Florida had also played something resembling soccer, the credit for formal introduction of the sport into America — at least with a stretch of the imagination — has to go to the 18th-century English soldiers.

In 1869 Rutgers and Princeton played a game. One hundred years later, American football fans celebrated the 100th anniversary of football, and to mark the date, Rutgers and Princeton squared off again. But the fans were wrong, because when the Scarlet of Rutgers went up against the Tigers of Princeton for the first time, they were actually playing soccer, not American football. Rutgers won that first game, 6–4; and over the next 15 years, colleges and universities in the eastern United States began to play soccer, even though American football backers might disagree. Officials from several leading universities, fearful that the game was too rough, put a ban on the sport; but just like today, the students violated the ban, playing unofficial games on fields in public parks instead of on their university grounds.

AMERICAN BEGINNINGS

In 1884 several colleges sent representatives to a meeting and formed the American Football Association, working out rules that were mostly the same as the rules in effect in England at the time. In 1886 the United States played its first international match, against a team of Canadian all-stars. Central Park in New York became a famous soccer center, as members of different ethnic groups would venture onto its lush, green lawn and play matches against one another. Soccer was a game solely for immigrants at the time; but in the next few years, the sons of the immigrants began to follow in their fathers' footsteps and organized teams of their own.

As was the case until recently, the biggest boom in soccer in the 1880s was in St. Louis, where the Italian immigrants played a regular schedule. Their children also took part in the game, and in 1890 a team called Kensington trotted onto the pitch to play another local team. American soccer was really born on that day, as the entire Kensington squad was composed of American citizens. The Kensington team, still remembered by many, did well its first year, winning more than 60 percent of its matches against teams made up entirely of foreign players. The following year two other all-American teams were formed in the St. Louis area; and, even today, with its vast Catholic Youth Council program, St. Louis is the one area where the American soccer professional stands a better chance of gaining a spot on a team than anywhere else in the nation.

A year after FIFA was founded in 1904, a meeting was held between members of Columbia, Cornell, Harvard, Haverford, and Pennsylvania, and the Intercollegiate Association League was founded. Many of the rules that were adopted then are still on the books. Other prestigious universities, such as Yale, Princeton, and Rutgers, quickly asked to join the organization, and the league was opened to anyone who promised to uphold the regulations that were set down.

U.S. Dewar's Cup
On a regular club level, the most prestigious soccer competition in the United States is the annual battle for the United States Dewar's Open Challenge Cup. Because of his love for soccer back in his native Scotland, in 1912 Sir Thomas Dewar decided to donate the Dewar's Challenge Cup, which would go to the winner of an annual Cup competition. Because the United States Soccer Football Association—which later changed its name to the United States Soccer Federation (USSF)—had not yet been founded, the competition was to be run by a group of supervisors. When the U.S. organization was founded a year later, Sir Thomas gave it the right to run the Dewar Cup competition.

United States Soccer Federation
Immediately after it was started in 1913, USSFA affiliated itself with FIFA and has been a member of the worldwide ruling body ever since. Such men as James P. McGuire and secretary Kurt Lamm have been appointed to numerous committees on the FIFA board and also have represented FIFA as observers at various international functions.

Around the same time that the USSFA and the Dewar's Cup were set up, numerous business firms began to find that their immigrant workers were homesick. One way the business officials hoped to solve the problem was to bring to the workers some of the activities they had enjoyed in their native lands. Soccer was the natural answer, and firms such as Bethlehem Steel started importing coaches from England and Italy to teach and coach their workers. The solution didn't work for everyone, but it was successful enough to prompt other companies throughout the nation to duplicate the move. This presented the USSFA with a minor dilemma: Were these teachers and coaches to be considered amateurs or professionals? They clearly were being paid for doing nothing more than coaching and teaching. It took several hours of meeting time to decide, but when the USSFA meeting was adjourned, the word was clear—they were professionals. Bethlehem Steel and other companies then decided to go all out and organize their own professional teams. Their teams faced clubs from other steel companies and other types of industry. The Bethlehem team was so powerful that when it won the U.S. championship in 1919, the firm rewarded it with a trip to Europe, where it competed against teams in Stockholm and Norway. In its biggest effort overseas, it defeated a Stockholm all-star team, 3-0, and drew wide approval for its aggressive and entertaining style of play.

The designation of the professional player by the USSFA drew loud protests from many players who claimed that because they had to work, they would not be able to compete in the U.S. Dewar's Cup on an equal basis with the professionals. They further argued that the professionals in the United States should have their own competition, while the amateurs should have their own competition. Clearly, the USSFA had to make arrangements to accommodate the amateurs. In 1922 there were two distinct factions battling and in a strong move, the amateur clubs threatened to bolt from the USSFA if they were denied the chance to compete for a cup against teams of similar player status. The threat worked, and the national federation ruled that no professional clubs would be allowed to compete in the Amateur Cup, which was set up that year, while all clubs would be allowed a chance to compete for the Dewar's Challenge Cup. That arrangement remains in effect today.

American Soccer League

A limited professional league called the American Soccer League was organized in 1933, and this loop—with teams from Los Angeles, Sacramento, Oakland, Salt Lake City, Tacoma, Hartford, Chicago, Cleveland, New Jersey, New York, and Rhode Island—is still in operation today. Former basketball great Bob Cousy became its commissioner at the start of the 1975 season, and until 1976 the loop was limited strictly to the East and Midwest. Play has been hectic, but many stars of the U.S. National Team in the late 1950s came from that league. The history of the loop shows that on more than one occasion, the championship remained undecided because the teams involved in the title game couldn't agree on either the time or the place to decide the match. When Cousy took over, however, he changed all that, and under his guidance the league has started to gain popularity. The league has gained political power as well. Before the start of the 1976 campaign, the league went to court and was able to stop the USSFA from charging what it termed "exorbitant entrance fees" from new members.

Before World War II, various teams from abroad came in for exhibition games at such old baseball parks as Ebbets Field in Brooklyn and the Polo Grounds in Manhattan. Teams like Rapid Vienna would draw crowds exceeding 20,000 for one or two matches. Before Pearl Harbor, almost all the visitors came from Europe, with England and Germany sending such teams as Liverpool and Hamburg, respectively. In March 1941, however, the first South American team appeared in the United States, when Botafoga FC of Rio de Janeiro played against a team of hastily selected U.S. all-stars. America's intervention in World War II curtailed international appearances by foreign clubs here; but in 1948 a team from Israel, celebrating that nation's emergence as a state, came to play the New York All-Star team, and 45,000 turned out at the Polo Grounds. Meanwhile, teams from all over Europe started making appearances here and in late June 1976, there were 24 foreign matches played in the United States.

INTERNATIONAL VISITORS

In 1950 the United States made its greatest showing in World Cup competition, when it defeated England, 1-0, but the drawing power of foreign clubs in the United States remained a big question mark. Although some promoters were able to bring in crowds of 20,000 for exhibition games, the spectators were mainly immigrants or first-generation Americans who were drawn to the teams from their native countries. In 1952 the English arrived for a match at Yankee Stadium. Although winning, 6-3, they drew only 7,000 fans, and it was evident that America was not yet ready for national soccer team appearances.

In the following few years there were sporadic appearances by such teams as München 1860 of Germany, Celtic of Scotland, and a Chilean select team. Then Bill Cox, a former owner of the Philadelphia Phillies of the National Baseball League, came onto the scene. Cox believed that a league comprised of foreign teams would be able to draw fans to see top-flight soccer. In late 1959, Cox called a press conference at the famed Yale Club in New York and announced that he was ready to promote an international soccer competition (the International Soccer League) with high-ranking foreign teams competing on an equal basis on an international point system. There were skeptics in the crowd who felt that a one-shot appearance by a team would be fine but that no one was going to shell out money on a regular basis to see teams compete.

Cox went ahead anyway and rented out the Polo Grounds for his initial tournament. Such famous world clubs as Nice of France, Glentoran of Ireland, and Kilmarnock of Scotland, besides Everton, Burnley, and later West Ham United from England took part in tournaments held over the five years that the loop was in operation. Because baseball had the first claim on the Polo Grounds, where the New York Giants played before they moved to San Francisco, Cox had to have backup facilities to play in, and he selected ancient Roosevelt Stadium in Jersey City and Randall's Island in New York City. Crowds generally were large for the first couple of years, and it was evident that soccer did have a future in the United States. But when it also became apparent that many of the foreign clubs were coming here without their stars and that the players seemed to take it too easy, the crowds started to dwindle. (In all fairness, it should be mentioned that clubs like Gornik of Poland, Dukla of Czechoslovakia, and Bangu of Brazil did go all out in an effort to lure spectators.)

The ISL's first championship was decided on August 6, 1960, when Bangu—which had bested Yugoslavia's Red Star, Italy's Sampdoria, Sporting Club of Portugal, Norrköping of Sweden, and Austria's Rapid Vienna to win the Second Division title—beat First Division champion Kilmarnock, 2-0. The Scots had bested England's Burnley, France's Nice, the New York Americans, Bayern-Münich of West Germany, and Glenavon of Northern Ireland.

In the league's second season, Everton bested Bangu, the NY Americans, Karlsruhe of West Germany, Kilmarnock, Concordia of Canada, Dynamo Bucharest of Rumania, and Turkey's Besiktas to win the First Division; while Czechoslovakia's Dukla swept the slate almost clean in the Second Division, winning six games and tying one to dominate the action. Dukla beat Concordia, Sportif Monaco of France, Red Star, Deportivo Español of Spain, Rapid Vienna, the Shamrock Rovers of Ireland, and Hapoel Petah Tiquva of Israel. In the championship, a two-game, total-goal series, Dukla ripped Everton, 7-2, in the first game and won the second match, 2-0, to claim the championship.

America FC of Brazil took the 1962 First Division crown, beating such contenders as SSV Reutlingen of West Germany, Guadalajara of Mexico, Sportivo Palermo of Italy, Dundee of Scotland, and Hajduk of Yugoslavia. In the Second Division, Portugal's Belenenses won the crown over Wiener of Austria, Panathinaikos of Greece, MTK of Hungary, Elfborg of Sweden, and Real Oviedo of Spain. In the play-offs between the two divisional champions, America beat Belenenses, 2-1 and 1-0. Since Dukla had won the championship a year earlier, it was invited to face America for the American Challenge Cup. The Czechs won the second game, 2-1, after the teams had tied, 1-1, in the first meeting of the two-game, total-goal series. The opening game of the Challenge Cup was held at Soldier Field in Chicago as an experiment, but the crowd of 12,000 was far less than had been anticipated.

In the 1963 season, several new teams invaded the United States, as Cox tried to get more ethnic groups out to see the games. The matches were held in New York; Chicago, Illinois; Detroit, Michigan; and Chicopee, Massachusetts, which Cox felt would one day be to soccer what Green Bay was to football. West Ham United won the First Division title over Italy's Mantua, Scotland's Kilmarnock, Brazil's Recife, West Germany's Preussen Münster, Mexico's Oro, and France's Valenciennes. In the Second Division, Gornik of Poland topped Dynamo of Yugoslavia, Wiener, Újpest, Balenenses, Valladolid of Spain, and Halsingborg of Sweden. West Ham United and Gornik waged a bitter battle for the championship, playing a 1-1 tie followed by a 1-0 win for West Ham. Then Dukla came back and successfully defended its American Challenge Cup by beating West Ham, 1-0, and then playing a 1-1 deadlock.

Ten teams competed in the 1964 season, and West Germany's Werder Bremen won the First Division crown over Scotland's Hearts, Italy's Lanerossi, Blackburn of England, and Bahia of Brazil. Zaglebie of Poland captured the Second Division title over Schwechater of Austria, Red Star, Guimaraes of Portugal, and AEK of Greece. In the battle for the overall league championship, Zaglebie blanked Werder, 4-0 and 1-0, to take the title. But then Dukla took its third straight American Challenge Cup by defeating the Polish team, 3-1, and then playing a 1-1 deadlock. In addition to playing games at some of the old sites, the ISL also experimented with matches in Boston and Los Angeles. But a rapid decline in fan turnout made it evident that the following year would be the loop's last.

In the 1965 campaign, indeed a fitting finale for the league, the New Yorkers topped Portuguesa of Brazil, Varese of Italy, München 1860 of West Germany, and West Ham United to win the First Division crown. In the Second Division, only four teams competed, with Polonia of Poland winning the title by beating Ferencvaros of Hungary, West Bronwich Albion of England, and Kilmarnock. Polonia defeated the New Yorkers, 3-0 and 2-1, and finally stopped even Dukla by defeating the Czechs, 2-0, and playing a 1-1 tie to capture the two-game, total-goal series, 3-1.

The caliber of play in the loop had, however, given American fans a taste of top-flight league competition, and many were indeed disappointed when the league officials announced at a special press conference that they were abandoning the plans they had announced midway through the 1965 campaign to try one more season. A crowd of 20,000 did turn out to see an exhibition in which AC Milan tied Santos, playing without fabled star Pelé.

Heavy financial losses and conflicts with the USSFA over fees and expenses had forced Cox to give up late in 1965, and with the folding of the league went the dreams of the Americans who had played for the New York Americans against teams like Bayern-Münich of West Germany and Újpest of Hungary. Would there ever be another professional soccer league in the United States? Fans were asking that question, too, when the following year they were able to see only an occasional exhibition match by a foreign club or games between local clubs that were fighting to keep their heads above water. These local teams, with names like Eintracht and Blau-Weiss Gotshee, often would have to pass the hat in order to pay the expenses of their players.

The World Cup was held in England in 1966, and even before the first ball was kicked out in that competition, rumors were circulating in soccer circles that professional soccer might well be on its way back in the United States—not just in one city like New York, but on a nationwide basis. A national television network decided to televise the final game of the World Cup competition, in which England defeated West Germany in overtime. So great was the response of the television audience, that steps were taken to start a national league the following year. Many sports personalities, such as the Allyn Brothers of Chicago and Lamar Hunt of the Kansas City Chiefs from the Old American Football League, were quick to jump on the bandwagon; and not one but two professional groups applied for sanction from the USSFA to promote leagues in North America. The groups also had to get the approval of the Canadian Football Federation, since franchises were to be awarded north of the border as well.

ASSOCIATIONS AND LEAGUES

The USSFA was sent into a quandary. It could get away with sanctioning one league, but there would be trouble with FIFA if it approved two leagues. Behind the scenes, talks between members of both proposed leagues and officials of the USSFA failed to resolve the dilemma. The USSFA finally decided to sanction the league known as the United Soccer Association (USA), which proposed to import whole teams for its first year to play under the banners of its member cities. The other league was known as the National Professional Soccer League (NPSL), and although it was declared an outlaw league by the USSFA and eventually by FIFA, it announced that it was ready to play. Under FIFA regulations, all players competing in the league were declared outlaws and would have to be reinstated by FIFA if later they wanted to play in an organized soccer league anywhere in the world. The NPSL would also find it impossible to schedule exhibition games against teams whose national associations belonged to FIFA. In an effort to get some top players, officials of the NPSL ventured overseas, but it was soon clear that a player with a good future in his own nation would not take the chance of being banned. So the players that came to the league were either unproven young players or older players who were clearly over the hill.

Even before the official beginning of both leagues, however, Americans were presented with top-flight soccer, as a former boxer Enzo Magnozzi decided that the time was right to bring the great Pelé to America for the first time. Since Pelé had been injured while playing in the World Cup, and Eusebio had walked off with the tournament's Most Valuable Player Award, a match was set up between Pelé's Santos team from Brazil and Eusebio's Benfica team from Portugal. From all over the East Coast, buses were arriving for hours before the kickoff at Randall's Island. The Portuguese contingent came from as far away as Illinois and Rhode Island, while Brazilians and other soccer fans were flooding in from all over. The game was delayed over 45 minutes when police reported a huge traffic jam on the one road leading to the stadium from the Triborough Bridge. Although Randall's Island can seat only about 22,000 fans, police and park department officials estimated that somehow over 30,000 had poured into the stadium to see the match. Thousands of fans, unable to get a seat, lined the perimeter of the field, while many others climbed on the bridge, where they could see most of the action without paying. Other fans, with tickets and without, broke down steel gates trying to get into the stadium. Soccer had finally come of age in the United States because Pelé, the man known around the world as the greatest soccer player of all time, was coming to defend his title against the challenge of Eusebio. (It is interesting to note that a few days earlier Eusebio had said at a press conference that if he could become the second greatest soccer player of all time he would be happy.) Pelé, fully recovered from the knee injury he received in the World Cup competition, proved to be the master, scoring once and assisting twice as Santos won, 4-0. With time running out, he went upfield and intercepted a dribble by Eusebio and the entire crowd cheered, even those who had brought flowers for the Benfica players. Then he approached the entrance to the dressing room and was gone. By prearranged plan the police had formed a tunnel for him, and with seven minutes still left to play, Pelé was in the dressing room and safe.

After Benfica, Santos, and Greece's AEK had finished their scheduled round-robin, Magnozzi figured that the time was right to bring Santos to Yankee Stadium for a Labor Day match against Inter-Milan of Italy. He proved right again, as a crowd of over 42,000, most of whom bought their tickets the day of the game, witnessed the match in which Santos won, 4-1, with a brilliant display of dribbling and passing. Magnozzi then invaded the West Coast, and Santos played a tie game against Argentina's River Plate before 30,000 at the Los Angeles Memorial Coliseum. Over the next few years, Magnozzi, and later Tony Doria of New Jersey, brought Pelé to the United States several times, and the crowds usually averaged between 20,000 and the 48,000 who saw Santos beat Napoli in 1969.

The average American soccer fan approached 1967 with enthusiasm, because now he would have not one but two leagues playing a full schedule of soccer. Last-minute threats of lawsuits from members of the NPSL and from Bill Cox, who claimed that he was being stopped by the USSFA in his attempts to promote international games, didn't budge the national ruling body from its decision that the United Soccer Association was the only league sanctioned to play in the United States, and since the USSFA had the backing of the Canadian body, naturally FIFA went along.

In the USA league, New York's Skyliners were represented by Cerro of Uruguay; the Shamrock Rovers played under Boston's banner; Aberdeen of Scotland competed in the uniforms of Washington, D.C.; the Hibernians of Edinburgh played as Toronto's representatives; Stoke City of England represented the Cleveland franchise; Glentoran of Northern Ireland played at Tiger Stadium in Detroit; the Wolverhampton Wolves of England played for Los Angeles (replacing America of Mexico); ADO of the Netherlands played under the banner of San Francisco; Bangu of Brazil represented Houston; Dundee United of Scotland played for Dallas; Vancouver had Sunderland of England as its team; and Cagliari of Italy wore the colors of Chicago in the 12-team league. Rivalries between clubs became common, and scenes like the pitched battle between the New York Skyliners and Chicago (really Cerro and Cagliari) rocked Yankee Stadium, with the fans leaping onto the field to join the players in combat. The season championship went to Los Angeles' Wolverhampton Wolves, with a 6-5 overtime win over Washington's Aberdeen club in a game in which both clubs threw defensive caution to the wind.

Meanwhile, even though it didn't have the sanction of the ruling body, the NPSL did get a national television contract, with such players as former Welsh great Phil Woosnam (now the NASL commissioner) playing for Atlanta. Although attendance at NPSL games was far below that of the rival USA organization, the TV money helped the league through its first season. Purist soccer fans were angered, however, over the stoppage for commercials during the telecasts, and when a referee revealed that he was sometimes forced to order players to fake injuries so that the advertisements could be broadcast, a scandal loomed. Since the USSFA did not have any say over the league, however, the stoppages continued.

There were a total of 10 teams in the NPSL, with the Eastern Division consisting of the Atlanta Chiefs, owned by baseball's Atlanta Braves; the Baltimore Bays, who were owned by baseball's Baltimore Orioles; the New York Generals, owned by RKO General; the Philadelphia Spartans; and the Pittsburgh Phantoms. Competing in the Western Division were the California Clippers, who represented both San Francisco and Oakland; the Toronto Falcons; the Chicago Spurs; the St. Louis Stars; and the Los Angeles Toros.

The California Clippers won the first-season championship, beating the Bays, 4-1, after Baltimore had won the opening match, 1-0. The title was decided as a two-game, in which two players were ejected and three cautioned, the Clippers had a 4-2 advantage in aggregate goals.

NORTH AMERICAN SOCCER LEAGUE

A multimillion dollar lawsuit was initiated by the NPSL against FIFA, the USA league, and the USSFA. Sir Stanley Rous, the head of FIFA, made a quick trip to the United States and urged the USSFA to try to avoid the pending suit. Meanwhile, various owners in both leagues were fed up with losing large sums of money, estimated by some to be as much as $1 million per club. A committee was formed with representatives from both sides of the fence to discuss the possibility of setting up a merger. After a couple of months, a merger agreement was worked out, and the resulting league called itself the North American Soccer League (NASL). Seventeen teams, broken into four divisions, competed in the loop's first season in 1968, with Atlanta winning the Atlantic Division; Cleveland taking the Lakes Division; Kansas City,

45

the Gulf Division; and San Diego winning the Pacific Division. John Kowalik of Chicago was the top scorer, with 30 goals and nine assists in 28 games for a total of 69 points, two more than Cirilo Fernandez of San Diego. Leading goalie was Ataulfo Sanchez of San Diego, who allowed an average of 0.93 goals per game. In the playoffs, held on a two-game, total-goal aggregate, Atlanta eliminated Cleveland, winning, 2-1, in sudden-death overtime after the two teams had tied their first game, 1-1; San Diego beat Kansas City, 1-0, in overtime, after the two teams tied their first match, 1-1. In the championship finale, Atlanta bombed San Diego, 3-0, after the first meeting produced a scoreless deadlock.

If there was a really black year for professional soccer, it had to be 1969, as the NASL found itself with only five of the original 17 teams still in business. Backers in Washington, New York, Boston, Cleveland, Chicago, Toronto, Detroit, Houston, San Diego, Oakland, Los Angeles, and Vancouver simply gave up the fight. The five remaining teams were placed in one division, with the schedule calling for each club to play 16 matches. No playoffs were scheduled, and Kansas City, with a record of 10 wins, two defeats, and four deadlocks, won the title with 110 points, one point more than Atlanta. If the NASL had used the internationally accepted point values of two points for a win, one for a tie, and none for a defeat, Atlanta would have won with 25 points, one more than Kansas City. The league used the same bonus system then that it does today, however, with a win worth six points, a tie worth three, and each goal worth one bonus point, up to three per match. Later, the ties were eliminated, but backers in Atlanta were bitter about losing because of the different point system. Kaizer "Boy Boy" Moutang, playing for Atlanta, won the scoring title, with 16 goals and four assists for 36 points, one point more than the score accumulated by Kansas City's George Benitez. Manfred Kammerer of Atlanta was the top goalie, with a 1.07 goals-against average.

Rochester and Washington, D.C., came into the league the following season, while Baltimore, under great pressure from backers of baseball's Orioles, folded up shop. Thus, at the start of the 1970 season, the third without a national TV pact, there were six teams in operation. All teams played a 24-game schedule, and Rochester won in the Northern Division, beating both Kansas City and St. Louis, while Washington, D.C., took the Southern Division crown, beating Atlanta and Dallas. In the championship playoff—a two-game, total-goal series—Rochester defeated Washington, 3-0, while the return game was won by Washington, 3-1, to give Rochester a 4-3 championship triumph. Kirk Apostolidis of Dallas and Carlos Metidieri of Rochester shared scoring honors, each with 35 points. On the basis of two points for a goal and one for an assist, Apostolidis earned his total on 16 goals and three assists, while Metidieri's total came from 14 goals and seven assists. Lincoln Phillips, the former member of Trinidad's national team (who later went on to coach Howard University to the NCAA championship), was the leading goalie, with an 0.95 goals-against average.

Many people considered the 1971 season to be the real turning point of the league. Although Kansas City decided to suspend operations, the loop was still able to expand to eight teams as Toronto, Montreal, and the New York Cosmos—then owned by a group that later put its operation under the umbrella of the multimillion-dollar Warner Communications company—joined the league. In addition to arranging for all eight clubs to play a regular seasonal schedule, NASL Commissioner Phil Woosnam also worked out an international cup schedule in which Portuguese Rio of Brazil, Apollo of Greece, and Italy's Lanorassi Vicenza would play against all eight of the NASL clubs, with the league's results against the foreign teams counting in the overall loop schedule.

The expansion to eight clubs also gave the league the opportunity to expand its playoff schedule to bring in extra revenue. A bid to get a major network to televise the playoffs proved futile, however, even though the Cosmos had proved themselves able to compete against the foreign clubs that had appeared during the regular season. CBS, which held the loop's option to televise, was not interested, nor were the other major networks. During the regular season competition, Rochester and New York placed first and second, respectively, in the Northern Division to make the playoffs; while Atlanta, with 120 points, edged Dallas, with 119 points, to win the Southern Division crown. In the semifinals of the four-team playoff, Dallas came back from an initial 2-1 overtime defeat at the hands of Rochester to win the next two games of the best-of-three series, 3-0 and 2-1, in sudden-death overtime and made the final round. In the other semifinal series, Atlanta blanked New York, 1-0, in overtime and won the return match, 2-0. Dallas, attempting to return from the brink of defeat, lost a 2-1 overtime decision to Atlanta in the opening game of the best-of-three series but then rallied to post 4-1 and 2-0 wins and win its first league title. Lamar Hunt's desire to stay in the soccer business, where he was losing a great deal of money, had paid off, and the Dallas team was congratulated by both town officials and fans. The makeup of the Tornado team, as it is still called, was basically English with a few Americans tossed into the squad. Rochester's Carlos Metidieri won the league scoring crown easily, with 19 goals and eight assists in 24 games for 46 points, nine more than rookie Randy Horton of New York, who had been a member of the Bermuda National Team. Goalie Mirko Stoja-novic of Dallas finished with the best goals-against average, allowing only 11 goals in the 1,359 minutes he played, for an average of 0.79.

The league continued with eight teams during the 1972 campaign, although Washington was purchased and moved to Miami. But in an effort to regain part of the huge financial loss from the seasons before, the schedule was curtailed to 14 games. Unfortunately, this seemed to cause some of the fans to turn away. Many felt that the schedule was too short and that any major soccer league had to play at least 20 games. Several top players also left since the shorter schedule meant that their salaries would be reduced. Still, the loop went ahead without delay. The New York team won the Northern Division title, with its record of seven wins, three losses, and four ties, giving it a total of 77 points. The St. Louis Stars captured the Southern Division crown, with seven wins, four defeats, and three ties for a total of 69 points. The St. Louis team was comprised mainly of native Americans, many of whom had learned the game at the Catholic Youth Council in St. Louis and had played with the St. Louis University Billikens, the perennial NCAA champions.

In an effort to reduce the financial losses, further playoffs were set up with only one semifinal game in each section. St. Louis defeated Rochester, 2-0, and New York took Dallas, 1-0. Rochester and Dallas had made the playoffs by finishing as the runners-up to New York and St. Louis, respectively. In the championship game, the New York Cosmos defeated the St. Louis Stars, 2-1, to claim the crown. The Cosmos' Randy Horton scored nine goals and added four assists to win the loop's scoring title with 22 points, four more than runner-up Mike Dillon of Montreal, who made eight goals and two assists in only 10 games. Ken Cooper, another Englishman playing with Dallas, was the top goalie in the loop, allowing 12 goals in 1,260 minutes for a 1.00 average.

Although the loop had established a player draft among graduating collegians, many teams drafted but did not sign their picks. This irri-tated fans, and some of the college coaches, who felt that the league was not making an attempt to Americanize the sport in this country. Then Al Miller, who had been a successful college coach at powerful Hartwick, came onto the scene. Miller was named head coach for the newly formed Philadelphia Atoms who, along with Toronto, had joined the operation for the 1973 season, and he was able to turn the predominantly American team into a major power. The teams, now numbering nine, were placed in three divisions, and the schedule was expanded to 19 games. Philadelphia, playing with Americans like Bob Rigby as goalie and Bob Smith as fullback (both of whom were later purchased by the Cosmos), won the Eastern Division title, compiling a total of 104 points in their impressive nine-win, two-defeat, and eight-tie record. Toronto captured the Northern Division title, with six wins, four defeats, and nine ties for a total of 89 points. Dallas won the Southern crown, with 11 wins, four defeats, and four ties for a total of 111 points. By placing second to Philadelphia, New York was the divisional team with the best point total of the second-place finishers, which included Montreal and St. Louis.

When the collegiate draft was held a few months before the start of the season, many skeptics laughed when Dallas selected Kyle Rote, Jr., the son of former football star Kyle Rote. Some claimed that it was being done strictly as a publicity gimmick. Young Rote proved them wrong, however, as the man who had turned down a college football scholarship led the league in scoring, with 10 goals and 10 assists for a total of 30 points, one more than the total recorded by Miami's Warren Archibald, a star for the Trinidad and Tobago National Team, and two more than that of Philadelphia's Andy Provan, one of three English players acquired by Miller to steady some of his American players. Rigby was the top goalie, with a league record mark of 0.62 goals against, allowing only eight goals in 1,157 minutes.

In the playoffs Dallas blanked New York, 1-0, while Philadelphia took the Toronto Metros, 3-0. The championship game was set for Dallas, with the hometown Tornado considered a slight favorite. The Atoms, however, became the first major sports franchise to win the title in its first season, as they stopped the Tornado, 2-0. On arriving home from Dallas, they were mobbed by several thousand fans at the airport and were given an official city welcome. The Atoms had proven to the soccer world that Americans can indeed play soccer. Rigby immediately received offers from several foreign teams, which he turned down. Other native Americans who performed well that year were forwards Joe Fink of New York and Gene Geiman of St. Louis, while goalie Mike Winter of St. Louis ended with an impressive 1.42 goals-against average.

The league's biggest expansion came before the start of the 1974 campaign, when the size of the loop increased from nine to 15. Boston, Denver, Washington, and Baltimore were added; and the entirely new Western Division—consisting of Los Angeles, San Jose, Seattle, and Vancouver—was formed. Montreal, however, backed mostly by the Alouettes of the Canadian Football League, dropped by the wayside, claiming financial losses of over $750,000 from the previous year. Under the four-division setup, each team would play 20 games, and tie games would no longer be left unsettled. In the event that the score was deadlocked after regulation play, the teams would each take five penalty shots. If they remained tied, then they would alternate penalty shots until one team scored and the other was unsuccessful. A team that won a match in this manner, however, would not receive the standard six points given for a regulation-time victory. Instead, it would receive three points plus one point per goal, up to three. The defeated team would receive one point for each goal it scored, up to three.

Boston won the Northern Division crown that year, with 94 points accumulated on a record of 10 wins, nine defeats, and one tie-win. Miami emerged as the Eastern Division champion, with a record of nine wins, five defeats, and six tie-wins for a total of 107 points, two more than divisional runner-up Baltimore, which was able to gain a wild-card spot* in the playoffs. Dallas' nine wins, eight defeats, and three tie-wins added up to 100 points, far above the totals of St. Louis and Denver, to capture the Central Division title; while in the Western Division, Los Angeles had a record of 11 wins, seven defeats, and two tie-wins for a 110-point total. In the battle for runner-up honors, San Jose placed second with 103 points and won the wild-card spot in the playoffs, while third-place finisher Seattle had 101 points but did not make the playoffs.

Even before the final ball had been kicked in the regular season, many of the league's owners were complaining that overtime play should be instituted and that the penalty shooting should be used only if a set time limit of sudden-death overtime failed to resolve the situation. Several owners also were angry that a tie-win was limited to three points, and some, possibly persuaded by soccer traditionalists, wanted the controversial offside rule abolished. In 1973 the league had changed the offside rule accepted worldwide. According to the accepted rule, a player in the other team's half of the field is considered offside if there are not two defenders between him and the goal at the time the ball is played to him. According to the NASL rule, however, a player cannot be considered offside, even in his opponent's half of the field, until he commits the standard offside violation less than 35 yards from the opponent's goal. Opponents of the rule said that NASL players engaging in international competition found it extremely difficult to adjust their game from the league rule to the international rule, and although there were many reasons why the United States National Team was unable to qualify for the 1974 World Cup, the offside factor had played a role when the United States was humbled by Mexico in the qualifying eliminations.

*When a team finishes either second or third in its own division and has a higher point total than the other second- or third-place finishers in the other divisions of the same conference, it gains the wild-card spot.

Paul Child of San Jose won the scoring title with 15 goals and six assists for 36 points while Seattle's Barry Watling was the top keeper with an average of 0.80 allowing 16 goals in 1,800 minutes of action.

Before the outdoor loop got underway in 1975, NASL experimented with a modified indoor tournament schedule. Even though the Tampa Bay Rowdies had not yet competed in a regular league game, they made it to the finals, where they were defeated by San Jose, 8-5.

By 1975 the league had expanded to 20 teams, making it the third largest sports loop in North America. Franchises were awarded to Hartford, Tampa Bay, Chicago, San Antonio, and Portland. The league also increased the number of American or Canadian citizens each team is required to have from four to five. Last-minute entrant Portland was exempt from this regulation, but at the end of the season, the team was almost forced to withdraw from the playoffs because the clubs from which it had borrowed players insisted that the players return to England to get ready for the start of their national soccer schedules.

Despite the protests, Commissioner Woosnam was able to maintain the controversial offside rule in 1975, and it now seems as though the rule will remain for years to come. In the quarterfinals, Dallas blasted San Jose, 3-0, while Boston took Baltimore, 1-0. In the semifinals Los Angeles blanked Boston, 2-0, and Miami ousted Dallas, 3-1, setting the stage for a game between Los Angeles and Miami in the Orange Bowl in Miami. Los Angeles won the championship game, 4-3, on penalty shots after the teams had tied, 3-3, in regulation time. The displeasure of fans who had seen the game on national television was overwhelming. How could penalty shots alone decide a tie game? This time Woosnam had no choice, and he set up a committee to investigate different ways of determining the winner of a game. The league also drew criticism when the attendance figures originally included about 7,000 people more than were actually on hand.

Some NASL officials felt that the chances of getting a national television contract were still slim since the American teams did not have any world-class stars. Consequently, clubs began to seek top-flight players. The Cosmos went after George Best, sometimes called soccer's Joe Namath. Best is known as the game's bad boy, for his conduct on the field and off. He has had many memorable arguments with both referees and police and has a large following of women. Best assured the Cosmos that he was 99.9 percent certain that he would play for them, giving the NASL its first big name. But after returning to England, Best had a change of heart and notified the New Yorkers that he was not going to play. The Cosmos had already been involved in secret negotiations with Pelé, who had retired from Santos the year before, but because of the trouble and bad publicity they received when Best changed his mind, they still were not ready to announce anything. An attempt for a national television package fell on deaf ears. Without a big star the networks just weren't interested.

St. Louis made a big move in obtaining top-name foreigners with the signing of former English National Team goalie Peter Bonetti, while Boston obtained both Eusebio and Antonio Simoes of Portugal. After much negotiation, the Cosmos finally got Pelé to play for them for the estimated price of $4.7 million for three years, and he joined them in June 1975. Immediately a series of exhibition games was announced, and Pelé's first match in a Cosmos uniform — a 2-2 exhibition tie in which he scored and assisted on a tally by former Israeli star Mordechai Sphigler — was nationally televised and carried live to 13 foreign nations. Pelé and the Cosmos were kept busy during the remainder of the season, playing exhibition games in addition to their regular matches. Because of Pelé's great drawing power, the Cosmos were able to work out an arrangement to receive 50 percent of the gross receipts from each away game they played (computed on the number of fans the other team had drawn in its previous games). Many supporters of the Cosmos were disappointed that Pelé's presence was not enough to give the Cosmos the championship, but Pelé himself had said at the time of his signing that no man alone could provide a team with a championship. His main desire, he said, was to come to America as a missionary, citing a dream he had that soccer would one day become a major league sport in America, with teams of as high a caliber as those in the rest of the world.

But not only were the Cosmos unable to win the NASL championship — they weren't even able to make the playoffs. Pelé suffered a thigh injury toward the close of the season, and the team fell apart. Like other foreign players, he complained that the artificial surfaces of many stadiums hindered the game and made a top player no better than an average player on regular grass. On the artificial surfaces, the ball took strange bounces and made plays such as the wall pass, which is soccer's version of basketball's give-and-go, totally ineffective. Instead of slowing the ball down like regular grass, the artificial turf made some of Pelé's famous lead passes run wildly off the pitch.

In the regular 1975 season, each of the 20 teams played 22 games, and a change in the point system saw the elimination of tie-wins. Now, instead of penalty shots to break a tie after regulation time had ended, the loop adopted a 15-minute sudden-death overtime procedure. If the game was still tied after the extra 15 minutes, then penalty shooting was held, and the team that won that phase of the competition would get one more goal. And instead of getting three points for the tie-win, they received the same six points, given for a win within regulation time, besides one point for each goal, to a maximum of three.

Boston, Toronto, and New York waged a bitter battle for the top two spots in the Northern Division that year, and with a record of 13 wins and nine defeats, Boston finished with 116 points. Toronto was two points behind, even though it had finished with the identical record Boston had achieved. The difference in deciding the divisional winner came in bonus points; Boston's Minutemen had 38, while Toronto had only 36. New York, which at times seemed to have a revolving door for players as coach Gordon Bradley changed lineups every game, was third with 91 points.

In the Southern Division, Tampa Bay put together a record of 16 wins and six setbacks, as first-year coach Eddie Firmani, a former top player both in England and Italy, led his team to the divisional title with 135 points. Miami was second in the division, with a record of 14 wins and eight defeats for a total of 123 points. The Washington Diplomats were third, with 112 points, but also had the honor of playing Pelé and the Cosmos in the first sports event on the new pitch at RFK Stadium. Despite a crowd of over 35,000, however, the Diplomats lost the match, 9-2.

St. Louis captured the Central Division title with a record of 13 wins and nine defeats for a total of 115 points, nine more than runner-up Chicago. Meanwhile in the Western Division, Portland, Seattle, and Los Angeles were switching positions all season. Portland finally won the divisional crown, with 138 points compiled on a record of 16 wins and six losses. Seattle won runner-up honors with 15 wins and seven losses for a total of 129 points, while Los Angeles came in third, with a record of 12 wins and 10 defeats for a total of 107 points.

In the quarterfinals of the playoffs, St. Louis outshot Los Angeles, 5-4, in penalty shots, after the teams had deadlocked at 1-1 in 90 minutes of regulation time, and 15 extra minutes failed to see a goal scored. For their proficiency in penalty shots, the St. Louis team recorded a 2-1 victory. In another quarterfinal game, Miami defeated Boston, 2-1, in overtime; while in other matches, Tampa Bay blanked Toronto, 1-0, and Portland topped Seattle, 2-1, in overtime. The semifinal pairings had Portland matched against St. Louis, while Tampa Bay met Miami. In the game that many called the Battle of Florida, the Rowdies of Tampa Bay blasted Miami, 3-0; while in the other semifinal, Portland edged past St. Louis, 1-0.

For the first time, the league had decided in advance where the championship would be held, and on August 24, Soccer Superbowl I was held in San Jose. Although many in the league felt that it would have been great to have the Cosmos and Pelé in the championship,

Pelé did attend as the honored guest. The game was nationally televised, and the ratings were good as Tampa Bay stopped the Portland Timber machine, 2-0. Substitute Arsene Aguste scored with 21 minutes gone in the second half; and Clyde Best, the man who a couple of years earlier at Yankee Stadium had scored two goals for West Ham United to offset Pelé's two tallies for Santos, added the clinching goal with less than five minutes remaining.

Steve David, a former policeman and player for the Trinidad and Tobago National Team, was the scoring champ for the season. The Miami star scored 23 goals and added six assists in 21 games for 52 points. Gordon Hill of Chicago's Sting and Derek Smethurst of Tampa tied for second place in the scoring battle. Hill had 16 goals and seven assists, while Smethurst ended up with 18 goals and three assists. In the battle for top goalie, Shep Messing, who had been released from the Cosmos over the winter and had ended up playing for Boston, won the goalie crown, with an average of only 0.93 goals against, yielding 17 goals in 1,639.32 minutes. Seattle's Barry Watling was the runner-up, with a 1.15 goals-against average, and Graham Brown of Portland finished third, at 1.20 goals against.

After the season was over, the league shocked many when it announced its annual all-star team. Few could argue against the selection of David as the Most Valuable Player, or Penn State punter Chris Bahr of Philadelphia as the Rookie of the Year, or even John Sewell of St. Louis as the Coach of the Year. But when Peter Bonetti of St. Louis was named the loop's leading goalie, an outcry was heard not only from players who had finished with a better goal-against average, but from fans who complained that the voting was rigged. Pelé also made the all-star team, and many felt that although he certainly had done a great deal for the game, his overall play had not warranted such an honor, let alone placing second to David as the league's Most Valuable Player. The U.S. soccer fans now were echoing complaints heard whenever all-star teams were announced in Europe and South America.

Although the league remained at 20 teams for the 1976 season, there were three major changes. Philadelphia was purchased by a group of Mexican soccer officials who, for the time being, were denied the right to move the franchise south of the border. Meanwhile, Baltimore sold its interests, and the new owners moved the franchise to San Diego, while Denver was moved to Minnesota. Before the regular season got underway, the league held its second annual indoor tournament, and the Tampa Bay Rowdies defeated Rochester, 6-4, in the title game held in St. Petersburg.

All of the league's teams made bids to acquire the services of top foreign players, as the league implemented a regulation cutting the roster of each club from 18 to 16 and requiring each club to carry at least six American or Canadian citizens on its team. This made the collegiate draft even more important than it had previously been. Under the new rule, at least one American or Canadian would have to be in the lineup at all times. Brown University's three-time All-American Steve Ralbovsky was the number one draftee and was selected by the Los Angeles Aztecs (which now was owned partly by Elton John, who also owns a club in England). But Ralbovsky did not get a bonus offer and was signed by the rival Los Angeles Skyhawks of the American Soccer League. The Skyhawks were one of the franchises acquired by Cousy, as the loop, with 11 teams competing, finally became a coast-to-coast operation.

Among the top foreign stars enlisted for the NASL during the 1976 season were George Best, who changed his mind and signed with the Aztecs; Rodney Marsh, the great English forward, who went with Tampa Bay; Bobby Moore, the former captain of the English National Team, who signed to play with San Antonio along with his English teammate Bob McNabe; and defender Stewart Jump, who went to Tampa. By mutual agreement, Eusebio's contract with Boston was not renewed, and he signed with Toronto Metro-Croatians, parting company with teammate Antonio Simoes after many years together.

Chicago and Toronto each compiled records of 15 wins and nine defeats in the battle for the Atlantic Conference's Northern Division title, but on the basis of bonus points, Chicago won the divisional crown with 132 points, nine more than Toronto. Rochester finished third, followed by Hartford and Boston, which was plagued by player revolt and the sale of many top stars. In the Eastern Division, Tampa Bay had a record of 18 wins and six losses for a total of 154 points. New York, which early in the season had obtained Italian National Team player Giorgio Chinaglia, placed second to the Rowdies, with a record of 16 wins and eight losses, worth 148 points. Washington placed third, followed by Philadelphia and Miami. In the Pacific Conference's Southern Division, San Jose won the crown with 123 points and a record of 14 and 10. Dallas placed second, with 117 points; while Los Angeles had 108 points, one better than San Antonio. San Diego was last. Minnesota, which drew late-season crowds of over 35,000 four times, won the Western Division title, with a record of 15 wins and nine losses and 138 points. Seattle and Vancouver each won 14 and lost 10, but on the bonus point system, Seattle earned 123 points, three more than Vancouver. Portland placed fourth, and St. Louis was last, with its 5 and 9 mark the poorest in the league.

The playoffs were expanded, and in first-round action New York defeated Washington, 2-0; Seattle beat Vancouver, 1-0; Dallas took

Los Angeles, 2-0; and Toronto edged Rochester, 2-1. In the quarter-finals, Tampa Bay topped New York, 3-1; Toronto outshot Chicago in penalty shots to post a 3-2 victory; San Jose blanked Dallas, 2-0; and Minnesota took Seattle, 3-0. In the semifinals, Toronto beat Tampa Bay, 2-0; and Minnesota, before a home crowd of 49,572, beat San Jose, 3-1. In the championship game, held in Seattle's Kingdome, Toronto got a first-half goal by Eusebio and two second-half scores, by Ivan Lucacevic and Ferreira, to beat Minnesota, 3-0.

Chinaglia, who set a single-game league mark of five goals and two assists for 12 points, won the scoring title, with 19 goals and 11 assists for 49 points. Smethurst was second, with 45 points, one more than Pelé. Seattle's Chursky was the top goalie, with a 9.91 goals-against average. San Jose's Mike Hewitt was second at 0.92, and Toronto's Paolo Cimpiel, who missed the playoffs because of a contract dispute and was replaced by Zeljko Bilecki, was third, with an 0.96 goals-against mark. Pelé was the MVP winner; Firmani, the top coach; and Dallas' Steve Pecher, the top rookie. Total regular season attendance was over 2½ million, an increase of 20 percent over 1975.

U.S. DEWAR'S OPEN CHALLENGE CUP

Year	Winner		Runner-Up		Venue
1914	Bklyn, Field Club	2	Brooklyn Celtic	1	Pawtucket, R.I.
1915	Bethlehem Steel	3	Brooklyn Celtic	1	S. Bethlehem, Pa.
1916	Bethlehem Steel	1	Fall River Rovers	0	Pawtucket, R.I.
1917	Fall River Rovers	1	Bethlehem Steel	0	Pawtucket, R.I.
1918	Bethlehem Steel	2	Fall River Rovers	2	Pawtucket, R.I.
	Bethlehem Steel	3	Fall River Rovers	0	Harrison, N.J.
1919	Bethlehem Steel	2	Paterson	0	Fall River, Mass.
1920	Ben Millers	2	Fore River	1	St. Louis, Mo.
1921	Robbins Dry Dock	4	Scullin Steel	2	Fall River, Mass.
1922	Scullin Steel	3	Todd Shipyard	2	St. Louis, Mo.
1923*	Paterson	2	Scullin Steel	2	St. Louis, Mo.
1924	Fall River	4	Vesper Buick	2	Harrison, N.J.
1925	Shawsheen	3	Canadian Club	0	Tiverton, R.I.
1926	Bethlehem Steel	7	Ben Miller	2	Brooklyn, N.Y.
1927	Fall River	7	Holley Carburetor	0	Detroit, Mich.
1928	N.Y. Nationals	2	Bricklayers	2	New York, N.Y.
	N.Y. Nationals	3	Bricklayers	0	Chicago, Ill.
1929†	Hakoah All-Stars	2	Madison Kennels	0	St. Louis, Mo.
	Hakoah All-Stars	3	Madison Kennels	0	Brooklyn, N.Y.
1930	Fall River	7	Bruell Insurance	2	New York, N.Y.
	Fall River	2	Bruell Insurance	7	Cleveland, Ohio
1931	Fall River	6	Bricklayers	2	New York, N.Y.
	Fall River	1	Bricklayers	1	Chicago, Ill.
1932	New Bedford	3	Stix, Baer & Fuller	3	St. Louis, Mo.
	New Bedford	5	Stix, Baer & Fuller	2	St. Louis, Mo.

Year	Winner		Runner-Up		Venue
1933	Stix, Baer & Fuller	1	N.Y. Americans	0	St. Louis, Mo.
	Stix, Baer & Fuller	2	N.Y. Americans	1	New York, N.Y.
1934	Stix, Baer & Fuller	4	Pawtucket Rangers	2	St. Louis, Mo.
	Stix, Baer & Fuller	2	Pawtucket Rangers	3	Pawtucket, R.I.
	Stix, Baer & Fuller	5	Pawtucket Rangers	0	St. Louis, Mo.
1935	Central Breweries	5	Pawtucket Rangers	2	St. Louis, Mo.
	Central Breweries	1	Pawtucket Rangers	1	Pawtucket, R.I.
	Central Breweries	1	Pawtucket Rangers	3	Newark, N.J.
1936	Phila. Americans	2	St. Louis Sh'mr'cks	2	St. Louis, Mo.
	Phila. Americans	3	St. Louis Sh'mr'cks	1	Philadelphia, Pa.
1937	N.Y. Americans	0	St. Louis Sh'mr'cks	2	St. Louis, Mo.
	N.Y. Americans	4	St. Louis Sh'mr'cks	2	New York, N.Y.
1938	Sparta, Chicago	4	St. Mary's Celtic	0	Chicago, Ill.
	Sparta, Chicago	4	St. Mary's Celtic	2	New York, N.Y.
1939	St. Mary's Celtic, Brooklyn	1	Manhattan Beer	0	Chicago, Ill.
	St. Mary's Celtic, Brooklyn	4	Manhattan Beer	1	New York, N.Y.
1940‡	Baltimore, S.C.	0	Sparta, Chicago	0	Baltimore, Md.
	Baltimore, S.C.	2	Sparta, Chicago	2	Chicago, Ill.
1941	Pawtucket	4	Chrysler, Detroit	2	Pawtucket, R.I.
	Pawtucket	4	Chrysler, Detroit	3	Detroit, Mich.
1942	Gallatin, Pa.	2	Pawtucket	1	Pittsburgh, Pa.
	Gallatin, Pa.	4	Pawtucket	2	Pawtucket, R.I.
1943§	Brooklyn Hispano	2	Morgan Strasser	2	New York, N.Y.
§	Brooklyn Hispano	4	Morgan Strasser	2	New York, N.Y.
1944§	Brooklyn Hispano	4	Morgan Strasser	0	New York, N.Y.
1945	Brookhattan	4	Cleveland Americans	1	New York, N.Y.
	Brookhattan	2	Cleveland Americans	1	Cleveland, Ohio
1946	Chicago Vikings	1	Ponta Delgada, Fall River	1	Fall River, Mass.
	Chicago Vikings	2	Ponta Delgada, Fall River	1	Chicago, Ill.
1947	Ponta Delgada	6	Sparta, Chicago	2	Chicago, Ill.
	Ponta Delgada	3	Sparta, Chicago	2	St. Louis, Mo.
1948	Simpkins, St. Louis	3	Brookhattan	1	Philadelphia, Pa.
1949	Morgan, Pa.	0	Philadelphia Nats	2	Pittsburgh, Pa.
	Morgan, Pa.	4	Philadelphia Nats	0	St. Louis, Mo.
1950	Simpkins	2	Ponta Delgada	1	Tiverton, R.I.
	Simpkins	1	Ponta Delgada	4	Bridgeville, Pa.
1951	German Hungarian	2	Heidelberg	2	Brooklyn, N.Y.
	German Hungarian	6	Heidelberg	2	Pittsburgh, Pa.
1952	Harmarville, Pa.	3	Philadelphia Nats	1	Philadelphia, Pa.
	Harmarville, Pa.	4	Philadelphia Nats	1	Chicago, Ill.
1953	Falcons, Ill.	2	Harmarville, Pa.	0	Harmarville, Pa.
	Falcons, Ill.	1	Harmarville, Pa.	1	St. Louis, Mo.
1954	N.Y. Americans	1	Kutis, St. Louis	0	New York, N.Y.
	N.Y. Americans	2	Kutis, St. Louis	0	New York, N.Y.
1955	Eintracht, New York	2	Danish Americans	0	Los Angeles, Cal.
1956	Harmarville, Pa.	0	Chicago Schwaben	1	Chicago, Ill.
	Harmarville, Pa.	3	Chicago Schwaben	1	Harmarville, Pa.
1957	Kutis, St. Louis	3	Hakoah New York	0	St. Louis, Mo.
	Kutis, St. Louis	3	Hakoah New York	1	New York, N.Y.
1958	Los Angeles Kickers	2	Pompei Baltimore	1	Baltimore, Md.
1959	S. Pedro Canvasbacks	4	Fall River	3	Fall River, Mass.
1960	Phila. Ukrainian	5	Los Angeles Kickers	3	Philadelphia, Pa.
1961	Phila. Ukrainian	2	Los Angeles Scots	2	Philadelphia, Pa.
	Phila. Ukrainian	5	Los Angeles Scots	2	Philadelphia, Pa.

Year	Winner		Runner-Up		Venue
1962	N.Y. Hungaria	3	San Franc isco Scots	2	New York, N.Y.
1963	Phila. Ukrainian	1	L. Angeles Armenian	0	Philadelphia, Pa.
1964	L.A. Kickers	2	Phila. Ukrainian	2	Philadelphia, Pa.
	L.A. Kickers	2	Phila. Ukrainian	0	Los Angeles, Cal.
1965	N.Y. Ukrainian	1	Hansa Chicago	1	New York, N.Y.
	N.Y. Ukrainian	3	Hansa Chicago	0	Chicago, Ill.
1966	Phila. Ukrainian	1	Orange County	0	Los Angeles, Cal.
	Phila. Ukrainian	3	Orange County	0	Philadelphia, Pa.
1967	N.Y. Greek-Americans	4	Orange County	2	New York, N.Y.
1968	N.Y. Greek-Americans	1	Chicago Olympic	1	Chicago, Ill.
	N.Y. Greek-Americans	1	Chicago Olympic	0	New York, N.Y.
1969	N.Y. Greek-Americans	1	Montebello Armenians	0	Los Angeles, Cal.
1970	Elizabeth, N.J.	2	L. Angeles Croatia	1	New York, N.Y.
1971	N.Y. Hota	6	San Pedro Yugoslavs	4	Los Angeles, Cal.
1972	Elizabeth, N.J.	1	San Pedro Yugoslavs	0	Elizabeth, N.J.
1973	L.A. Maccabee	5	Cleveland Inter	3	Los Angeles, Cal.
1974	N.Y. Greek-Americans	2	Chicago Croatians	0	New York, N.Y.
1975	L.A. Maccabee	1	Inter-Giuliana, N.Y.	0	Los Angeles, Cal.
1976	S.F. Athletic Club	1	Inter-Giuliana, N.Y.	0	New York, N.Y.

* Awarded to Paterson by default.

† First year of deciding title by two- or three-game series.

‡ No deciding game played.

§ Single game played.

NATIONAL AMATEUR CUP

Year	Winner		Runner-Up		Venue
1924	Fleisher Yarn	3	Swedish-American	0	Chicago, Ill.
1925	Toledo	3	McLeod Council	1	Cleveland, Ohio
1926	Defenders	1	Heidelberg	0	Cleveland, Ohio
1928*	Swedish-Americans		Powers Hudson Essex		
1929	Heidelberg	9	1st German S.C.	0	Newark, N.J.
1930†	Raffies	3	Gallatin	3	Pittsburgh, Pa.
1931	Goodyear	1	Black Cats	1	N. Bedford, Mass.
	Goodyear	2	Black Cats	0	Akron, Ohio
1932	Clev. Shamrock	2	Stanto Christo	1	Cleveland, Ohio
1933	German-American	5	McKnight Beverage	1	Philadelphia, Pa.
1934	German-American	1	Heidelberg	1	Philadelphia, Pa.
1935	W. W. Riehl	3	All-Amer. Cafe	0	Pittsburgh, Pa.
1936	Brooklyn, S.C.	2	Castle Shannon	1	Brooklyn, N.Y.
1937	Trenton Highlander	1	Castle Shannon	0	Pittsburgh, Pa.
1938	Ponta Delgada	2	Heidelberg	0	Fall River, Mass.
1939	St. Michael	3	Gallatin	1	Fall River, Mass.
1940	Morgan Strasser	1	Fireston	0	N. Tiverton, Mass.
1941	Fall River	2	Chrysler	1	Fall River, Mass.
1942	Fall River	4	Morgan U.S.C.O.	3	Fall River, Mass.
1943	Morgan Strasser	4	Santo Maria	1	Baltimore, Md.
1944	Eintracht	5	Morgan Strasser	2	New York, N.Y.
1945	Eintracht	1	Rafterys	0	New York, N.Y.

Year	Winner		Runner-Up		Venue
1946	Ponta Delgada	5	Castle Shannon	2	Fall River, Mass.
1947	Ponta Delgada	4	Curry, Vets	1	Fall River, Mass.
1948	Ponta Delgada	4	Curry, Vets	1	Fall River, Mass.
1949	Elizabeth	6	Zenthoefer	1	Astoria, N.Y.
1950	Ponta Delgada	0	Harmarville	1	Tiverton, R.I.
	Ponta Delgada	4	Harmarville	1	Pittsburgh, Pa.
1951	German Hungarian	4	Harmarville	3	Brooklyn, N.Y.
1952	Raiders	3	Lusitano	1	Ludlow, Mass.
1953	Ponta Delgado	2	Chicago Slovaks	0	Tiverton, R.I.
1954	Beadling	2	Simpkins	5	St. Louis, Mo.
	Beadling	5	Simpkins	1	Pittsburgh, Pa.
1955	Heidelberg Tornados	2	Chicago Eagles	2	Chicago, Ill.
	Heidelberg Tornados	5	Chicago Eagles	0	Heidelberg, Pa.
1956	Kutis, St. Louis	1	Phil. Ukrainian	0	St. Louis, Mo.
1957	Kutis, St. Louis	1	Rochester Ukrainian	1	St. Louis, Mo.
1958	Kutis, St. Louis	2	Beadling	1	Pittsburgh, Pa.
1959	Kutis, St. Louis	5	St. Andrew Scots	0	St. Louis, Mo.
	Kutis, St. Louis	2	St. Andrew Scots	2	Detroit, Mich.
1960	Kutis, St. Louis	4	Patchogue, N.Y.	0	St. Louis, Mo.
1961	Kutis, St. Louis	1	Italian-Amer. Stars	0	St. Louis, Mo.
	Kutis, St. Louis	3	Italian-Amer. Stars	3	Hartford, Conn.
1962	Carpathia Kickers	4	Ameri. Hungarian	0	Detroit, Mich.
1963	Italian-Americans	1	St. Ambrose	0	Rochester, N.Y.
1964	Schwaben	4	German Hungarian	0	Chicago, Ill.
1965	German-Hungar., Phila.	6	St. Ambrose	0	Philadelphia, Pa.
1966	Chicago Kickers	5	Italian-Americans	2	Chicago, Ill.
1967	Hartford Italians	2	Kutis, St. Louis	0	St. Louis, Mo.
1968	Chicago Kickers	2	Carpathian Kickers	1	Detroit, Mich.
1969	British Lions	4	Kutis, St. Louis	1	Washington, D.C.
1970	Chicago Kickers	6	German Hungarian	5	Chicago, Ill.
1971	Kutis, St. Louis	4	Cleveland Inter-Italian	1	Cleveland, Ohio
1972	Busch, St. Louis	1	New Bedford Portuguese	0	St. Louis, Mo.
1973	Philadelphia Inter	3	San Jose Grenadiers	2	Philadelphia, Pa.
1974	Philadelphia Inter	4	Big 4 Chevrolet	3	St. Louis, Mo.
1975	Chicago Kickers	1	Scotland SC	0	Kearny, N.J.
1976	Bavarian Blue Ribbon	3	Trenton Ext.	1	Milwaukee, Wisc.

* Game not played.

† Awarded to Raffies; Gallatin failed to complete replay.

NATIONAL JUNIOR CHAMPIONSHIP†

Year	Winners	Runner-Up
1935	Reliable Stores, New Bedford	W. of Scotland, Brooklyn, N.Y.
1936	Hatkivoh F.C., Brooklyn, N.Y.	Bethlehem Midgets
1937	Hatkivoh F.C., Brooklyn, N.Y.	Beloise F.C., Pittsburgh
1938	Lighthouse, Philadelphia	Beading F.C., Pittsburgh
1939	Avella F.C., W. Penn.	Apache F.C., Baltimore
1940	Avella F.C., W. Penn.	Yorkville Ath., New York
1941	Mercerville, Trenton	Kensington Rec., E. Penn.

1942 through 1944 no competition

Year	Winners	Runner-Up
1945*	Pompei, Baltimore, and Hornets Chicago	
1946	Schumacher, St. Louis	Prague A.C., New York
1947	Heidelberg, Pa.	Baldwin Hill, Trenton
1948	Lighthouse B.C., Philadelphia	Schumacher, St. Louis
1949	Lighthouse B.C., Philadelphia	Windsor A.C., St. Louis
1950	Harrison B.C. (N.J.)	Seco B.C., St. Louis
1951	Seco B.C., St. Louis	Midway B.C., Philadelphia
1952*	Kollsman S.C., Brooklyn, and Lions, Chicago	
1953*	Newark, N.J., and Hansa, Chicago	
1954	Hansa, Chicago	Heidelberg, Pa.
1955*	Gottschee, New York, and Schwaben, Chicago	
1956*	St. Englebert, St. Louis, and Heidelberg, Pa.	
1957	Lighthouse, Philadelphia	Kriegshauser, St. Louis
1958	St. Paul, St. Louis	Gottschee, New York
1959	Ukrainian, N.Y.	Fichte, Chicago
1960	St. Paul, St. Louis	Elizabeth, N.J.
1961	Hakoah, San Francisco	Lighthouse, Philadelphia
1962	Schumachers, St. Louis	Good Counsel, Baltimore
1963	Kutis, St. Louis	Eintracht, New York
1964	Kutis, St. Louis	Lighthouse Celtic, Philadelphia
1965	I.M. Heart of Mary, St. Louis	Lighthouse Celtic, Philadelphia
1966	St. William, St. Louis	Knitters, Brooklyn
1967	Lighthouse, Philadelphia	St. Philip Neri, St. Louis
1968	St. Philip Neri, St. Louis	Hammsetts, Trenton
1970	St. Barts, St. Louis	Blau Weiss Gottschee, N.Y.
1971	Seco, St. Louis	Casa Bianca, Baltimore
1972	Seco, St. Louis	Casa Bianco, Baltimore
1973	St. Elizabeth S.C., Baltimore	Sparta, San Diego
1974	Florissant Celtic, St. Louis	Dico Rivera, San Diego
1975	Imos Pizza, St. Louis	Blau-Weiss Gotschee, N.Y.
1976	Annandale Cavaliers, Va.	Sparta, Chicago

* No champions declared.
† Called James P. McGuire Cup in 1976.

AMERICAN SOCCER LEAGUE CHAMPIONS

1934	Kearny Irish	1957	New York Hakoah
1935	Philadelphia Germans	1958	New York Hakoah
1936	New York Americans	1959	New York Hakoah
1937	Kearny Scots	1960	Colombo
1938	Kearny Scots	1961	Ukranian Nationals
1939	Kearny Scots	1962	Ukranian Nationals
1940	Kearny Scots	1963	Ukranian Nationals
1941	Kearny Scots	1964	Ukranian Nationals
1942	Philadelphia Americans	1965	Hartford S.C.
1943	Brooklyn Hispanos	1966	Roma S.C.
1944	Philadelphia Americans	1967	Baltimore St. Gerard's
1945	New York Brookhattan	1968	Ukranian Nationals
1946	Baltimore Americans	1968	Washington Darts
1947	Philadelphia Americans	1969	(First Summer Season)
1948	Philadelphia Americans		Washington Darts
1949	Philadelphia Americans	1970	Philadelphia Ukranians
1950	Philadelphia Nationals	1971	New York Greeks
1951	Philadelphia Nationals	1972	Cincinnati Comets
1952	Philadelphia Americans	1973	New York Apollo
1953	Philadelphia Nationals	1974	Rhode Island Oceaneers
1954	New York Americans	1975	Boston Astros–New York Apollo
1955	Uhrik Truckers	1976	Los Angeles Skyhawks
1956	Uhrik Truckers		

NASL CHAMPIONSHIPS

Year	Winner	Runner-Up
1967 (NPSL)	Oakland	Baltimore
1967 (USA)	Los Angeles	Washington
1968	Atlanta	San Diego
1969	Kansas City	Atlanta
1970	Rochester	Washington
1971	Dallas	Atlanta
1972	New York	St. Louis
1973	Philadelphia	Dallas
1974	Los Angeles	Miami
1975	Tampa Bay	Portland
1976	Toronto	Minnesota

CHAPTER 5

African Development

African soccer started to shed its backward and primitive organization during the early 1960s, and many feel that in the not-too-distant future several African nations will be able to challenge the European and South American soccer powers. Already the record books are starting to note the high-level performance of the continent's national team, and when Zaire defeated the touring Santos team of Brazil in 1972, the entire soccer world sat up and took notice.

In the more politically stable African nations, governments have backed the growth of the game, invited foreign teams to play exhibition matches at government expense, organized strong clinical programs run by top European and Asian players and coaches, and created incentives for players to score victories over opponents. In the countries with a lot of political unrest, however, the development of soccer has been relatively slow, and these nations have not been able to match the level of soccer played by their neighbors. If there is one major drawback to the entire African soccer scene, it is the political antipathy of several nations toward one another. The African Football Federation often has scheduled tournaments that could not be successfully completed because one nation was fighting another nation and would not send a soccer team to play.

Soccer has been played in Africa for over 75 years, and its development there actually started when troops from the various nations who were colonizing the continent played matches there. Slowly African youth began to pick up the game. In East Africa, where the great Eusebio first put on a pair of soccer boots, the game was played by youngsters who adopted, with some modifications, the soccer style of their

Portuguese rulers. The English and Dutch also introduced their style of play to their colonies; and everywhere on the continent, the style of a particular nation resembled that of its rulers. When the countries began to achieve independence, the governments of the emerging nations stressed the development of strong leagues and the importance of having their players develop styles of their own. This has been slow coming in many cases but has been aided by several top coaches from Yugoslavia. In 1969 Morocco hired the great former Yugoslavian coach Blagoje Vidinic to prepare its team for the battle to become the first African entry into the World Cup. Vidinic spent months getting the Moroccan team ready for the competition against seven other African entrants, and he brought in many top Yugoslavian players to work with him in trying to mix the best of the Moroccan style with that of Yugoslavia. Morocco did make it to the World Cup in Mexico, and the Moroccans offered Vidinic a chance to stay on as their national coach; but the Yugoslavian got a better offer from sports-minded President Mobuta of Zaire and took a job as that nation's national coach instead. In 1974 Zaire entered the elimination tourney for the World Cup, held in West Germany. The first black nation to play in a World Cup tourney, the African team beat 23 other nations to win a berth in the Cup.

NATIONAL PRIDE

Throughout Africa large new stadiums are being erected, and because of the extreme heat, several nations, like Algeria, have installed artificial turf. Because of the growth of African soccer, the African Confederation, the ruling body of the continent, has instituted junior tournaments and a Cup-Winners' Cup and interzonal competition.

Whereas once five or six entrants in the annual African Cup were considered a lot, today African soccer events are so crowded that elimination tournaments often must be held. The days when the rulers of the colonies played soccer on patches of cleared ground are over, and a strong feeling of national pride has started to develop among many of the players in the competing nations.

Zaire

Nowhere is pride in soccer more evident than in Zaire, where the team was honored at an official banquet and each team member received the equivalent of $20,000, a new house, and a new car from President Mobuta after they won the spot in the World Cup. Some say that Mobuta went overboard in his praise of the team, which was demolished in the opening rounds of the 1974 World Cup, but Mobuta (the man behind the Ali-Foreman heavyweight title fight) has replied to his critics that despite the amount of money being poured into the effort, putting Zaire on the international sports scene will reap great benefits not only in prestige but also in future international tourism, as nations will bring fans to the country whenever they are visiting to play an exhibition match.

The biggest problem facing Zaire's early soccer development was the bitter conflict between the two major football associations in the nation. For years, until the ministry stepped in at the request of the president, the national team of Zaire was composed of players who competed in the Kinshasa-Lubumbashi League, while those who belonged to the rival Mbuji-Mayi Association were overlooked. Now the Zaire football leaders are selecting players from both groups, however, and the response from both associations has been so positive that there is even talk of holding interleague competition by the beginning of the 1980s.

Among the leading teams in Zaire that have played not only in African Cup competition but also in Europe and Asia, are the FC Sanga Valende team, the Cercle Sportif Imana team of Kinshasa, Vita, and Tout Puissant Mazembe. As has been the case in many African nations, Zaire has been able to secure such renowned world-class stars as Pelé, who is doing clinical work for the Pepsi-Cola Company, to help develop its vast junior program. Not to be outdone, Coca-Cola is also now organizing junior leagues and clinics for juniors. Some big industrial companies have also been sponsoring full professional teams in leagues, which along with the strong backing of the government, will make it hard for the other African nations to surpass Zaire in its soccer success until they adopt similar backing proposals.

Morocco

In Morocco soccer developed during both English and Spanish domination, but the development, which at first was very rapid, has slowed down, and in 1976 the national association had to sit down and iron out some of the difficulties between the clubs. Most clubs were interested in competing on an international level, but each club wanted to have the final say in determining not only the makeup of the national team, but also who would be selected as coach, trainer, and administrative head. Morocco came close to drawing a suspension from FIFA when it forfeited its final match of the World Cup qualifying series in 1973; but after receiving a stern warning, it was back in FIFA's good graces after paying a fine that went to the African Confederation. Morocco is presently trying to regain its former prestige in the soccer world, and with the clubs now almost working together, it has resumed competing on a full-time basis with the likes of Zaire and Zambia.

Zambia
Zambia is another nation that utilizes foreign coaches, mostly from Europe, to build its soccer program. Unlike Morocco, in Zambia there has been little or no friction between competing clubs, as the teams are interested in giving their nation the strongest possible representation in international competition. Among the Zambian clubs that have been successful in Cup and international club matches are powerful Mulfulira Wanderers, a name taken from the Wolverhampton Wanderers who toured Africa in the early 1960s, and the Green Buffaloes, a team that has developed a strong junior program and has successfully brought its junior players to compete on the varsity team.

Algiers
Although its ties with the Asian soccer nations are often considered stronger than those with its rival African countries, under the leadership of Algerian Football Federation president Benaouda, Algerian soccer has been progressing well, as the nation has recognized the need for new facilities, such as the new stadium built for the Mediterranean Games. Both the French and English have played a strong part in building Algeria's soccer program, and creating a strong national team has become the top priority, overriding interclub competition. Disputes have arisen among the stronger clubs, who claim that they should be allowed to compete in both the African Cup and the African Cup-Winners' Cup; but in 1975, when the first annual African Cup of Cup-Winners tournament was held, there were no Algerian entrants in the field, nor competing for the adjoining African Cup. Algeria did field an impressive team for the African Nations Cup, however, and in the future may have one of the stronger national teams on the continent.

Arab Republic of Egypt
The Arab Republic of Egypt is another up-and-coming power on the African scene, although it also sends its club to international tournaments elsewhere, such as the Mediterranean Games. The Egyptian team has also competed in the World Military Championship and in the Olympic qualifying series. In club competition the Mehalla team and Union Recreation club are dominant, and both teams have played in various interclub tournaments in African Federation competition. Several new stadiums have been built in Egypt over the past 15 years, and the government was almost thrown into a political crisis in 1974 when one of the new stadiums collapsed, killing several persons. A

government inspector now examines the plans and construction of any new stadium to make sure that the increasing numbers of fans who are attending games will be safe. One of the biggest problems with Egyptian soccer appears to be the lack of competent Egyptian officials. Because of their questionable calls, the officials have often been the cause of riots, leading to death and injury not only to fans but on several instances to players who were attacked by irate fans of the opposing team.

Tunisia

Tunisia also is starting to emerge as one of the more powerful nations in African soccer, and although the rapid development it showed in the 1950s declined in the 1960s, in the early 1970s Tunisia started to emerge again with the success in international competition of such clubs as Tunisia FC and Inter-Tunisia. The two clubs originally were one, but because of disputes among various club members, the team voted to disband and form two separate organizations, both of which are now regarded as stronger than the original group. One of the greatest moments in Tunisian soccer came in 1975, when the Tunisian team eliminated Algeria in the opening round of the 10th African Cup. The nation declared a national holiday, and the players received awards from government leaders.

Uganda

The Express club has been the dominant power in Ugandan soccer and the major supplier of players for the National Team of Uganda. No one can accuse the National Federation of playing favorites, for Express is a fast-moving, well-backed club; four different players from its roster each scored a goal in the Ugandan National Team's 1975 victory over Mauritius.

Togo

Led by Club Sortif Lome team and its rival Omnisports Atapkame, Togo also is regarded as one of the stronger soccer nations in Africa. Utilizing a style of play that combines both English and Spanish techniques, teams from Togo have been successful in international matches against other African teams.

Nigeria

Nigeria is another hotbed of soccer—one that carries its passion for the game to extremes. During the civil war with Biafra, both sides declared a special ceasefire, since Pelé and his Santos team were playing an exhibition game. The ceasefire lasted three days, and the war resumed after Pelé left the country. In club competition, the Rangers

Club has won the national championship four times, more than any of the other clubs, and is also the chief supplier of talent for the national team, which although well financed is still not so strong as most of the other African national clubs. Another strong team from Nigeria is the Mighty Jet Club.

Cameroon
Cameroon is also on the rise as a national power, and its highly regarded Tonnerre de Yaoundé club has been successful in defeating several Asian clubs in intercontinental exhibition games.

Ethiopia
Ethiopian soccer also is starting to develop, thanks to a large investment of industrial money into the program, and such clubs as the Embassoira d'Asmara and Saint-George have been able to compete on an equal level with other African teams. For the most part, the national team has not been able to win any major titles. In the qualifying round for the 1974 World Cup, however, it was able to eliminate Tanzania before being defeated by Zambia.

Tanzania
Tanzania is also starting to emerge in African soccer, and its Jeshi FC club is one of the most entertaining teams of Africa, featuring a system that has six men on attack at all times.

Central Africa Republic
Fatima and Tempete Mocaf are the two strongest teams from Central African Republic and make up the nucleus of the national team that will be competing in the 1978 World Cup elimination tournament for the first time.

Senegal
On April 13, 1975, Senegal went wild when its national team was able to defeat Morocco for the first time in eight years. Although its 2-1 victory was not enough to offset Morocco's first-leg 4-0 triumph, the victory still marked a high spot in soccer development in Senegal; and since then such clubs as Jeanne d'Arc have been competing on a regular basis in inter-African club competition.

Ghana
Ghana has one of the better-developed national clubs in Africa and has been able to play competitively in both club and national competition. In fact, in the qualifying round for the 1974 World Cup, Ghana defeated Zaire in one of the elimination matches. Several players from

Ghana have come to the United States to learn different styles of playing from the English and South American players in the North American and American Soccer leagues. They then have gone home to teach the skills they learned, and consequently Ghana is a nation where almost all the world soccer styles have been blended together into one. The most successful club in Ghana is the Great Olympics.

Emerging into Soccer

Other African nations that are now competing on a regular international basis are Somalia, with its Horsed team; the Sudan, whose national team is made up mostly of players from the Merreickh club; Burundi, led by the Inter-Football club; Malagasy Republic, whose top club is the Tuléar team; Malawi, with the powerful Batta Bullets leading the way; Lesotho, led by the Matlama FC; Niger, which has two strong clubs—the Olympic Niamey FC and the Sahel SC; Dahomey, with the Étoile Sportive club the outstanding team; Mali, with the Djoliba Niamey team, which eliminated the strong Mighty Black Pool club, Sierra Leone's strongest side; Liberia, with top clubs Bame and Barolle Invincible; the Ivory Coast, with the bitter rivals ASEC d'Abidjan and Stella Club its two strongest teams; Gabon, with its Petro Sports Club; Gambia, with its Real de Banjul team and Wallidan SC as its top clubs; Guinea, led by its Haifa 11 team; and Kenya, which for the past 10 years has been playing a limited league schedule in order to build a strong national team that competes in Asia and on a European training tour.

With nations like Mauritius and many other new nations springing up almost yearly, there are sure to be more and more competitors in future international tournaments. And although many members of FIFA are opposed to it, with their large representation and lucrative FIFA dues, the Africans could well have two spots in the World Cup championships in the not-too-distant future.

The rise in African soccer goes on, and with its growth comes the quest for additional training procedures, not only on the part of players and coaches but also from trainers. European soccer schools that offer special courses in prevention of injuries have been getting many students from African nations. Although there is much that still needs to be done, the African youth today are often being trained not by foreigners but by their own people as African nations make a concentrated effort to enter the international soccer arena.

AFRICAN CHAMPIONSHIPS

Year	Winner	Runner-Up	Score
African Cup of Nations			
1957	Egypt	Ethiopia	4–0
1959	Egypt	Sudan	2–1
1961	Ethiopia	Egypt	4–2
1963	Ghana	Sudan	3–0
1965	Ghana	Tunis	3–2
1968	Zaire	Ghana	1–0
1970	Sudan	Ghana	1–0
1972	Congo	Mali	3–2
1974	Zaire	Zambia	2–0
1976	Morocco*	Guinea	1–1
African Cup of Champions Cup			
1964	Oryx, Cameroon	Kotoko, Ghana	
1966	State Abidjan, Ivory Coast	Stade, Mali	
1967	Englebert, Zaire	Kotoko, Ghana	
1968	Englebert, Zaire	Etoile Filante, Togo	
1969	Ismaili, Egypt	Englebert, Zaire	
1970	Kotoko, Ghana	Englebert, Zaire	
1971	Cannon, Cameroon	Kotoko, Ghana	
1972	Hafia, Guinea	Simba, Uganda	
1973	Vita, Zaire	Kotoko, Ghana	
1974	Cara, Congo	Mehallah, UAR	
1975	Hafia, Guinea	Rangers, Nigeria	
African Cup of Cup Winners Championship			
1975	First leg: Stella, Ivory Coast	Tonnerre, Cameroon	1–0
	Second leg:		
	Tonnerre, Cameroon	Stella, Ivory Coast	4–1
	Two-game, total-goal		
	champion: Tonnerre		4–2

* Morocco declared winner on round-robin basis.

CHAPTER 6
Asian Soccer

In the 1966 World Cup competition, held in England, a band of players from North Korea shocked the soccer world by upsetting powerful Italy, regarded as one of the top choices to take the title. Many soccer fans in Europe and South America were aware that soccer was being played in such nations as Israel, New Zealand, and Australia, which although not Asian, had been placed in the Asian Football Federation by FIFA. But the men from North Korea, which became the first Asian nation to participate in the World Cup, came as a real surprise. They had never won a major tournament before taking the Asian elimination series, but after losing, 3-0, to the Soviet Union and tying Chile, 1-1, they beat Italy, 1-0, forcing the Italians to find a secret way out of the stadium to avoid their irate fans. After that defeat, the Italian team even had to change its return plans, when word leaked out that thousands of fans were ready to meet the players at the original port, prepared not only to hurl insults, but anything else they had handy.

In the quarterfinal round of the World Cup, the play of such men as Yang Sung Kook, Pak Suen Jin, and Li Dong Woon was devastating, as they shocked Portugal, which had Eusebio on its roster. The North Koreans finally submitted, 5-3, but it took a four-goal performance from Eusebio to turn the trick for Portugal. Immediately interest from the rest of the soccer world skyrocketed, and the North Korean team was invited to play a series of matches to demonstrate just how far it could go in other tournament. Not only did North Korea benefit from the exposure, but all of Asia was becoming recognized as a potential stronghold of soccer.

As in many African nations, soccer in Asia had its beginning in foreign occupation; the English played the game while occupying Palestine. The British influence eventually spread throughout the Near East and throughout Asia, with Scottish and English players participating in Singapore, Hong Kong, Australia, and New Zealand.

Unfortunately, soccer in Asia has been plagued with discord. In addition to Mainland China's battle for acceptance by FIFA, the frictions between neighboring Arab nations, besides their battle to exclude Israel, have made planning most difficult. Except Mainland China, the various nations are all invited to play in the Asian Cup. If, as was the case in 1976, an English or other team wanted to accept a Mainland Chinese invitation to play a series of matches behind the bamboo curtain, it would have to first secure the permission of FIFA, or else face either a severe fine or being banned by the worldwide ruling body from future competition.

ASIAN LEAGUES

Besides Mainland China, which finally appears ready to make a formal bid to join FIFA to compete in the Asian zone elimination series for future World Cups, the biggest new power on the soccer horizon is Japan. Years ago, promoters had to beg people to take a free ticket to see a game in Japan; but now at many league games, and at just about every international exhibition match, it's standing room only. When Pelé first toured Japan with the Santos team in the late 1960s, only about 10,000 people turned out for the match. When he returned 10 years later, however, the 80,000 fans who turned out were seated in the stands two hours before the opening kickoff.

Japan
The biggest reason for the growth of interest in soccer in Japan is men like Mr. Honda, the head of the giant industrial plant that bears his name. Honda became interested in soccer development and spent a great deal of money bringing in top coaches to run clinics both for his workers and for his office staff. With close ties in Brazil, Honda was also able to secure the services of several children of Japanese men. He offered these youths, then in their teens, incentive to come to Japan by promising to provide employment for them after they were educated. The skills that the youths had learned in Brazil while playing junior soccer were soon picked up by those who had never even seen a soccer ball before, and as a result, today children in Japan are taking to soccer in even greater numbers than they are to baseball and gymnastic competition.

When it came time for the entry box to be opened prior to the start of the elimination series for the 1974 World Cup, the tournament organizers were shocked when they learned that although its national soccer association was only a few years old, Japan was entering a team in the competition. The Japanese played well, however, even though they were eliminated. First they lost to Hong Kong, 1-0, but they re-

71

bounded to sink South Vietnam, 4-0, before finally being ousted, 1-0, by Israel. (To avoid political problems, the tournament organizers placed the two Koreas in separate brackets and this worked out well, since neither of them was able to advance beyond the opening.)

The growth of Japanese soccer is evident even at the high school level. At the beginning of 1976, there were a total of 2,676 high schools playing the sport, as compared to less than 200 when the Japanese Soccer League was formed in 1965 following the Tokyo Olympic Games. The league added a second division of 10 teams to go along with the 10 in the first division and adopted a regulation that provides for the two lowest teams in the first division to be placed in the second division the following year, with the top two clubs in the second division advancing into the first division for the following season. Toyo Kogyo was the most successful team in the early stages of the league, winning the title four times straight between 1966 and 1970, placing second the following year, and then again climbing into the winner's circle the next year. Other strong teams are Osaka's Yanmar Diesel, Toyota Textile Machines, Hitachi FC of Tokyo, and Mitsubishi FC of Tokyo, which finally took the title away from Toyo Kogyo of Hiroshima.

Iran

Another progressive soccer nation in Asia is Iran, which not only has often been called on to run the Asian Cup, but also holds an annual Iran Invitational Cup, with such non-Asian teams as Algeria, Poland, Egypt, Zaire, Czechoslovakia, and the Soviet Union joining in the heated competition. The Iranian Football League was started in 1973, and from its humble beginning of 12 teams, it had grown to two separate divisions with 23 teams competing in 1976. The two most powerful clubs have been Persepolis and Taj, both from Tehran, but provinces and cities such as Abadan, Isfahan, Pahlevi and Bandar now have teams competing in both divisions.

Malaysia

Another nation in Asia that has developed tremendously since the early 1970s is Malaysia. Arsenal, one of the most powerful clubs in England's history, was shocked at a series of exhibition matches it played in Malaysia in 1975. At Kuala Lumpur, the team was defeated, 2-0, by the Malaysian Selection and then was hard-pressed to salvage a 1-1 tie in the return game held in Penang. After the two games, Bertie Mee, the Arsenal manager said, "Let me say straightaway that I have not and I will not make any excuses for our defeat in Kuala Lumpur. The improvement in soccer standards amongst the Malaysians is, I consider, quite phenomenal when compared to the last time we visited back in 1968."

Among the better teams in the nation are Negri Sembilan and Trengganu, and the growth of the game is evident by the number of teams applying each year for admission to the first division, which now numbers 12 clubs. Plans call for a second division to be started by the beginning of 1980, and with the success of the national team against Thailand and North Korea, the future of soccer in Malaysia looks brighter than one could even have hoped for 10 years ago.

Israel

Israel has had problems in soccer, but not on a competitive level against teams from Europe and its neighboring nations. The troubles stem from the many scandals involving top teams, which have been accused of losing games on purpose when they were low in the standings to avoid close ties and being sent to a lower division. Before they were forced out because of pressure by the Arab nations, who threatened to boycott, the Israelis won the old Asian Cup for several years. Powerhouse teams such as Hapoel Petah-Tiquva, Hapoel Tel Aviv, and Maccabi-Tel Aviv, have been among the top squads in the 25-year history of the Israeli League, but top players are hard to keep. Because theoretically all players in Israel are amateurs, the wages they receive are minimal, and players like Mordechai Sphingler, who was a teammate of Pelé with the Cosmos in 1975, have left Israel for nations like Switzerland, Belgium, and West Germany. The Israeli parliament has discussed the situation in an attempt to curb the flow of players abroad, and there have been many discussions about the alleged incidents of throwing games. It has also been brought out that there has to be a national curb against the increasing violence during soccer matches. Still, despite all these troubles, the Israelis did manage to score a major triumph when their team qualified for the 1976 Olympic Games in Montreal.

Iraq

Another nation that has started to emerge in international soccer is Iraq, which has spent a great deal of money in an effort to build up the youth soccer program. The Iraqi National Team currently has scheduled a full series of European games, both home and away, in an effort to give its players more exposure to different styles of play. As is the case in many other nations, however, several of the top clubs have bitterly opposed requests from the national federation to release their players for national team practice. The two most powerful clubs in the nation are Air Force Blues and the Transport Greens. Hazzim Jassam has been sought by many foreign teams, but he has expressed the desire to stay with Iraq at least until he wins an International Cap in World Cup competition.

India

Disgusted with its failure to win any significant events in the international soccer arena, in 1976 the Indian Football Federation took several steps to try to attain more success in the future. After a lengthy meeting, in which every major and junior association was represented, the committee voted to invite more foreign players and coaches to India to try to build up the soccer program. Representing such clubs as Bengal and Kerala, many of the top junior players have been placed in a special development program that will permit them to be added to the rosters of top clubs in the higher age brackets and used during friendly or exhibition matches. India then, appears ready to take hold of its soccer problems and work out a solution.

Indonesia

The humiliation of dropping a 6-0 World Cup elimination game to Australia was all that critics of the Indonesian Football Association needed to ask for and get a change in the way the soccer program is run in that nation. Following that disaster at Sydney in 1973, the Indonesians decided that they could no longer afford to limit their international soccer activity to such events as the Burma Cup and the Djakarta Cup. They started inviting six or seven European teams to come each year and play exhibition matches, and to give clinics for not only the youngsters but for players who play in the big leagues as well. Although it was still too early to see how successful the new program would be, in 1976 the many teams in the major league held a conclave, where they agreed not to force players selected to play with the national team.

Australia

The influence of English and Scottish soccer stars in Australia became evident when the Aussies surprised everyone and won the Asian elimination series to gain a spot in the 1974 World Cup in West Germany. The Australians granted immediate citizenship to players from Great Britain who came to Australia to play on one of the many Australian teams, and players like Jimmy Mackay of Scotland were made overnight heroes after the Aussies survived a rugged elimination series and gained a spot in the competition in West Germany. Their hopes of glory were shortlived, however, as they lost, 2-0, to East Germany and, 3-0, to West Germany, before playing a scoreless tie with Chile. They did play a strong defensive game, with Jack Reilly of the Hakoah team making several brilliant saves. Coach Rale Rasic, a Yugoslavian, said that he had stressed the defense, because he knew that most of his foreign players had been accustomed to this style of play in their native nations. Among the top clubs in Australia are Just, Sutherland,

Western Suburbs, St. George, Budapest, Safeway United, Marconi, Apia, and Pan Hellenic, and there has often been bitter conflict between groups from Melbourne, Sydney, and Victoria. Under the able direction of Michael Weinstein, the vice-president of the Australian Soccer Federation, a strong move has been made to form a true national league instead of the earlier provisional leagues. Also under Weinstein's direction, Australia has been fortunate to have many foreign teams tour there. Such world powers as Santos (with Pelé), Ajax, Everton, Glasgow Rangers, Dynamo Moscow, Torpedo Moscow, AS Roma, Ferencvaros, and Manchester United and its cross-town rival Manchester City, have appeared in Australia at great cost to the Australian government in an effort to expose the Aussies to the best possible competition.

New Zealand
New Zealand is also trying to raise the level of its soccer playing, and, like Australia, it is relying mainly on players imported from Great Britain. Nonetheless, the New Zealanders appear to be several years behind their Australian counterparts.

Other Countries
Other nations that seem to be making more concentrated bids for soccer success are Kuwait—which lost the finals of the Asian Cup that year, 1-0, to Iran—Burma; Yemen; Jordan; and the Philippines, which competed in the first annual Aloha Festival in Hawaii and lost a hard-fought 1-0 match to Nationalist China.

Hong Kong, Syria, Bangladesh, Singapore, Bahrein, and Brunei appear to be basing their soccer futures on their top youth players, putting them into youth tournaments in Asia. Yemen did look impressive in one such youth event, beating Malaysia, 4-2; while Afghanistan, another up-and-coming soccer nation, tied Mainland China, which had received special permission from FIFA to compete. A team like Brunei's, however, is to be pitied, for it dropped back-to-back 10-0 decisions against Iran and Iraq.

Sri Lanka drew FIFA's criticism when its team withdrew only 14 days before the start of the 17th annual Asian Youth Tournament. No suspension was issued, however, when it was explained that there simply were not enough players who could be enticed to come out for practice.

With many nations paying the expenses of the foreign teams that came into the countries for games, and with FIFA spending a great deal of time and money sending out various player forms, there has been talk that in the near future there will be more than just one team from Asia in World Cup competition. The request for more than one

Asian team has been made to FIFA, and the backers of this idea feel that they have a solid case, pointing out that in South America qualifying tourneys can have as few as three teams, while in order to qualify from Asia the winning team has to beat as many as 20 teams to gain a spot in the World Cup finals.

But no matter what team or teams do qualify in the future, they will be far better teams than the previous Asian representatives because of the vast experience they have been garnering all over Asia, Europe, and South America. Eventually, the day may come when an Asian team enters the World Cup competition the favorite to take the title.

MAJOR ASIAN TOURNAMENTS

Year	Venue	Winner	Runner-Up	Result
Asian Cup				
1956	Hong Kong	Korea Republic	Israel	round-robin
1960	Seoul	Korea Republic	Israel	round-robin
1964	Tel-Aviv	Israel	India	round-robin
1968	Teheran	Iran	Burma	round-robin
1972	Bangkok	Iran	Korea Republic	2–1
1976	Teheran	Iran	Kuwait	1–0
Asian Games				
1951	New Delhi	India	Iran	2–1
1954	Manila	Nationalist China	Korea Republic	5–2
1958	Tokyo	Nationalist China	Korea Republic	3–2
1962	Djakarta, Indonesia	India	Korea Republic	2–0
1966	Bangkok	Burma	Iran	1–0
1970	Bangkok	Burma and Korea Republic		0–0
1974	Teheran	Iran	Israel	1–0
SEAP* Games				
1959	Bangkok	Vietnam Republic	Thailand	3–1
1961	Rangoon	Malaysia	Burma	2–0
1965	Kuala Lumpur	Burma and Thailand		2–2
1967	Bangkok	Burma	Vietnam Republic	2–1
1969	Rangoon	Burma	Thailand	3–0
1971	Kuala Lumpur	Burma	Malaysia	2–1
1973	Singapore	Burma	Vietnam Republic	3–2
1975	Bangkok	Thailand	Malaysia	2–1

*Southeast Asian Peninsula.

Year	Venue	Winner	Runner-Up	Result

Asian Youth Tournament

Year	Venue	Winner	Runner-Up	Result
1959	Kuala Lumpur	Korea Republic	Malaysia	2-1
1960	Kuala Lumpur	Korea Republic	Malaysia	4-0
1961	Bangkok	Indonesia and Burma		0-0
1962	Bangkok	Thailand	Korea Republic	2-1
1963	Pinang	Korea Republic and Burma		2-2
1964	Saigon	Israel and Burma		0-0
1965	Tokyo	Israel	Burma	5-0
1966	Manila	Burma and Israel		1-1
1967	Bangkok	Israel	Indonesia	3-0
1968	Seoul	Burma	Malaysia	4-0
1969	Bangkok	Burma and Thailand		2-2
1970	Manila	Burma	Indonesia	3-0
1971	Tokyo	Israel	Korea Republic	1-0
1972	Bangkok	Israel	Korea Republic	1-0
1973	Teheran	Iran	Japan	2-0
1974	Bangkok	Iran and India		2-2
1975	Kuwait	Iran and Iraq		0-0
1976	Bangkok	Iran and Korea DPR		0-0

Champion Clubs' Tournament

Year	Venue	Winner	Runner-Up	Result
1967	Bangkok	Hapoel Tel-Aviv	Selangor	2-1
1968	Bangkok	Maccabi-Tel Aviv	Yang Zee	1-0
1970	Teheran	Taj Club	Hapoel Tel Aviv	2-1
1971	Bangkok	Maccabi-Tel Aviv	Iraq Police Club	2-0

Merdeka Football Tournament of Malaysia

Year	Venue	Winner	Runner-Up	Result
1957	Kuala Lumpur	Hong Kong	Indonesia	League comp.
1958	Kuala Lumpur	Malaysia	Hong Kong	League comp.
1959	Kuala Lumpur	Malaysia	India	League comp.
1960	Kuala Lumpur	Malaysia and Korea Republic		0-0
1961	Kuala Lumpur	Indonesia	Malaysia	2-1
1962	Kuala Lumpur	Indonesia	Pakistan	2-1
1963	Kuala Lumpur	Nationalist China	Korea Republic	1-0
1964	Kuala Lumpur	Burma	India	1-0
1965	Kuala Lumpur	Nationalist China and Korea Republic		1-1
1966	Kuala Lumpur	South Vietnam	Burma	1-0
1967	Kuala Lumpur	Korea Republic and Burma		0-0
1968	Kuala Lumpur	Malaysia	Burma	3-0
1969	Kuala Lumpur	Indonesia	Malaysia	3-2

Year	Venue	Winner	Runner-Up	Result
1970	Kuala Lumpur	Korea Republic	Burma	1-0
1971	Kuala Lumpur	Burma	Indonesia	1-0
1972	Kuala Lumpur	Korea Republic	Malaysia (A)	2-1
1973	Kuala Lumpur	Malaysia	Kuwait	3-1
1974	Ipoh	Malaysia	Korea Republic	1-0
1975	Kuala Lumpur	Korea Republic	Malaysia	1-0

Kings Cup Tournament of Thailand

Year	Venue	Winner	Runner-Up	Result
1968	Bangkok	Indonesia	Burma	1-0
1969	Bangkok	Korea Republic	Indonesia	1-0
1970	Bangkok	Korea Republic	Thailand	1-0
1971	Bangkok	Korea Republic	Thailand	1-0
1972	Bangkok	Malaysia	Thailand	1-0
1973	Bangkok	Korea Republic	Malaysia	2-1
1974	Bangkok	Korea Republic	Thailand	3-1
1975	Bangkok	Korea Republic	Burma	1-0

Djakarta Anniversary Tournament of Indonesia

Year	Venue	Winner	Runner-Up	Result
1970	Djakarta	Malaysia	Korea Republic	2-0
1971	Djakarta	Burma	Indonesia	1-0
1972	Djakarta	Indonesia	Korea Republic	5-2
1973	Djakarta	Burma	Indonesia	round-robin
1974	Djakarta	Burma	Indonesia	round-robin
1975	Djakarta	Burma	Malaysia	2-0
1976	Djakarta	Korea Republic	Burma	1-0

Vietnam National Day Tournament

Year	Venue	Winner	Runner-Up	Result
1970	Saigon	South Vietnam	Thailand	1-0
1971	Saigon	South Vietnam and Malaysia		1-1
1972	Saigon	Khmer Republic	South Vietnam	2-1
1973	Saigon	Indonesia	Malaysia	3-2

President's Cup of Korea

Year	Venue	Winner	Runner-Up	Result
1971	Seoul	Burma and Korea Republic		0-0
1972	Seoul	Burma	Indonesia	3-1
1973	Seoul	Burma and Khmer Republic		0-0
1974	Seoul	Korea Republic	Indonesia	7-1
1975	Seoul	Korea Republic	Burma	1-0

Singapore Pesta Sukan Tournament

Year	Venue	Winner	Runner-Up	Result
1971	Singapore	India and South Vietnam		0-0
1972	Singapore	Indonesia (A)	Indonesia (B)	2-1

CHAPTER 7

Caribbean Soccer

In Mexico, Guatemala, and Cuba there is the Spanish influence; in Haiti, the French influence; and in Jamaica, Bermuda, and Honduras the English influence is dominant. The different influences on not only the people of the Caribbean but on their soccer techniques make the North, Central American, and Caribbean soccer association (known as CONCAF) one of the most interesting in the world. The organization is further enhanced by the membership of both the United States and Canada.

Throughout the history of the association, there has been a tradition of bitter matches. War even resulted from a soccer competition between Honduras and El Salvador, when the two teams were battling for a spot in the 1970 World Cup. Professionalism is intense in Mexico, while in Bermuda it is almost nonexistent. The sport is played throughout the association in well-organized leagues, and each country takes great pride in its national team. Government heads have almost rolled as a result of decisions regarding the soccer field, the most noteworthy being the criticism that Mexican officials received when they sanctioned a round-robin series of games between their local federation and six other nations in the association's 1974 World Cup elimination series. The games were well organized, except Haiti, the host nation, got just about every possible break from game officials, including the disallowing of three goals made by their Trinidadian opponents in one game. Although Mexico beat Haiti in the round-robin, by the time the game was played, Haiti had already advanced too far, and Mexico was unable to salvage its second straight trip to the World Cup, much to the dismay of the other participating nations.

The organizing committee was deluged with protests but, of course, a referee's decision can't be changed. After the round-robin, all the competing nations except Haiti voted to revert to the old format of home-and-away competition, and no further round-robin farces would be held again.

NATIONAL TEAMS

Soccer has been played for 50 years throughout the Caribbean and Central America, and if there is one thing to be said for the area, it is that there is no conformity in the region. Although the teams get together on a national basis for invitational events in addition to World Cup elimination, Olympic Trials, the Mexican Cup, and special CONCAF events, there is no regular schedule of games between the competing nations. Club competition in the area is almost as popular as international events; and the Mexican First Division, featuring such renowned clubs as Cruz Azul, Universtaad, and Club America, is one of the best leagues in the world. The competition is strong, there are numerous arch rivalries; teams from Mexico City invariably draw large crowds when they play other Mexico City teams at Azteca Stadium. Travel is a great inconvenience for some of the clubs. Whenever Cruz Azul goes to Vera Cruz for a battle, for example, the trip usually takes seven or eight hours by bus, the way most Mexican teams travel.

Mexico

One of the highlights of the international season in Mexico is the annual Mexico City Cup, in which host Mexico plays against Costa Rico, Argentina, and the United States. Although in 1976 the Mexicans were regarded as underdogs to Argentina, the two teams battled to a 1-1 tie; and Mexico won the tournament when it defeated the U.S., 2-0, after remaining scoreless in the first half. The Mexicans had the best goal average, scoring 10 goals and yielding only one, while the Argentinians scored nine goals and yielded one. Officials of Argentina became outraged when the decision that goal average would determine the tourney winner was announced, claiming that they were not notified in advance. But FIFA ruled the goal-average clause was mentioned in the plans for the tournament. The Mexican Football Federation says that in the future it will invite different countries for the competition, thus giving its own fans a better opportunity to see all the region's teams. In the past, several nations have turned down the invitation, however, because their players have complained about the high altitude and the breathing problems that it causes.

Among the better-known teams that have been invited to compete in the annual CONCAF Championship of Champion Club tournament are the Mexican pair Club Deportivo Toluca and Club Social y Deportivo León, both of which feature the fast style of wing play and rugged defense around the midfield area, which is one of the keys to Mexico's success in international competition. Many of the clubs are wealthy and have been able to buy such top South American stars as Edu, who was a teammate of Pelé at Santos, and Lima, another Santos player. When Uruguayan football teams were unable to meet the demands of some of their players for fair wages, the players went to Mexico and played for many of the top teams there. This angered some of the less affluent teams, but the Mexican Football Federation never put a limit on the number of foreign players a team could have on its roster.

In 1975 the Mexican club Español showed its dominance in the CONCAF tourney by defeating five opponents and tying its other match to win the championship title. With close to a million competitors on all age levels, soccer in Mexico has been progressing rapidly. There was talk in the early 1960s that the game would be replaced by baseball; but by the end of the decade, there were twice as many soccer clubs registered as before while fan participation in baseball had dropped and a couple of clubs had folded.

Costa Rica

Based on a well-organized junior program, which in 1976 captured the first Youth Tournament Union Centroamericana Cup, soccer is once again well on the upswing in Costa Rica. Between the late 1950s and late 1960s, Costa Rican soccer was dependent on foreign players; and when the clubs found that they could no longer compete with other nations for top players, the interest of the fans started to decline sharply. But with a strong youth program, Costa Rican soccer is regaining its past high form. Of the top teams in Costa Rica, where almost every major factory and foreign business supports a team, the Saprissa Club has been the most successful. Is Costa Rica ready for full participation on a regular basis with some of the other Caribbean teams? The answer may not be known until those now being introduced to the game come of age and represent the top clubs. Hopefully, they will fulfill Costa Rica's dream of competing successfully in international competition.

Guatemala

Guatemala is another country that has had its ups and downs since the end of World War II. In the early 1960s, the Guatemalan National Team went on a tour of South America and upset Uruguay. But when the same men went back to their respective clubs, they lost a couple of games to teams of all-stars from the United States. That slump continued until the beginning of the 1970s, when a strong national federation devised a rugged training program and ordered all clubs to field at least three junior teams in order to remain in good standing. Now many of the younger players on the Guatemalan National Team are starting to reach maturity, and their advancement from the junior level to the varsity has created excitement among the nation's youth, who once never bothered turning out for games. The slots vacated by the young players who have moved up have been filled by players just out of grade school, and the program has been a model for other nations. The nucleus of the national team is made up of players from Club Comunicaciones, which won the title of the Premier League six times running during the late 1960s and early 1970s, and from the Aurora FC, which has been a strong challenger to the Comunicaciones organization. Club Comunicaciones is so powerfully organized that when Guatemala selected its junior team for the Union Centroamericana Cup, all but five members of the team were from that club, which was originally formed by a group of communication workers who believed that they had the ability to play against some of the older, established teams.

Haiti

Haitian soccer is one of the fastest growing in the area, and government support has been outstanding. Under the reign of Jean-Claude Duvalier, the government has spared no expense in getting such top foreign clubs as the Cosmos with Pelé to come and play a series of matches against Haitian teams Victory and Viollet. When Haiti won the controversial round-robin tourney over Mexico, Trinidad and Tobago, Netherlands Antilles, Guatemala, and Honduras to earn a spot in the 1974 World Cup, all players and managers, including the old New York Generals' Phillipe (White Devil) Vorbe were given luxurious gifts, and the team was promised $100,000 per player if it defeated Italy and $50,000 each if it tied. Although they lost, the Haitians displayed a fiery style of play (resembling French soccer), and Haiti is undoubtedly destined to become a soccer power. Its league is one of the best in the area, with such teams as the Racing Club, Aigle Noir, and Don Bosco de Pétionville joining Viollet and Victory as the top clubs in the nation.

In 1976 Haiti sent its Viollet club across the mountains to Santo Domingo, Dominican Republic, for an exhibition game against the Cosmos. The game would have been a sure sellout in Port-au-Prince, but realizing that their neighbors weren't very soccer oriented, the Haitians decided to play the game in Santo Domingo. Although there is only very limited soccer activity in Santo Domingo, Pelé was still able to draw 20,000 fans on a rainy night for the Cosmos game against Viollet, and Haitian officials offered to help their neighbors build up soccer. Not too much earlier, the two nations weren't even engaging in diplomatic relations, but it was another example of soccer helping to secure friendship and bridge a gap between cultures.

El Salvador

Following a short but bloody war with Honduras, El Salvadorian soccer started to decline. The national team, which had done poorly, lost all three of its games in the first round of the 1970 World Cup and failed to score a single goal while yielding nine. The team was shunted aside, and the emphasis was put on youth development. The backers of the two major clubs in the nation—Club Águila and Club Alianza—finally were brought together for a meeting after refusing to talk with one another for many years. The two clubs agreed to put more time and effort into organizing and working with younger boys and would try to point the nation in the right direction to regain the prestige it had enjoyed in the soccer world when it qualified for the 1970 World Cup competition in England. The youth movement was only three years old when the nation entered a junior tournament. At the time the tournament was announced, it was scheduled for Guatemala, but the earthquake that devastated that nation forced the organizers to look for another playing site. El Salvador volunteered its stadium (called Estadio Flor Blanca) in San Salvador, and the well-run tournament was well received by all the competing junior teams and by the members of the visiting national associations. The El Salvador junior team didn't win the event, but it did score an impressive 4-1 win over Guatemala, which eventually lost the final round to Costa Rica. With well-run junior programs spreading throughout the country and the importation of several youth coaches from abroad, El Salvadorian soccer is another bright spot in the soccer future of CONCAF.

Bermuda, Jamaica, and Barbados
The same, unfortunately, cannot be said about some of the former British colonies such as Bermuda, Jamaica, and Barbados. Here, for the most part, soccer takes a back seat to track and field and even cricket, although all three nations at one time or another put a lot of effort into trying to build up their soccer programs, at times even enjoying success. Bermudian soccer is primarily dominated by the Police Club and Somerset teams. Because players receive little or no money, however, the better competitors leave the country to play elsewhere. Examples of this are Randy Horton, Clyde Best, and Sam Nusum, who are regarded by many as the top three players of the past 20 years. Horton, now back in Bermuda as an educator, played for the New York Cosmos. The tall forward was regarded as one of the top players in Bermuda but said that although he hated leaving the island, he had to play in the United States in order to finance his continuing education. Nusum, a top goalie, went to the United States and Canada to play with top clubs there. Best went to England, where he was one of the stars of the powerful West Ham United Club before he left to play with the Tampa Bay Rowdies of the NASL.

Soccer action in Barbados is limited, with only a small, five-team league and a few junior programs. Jamaica, once regarded as a stronghold of soccer, has experienced a steady decrease in the number of clubs and players. The decline of Jamaican soccer was made evident when the team withdrew at the last minute from the qualifying rounds of the 1970 World Cup, and, except for a few international exhibition games, in the following six years nothing was done to improve the plight. In late 1976, however, a meeting was held. Some wealthy backers promised to put money into the junior program, and there is new hope for success. Players like the Washington Diplomats' Leroy Deleon are fine examples of the Jamaican style of soccer, which stresses fast and long runs by the wingers, while defense almost always uses excessive pushing and fouling in the midfield area.

Honduras
Honduras appears to be maintaining a growing pace, with a fine professional league led by Club España and Club Olimpia. There is also a well-run junior program, which has about 75,000 youngsters registered. The style of play is similar to Mexican football undoubtedly because many of the Honduran coaches attended a clinic in Mexico in 1975.

Trinidad and Tobago
Trinidad and Tobago have produced some fine teams and excellent players since 1960, and their rugged, hard-tackling style of play is what soccer was like back in the 1930s in Europe. Players like Lincoln Phillips, a top goalie, played in the United States and then went on to coach the Howard University team to success, including an NCAA title. Former policeman Steve David led the NASL in scoring in 1975, and Warren Archibald is regarded by many as the fastest winger in the history of the NASL. The top two clubs in Trinidad and Tobago are the Palo Seco team and Malvern SC, while the youthful Santos team is also highly regarded.

Nicaragua
Nicaragua is another nation building its soccer program slowly, emphasizing not professional play but rather youth development. The top two clubs in the nation are Club Diriangen and Club Gatala, both of which sponsor so much junior soccer that they each have as many as 15 teams registered in various junior leagues throughout the nation.

Netherlands Antilles
Although its caliber of play still is not up to that of its former Dutch rulers, the Netherlands Antilles is on the way up the ladder with such clubs as Jong Colombia and Doort Unie Brion Trappers. Surinam, Guyana, Panama, Puerto Rico, and Antigua are just starting to develop in soccer; and with the governments contributing not only money but the time to build well-organized junior programs, these five nations should be successful by the early 1990s.

Surinam
Robin Hood and Voorward are the best teams in Surinam, and by agreement they each let players from the junior movement try out with them without losing their amateur status. The youthful players also

play in nonleague exhibition games along with the older stars, and it is this junior experience program that league officials hope will lead not only to a stronger national team but also to an increase in the total league membership from the 10 teams it had at the start of the 1976 campaign.

Guyana

Thomas United and Christianburg top the 12-team Guyana League, and each of these clubs has a strong junior movement. The best of the juniors from both clubs dominate the National Junior Team for intenational competition; and the outlook for soccer in Guyana is bright because at the beginning of 1975, there were already 20,000 junior players, many of them under age eight, playing in regular leagues throughout the country.

Panama

Panamanian soccer was slow to get started, but one of the real drives for soccer growth came from the fans themselves, who used to go out and watch games between the crews of ships waiting to pass through the canal. The youngsters quickly became interested in the game, and whenever exhibition clinics were given by the seamen, adults would be instructed in how to help the youngsters learn the game. A small pro league of only six clubs is in operation, but with the increased interest of the youngsters, the future is indeed looking good for soccer in Panama. In the 1975–76 CONCAF Junior Tournament, the Panamanian youth team jolted Nicaragua and was able to tie Costa Rico, a possibility that even a few years yearlier would have been unthinkable.

Antigua

Antigua also stresses junior development, with many top foreign players giving exhibitions and clinics. Puerto Rico still concentrates on older leagues, but following its disastrous 7–0 and 5–0 defeats to Haiti in the qualifying round of the 1974 World Cup, a move for junior development started. It will take at least until the mid-1980s for the effects of the youth program to be felt, but with teams like the Cosmos and Miami Toros making annual exhibition visits, the future is somewhat brighter than it was at the time of the World Cup fiasco.

Throughout the area, soccer attendance is generally on the upswing, and the caliber of competition seems to have improved. CONCAF has arranged to have its annual champion play the winner of the South American Cup, and although many feel that it would have been better to wait until the mid-1980s to play these matches, when the announcement was made in 1975, the enthusiasm was overwhelming, and it is hoped that the challenge will speed up soccer development throughout the Caribbean zone.

CHAPTER 8

The World Cup

I have played in many, many games both on a league level as well as on an international level; but unless I had played in the World Cup, I wouldn't have been able to call my career complete. The World Cup is the ultimate accomplishment for a player. It is the dream of youngsters everywhere just starting out in the sport, as well as the dream of old-timers still hanging on no matter where they play soccer, be it in Europe, South America, the United States or even in Africa, that they one day get the chance to play for their nation in the World Cup. I have engaged for my own club in two English Football Association Cup finals at Wembley and competed for England in several Home Championships against Wales, Scotland, and Northern Ireland; but all these forms of competition can't nearly compare with my games for England in the World Cup.

Unless one plays in the World Cup, it is impossible to know the feeling one experiences. When you play and do well, you are at the peak of ecstasy, while losing or doing poorly sends you to the depths of despair. It is these feelings, not only on the part of the players and coaches but also on the part of the fans, that make the World Cup in my opinion the greatest team event in the worldwide spectrum of sports. I have experienced both the joys and sorrows of competing in this type of competition, so I can say that I speak from my heart when I tell you that there is nothing that can match the World Cup.

That is how Bobby Moore, who captained (or "skippered") the English National Team to the World Cup, described his feelings nearly 10 years later when he was interviewed at a press conference in San Antonio after signing a contract to play for the San Antonio Thunder in the North American Soccer League. It is the World Cup, which is held every four years, that draws more worldwide focus than any other team championship. It is the championship tournament that has caused nations to break off diplomatic relations with one another as the result of an incident on the field of play. It is the championship, and the various qualifying matches that led up to it, that once touched off the Soccer War between two nations. It is the tournament that has enabled a shaky government in one country to hold on to its power, because that nation's team was successful in the competition and the people forgot their problems as they celebrated their team's victory over another nation in the soccer arena. As a result of one unfavorable decision in a World Cup game, an entire nation went into mourning. It is the quest for the World Cup championship that has caused nations to spend millions of dollars, even though they were really unable to afford it, in order for their team to build the best possible squad.

The World Cup was the brainchild and dream of two Frenchmen, Jules Rimet and Henri Delaunay, neither of whom ever played professional soccer. In 1904 in Paris they sat down and decided that the Olympic Games was not the proper way to prove world soccer supremacy. They felt that since professional soccer was starting to become popular in Europe and South America, and because the International Olympic Committee was cracking down against nations using professional soccer players, a new type of international soccer tournament was desperately needed. The Olympic Committee knew that for several years many professional soccer players had been representing their nations in the Olympic Games, and the committee threatened that strong measures, including expulsion from the games, would be taken against countries allowing this practice to continue.

Rimet and Delaunay could never have dreamed of the trouble they would face in the following years, as they tried to get their plan off the drawing board and into the field. But they also could never have imagined just how great the tournament would ultimately become.

Rimet, who was later to become the president of the French Football Federation and also the head of FIFA, and Delaunay, who was to be the secretary of the French Football Federation from 1919 until his death 37 years later, wrote letters to all the top football associations in Europe and South America to find out how they felt about forming a tournament called the World Cup. Almost immediately they learned that getting the idea into operation would not be an easy task. England, long considered the stronghold of European soccer, was opposed to the idea and even threatened to break off soccer ties with any nation that backed the idea.

Although Rimet and Delaunay continued to press for their idea of a World Cup, progress was indeed slow, and with the advent of World War I, the idea was shelved. After the war, however, many nations expressed a desire to see how such a tournament would work, and a meeting was held in 1920 in Antwerp. Although the meeting was officially FIFA's annual convention, strong pressure came from previously uncommitted nations to get the World Cup underway. Rimet and Delaunay were assigned a group of men to work with to plan the first

World Cup tournament. Although no date was set, Rimet and Delaunay were confident that they would see their dream fulfilled in about five years. In reality it took twice as long before the first ball was booted in competition.

FIFA held another meeting in 1924 in conjunction with the Olympic Games, and several nations there were disturbed at how the soccer competition at the Olympics was going, complaining that their best players were banned from playing in the Olympics. Delaunay's comment that the Olympics no longer indicated a nation's soccer prowess was all that was needed to get various nations still sitting on the fence into the World Cup camp. Four years later in Amsterdam, FIFA decided to hold the first World Cup in 1930. When the question of where to hold the tournament arose, Uruguay, which had won the 1928 Olympic title, entered its bid as did Italy, Holland, Spain, and Sweden.

1930

Promising to pay all the traveling and hotel expenses of the competing nations, Uruguay was awarded the tournament. It also had promised to build a special stadium just for the event. Italy, Holland, Spain, and Sweden were bitterly disappointed and agreed to boycott the event. They were joined in their refusal to play by England (which had never joined FIFA), Austria, Hungary, Switzerland, Germany, and Czechoslovakia. France, Yugoslavia, Belgium, and Rumania, however, decided to enter the event, giving Europe four representatives. Meanwhile, several South American nations were bitter over Italy and Holland's refusal to play and openly threatened to withdraw from FIFA. The United States, with a team composed mostly of Scottish and English professionals, surprised many when it accepted the invitation to play.

In all, 13 nations were entered in the first World Cup competition. Getting to Uruguay from Europe was a three-week journey, and the four European participants left together. Their ship picked up the Brazilians en route, and a wild celebration greeted the five teams as they arrived together in Uruguay.

The format for the first World Cup called for the 13 teams to be broken into four separate divisions or pools, as they were called then. Argentina, Chile, France, and Mexico were in Pool One; Pool Two had Brazil, Yugoslavia, and Bolivia; Uruguay, Rumania and Peru comprised Pool Three; and the United States, Belgium, and Paraguay made up Pool Four. Uruguay and Argentina were regarded as the two strongest teams in the tournament, as it was felt that their fast-moving style and fancy passing would give them an advantage over the European competitors. Argentina defeated France, 1-0, Mexico, 6-3, and Chile, 3-1, to win Pool One and advance to the semifinals. Chile finished second in the group, followed by France and Mexico. In Pool Two, each of the three competitors had to play only two games. Yugoslavia defeated Brazil, 2-1, and Bolivia, 4-0, to advance to the semifinals, while in the battle for second place in the group, Brazil ripped Bolivia, 4-0.

Uruguay showed great form in Pool Three, and its team enjoyed great fan support. Strong discipline marked the team both on and off the field, but goalie Mazzali, regarded by many at the time as the outstanding keeper in South America, found out that the officials of the Uruguayan team meant business when they imposed a curfew. He was caught before the semifinals sneaking into the training camp late one night and immediately was bounced from the team, replaced by Enrique Ballesteros.

In its Pool Three matches, Uruguay showed great defensive ability, blanking a strong Peruvian team, 1-0, and then demolishing Rumania, 4-0. Rumania defeated Peru, 3-1, in the battle for runner-up honors. The United States was the surprise of Pool Four competition, beating both Belgium and Paraguay by identical 3-0 scores, as in each game the team leaped to a 2-0 halftime lead and then coasted home. Paraguay took second place in the division by beating Belgium 1-0. The semifinal drawings found Argentina matched against the United States and Uruguay against Yugoslavia. Both matches were rated as pretty much even, but both turned into runaways. Argentina showed too much speed for the North Americans and won, 6-1, as Stabile and Peucelle each scored twice and Monti and Scopelli added single tallies. U.S. goalkeeper Douglas was under constant barrage, and even though he allowed six goals, he still received an ovation when he left the field for the 25 saves he made. For most of the first half, the United States was able to contain the Argentinian attack; and at the end of the first half, the score was only 1-0. But then a three-goal outburst within a nine-minute span dashed all the U.S. hopes.

In the other semifinal, Uruguay completely dominated the action and defeated Yugoslavia, 6-1. Its great inside left Cea scored three goals, and Anselmo added two tallies, while Iriarte added the final score. Seculic prevented a shutout for Yugoslavia by scoring one goal, just as Brown had done for the United States in its losing effort against Argentina.

Now the stage was set for the championship match between Uruguay and Argentina, two teams that had already played many rough games together. Thousands of Argentinian fans came by boat from River

Plate to see the game. Although the Centenary Stadium grounds could hold 100,000 spectators, the police, fearful of a gate crash like that on opening day, limited attendance to 90,000. The Argentinian team had police security both in training sessions and on its way to the stadium for the finale. Equipped with fixed bayonets and backed up by soldiers, police formed a circle around the stadium, forcing fans to keep moving and keep the entrances clear for the players. Referee John Langenus had his own bodyguards, and just before the match got underway he was forced to make a decision. Both the Uruguayans and the Argentinians wanted to use a ball from their respective countries. While officials stood and waited, the referee made his decision: a coin flip would decide. The Argentinians won the right to use their ball, and throughout the stands immediately many Argentinians made bets with Uruguayans that, using its own ball, Argentina would win. Although Uruguay was the favorite because the match was being played on its home grounds, the team entered the game shorthanded, as Anselmo was out of action with a pulled leg muscle.

The game got underway with a wild barrage of firecrackers, something that even then soccer officials tried to discourage but weren't too successful at stopping. With 12 minutes gone in the match, Uruguay scored, as right winger Pablo Dorado put a 15-yarder past Argentinian goalie Botasso. The Uruguayan crowd went wild, bringing noisemakers to the front. Since this was the country's 100th anniversary, one might well have believed that there was a birthday celebration going on. Then 18 minutes later, the crowd was sent into near silence as outside right Paucelle tied the game for Argentina. Referee Langenus kept tempers under control both on and off the field, but with only 12 minutes left in the first half, he allowed a goal by Argentina's center forward Stabile to stand, even though there was some justification to the Uruguayan claim that the play was offside. Although they were restrained from going onto the field, the Uruguayan fans were bitter as the first half came to an end with their nation trailing, 2-1.

Jubilation exploded in the stadium 10 minutes into the second half, however, when from his inside left position, Cea dribbled past two defenders and drew Argentinian goalie Botasso out of position before firing a six-yarder into the upper left corner to give Uruguay a 2-2 deadlock. The Argentinians were a beaten club as the short, swift passes of Uruguay's front line cut their defense to ribbons. Ten minutes after it had tied the score, Uruguay jumped into the lead as left winger Santos Iriarte scored. Then, with less than a minute remaining to play, Castro put the icing on the cake with a blast from 20 yards out, which Botasso appeared to misplay.

Jules Rimet was in all his glory as he entered the playing field and presented Uruguayan team captain Nasazzi with the first Jules Rimet Trophy with the understanding that the actual championship trophy would be returned to FIFA prior to the next World Cup championship. Only after a nation had won the title three times could it retain the coveted trophy in soccer permanently. Each member of the Uruguayan squad received a replica of the larger trophy to keep.

Uruguay went wild as the final whistle sounded. Motorcades formed throughout Montevideo. Ships in port blew their horns, and the following day was declared a national holiday.

1934

Italy made a successful bid to host the following World Cup, held in 1934; and Uruguay, remembering Italy's boycott four years earlier, bitterly refused to defend its title. Even if Uruguay had attempted to defend its crown, however, there was doubt that it could have won its second straight championship. Soccer in Uruguay was in crisis. Player strikes had hit the soccer scene for two straight years. The Uruguayan Federation appealed to its players to sit down and discuss the problems, but the plea fell on deaf ears. Meanwhile, response from around the world to the tournament was greater than had been expected, and the World Cup Committee found that a total of 32 nations desired to compete. Qualifying matches were held, and even host Italy had to battle to become one of the 16 teams to make the final stages of the competition, defeating Greece, 2-0. The United States found itself the 16th and final team in the competition when it defeated Mexico, 3-1, in Rome.

The committee abandoned the format used four years earlier, and the opening round was a single-game affair. A win advanced a team to the second round, while a single defeat eliminated a team from further competition. In the opening game of the tournament, Italy was matched against the United States, and almost from the opening whistle, it was no contest as the Italians outhustled, outdribbled, and outshot the Americans to a 7-1 win. The only goal for the Americans came from Donelli. Schiavio, who scored three times, and Orsi, who scored twice, were heroes on the Italian team, which was cheered on by many dignitaries including Mussolini himself.

In an exciting contest, Czechoslovakia rallied from a 1-0 halftime deficit to topple Rumania, 2-1; while in a walkaway, Germany ripped Belgium 5-2, although the Belgians did maintain a shaky 2-1 halftime advantage. Austria, regarded by many as one of the best teams in Europe at the time, was hard pressed to defeat France, 3-2, in overtime on a goal by Bican. Spain toppled Brazil, 3-1, and Argentina lost to Sweden, 3-2. Both South American entrants had traveled a long distance only to be eliminated after one game. Hungary topped Egypt, 4-2, and Switzerland advanced to the second round with a hard-fought 3-2 win over Holland.

The highlight of the second round was a bitter two-game struggle between Italy and Spain. Italy squandered a 1-0 halftime lead in the first game and had to settle for a 1-1 tie and a replay. In the replay, Orsi's first-half goal was the only tally of the match, as the Italians gained a spot in the semifinals.

Turin was the scene of the most spectacular game of the second round, with Czechoslovakia and Switzerland engaging in a match in which each team penetrated its opponent's defense. With 18 minutes gone, Kielholz scored on a breakaway for Switzerland, but the Czechs countered with a tying goal six minutes later, as Sobotka passed to Svoboda for the score. Cambal, a rarity in those days as an attacking center halfback, passed to Sobotka to set up another goal for the Czechs shortly after the second half got underway. Now it was the Swiss' turn to attack, and they pounded away until Trello Abegglen tied the score. But the Czechs were not to be denied, and with only seven minutes remaining in regulation time, Nejedly scored the winning goal to place Czechoslovakia in the semifinal round.

Germany, cheered on by Italian rooters who had umbrellas covered with swastikas, defeated Sweden, 2-1, as Hohmann scored both goals for the winners. In the final second-round game, Horwath and Zischek gave Austria a 2-0 lead, and a goal by the Hungarians' Sarosi on a penalty shot came too late to save Hungary from defeat. Many Hungarian fans were bitter that one of their stars, Maekos, was ejected with 20 minutes remaining when he committed two flagrant fouls.

In the opening semifinal game held in Rome, Czechoslovakia had an easy time, completely outplaying Germany and winning, 3-1, as Nejedly scored twice and Kreil scored once. Noack, the brilliant inside left, saved Germany from a shutout. The other semifinal game was a classic. The Italians, stressing a third fullback, went against the offensive-minded Austrians, and it was an exciting encounter. Guaita's goal in the first half was the only tally of the match, as Italy won, 1-0. Combi, the Italian captain, was brilliant in the nets, saving 22 shots; and as he left the field in Milan, thousands of Italian fans invaded the pitch and helped carry him off.

Prior to the finals between Italy and Czechoslovakia, a game was held to decide third place, and Germany got two goals from Lehner en route to a 3-2 win over Austria.

The final match was held in Rome, and some soccer experts still claim that it was one of the best-played games ever held in the World Cup history. The Czechs appealed to their fans to back them, and trains and buses arrived from Prague, carrying thousands of fans to the game.

Playing a short-passing game, the Czechs dominated the early action but were unable to put a shot past Combi until Puc, who earlier had been forced to the sidelines with a leg cramp, fired a 20-yarder into the lower corner with only 20 minutes left in regulation play. The Czechs, spurred on by the goal, continued to pound away at the Italians but were unsuccessful. Then with eight minutes remaining, Orsi tied the score for the Italians as his curving right-footed shot from 12 yards out got past Planicka. The regulation time ended with the two teams even at one score apiece. In the seventh minute of the 30-minute overtime session, Guaita, who was switched by coach Pozzo from his starting outside right position to the center forward spot, found Schiavio free on the right side and placed a nifty pass to him. Schiavio seized the opportunity, and as he scored, fireworks exploded in the stadium. The Czechs made some fireworks of their own late in the overtime session, but a spectacular diving save by Combi on a shot off Svoboda's left foot saved the 2–1 win for the Italians.

1938

There was an atmosphere of despair as the 1938 World Cup got underway in France. With war clouds hanging over Europe and several South American nations angry that Europe would be the scene of the competition for the second straight time, the tournament did not receive the recognition it deserved. Uruguay and Argentina boycotted the event, leaving Brazil as the only South American representative. Austria had been swallowed up, and its top players were now wearing the uniforms of Germany. Some critics said that the event should be canceled, but FIFA ruled that the World Cup should be played as scheduled. Only 15 teams competed, and the format called for seven first-round games, with the winners joining Sweden in the second-round competition. Several countries immediately protested that they should have received the bye, but they were overruled by the organizing committee, which was kept busy trying to pacify all participants.

Close competition marked the opening round with pretourney favorite Italy just barely getting by a stubborn and surprisingly tough Norwegian team. Italy took the field to the thunderous jeers of French fans, and this seemed to spur the team on. With only two minutes gone in the match, Norwegian goalie H. Johansen let a shot by Ferrari bounce out of his hands onto the waiting left foot of Ferraris II, who booted it home for the game's first tally. Norway's defense was able to contain the Italian star winger Colaussi, and slowly Norway started to display its aggressive form. Brustad got the tying tally for Norway midway through the second half; and then, with less than four minutes to play in regulation time, Brustad again scored, only to have the goal nullified because of an offside call. The crowd roared its disapproval, but the decision stood, and in the 30-minute overtime session, with five minutes gone, Piola scored to give Italy a hard-earned 2-1 win.

Switzerland had to play two games against Germany before advancing to the second round. In the first game, a goal by German star Gauchel was offset late in the first half by one from Swiss winger Trello Abegglen. The second half and the ensuing 30-minute overtime session failed to produce any more goals, and a replay was held five days later. In this match, Germany took a 2-0 halftime lead on a goal by Hahnemann, who had played for Austria, and a self-goal by Swiss defender Loertscher. Wallascheck, who had been injured in the first game, cut the German lead to one goal, and after Bickel tallied the tying score, Abegglen hit the nets twice within seven minutes to give Switzerland a 4-2 come-from-behind victory.

Cuba, which had entered the tournament after Mexico withdrew, tied powerful Rumania, 3-3, in the first match and then rallied from a 1-0 halftime deficit to win the replay, 2-1, on a goal that the Rumanians futilely protested was offside. Brazil and Poland waged a wild match, with 11 goals entering the nets. Playing a fast wing game with their fullbacks coming upfield, the Brazilians shot out to a 3-1 halftime lead as Leonidas scored all three of their tallies. But the Poles, playing a deliberate, well-organized passing game, recovered to gain a regulation 4-4 tie as Willimowski scored twice. In the overtime session, Leonidas and Romeo scored for Brazil; while Poland could manage only one tally by Willimowski, and Brazil won, 6-5. In other first-round games, Czechoslovakia blanked Holland with three goals in overtime; France took Belgium 3-1; and Hungary had a 6-0 field day against the Dutch East Indies.

Sweden, as expected, got past its second-round foe Cuba with no trouble, finding the range for eight goals while holding the Cubans to only four. Gustav Wetterstroem led the assault with four goals. The second-half goals by Piola carried Italy to a 3-1 win over host France, while Hungary took Switzerland, 2-0. In the other second-round game, Brazil and Czechoslovakia engaged in a fisticuff first game in which two players from each team were sent off the field. The game ended in a 1-1 deadlock; but in the replay Brazil won, 2-1.

In the semifinal round, Italy defeated Brazil, 2-1, as Colaussi, on a breakaway, and Meazza, on a conversion of a penalty shot, gave Italy a 2-0 halftime lead. Romeo averted a shutout when he scored for Brazil late in the second half. Hungary ripped Sweden, 5-1, in the other semifinal, as Szengeller led the assault with three goals. Prior to the finale between Italy and Hungary, Brazil won the third-place trophy with a 4-2 win over a disheartened Swedish team. Leonidas scored twice for the winners.

The final match was held in Paris, and the Italians had little trouble beating the Hungarians, 4-2. Colaussi scored early in the match and Titkos then tied the game for Hungary; but Colaussi made it 2-1, and Piola scored the first of his two goals to send the Italians off the field at the break with a 3-1 lead. Piola got his second goal midway in the final half, with Sarosi countering for the losing Hungarian side.

After the game, Italian manager Pozzo stood facing the crowd and gave the Fascist salute, as the crowd roared its disapproval. The winning Italian team returned home and was greeted by a wild mob led in its cheers by Mussolini, who gave the team gifts and awarded each of the players a substantial sum of money for winning Italy's second World Cup championship. It would be 12 years before the next World Cup was to be held, and for that period of time, Italy was considered the defending titlist.

1950

England entered the competition for the 1950 World Cup, which was held in Brazil, and provided the United States with its greatest soccer triumph ever. There were 13 teams in the tournament, broken into four first-round pools. In its first match, the United States was matched against Spain and lost, 3-1, as was expected. Then the team came up against England, which had beaten Chile, 2-0, in its first encounter. The United States looked disorganized in the game played at Belo Horizonte. The English seemed to be standing back to allow the Americans to start shaping up—something that proved fatal when late in the first half Joe Gaetjens, who later returned to his native Haiti and was never heard of again, scored a rebound off a shot by Joe Bahr, whose son later played with the NASL's Philadelphia Atoms.

Sir Stanley Matthews recalled,

> In the beginning we laughed and decided to allow the Americans some time to get organized. But after they scored that goal and we couldn't get a clean shot on goal, I became so frustrated and angry that I kept digging my nails into my palms, and after the game was over and we had lost, 1-0, I looked at my hands and blood was flowing from them.

In Europe, when the score was announced over the wires, operators receiving the message wired back that there had to be some mistake. But it was no mistake; the Americans really had defeated the powerful English. England returned to repay the Americans seven years later, however, by beating them, 11-0, in an exhibition game played in New York. Nevertheless, the United States' defeat of England is remembered and talked about in soccer circles whenever World Cup competition is taking place.

Brazil won the Pool One title over Yugoslavia, Switzerland, and Mexico; while in Pool Two the winner was Spain, which swept all three of its matches against the United States, Chile, and England. Only Sweden, Italy, and Paraguay were entered in Pool Three, and the Swedes won the title with a 3-2 win over Italy. Pool Four was a farce, with only Uruguay and Bolivia entered; and when Uruguay won the match, 8-0, it was placed with Brazil, Spain, and Sweden into a four-team round-robin playoff for the overall World Cup championship.

Brazil and Uruguay were regarded as the favorites to meet in the last match of the round-robin; and in its first game of the final round, the Brazilians, with the cheers of their followers ringing in their ears, trounced Sweden, 7-1. Ademir, their brilliant center forward, scored four times, and Chico added two and Maneca one more goal. Meanwhile, Uruguay was forced to tally late in its game to tie Spain, 2-2. It then had to again resort to last-minute heroics by Miguez, who scored two late goals to give his nation a 3-2 victory over Sweden. Brazil, however, had an easy time against Spain, winning 6-1, as Chico and Jair each scored twice. In the final game of the round-robin, a crowd of over 200,000 jammed Maracana Stadium. A tie was all Brazil needed to win the championship, but after a scoreless first half, Friaca came in on a breakaway to give Brazil a 1-0 lead. The Uruguayans, however, would not be denied, as they started to press the Brazilian goal. They gained a tie 10 minutes after the Brazilian goal as Schiaffino took a pass from Perez and sent a shot past the fingertips of Brazilian goalie Barbosa. Uruguay could sense victory while the Brazilians mistakenly were playing for the deadlock. With only 11 minutes left to play, Ghiggia took a long run down the wing and passed to Perez, who then returned the ball to Ghiggia, who had cut toward the goal. Ghiggia sent a shot home for the winning tally.

Since the game was on Brazilian home ground, many of the Uruguayans who had come from their nation celebrated the victory quietly instead of going out and celebrating in public. Brazil was indeed in a state of shock, as it had desperately wanted its first World Cup championship.

Brazil's time was not that far away, however, and immediately the Brazilian Federation started plans to field the strongest team possible for the 1954 World Cup championship, which would be held in Switzerland, the home base of FIFA.

Even before the first ball was kicked, there was controversy, as many of the 16 teams entered complained that the Swiss police were harassing their players.

The format called for the 16 teams to be broken into four brackets of four teams each, with the top two teams in each bracket or pool gaining the knock-out quarterfinal round. Brazil and Yugoslavia played a 1-1 deadlock, after which Brazil was declared the group winner by virtue of its earlier 5-0 win over Mexico. Yugoslavia also advanced, and Mexico joined France on the sidelines. Led by the great Ferenc Puskas, Hungary ran away with Pool Two, trouncing Korea, 9-0, and West Germany, 8-3. West Germany was able to advance when it defeated Turkey, 7-2, in a special playoff for the second spot. Turkey and Korea were eliminated. In Pool Three, Uruguay and Austria advanced, while Scotland, making its first World Cup appearance, was humiliated, losing, 7-0, to Uruguay. After dropping a 1-0 decision to Austria, the Scots found themselves out of the running for the title altogether, along with Czechoslovakia. In Pool Four England, by virtue of its 4-4 tie against Belgium and its 2-0 win over Switzerland, advanced to the quarterfinals; while Switzerland beat Italy, 4-1, in a special playoff after the two nations had each finished with one win and one defeat. The Italians were eliminated and immediately protested that since they had compiled a better goal average than the Swiss in the regular phase of the pool competition, they should have been given the place in the quarterfinals.

In the first quarterfinal game, West Germany defeated Yugoslavia, 2-0, as Horvat, the Yugoslavian midfielder, accidentally sent a header into his own goal and Rahn scored the clincher in the second half. In a wild match, Austria came from a 4-2 halftime deficit to topple Switzerland, 7-5, as Wagner propelled two late goals past Swiss goalie Parlier. Uruguay had little trouble ousting England, 4-2. The final quarterfinal game, involving Brazil and Hungary, was so memorable that it is still called the Battle of Berne. Throughout the match, tempers flared violently. With 17 minutes gone, Brazilian player Indio suffered an injury when he was pushed and then stepped on inside the penalty area. Djalmo Santos converted the penalty shot, and then the Brazilians started to hit back whenever they were fouled by the

Hungarians, who were playing without Puskas because he had suffered a leg injury.. After Brazilian Julinho was injured, the Hungarian star M. Toth got trampled, which injured his left leg. Hungary won, 4-2, mainly on the strength of the wing play of Kocsis and the center forward performance of Hidegkuti, who scored one and two goals, respectively. After the game Puskas was reported to have cut Brazilian star Pinheiro with a broken bottle just as the team was ready to enter its dressing room. A free-for-all broke out near the dressing room, and players and fans alike joined in for over an hour until Swiss police were able to gain the upper hand and stop the melee.

In the semifinals F. Walter converted two penalty shots and O. Walter added two more goals, as West Germany ripped Austria, 6-1. In the other semifinal, Kocsis headed in two goals in overtime to give Hungary a 4-2 win over Uruguay.

The final was played after Austria beat Uruguay, 3-1, for third place. In the championship game, Puskas, although hobbling, played and scored the first goal of the match after only six minutes. Then the Hungarians made it 2-0 on a goal by Czibor. Within 12 minutes, however, West Germany tied the score with goals by Morlock and Rahn. Rahn scored the winning tally five minutes from the end of regulation time, as he took a pass from Hans Schaefer and sent a short five-yarder with his left foot past desperately diving goalie Grosics. German goalie Turek saved the victory when, with 25 seconds left, he stopped a breakaway by Czibor.

When the West Germans arrived home, manager Sepp Herberger was congratulated by many political and civil dignitaries, and West Germany, which only a few years earlier had started to rebuild its soccer program, was in a state of jubilation.

1958

What happened in the following four World Cup tournaments is in reality the story of Pelé and Brazil. The 1958 World Cup was held in Sweden, and the 16 teams, most of whom had survived rugged zone elimination tourneys, were once again placed in four brackets of four teams each, with the top two advancing to the quarterfinals. Pelé did not score in the Pool Four competition, although the 17-year old was all over the field with his brilliant passing and dribbling. His playing enabled Brazil to defeat the Soviet Union, 2-0; and when the Brazilians added a 3-0 win over Austria and a scoreless deadlock against England to their total, they won the Pool Four competition.

In the next round the Brazilians were joined by the USSR who had eliminated England, 1-0, after both teams had won out over Austria because of point total. England had tied all three of its games, while the Soviets were 1-1-1. West Germany topped Pool One, with one win and two ties. Czechoslovakia and Ireland were tied for second place, but Ireland gained the next round by defeating the Czechs, 2-1, in overtime on a goal by McParland; and the Czechs, along with Argentina, were out of the competition.

In Pool Two France beat Paraguay, 7-2, and gained the quarterfinals, along with Yugoslavia; joining Paraguay on the sidelines, however, was Scotland. Sweden won two games before its home fans, tied one to win Pool Three, and was joined in the quarterfinals by Wales, which had defeated Hungary, 2-1, on two second-half goals, to gain the next round. Hungary, along with Mexico, was eliminated.

Pelé's second-half goal was the lone tally of Brazil's match against Wales in their quarterfinal-round game. In the other matches, Fontaine's two goals paced France to a 4-0 win over Ireland; Rahn scored the lone goal of West Germany's 1-0 win over Yugoslavia; and second-half goals by Hamrin and Simonsson gave Sweden a 2-0 win over the Soviet Union.

Pelé drew worldwide acclaim for his three-goal performance in the semis, as Brazil defeated France, 5-2. In the other semifinal, Sweden broke a 1-1 halftime deadlock to defeat West Germany, 3-1. In the battle for third place, Fontaine scored four goals, giving him 13 for the tourney, as France beat West Germany 6-3.

The championship game was no contest as Brazil toppled Sweden, 5-2. Pelé and Vava each scored twice to lead the victory and one of Pelé's goals was probably the most spectacular scored in any World Cup final (see chapter 13).

1962

Four years later Brazil again was one of 16 nations competing for the World Cup, which was held in Chile. The Soviet Union and Yugoslavia advanced to the quarterfinals from Group One, while Uruguay and Colombia were eliminated. West Germany won the competition in Group Two, but Chile also made the next round. Italy, which had been beaten, 2-0, by Chile in a game marked by seven separate fights, two ejections, and five cautions, was eliminated, as was Switzerland. With a goal and an assist from Pelé, Brazil won its opening game over Mexico, 2-0, but then lost Pelé because of a torn thigh muscle in its 0-0 game against Czechoslovakia. It still had enough points to lead the division, however, with a 2-1 win over Spain. The Czechs also advanced, while Spain and Mexico were eliminated. Hungary topped

England, 2-1, and the two nations made it to the quarterfinals, while Argentina and Bulgaria were eliminated.

Radakovic's goal was the lone tally in the quarterfinal game between Yugoslavia and West Germany, and the Yugoslavians won, 1-0. Meanwhile Garrincha, called the Little Bird, scored twice and Vava scored once as Brazil eliminated England, 3-1. Chile toppled the Soviet Union, 2-1, on goals by Sanchez and L. Rojas, but Soviet goalie Lev Yachin was great covering the nets. In the last quarterfinal game, Scherer scored the only goal of Czechoslovakia's 1-0 win over Hungary.

Two goals each by Garrincha and Vava paced Brazil to a 4-2 semifinal-round victory over Chile; while in the other semifinal game, Scherer scored twice in the second half to lead the Czechs to a 3-1 win over Yugoslavia. Before the finale, Rojas's second-half goal gave Chile third place with a 1-0 win against Yugoslavia.

The championship game between Brazil and Czechoslovakia was played in Santiago, and Brazil was regarded as a strong favorite. The Czechs shocked the Brazilians early in the contest, however, when Josef Masopust took a cross from Scherer and sent a shot past Brazilian goalie Gilmar. Brazil matched the score late in the half, with Amarildo outguessing goalie Schroiff and blasting a shot into the gap left by the keeper. In the second half, the Brazilians completely dominated the action, and goals by Zito and Vava gave them their second consecutive World Cup championship.

1966

The 1966 World Cup championship, held in England, will go down as the most disputed and one of the most brutal World Cups ever held. Brazil lost Pelé early in the tournament, when he was brutally fouled and then trampled on by a Bulgarian defender, whose main job appeared to be to make sure that *Ie Re,* as Pelé was now being called, would not score. The crowds in England reacted bitterly whenever flagrant fouls were committed, and the English players themselves were often forced to retaliate when they were excessively fouled.

In Pool One, England's defense was unbeatable, as the team won, 2-0, over both Mexico and France and deadlocked Uruguay, 0-0. The Uruguayans also gained the quarterfinals by beating France, 2-1, and tying Mexico, 0-0. Mexico and France were eliminated. In Pool Two, West Germany and Argentina advanced to the quarterfinals, each beating Spain and Switzerland, while playing a scoreless match between themselves.

Portugal, with Eusebio (known as the Black Panther from Mozambique and called the new Pelé after the tournament), won Pool Three;

and Hungary also advanced to the next round. Defending champion Brazil was out of the running without a healthy Pelé, and there were riots in Rio de Janeiro. Church services were held with prayers for his recovery so that he could play in his team's do-or-die game against Portugal. He tried to play but had to leave the game because of his injury. Following Brazil's 3-1 defeat at the hands of Portugal, there were reports that bridges in Rio and other Brazilian cities were closed because of several suicides. Portugal and Hungary advanced to the quarterfinals, while Brazil was joined on the sidelines by Bulgaria.

In the Pool Four competition, Italy suffered one of the most humiliating setbacks in its long soccer history. Favored to win the division, the Italians started out strongly by beating Chile, 2-0, but then lost to the Soviet Union, 1-0, and were beaten, 1-0, by North Korea. The Italians knew what awaited them on their return home, and instead of arriving as scheduled in Rome, they flew to Milan, only to be greeted by thousands of angry rock- and tomato-throwing "fans." USSR swept all three of its division games and was joined in the quarterfinal round by North Korea. Italy and Chile were eliminated.

Geoff Hurst scored in the second half to give England a 1-0 win over Argentina in one of the quarterfinal-round games, while West Germany showed a well-balanced attack with Horst Held, Franz Beckenbauer (called the General), Uwe Seeler, and Haller scoring for a 4-0 win over Uruguay. The Soviet Union toppled Hungary, 2-1, on goals by Chislenko and Parkujan to advance to the semifinals; while in the other quarterfinal-round game, North Korea leaped out to an early 3-0 lead on goals by Pak Seung Jin, Li Dong-Woon, and Yang Sung Kook. Portugal, however, managed to cut the halftime deficit to 3-2 on a goal set up by Simoes on a breakaway, with a pass to Eusebio, and a goal scored on a conversion of a penalty shot after Torres had been brought down inside the penalty area. In the second half, Eusebio scored twice again, once on a penalty shot, and José Augusto added one more to give Portugal a 5-3 victory. The North Koreans received a standing ovation from the crowd attending the game in Everton, however, for their fine performance.

In the semifinals, Haller and Beckenbauer scored to give West Germany a 2-1 win over the Soviet Union, while Bobby Charlton's two goals paced England to a 2-1 win over Portugal, whose lone tally was scored by Eusebio. After the game, Eusebio was in tears, and the crowd showed its appreciation for his fine play by giving him a standing ovation.

Eusebio and Torres, on a penalty shot and a 12-yarder, respectively, provided Portugal with its 2-1 win over the USSR in the battle for third place, setting the stage for the championship contest between host England and West Germany before over 100,000 at famed Wembley.

With German flags flying high in the stadium, the West Germans took an early lead when Ray Wilson, considered one of the best defenders in English history, cleared a shot poorly and the ball came down at the feet of Haller, who sent it past goalie Gordon Banks. England tied the game shortly afterward, however, as Geoff Hurst sent a shot past West German goalie Tilkowski. In the second half, Peters scored for England with 13 minutes left, but the West Germans would not be denied, and, pressing the English goal, they gained a 2-2 tie on a tally by Weber, forcing a 30-minute overtime session.

Alan Ball, who had played a brilliant game throughout the finale, found Hurst free near the left side of the West German goal, and Hurst blasted a powerful right-footed shot that hit the upper crossbar and bounced straight down. Referee Dienst ruled a goal, but the West Germans claimed the ball had not crossed the goal line when it came down. After consulting with Soviet linesman Bahramov, however, the goal was declared legal, and England led, 3-2, clinching the win minutes from the end on Hurst's third tally, thus making him the only man ever to score three goals in the championship World Cup match.

England, which had maintained its 65-year winning streak over Germany, went wild as captain Bobby Moore accepted the trophy from Queen Elizabeth and then took a victory lap around the stadium. Picadilly Circus was crowded that night, and the pubs stayed open later than usual, with fans drinking almost as much as when World War II ended.

1970

The 1970 World Cup was held in Mexico, despite arguments that it was not the best place to hold the event. Because of television obligations, many of the games were held in the middle of the afternoon, and the altitude played havoc with some of the visiting teams. With several qualifying tournaments behind them, the 14 teams that joined defending champ England and host Mexico were exhausted even before the first ball was kicked.

In one of the elimination events prior to the tournament, El Salvador played Honduras. While returning to El Salvador from Honduras, where the second game of the two-game total-goal scores was held, fans were attacked, and the Soccer War broke out. As the two nations were winding down their military action against each other, a third game was played at a neutral site, and El Salvador won and qualified.

Brazil was in the midst of controversy only months before the start of the tournament. Pelé, who earlier had said that he would not play in the World Cup, changed his mind, but coach Saldanha threatened to drop him off the team. Because of this and other, earlier controversial decisions, Saldanha was replaced by Zagalo.

Except for the Mexican fans' love for Brazil, there was no real sign of friendship in Mexico as the tournament got underway. England was harassed by the Mexican press after coach Alf Ramsey had called the Argentinians a group of animals, and tensions were high all around.

In Group One, the Soviet Union and Mexico opened the competition with a scoreless tie. Each then defeated Belgium and El Salvador to advance to the quarterfinal round. In Group Two, Italy defeated Sweden, 1-0, and then played a scoreless match against Israel and Uruguay to win the group title. Uruguay finished as the runner-up on goal average, even though it was tied with Sweden in total points.

Brazil and England advanced to the quarterfinals from Group Three, with Brazil's 1-0 win over England the highlight of the round. In that game Banks made the most spectacular save in World Cup history, somehow stopping a bouncing shot by Pelé. Rumania and Czechoslovakia were eliminated. In Group Four competition, West Germany defeated Morocco, 2-1, after trailing, 1-0, at the half, ripped Bulgaria, 5-2, and won a 3-1 decision over Peru, which also made the quarterfinals over Morocco and Bulgaria.

England had registered a protest to tournament officials following its defeat by Brazil, claiming that police did not protect English players or disperse the noisemakers outside their hotel who had kept the players awake the eve of the game. There was nothing FIFA or Cup officials could or would do, however, to alter the final decision.

The quarterfinals were well contested, with two of the matches decided in overtime. With 30 minutes gone, England struck for a splendid tally as Mullery took a cross from Newton and sent a shot past West German goalie Sepp Maien. Then five minutes into the second half, England found itself ahead, 2-0, as Martin Peters scored. Helmut Schoen then gambled, replacing Libuda with Grabowski, and all of a sudden the West Germans were controlling the tempo of the match. Beckenbauer, who was switched from fullback to halfback as Grabowski entered the game, scored as Peter Bonetti went down too late. Bonetti was a last-minute replacement for Gordon Banks, who had become ill after drinking a bottle of beer the night before. Uwe Seeler made a goal late in the game to send the match into overtime, and English fans were jubilant as Hurst scored. But the goal was disallowed, and it was never explained whether it was offside or if a foul had been charged. Gerd Müller scored the lone tally in overtime to give West Germany a 3-2 win and a spot in the semifinals.

In another overtime contest, Esparrago's goal, made with a few seconds remaining in the extra time, gave Uruguay a 1-0 victory over a Soviet team that played a lackluster match.

In another quarterfinal game, Italy powered three goals into the net within 45 minutes in the second half to top Mexico, 4-1, after the two teams had been tied 1-1 at the halftime break. Riva, considered the darling of Italian soccer fans, scored twice and Rivera scored once. In the final game of the round, Tostao, recovered from a serious eye injury that forced his retirement a year later, scored twice, and Jairzinho and Rivelino each added single tallies to advance Brazil to the semifinals with a 4-2 win over a hard-fighting Peru side that included Ramon Mifflin.

In the semifinals Brazil was pitted against Uruguay in Guadalajara and Italy against West Germany in Mexico City. The Uruguayan Federation asked the World Cup Committee to change the site of Uruguay's match, claiming that the population in Mexico City was too hostile toward opponents of Brazil. As expected, the Uruguayans lost both the appeal and the game. Early in the match, Brazil's greatest weakness—having Felix in goal—was revealed, as Cubilla hit a weak rolling shot that bounced right past Felix to give Uruguay an unexpected lead. Clodoaldo equalized for Brazil late in the half, and the two teams left the field at the halftime break tied at 1-1. In the second half, Brazil's speed, passing, and dribbling proved too much for Uruguay to handle. Tostao found Jairzinho alone on the right side and fed him a rolling pass that Jairzinho caught in full stride. Jairzinho then sent a cannonlike shot past Uruguayan goalie Mazurkiewiecz. Next, Pelé came in all alone on the Uruguayan goal, and as Mazurkiewiecz came out to challenge him, Pelé passed to a charging Rivelino, who put the ball into an almost empty net. The goalie, clearly out of position, was unable to do anything but watch the ball go into the net for the final tally of the game.

The other semifinal was a bitterly disputed confrontation, with each team at times playing brilliantly and at other times making foolish errors. With eight minutes gone, Boninsegna broke through the West German defense and from 18 yards out sent a left-footed shot past goalie Maier for the only goal of the first half. With time apparently having expired, the referee continued the game because of injury time he had taken earlier. In the match, Karl-Heinz Schnellinger took a cross from Grabowski and sent a shot past Italian goalie Albertosi to send the game into overtime—an overtime session in which both clubs completely abandoned defense in favor of attack. Five minutes into overtime, a defensive foul-up by Italian fullback Poletti allowed Müller to intercept a loose ball and send a shot into the net to give West Germany a 2-1 lead. Italy then countered with two quick goals by Tarcisio

Burgnich and Riva. West Germany still was not beaten, however, as Müller headed in a pass from Seeler. With nine minutes left to play in the 30-minute extra time, Rivera took a pass from Boninsegna and scored the winning tally as Italy defeated West Germany, 4-3. In the match for third place, however, West Germany defeated Uruguay, 1-0.

The Brazilians were heavily favored to take the title, and, with Mexican fans waving Brazilian banners, they took the field at Azteca Stadium. A huge crowd was on hand as the players walked onto the field for the championship game. This would be the last time the Jules Rimet Trophy would be contested. Since each team had won the World Cup twice, the winner of the game would retire the trophy.

Italy couldn't hope to match the fine speed and passing of its Brazilian opponents, and the Italians started the game by going into a defensive shell to try to cut off the Brazilian speed. They hoped to catch the Brazilian fullbacks too far upfield and then score with a long pass to a breakaway forward. With 18 minutes gone, Rivelino sent a cross near the Italian goal and Pelé, although guarded by three defenders, leaped high in the air to head the ball into the net and give Brazil a 1-0 lead. The Italians were in a state of shock and then tried to have four men guard Pelé, who would take a pass and find a free man for a shot on goal. Then Brazil committed its only serious error of the game as it gave away a foolish goal. It came as Clodoaldo back-passed the ball deep in his own territory and Boninsegna came running in to intercept the pass. Felix never had a chance to get the ball, but he came out, made a sharp turn, lost his balance, and Boninsegna placed the ball past him into the empty net to give the Italians a 1-1 tie just minutes before the halftime break. That was the only joy of the game for the Italians, however, as Pelé completely dominated the second half. Gerson exploded a left-footed 20-yarder into the net 22 minutes into the second half, and Brazil was ahead, 2-1. Then Pelé tipped Gerson's free kick over to Jairzinho, who blasted the ball home from the left side. The final tally in Brazil's 4-1 win was made with three minutes left to play, when Jairzinho passed to Pelé, who put the ball right at the feet of Carlos Alberto, who in turn kicked it home for victory and the permanent possession of the Jules Rimet Trophy. In Rio, where many had watched the game on television, the streets filled with merrymakers, while the Mexicans in the stadium and on the streets started parading around, yelling, *"Brasil! Brasil!"*

1974

Elaborate plans were made for the 10th World Cup in 1974, to be held in West Germany. A total of 126 teams sent in applications for the 14 spots in the final rounds; the other two sides were host West Germany and defending champion Brazil. A complicated series of zone elimination tournaments was organized, and the battles for the 14 spots got underway 30 months before the 16 finalists were to assemble in West Germany. The qualifying competition was heated and sometimes controversial. FIFA shelved an appeal made by some nations to allow 20 teams to be represented instead of 16. The federation also decided that since the Jules Rimet Trophy was no longer up for grabs, the new cup would be called the FIFA Cup.

In addition, FIFA decided to change the old format of the quarterfinal round. Under the new rule, a team would not be eliminated simply because of one defeat. The teams advancing to the quarterfinals would play a round-robin set amongst themselves, and in the event of a tie, each team would be awarded one point. There would be no overtime..

Haiti and Zaire both made it through the elimination tourneys to the West German showdown, thus giving the World Cup its first two black-nation entrants ever. In European Group One, Austria and Sweden came out deadlocked both in total points and goal average. In a playoff, however, a penalty shot by Larsson sent Sweden into the finals. Italy was an easy qualifier from Group Two in Europe, while the Netherlands and Belgium dominated Group Three. After both teams had battled through two scoreless ties, however, the Netherlands got the spot on goal average, as it scored 24 times while yielding only two goals. Belgium, led by its great goalie Piot, had yielded no tallies but scored only 10 times in its matches against Norway and Iceland. In Group Four, East Germany, now on a tremendous soccer buildup campaign, easily outclassed Rumania, Finland, and Albania to win a spot.

The biggest surprise of the various European zone eliminations, however, took place in Group Five, when Poland tied England, 1–1, in the last match, which was held before over 100,000 fans at Wembley. Because of its earlier shocking 2–0 win before 100,000 in Chorzów on goals by Gadocha and Waldimir Lubanski, Poland qualified while England joined Wales on the sidelines. The English press said that Poland would be a poor competitor in West Germany, but later proved to be very wrong.

Bulgaria ousted Portugal, Northern Ireland, and Cyprus to win the spot from Group Six, while Spain and Yugoslavia tied for the Group Seven place, necessitating a playoff. Yugoslavia was trailing Greece, 2–0, but made three late goals to win, 4–2. There were unproved accusations that Greece had allowed Yugoslavia to score its last goal almost without opposition in order to make the playoff necessary. In the playoff, however, a second-half goal by Katalinski gave Yugoslavia a 1–0 victory over Spain before 62,000 fans in Frankfurt. Scotland beat both Czechoslovakia and Denmark to advance from Group Eight, while in Group Nine the Soviet Union beat France and the Republic of Ireland.

Under the qualifying structure, the Soviets had to face Chile in a two-game playoff, with the winner making the final round in West Germany. After the two teams had battled to a scoreless deadlock in Moscow, however, Allende was overthrown in Chile; and Soviet officials ordered their team not to appear in the second game scheduled for Santiago. The Soviets appealed to FIFA to move the game to a neutral country, but the Chileans objected, saying that they would guarantee the safety of the Soviet players and officials. FIFA ruled that the Soviets would forfeit the match if they didn't play in Chile, and the Soviets did indeed forfeit, sending Chile, which in its earlier qualifying round had eliminated Peru, to West Germany. In other South American zone eliminations, Uruguay and Colombia tied, with the Uruguayans getting the position in West Germany on goal average, while Argentina eliminated both Paraguay and Bolivia.

In the North American and Central American zone elimination series, Mexico eliminated both Canada and the United States to become one of the six nations that would later battle for the right to go to West Germany: Guatemala qualified over El Salvador; Honduras eliminated Costa Rica; the Netherlands Antilles won when its opponent Jamaica failed to show up; Haiti ripped Puerto Rico; and Trinidad and Tobago took both Antigua and Surinam. Mexico was the clear favorite, but because of a huge financial commitment on the part of Haiti, the six-team tourney was held in Port-au-Prince. The Mexican press blasted its soccer officials for allowing such a thing to happen but to no avail.

Trinidad and Tobago soon found that it was not easy to win in Haiti, as three of its goals were called back and it dropped a 2–1 decision to the Haitians. When Mexico lost to Trinidad and Tobago, 4–0, after tying Guatemala and Honduras, the Haitians clinched the title; and even though they still lost their finale to Mexico, 1–0, they were on their way to West Germany.

The African zone elimination series was a long, drawn-out affair, with 12 separate groups holding competitions. In the final grouping, Zaire went against Zambia and Morocco. After Morocco forfeited and Zaire qualified without having to play its final game, President Mobuta held a wild palace celebration and gave each player a car, a house, and thousands of dollars. He also promised to have his palace chef set up a kitchen in West Germany and fly monkeys in to be slaughtered so the players could eat one of their native delicacies.

The Asian zone competition also took a long time to settle, but the Australians beat South Korea, 1-0, in a special playoff and made it to their first World Cup. After more than two years, then, the field of 16 was set, and worldwide television coverage was set up.

West and East Germany, which had never met in an international soccer game, were bracketed in Group One, along with Chile and Australia. Despite its opening 7-0 victory over Chile, the West German spectators booed their team because of what many felt was a lackluster performance that overstressed defense after Paul Breitner's goal at the 16-minute mark. East Germany didn't play any better in its 2-0 victory over Australia. The East Germans appeared bothered by the huge crowd and the gestures of some of the fans. Twelve minutes into the second half, Australian halfback Col Curran gave the East Germans their first goal, when he accidentally deflected a shot into his own goal. Thirteen minutes later Joachim Streich scored on a 20-yarder.

West Germany then played Australia, and manager Helmut Schoen tried an unsuccessful double-wing system on the right side, with twin wingers interweaving with one another and then cutting in toward the goal. It was only when he abandoned this system that the West Germans started to play the type of game that had made them the favorite among oddsmakers. Overath scored 12 minutes into the first half of the match, and when Bernd Cullmann added another tally 22 minutes later, the game was essentially over. A final West German goal by Müller early in the second half made the final score 3-0.

Next, the East Germans were pitted against Chile, and in a bitter battle that Italian referee Angonese somehow managed to keep under control, the two teams tied, 1-1, with Martin Hoffman's goal early in the second half offset by one from Chile's Sergio Ahumada. Chile and Australia played a scoreless deadlock, and then came the game between the two Germanys.

The match between East and West Germany was a hard-fought match in which emotions ran high. After Jurgen Sparwasser's only goal of the game midway through the second half, the East Germans went wild, with manager George Buschner hugging his players and weeping openly. East Germany had won the Group One title and, along with the West Germans, had made it to the next round.

Yugoslavia, Brazil, Scotland, and Zaire were bracketed in Group Two, and in this competition Zaire lost all three of its games. Brazil played scoreless ties against both Scotland and Yugoslavia; while in their game against Scotland, the Yugoslavians took the lead with a goal by halfback Stanislav Karasi nine minutes from the end of the match. With one minute remaining to play, however, Scotland made it a 1-1 deadlock on a goal by Joe Jordan. In their matches against Zaire, the other three teams in the bracket had no defensive problems. Peter Lorimer and Jordon gave Scotland its 2-0 victory, while Yugoslavia put nine goals past goalie Kazadi and his replacement Tubilando, with Dusan Bajevic scoring twice. The game between Brazil and Zaire was important, as it would determine which of the top three teams in the group would be eliminated. The Brazilians needed at least three goals to make the next round, and they went onto the field confident. With 13 minutes gone Jairzinho scored, but then Kazadi made some brilliant saves and shut off the Brazilians. It took Brazil 22 minutes of action in the second half before Rivelino scored, making it 2-0; but with 11 minutes remaining, substitute Valdomiro gave Brazil its long-awaited third goal and a spot in the next round along with Yugoslavia. Scotland was disappointed and left feeling that it was unfair to be eliminated simply because of goal average.

In Group Three, the Netherlands emerged as a world soccer power. Playing total football, in which they had 10 men on attack whenever they got the ball and 10 men aiding their goalie while on defense, the Dutch were brilliant, and the play of Johann Cruyff delighted the crowd. Johnny Rep scored both of the Netherlands' goals in the team's opening 2-0 win over Uruguay. Sweden and the Netherlands both played brilliantly in their scoreless deadlock; and in its final game the Netherlands defeated Bulgaria, 4-1, as Johan Neeskens converted two penalty shots and Rep and Theo De Jong each added single tallies. The Bulgarians had tried to resort to fouls in order to stop the Dutch attack, but referee Boskovic of Australia did not tolerate it and granted the two penalty shots. Two goals by Rald Edstrom gave Sweden a 3-0 win over Uruguay and a spot in the next round along with the Netherlands, while Bulgaria and Uruguay were eliminated.

Italy was the favorite to win Group Four, while Argentina and Poland were expected to battle it out for second place and a spot in the next round of competition. In the group's opening game, Italy was matched against Haiti, and Italian fans were predicting a runaway, but they were disappointed. With five minutes gone, Haiti stunned the Italians as they mounted a strong drive. Italian keeper Dino Zoff, who had entered the World Cup competition with 13 straight international shutouts to his credit, repelled them, but one minute into the second half Emannanuel Sanon eluded the Italian defense and sent a bullet shot past Zoff, who had come out to meet the challenge. Television viewers were treated to a spectacle as coach Antoine Tassy and his players on the bench rejoiced. The Haitian government had promised each player $100,000 if they defeated Italy and $50,000 each if they tied. The Italians regrouped, however, and came back to win as Rivera, Romeo Benetti, and Pietro Anastasi each scored for a 3-1 victory.

Poland and Argentina then played a match and goals by Grzegorz Lato, who was the tourney's high scorer with seven goals, and by Andrzej Szarmach in the opening eight minutes offset a late drive by Argentina as Poland won, 3-2. Argentina and Italy then played a bitter game marred by fouls, which ended in a 1-1 tie. After Poland eliminated Haiti with a 7-0 win, led by three tallies by Szarmach and two by Lato, it was obvious that Poland would win the grouping. Haiti had been forced to play the match without fullback Jean Joseph, who was banned from further competition after a urine test showed that he had taken drugs. Argentina also defeated Haiti, 4-1. Italy had needed at least a tie with Poland to advance, but Szarmach and Kazimierz Deyna scored in the first half, and Italy was able to score only once (on a goal by Favio Capello four minutes before the end of the match). Poland's 2-1 win gave it the Group Four crown, while Argentina advanced on goal average after it tied Italy in point total. Italian fans both in Germany and in Italy were furious with their team's play and stoned the bus and the players as they left the field and when they arrived home in Rome.

The stage was set for the second round, which was to be played on a round-robin basis. The Netherlands, Brazil, East Germany, and Argentina were in Group A; while West Germany, Poland, Sweden, and Yugoslavia were bracketed in Group B. The two group winners would later play for the championship, while the runners-up in each group would battle for third place.

The Netherlands made a shambles of the other Group A teams. Cruyff scored twice, and Rep and Rudi Krol each added a tally as the Dutch swamped Argentina, 4-0. Goals by Neeskens with eight minutes gone and by Rob Rensenbrink 14 minutes into the second half gave the Netherlands a 2-0 win over East Germany; while in its final group match, the Netherlands had to overcome a vicious series of fouls by Brazil before winning, 2-0, on second-half goals by Neeskens and Cruyff. Brazil, which beat East Germany, 1-0, on a second-half goal by Rivelino, and edged Argentina, 2-1, finished second, with East Germany third and Argentina fourth.

Poland opened the Group B competition with a 1-0 win over Sweden on a goal by Lato with two minutes left in the first half. West Germany defeated Yugoslavia, 2-0, on goals by Breitner and Müller. Poland was hard pressed, however, before beating Yugoslavia, 2-1. A penalty shot by Deyna gave the Poles a 1-0 lead with 27 minutes gone, but a defensive foul-up enabled the Yugoslavians to tie the score on a goal by Karasi with one minute left in the first half. Poland won the game when Lato scored midway in the second half. At Düsseldorf, Sweden and West Germany were matched, and the Swedes grabbed a 1-0 halftime lead as Edstrom put a shot past goalie Maier. Overath tied the score at 1-1 five minutes into the second half, and a minute later, the West Germans found themselves ahead, 2-1, as Rainer Bonhof scored past sprawling Swedish goalie Ronnie Hellstrom. Two minutes after Bonhof's goal, the Swedes got the tying tally on a goal by Roland Sanberg. With 12 minutes remaining, Grabowski scored, bringing the crowd of 68,000 to their feet, and a penalty shot by Breitner with a minute left was just extra gravy as the West Germans defeated Sweden, 4-2.

On July 3 it was pouring rain, and for over two hours the ground crew in Frankfurt worked to get the water off the field so Poland and West Germany could meet. Hoses from fire trucks were brought in to soak up the excess water. The winner of the match would advance to the finals, but slowed by the wet fields, for 75 minutes the two teams missed numerous opportunities. Lato lost his balance twice as he was coming in unopposed on the West German goal, while in the second half Uli Hoeness's penalty shot was saved by Polish goalie Jan Tomaszewski. With only 14 minutes remaining, Bonhof came roaring into the penalty area. As he was pushed, he passed to Müller, who sent the ball past Tomaszewski to give West Germany a 1-0 victory and a match against the Netherlands for the championship battle.

The final was set for July 7 in Munich. The day before, in the battle for third place, a crowd of 70,000 — only 7,833 less than would show up for the final — was on hand. Lato scored with 14 minutes left to give Poland a 1-0 victory over Brazil.

The championship game started with a surprise. With only one minute gone, English referee Jack Taylor awarded the Netherlands a penalty shot after Hoeness knocked Cruyff to the ground inside the penalty area. Neeskens sent the ball home past Maier, who had gambled by diving to his right while the ball actually was sent straight into the middle of the net. This was the first penalty shot ever awarded in a championship game of the World Cup, and the Dutch fans in the stadium went wild. The many dignitaries on hand, including U.S. Secretary of State Henry Kissinger, remained neutral, however, With 26 minutes gone, Taylor awarded another penalty shot, when Dutch defender Wim Jansen weakly pushed Bernd Holzenbein inside the penalty area. Breitner sent the ball past Dutch goalie Jan Jongbloed to tie the score at 1-1. With two minutes remaining in the first half, Müller scored a spectacular technical goal. Bonhof's pass from the right ended up behind Müller, but with a swift pivot Müller turned and took control of the ball and then pivoted again, propelling a shot

111

past a stunned Dutch goalie, who seemed to have let up momentarily. The Netherlands dominated the second half, although Maier made some unbelievable saves, once flat on the ground, when he tipped the ball gently upward and leaped off the turf to grab it. Jongbloed also was brilliant as he made a save when he came out of the area and headed the ball away. But then the final whistle was blown, and West Germany was a 2–1 winner. Although the Dutch hadn't won the title, they did win the respect of the entire soccer world, and their coach Rinus Michels was hailed as one of the best in the history of soccer.

Within a few weeks of the end of the 1974 tournament, the various teams who planned to enter the next championship game in Argentina in 1978 were busy making plans, picking new coaches and starting scouting operations to see if somewhere on a small team they could find a player who would carry them to the championship. The quest to win the World Cup never ends.

WORLD CUP I
Uruguay, 1930

Pool One

	Won	Drew	Lost	Goals For	Goals Against	Points
Argentina	3	0	0	10	4	6
Chile	2	0	1	5	3	4
France	1	0	2	4	3	2
Mexico	0	0	3	4	13	0

France, 4	Mexico, 1
Argentina, 1	France, 0
Chile, 3	Mexico, 0
Chile, 1	France, 0
Argentina, 6	Mexico, 3
Argentina, 3	Chile, 1

Pool Two

	Won	Drew	Lost	Goals For	Goals Against	Points
Yugoslavia	2	0	0	6	1	4
Brazil	1	0	1	5	2	2
Bolivia	0	0	2	0	8	0

Yugoslavia, 2	Brazil, 1
Yugoslavia, 4	Bolivia, 0
Brazil, 4	Bolivia, 0

Pool Three

	Won	Drew	Lost	Goals For	Goals Against	Points
Uruguay	2	0	0	5	0	4
Rumania	1	0	1	3	5	2
Peru	0	0	2	1	4	0

Rumania, 3	Peru, 1
Uruguay, 1	Peru, 0
Uruguay, 4	Rumania, 0

Pool Four

	Won	Drew	Lost	Goals For	Goals Against	Points
United States	2	0	0	6	0	4
Paraguay	1	0	1	1	3	2
Belgium	0	0	2	0	4	0

United States, 3	Belgium, 0
United States, 3	Paraguay, 0
Paraguay, 1	Belgium, 0

Semifinals

Argentina, 6	United States, 1
Uruguay, 6	Yugoslavia, 1

Championship
(Boldface indicates scorers)

Uruguay, 4	Argentina, 2

Uruguay—Ballesteros; Nasazzi, Mascheroni; Andrade, Fernandez, Gestido; **Dorado**, Scarone, **Castro, Cea, Irarte.**

Argentina—Botasso; Della Torre, Paternoster; J. Evaristo, Monti, Suarez; **Peucelle**, Varallo, **Stabile**, Ferreira, M. Evaristo.

* Overtime.
** Replay.
‡ Round-Robin.

WORLD CUP II
Italy, 1934

First Round

Italy, 7	United States, 1
Czechoslovakia, 2	Rumania, 1
Germany, 5	Belgium, 2
Austria, 3	France, 2*
Spain, 3	Brazil, 1
Switzerland, 3	Holland, 2
Sweden, 3	Argentina, 2
Hungary, 4	Egypt, 2

Second Round

Germany, 2	Sweden, 1
Austria, 2	Hungary, 1
Czechoslovakia, 3	Switzerland, 2
Italy, 1	Spain, 1*
Italy, 1	Spain, 0**

Semifinals

Czechoslovakia, 3	Germany, 1
Italy, 1	Austria, 0

Third Place

Germany, 3	Austria, 2

Championship

Italy, 2	Czechoslovakia, 1*

Italy—Combi; Monzeglio, Allemandi; Ferraris IV, Monti, Bertolini; Guaita, Meazza, **Schiavio,** Ferrari, **Orsi.**

Czechoslovakia—Planicka; Zenisek, Ctyroky; Kostalek, Cambal, Kreil; Junek, Svoboda, Sobotka, Nejedly, **Puc.**

WORLD CUP III
France, 1938

First Round

Switzerland, 1	Germany, 1*
Switzerland, 4	Germany, 2**
Cuba, 3	Rumania, 3
Cuba, 2	Rumania, 1**
Hungary, 6	Dutch East Indies, 0
France, 3	Belgium, 1
Czechoslovakia, 3	Holland, 0*
Brazil, 6	Poland, 5*
Italy, 2	Norway, 1*

Second Round

Sweden, 8	Cuba, 0
Hungary, 2	Switzerland, 0
Italy, 3	France, 1
Brazil, 1	Czechoslovakia, 1*
Brazil, 2	Czechoslovakia, 1**

Semifinals

Italy, 2	Brazil, 1
Hungary, 5	Sweden, 1

Third Place

Brazil, 4	Sweden, 2

Championship

Italy, 4	Hungary, 2

Italy—Olivieri; Foni, Rava, Serantoni, Andreolo, Locatelli; Biavati, Meazza, **Piola**, Ferrari, **Colaussi**.

Hungary—Szabo; Polgar, Biro; Szalay, Szucs, Lazar; Sas, Vincze, **Sarosi**, Szengeller, **Titkos**.

*Overtime.
**Replay.
‡Round-Robin.

WORLD CUP IV
Brazil, 1950

Pool One

	Won	Drew	Lost	Goals For	Goals Against	Points
Brazil	2	1	0	8	2	5
Yugoslavia	2	0	1	7	3	4
Switzerland	1	1	1	4	6	3
Mexico	0	0	3	2	10	0

Brazil, 4	Mexico, 0
Yugoslavia, 3	Switzerland, 0
Yugoslavia, 4	Mexico, 1
Brazil, 2	Switzerland, 2
Brazil, 2	Yugoslavia, 0
Switzerland, 2	Mexico, 1

Pool Two

	Won	Drew	Lost	Goals For	Goals Against	Points
Spain	3	0	0	6	1	6
England	1	0	2	2	2	2
Chile	1	0	2	5	6	2
United States	1	0	2	4	8	2

Spain, 3	United States, 1
England, 2	Chile, 0
United States, 1	England, 0
Spain, 2	Chile, 0
Spain, 1	England, 0
Chile, 5	United States, 2

Pool Three

	Won	Drew	Lost	Goals For	Goals Against	Points
Sweden	1	1	0	5	4	3
Italy	1	0	1	4	3	2
Paraguay	0	1	1	2	4	1

Sweden, 3	Italy, 2
Sweden, 2	Paraguay, 2
Italy, 2	Paraguay, 0

Pool Four

	Won	Drew	Lost	Goals For	Goals Against	Points
Uruguay	1	0	0	8	0	2
Bolivia	0	0	1	0	8	0

Uruguay, 8	Bolivia, 0

Final Pool‡

	Won	Drew	Lost	Goals For	Goals Against	Points
Uruguay	2	1	0	7	5	5
Brazil	2	0	1	14	4	4
Sweden	1	0	2	6	11	2
Spain	0	1	2	4	11	1

Uruguay, 2	Spain, 2
Brazil, 7	Sweden, 1
Uruguay, 3	Sweden, 2
Brazil, 6	Spain, 1
Sweden, 3	Spain, 1
Uruguay, 2	Brazil, 1

* Overtime.
** Replay.
‡ Round-Robin.

WORLD CUP V
Switzerland, 1954

Pool One

	Won	Drew	Lost	Goals For	Goals Against	Points
Brazil	1	1	0	6	1	3
Yugoslavia	1	1	0	2	1	3
France	1	0	1	3	3	2
Mexico	0	0	2	2	8	0

Yugoslavia, 1	France, 0
Brazil, 5	Mexico, 0
France, 3	Mexico, 2
Brazil, 1	Yugoslavia, 1*

Pool Two

	Won	Drew	Lost	Goals For	Goals Against	Points
Hungary	2	0	0	17	3	4
West Germany	1	0	1	7	9	2
Turkey	1	0	1	8	4	2
North Korea	0	0	2	0	16	0

Hungary, 9	North Korea, 0
West Germany, 4	Turkey, 1
Hungary, 8	West Germany, 3
Turkey, 7	North Korea, 0
West Germany, 7	Turkey, 2**

Pool Three

	Won	Drew	Lost	Goals For	Goals Against	Points
Uruguay	2	0	0	9	0	4
Austria	2	0	0	6	0	4
Czechoslovakia	0	0	2	0	7	0
Scotland	0	0	2	0	8	0

Austria, 1	Scotland, 0
Uruguay, 2	Czechoslovakia, 0
Austria, 5	Czechoslovakia, 0
Uruguay, 7	Scotland, 0

Pool Four

	Won	Drew	Lost	Goals For	Goals Against	Points
England	1	1	0	6	4	3
Italy	1	0	1	5	3	2
Switzerland	1	0	1	2	3	2
Belgium	0	1	1	5	8	1

England, 4	Belgium, 4
England, 2	Switzerland, 0
Switzerland, 2	Italy, 1
Italy, 4	Belgium, 1
Switzerland, 4	Italy, 1**

Quarterfinals

West Germany, 2	Yugoslavia, 0
Hungary, 4	Brazil, 2
Austria, 7	Switzerland, 5
Uruguay, 4	England, 2

Semifinals

West Germany, 6	Austria, 1
Hungary, 4	Uruguay, 2*

Third Place

Austria, 3	Uruguay, 1

Championship

West Germany, 3	Hungary, 2

West Germany—Turek; Posipal, Kohlmeyer; Eckel, Liebrich, Mai; **Rahn (2), Morlock,** O. Walter, F. Walter, Schaefer.

Hungary—Grosics; Buzansky, Lantos; Bozsik, Lorant, Zakarias; **Czibor,** Kocsis, Hideguti, **Puskas,** J. Toth.

* Overtime.
** Replay.
‡ Round-Robin.

WORLD CUP VI
Sweden, 1958

Pool One

	Won	Drew	Lost	Goals For	Goals Against	Points
West Germany	1	2	0	7	5	4
Czechoslovakia	1	1	1	8	4	3
Ireland	1	1	1	4	5	3
Argentina	1	0	2	5	10	2

West Germany, 3	Argentina, 1
Ireland, 1	Czechoslovakia, 0
West Germany, 2	Czechoslovakia, 2
Argentina, 3	Ireland, 1
West Germany, 2	Ireland, 2
Czechoslovakia, 6	Argentina, 1

Pool Two

	Win	Drew	Lost	Goals For	Goals Against	Points
France	2	0	1	11	7	4
Yugoslavia	1	2	0	7	6	4
Paraguay	1	1	1	9	12	3
Scotland	0	1	2	4	6	1

France, 7	Paraguay, 3
Yugoslavia, 1	Scotland, 1
Yugoslavia, 3	France, 2
Paraguay, 3	Scotland, 2
France, 2	Scotland, 1
Yugoslavia, 3	Paraguay, 3

Pool Three

	Won	Drew	Lost	Goals For	Goals Against	Points
Sweden	2	1	0	5	1	5
Hungary	1	1	1	6	3	3
Wales	0	3	0	2	2	3
Mexico	0	1	2	1	8	1

Sweden, 3	Mexico, 0
Hungary, 1	Wales, 1
Wales, 1	Mexico, 1
Sweden, 2	Hungary, 1
Sweden, 0	Wales, 0
Hungary, 4	Mexico, 0
Wales, 2	Hungary, 1**

Pool Four

	Won	Drew	Lost	Goals For	Goals Against	Points
Brazil	2	1	0	5	0	5
England	0	3	0	4	4	3
USSR	1	1	1	4	4	3
Austria	0	1	2	2	7	1

England, 2	USSR, 2
Brazil, 3	Austria, 0
England, 0	Brazil, 0
USSR, 2	Austria, 0
Brazil, 2	USSR, 0
England, 2	Austria, 2
USSR, 1	England, 0**

Quarterfinals

France, 4	Ireland, 0
West Germany, 1	Yugoslavia, 0
Sweden, 2	USSR, 0
Brazil, 1	Wales, 0

Semifinals

Brazil, 5	France, 2
Sweden, 3	West Germany, 1

Third Place

France, 6	West Germany, 3

Championship

Brazil, 5	Sweden, 2

Brazil—Gilmar; D. Santos, N. Santos; Zito, Bellini, Orlando; Garrincha, Didi, **Vava (2)**, **Pele (2)**, **Zagalo**.

Sweden—Svensson; Bergmark, Axbom; Boerjesson, Gustavsson, Parling; Hamrin, Gren, **Simonsson, Liedholm**, Skoglund.

* Overtime.
** Replay.
‡ Round-Robin.

WORLD CUP VII
Chile, 1962

Group One

	Won	Drew	Lost	Goals For	Goals Against	Points
USSR	2	1	0	8	5	5
Yugoslavia	2	0	1	8	3	4
Uruguay	1	0	2	4	6	2
Colombia	0	1	2	5	11	1

Uruguay, 2	Colombia, 1
USSR, 2	Yugoslavia, 0
Yugoslavia, 3	Uruguay, 1
USSR, 4	Colombia, 4
USSR, 2	Uruguay, 1
Yugoslavia, 5	Colombia, 0

Group Two

	Won	Drew	Lost	Goals For	Goals Against	Points
West Germany	2	1	0	4	1	5
Chile	2	0	1	5	3	4
Italy	1	1	1	3	2	3
Switzerland	0	0	3	2	8	0

Chile, 3	Switzerland, 1
West Germany, 0	Italy, 0
Chile, 2	Italy, 0
West Germany, 2	Switzerland, 1
West Germany, 2	Chile, 0
Italy, 3	Switzerland, 0

Group Three

	Won	Drew	Lost	Goals For	Goals Against	Points
Brazil	2	1	0	4	1	5
Czechoslovakia	1	1	1	2	3	3
Mexico	1	0	2	3	4	2
Spain	1	0	2	2	3	2

Brazil, 2	Mexico, 0
Czechoslovakia, 1	Spain, 0
Brazil, 0	Czechoslovakia, 0
Spain, 1	Mexico, 0
Brazil, 2	Spain, 1
Mexico, 3	Czechoslovakia, 1

Group Four

	Won	Drew	Lost	Goals For	Goals Against	Points
Hungary	2	1	0	8	2	5
England	1	1	1	4	3	3
Argentina	1	1	1	2	3	3
Bulgaria	0	1	2	1	7	1

Argentina, 1	Bulgaria, 0
Hungary, 2	England, 1
England, 3	Argentina, 1
Hungary, 6	Bulgaria, 1
Argentina, 0	Hungary, 0
England, 0	Bulgaria, 0

Quarterfinals

Yugoslavia, 1	West Germany, 0
Brazil, 3	England, 1
Chile, 2	USSR, 1
Czechoslovakia, 1	Hungary, 0

Semifinals

Brazil, 4	Chile, 2
Czechoslovakia, 3	Yugoslavia, 1

Third Place

Chile, 1	Yugoslavia, 0

Championship

Brazil, 3	Czechoslovakia, 1

Brazil—Gilmar; D. Santos, Mauro, Zozimo, N. Santos; **Zito,** Didi; Garrincha, **Vava, Amarildo,** Zagalo.

Czechoslovakia—Schroiff; Tichy, Novak; Pluskal, Popluhar, **Masopust**; Pospichal, Scherer, Kvasniak, Kadraba, Jelinek.

WORLD CUP VIII
England, 1966

Group One

	Won	Drew	Lost	Goals For	Goals Against	Points
England	2	1	0	4	0	5
Uruguay	1	2	0	2	1	4
Mexico	0	2	1	1	3	2
France	0	1	2	2	5	1

England, 0	Uruguay, 0
France, 1	Mexico, 1
Uruguay, 2	France, 1
England, 2	Mexico, 0
Uruguay, 0	Mexico, 0
England, 2	France, 0

Group Two

	Won	Drew	Lost	Goals For	Goals Against	Points
West Germany	2	1	0	7	1	5
Argentina	2	1	0	4	1	5
Spain	1	0	2	4	5	2
Switzerland	0	0	3	1	9	0

West Germany, 5	Switzerland, 0
Argentina, 2	Spain, 1
Spain, 2	Switzerland, 1
Argentina, 0	West Germany, 0
Argentina, 2	Switzerland, 0
West Germany, 2	Spain, 1

Group Three

	Won	Drew	Lost	Goals For	Goals Against	Points
Portugal	3	0	0	9	2	6
Hungary	2	0	1	7	5	4
Brazil	1	0	2	4	6	2
Bulgaria	0	0	3	1	8	0

Brazil, 2	Bulgaria, 0
Portugal, 3	Hungary, 1
Hungary, 3	Brazil, 1
Portugal, 3	Bulgaria, 0
Portugal, 3	Brazil, 1
Hungary, 3	Bulgaria, 1

Group Four

	Won	Drew	Lost	Goals For	Goals Against	Points
USSR	3	0	0	6	1	6
North Korea	1	1	1	2	4	3
Italy	1	0	2	2	2	2
Chile	0	1	2	2	5	1

USSR, 3	North Korea, 0	USSR, 1	Italy, 0
Italy, 2	Chile, 0	North Korea, 1	Italy, 0
Chile, 1	North Korea, 1	USSR, 2	Chile, 1

Quarterfinals

England, 1	Argentina, 0
West Germany, 4	Uruguay, 0
Portugal, 5	North Korea, 3
USSR, 2	Hungary, 1

Semifinals

| West Germany, 2 | USSR, 1 |
| England, 2 | Portugal, 1 |

Third Place

| Portugal, 2 | USSR, 1 |

Championship

| England, 4 | West Germany, 2* |

England — Banks; Cohen, Wilson; Stiles, J. Charlton, Moore; Ball, **Hurst (3)**, Hunt, B. Charlton, **Peters.**

West Germany — Tilkowski; Hottges, Schulz; **Weber,** Schnellinger; **Haller,** Beckenbauer, Overath; Seeler, Held, Emmerich.

* Overtime.
** Replay.
‡ Round-Robin.

WORLD CUP IX
Mexico, 1970

Group One

	Won	Drew	Lost	Goals For	Goals Against	Points
USSR	2	1	0	6	1	5
Mexico	2	1	0	5	0	5
Belgium	1	0	2	4	5	2
El Salvador	0	0	3	0	9	0

Mexico, 0	USSR, 0
Belgium, 3	El Salvador, 0
USSR, 4	Belgium, 1
Mexico, 4	El Salvador, 0
USSR, 2	El Salvador, 0
Mexico, 1	Belgium, 0

Group Two

	Won	Drew	Lost	Goals For	Goals Against	Points
Italy	1	2	0	1	0	4
Uruguay	1	1	1	2	1	3
Sweden	1	1	1	2	2	3
Israel	0	2	1	1	3	2

Uruguay, 2	Israel, 0
Italy, 1	Sweden, 0
Uruguay, 0	Italy, 0
Sweden, 1	Israel, 1
Sweden, 1	Uruguay, 0
Italy, 0	Israel, 0

Group Three

	Won	Drew	Lost	Goals For	Goals Against	Points
Brazil	3	0	0	8	3	6
England	2	0	1	2	1	4
Rumania	1	0	2	4	5	2
Czechoslovakia	0	0	3	2	7	0

England, 1	Rumania, 0
Brazil, 4	Czechoslovakia, 1
Rumania, 2	Czechoslovakia, 1
Brazil, 1	England, 0
Brazil, 3	Rumania, 2
England, 1	Czechoslovakia, 0

Group Four

	Won	Drew	Lost	Goals For	Goals Against	Points
West Germany	3	0	0	10	4	6
Peru	2	0	1	7	5	4
Bulgaria	0	1	2	5	9	1
Morocco	0	1	2	2	6	1

Peru, 3	Bulgaria, 2
West Germany, 2	Morocco, 1
Peru, 3	Moroccco, 0
West Germany, 5	Bulgaria, 2
West Germany, 3	Peru, 1
Morocco, 1	Bulgaria, 1

Quarterfinals

West Germany, 3	England, 2*
Brazil, 4	Peru, 2
Italy, 4	Mexico, 1
Uruguay, 1	USSR, 0*

Semifinals

Italy, 4	West Germany, 3*
Brazil, 3	Uruguay, 1

Third Place

West Germany, 1   Uruguay, 0

Championship

Brazil, 4   Italy, 1

Brazil—Felix; **Carlos Alberto,** Brito, Piazza, Everaldo; Clodoaldo, **Gerson; Jairzinho,** Tostao, **Pelé,** Rivelino.

Italy—Albertossi; Cera, Burgnich, Bertini (sub-Juliano), Rosato, Facchetti; Domenghini, Mazzola, De Sisti; **Boninsegna** (sub-Rivera), Riva.

*Overtime.
**Replay.
‡Round-Robin.

WORLD CUP X
West Germany, 1974

Group One

	Won	Drew	Lost	Goals For	Goals Against	Points
East Germany	2	1	0	4	1	5
West Germany	2	0	1	4	1	4
Chile	0	2	1	1	2	2
Australia	0	1	2	0	5	1

West Germany, 1	Chile, 0
East Germany, 2	Australia, 0
West Germany, 3	Australia, 0
East Germany, 1	Chile, 1
East Germany, 1	West Germany, 0
Chile, 0	Australia, 0

Group Two

	Won	Drew	Lost	Goals For	Goals Against	Points
Yugoslavia	1	2	0	10	1	4
Brazil	1	2	0	3	0	4
Scotland	1	2	0	3	1	4
Zaire	0	0	3	0	14	0

Brazil, 0	Yugoslavia, 0
Scotland, 2	Zaire, 0
Brazil, 0	Scotland, 0
Yugoslavia, 9	Zaire, 0
Scotland, 1	Yugoslavia, 1
Brazil, 3	Zaire, 0

Group Three

	Won	Drew	Lost	Goals For	Goals Against	Points
Netherlands	2	1	0	6	1	5
Sweden	1	2	0	3	0	4
Bulgaria	0	2	1	2	5	2
Uruguay	0	1	2	1	6	1

Netherlands, 2	Uruguay, 0
Sweden, 0	Bulgaria, 0
Netherlands, 0	Sweden, 0
Bulgaria, 1	Uruguay, 1
Netherlands, 4	Bulgaria, 1
Sweden, 3	Uruguay, 0

Group Four

	Won	Drew	Lost	Goals For	Goals Against	Points
Poland	3	0	0	12	3	6
Argentina	1	1	1	7	5	3
Italy	1	1	1	5	4	3
Haiti	0	0	3	2	14	0

Italy, 3	Haiti, 1
Poland, 3	Argentina, 2
Argentina, 1	Italy, 1
Poland, 7	Haiti, 0
Argentina, 4	Haiti, 1
Poland, 2	Italy, 1

Second Round
Group A

	Won	Drew	Lost	Goals For	Goals Against	Points
Netherlands	3	0	0	8	0	6
Brazil	2	0	1	3	3	4
East Germany	0	1	2	1	4	1
Argentina	0	1	2	2	7	1

Brazil, 1	East Germany, 0
Netherlands, 4	Argentina, 0
Netherlands, 2	East Germany, 0
Brazil, 2	Argentina, 1
Netherlands, 2	Brazil, 0
Argentina, 1	East Germany, 1

Group B

	Won	Drew	Lost	Goals For	Goals Against	Points
West Germany	3	0	0	7	2	6
Poland	2	0	1	3	2	4
Sweden	1	0	2	4	6	2
Yugoslavia	0	0	3	2	6	0

Poland, 1	Sweden, 0
West Germany, 2	Yugoslavia, 0
Poland, 2	Yugoslavia, 1
West Germany, 4	Sweden, 2
Sweden, 2	Yugoslavia, 1
West Germany, 1	Poland, 0

Third Place
Poland, 1   Brazil, 0

Championship
West Germany, 2   Netherlands, 1

West Germany—Maier; Vogts, Schwarzenbeck, Beckenbauer, **Breitner**; Bonhof; Höness, Overath, Grabowski, **Müller**, Holzenbein.

Netherlands—Jongbloed; Suurbier, Rijsbergen (sub–De Jong), Haan, Krol; Jansen, Van Hanegem, **Neeskens**; Rep, Cruyff, Rensenbrink (sub–Van der Kerkhof).

* Overtime.
** Replay.
‡ Round-Robin.

CHAPTER 9

European Titles

When almost any club in any nation in Europe plays in a regular season game, for the most part the match will go on without major difficulties either among the players or the fans in attendance. But it's almost war time when clubs from different nations engage in one of the three big annual tournaments—the European Cup, the Cup-Winners' Cup, and the Union of European Football Associations tournament, which replaced the old Inter-Cities Fairs Cup. These events were designed to settle arguments among fans and national associations about who plays soccer best.

These three tournaments are strictly club events and should not be confused with the Henri Delaunay Cup (better known as the European Nations Football Championship), which was originally referred to as the European Nations Cup. In this competition, all the nations in Europe enter their national teams for a series of elimination events that take about two years to complete.

EUROPEAN CUP

The first European Cup was held in the 1955-56 season, and with 16 teams competing, it proved the power of Spain's Real Madrid. Fielding a team with such players as goalie Alonso, fullback Zarraga, halfbacks Joseito and Marchal, and forwards di Stefano, Rial, and Gento, the Spanish opened the competition by beating the Swiss team Servette Geneva, 2-0 and 5-0. In the quarterfinals, they took the Yugoslavian powerhouse Partizan Belgrade, 4-0, and were able to win the total-goal series, 4-3, even though they lost the return match in Belgrade, 3-0. Then they waged two bitter battles with Italian power AC Milan, winning the first game in Spain, 4-2, and dropping the return match, 2-1; but they were still able to gain the final round by a 5-4 aggregate.

In the championship game, they faced Stade de Reims of France, which had advanced with victories over Asrhus of Greece, Voros Lobogo of Hungary, and the Hibernians of Scotland. The championship game was played in Paris, and Stade de Reims had such great forwards as Kopa and Templin. A disappointing crowd of only 38,000 saw Spain's Rial score two goals, with di Stefano and Marquitos each adding tallies to offset the three French goals recorded by Lebond, Templin, and Hidalgo. Toward the end of the game, the French crowd became nasty, tossing papers and even cushions onto the field whenever a Real Madrid player would appear near the touch line in an effort to get a ball. FIFA, as well as the French Association, warned fans in an open letter that was published throughout France that further action of this type would cause their team to be banned from future European tournaments.

Despite the poor attendance for the first-season finale, the popularity of the tournament was demonstrated the following season, when 22 teams entered the competition. Real Madrid made few changes in the lineup that had won it the title the previous year and was lucky to get past the first round. Matched against Rapid Vienna, the Spanish won the opening match in Madrid, 4-2, but dropped the return in Vienna, 3-1. On a neutral field, however, they were able to win a special third game, 2-0; and they made it to the quarterfinals, where they disposed of Nice, 3-0 and 3-2.

Manchester United, at the time regarded as the strongest English team, was Real Madrid's next opponent, and the Spanish machine won, 3-1, before deadlocking the second match at 2-2. Manchester United fans have never been overly courteous, and they showed their dissatisfaction not to the Real Madrid team but to their own club and game officials by rioting near the end of the second game.

In the championship final, Real Madrid's opponent was Fiorentina, which in its first round had had to work hard to beat Norrköping of Sweden, 1-0, after the clubs had played a 1-1 deadlock right in Italy's backyard. In the quarterfinals, Fiorentina defeated the Grasshoppers of Switzerland, 3-1, and tied the return game, 2-2, to gain the semifinals against Red Star Belgrade. Fiorentina's semifinal matches with Red Star have been called the dirtiest soccer games ever played in the tournament, and the officials blew their whistles for fouls almost every minute. Fiorentina won the first game, 1-0, and then the two teams battled to a scoreless deadlock. The championship game was played in Madrid, and a crowd of 124,000 was on hand. Spanish fans were not disappointed, as a penalty shot conversion by di Stefano and a breakaway goal by Gento gave Real Madrid a 2-0 victory. The fans celebrated long into the night, and the normally tough Spanish police were exceptionally lenient.

The field for the following tournament increased to 24, and once again the mastery of Real Madrid prevailed. In its first series against Antwerp, the team won, 2-1 and 6-0, and then disposed of Seville, one of its chief rivals in the Spanish First Division, 8-0. Using mostly substitutes, Real Madrid tied the return, 2-2, but had a comfortable 10-2 aggregate. Vasas Budapest was the team's semifinal opponent, and after winning the first match, 4-0, the Spanish coasted slightly and lost the return, 2-0. Meanwhile, AC Milan opened with a historic three-game series against Rapid Vienna, winning, 4-1, and then losing, 5-2, before winning the third encounter, 4-2. The Italians played superbly against the Glasgow Rangers, winning, 4-1 and 2-0; and they crushed West Germany's Borussia Dortmund, 4-1, after the first game had ended in a 1-1 deadlock. In the semifinals they played a rugged, fight-filled match and lost to Manchester United, 2-1, in Manchester. On their home field in Milan, however, they were outstanding and won the game, 4-0, to take a spot in the finals to be held in Brussels. Some say that it is too bad there couldn't have been two champions that year since both teams were so good. Real Madrid and AC Milan played a tough and often rough game, but it was also a clean game—something few had expected. Goals by di Stefano and Gento for Real Madrid and by Schiaffino and Grillo for AC Milan made it 2-2 at the end of regulation time, but in overtime Gento scored off passes from Rial and di Stefano to give the Spanish their third consecutive title. Although he didn't score in the match, the player who caught the eyes of the press was AC Milan's Liedholm, a native of Sweden, who swept up and down the wings.

The major change in Real Madrid's lineup for the following tournament was Dominguez, who replaced Alonso in the nets. But the Spanish remained the champions. The team first conquered Mesiktas of Turkey, 2-0, in Madrid and tied the return in Turkey at 0-0. After deadlocking Wiener, 0-0, in Vienna, the Spanish went to Madrid, where di Stefano scored three goals in Real Madrid's 7-1 victory. They then were scared by their crosstown rival, Atletico Madrid. Real won the first game, 2-1, and lost the next game, 1-0, but then won the third game, 2-1, to make the finals.

Stade de Reims had advanced with 4-1 and 6-2 wins over Arad of Rumania and then demolished Finland's Palloseura, 4-0 and 3-0, before playing the strong Standard Liège team of Belgium. The Belgians won the opening game of the two-match series, 2-0; but Stade de Reims rallied on its home pitch to a 3-0 victory and won the series, 3-2, in aggregate goals. The Young Boys Berne, considered by many to be the strongest Swiss team ever, defeated Reims, 1-0, in Switzerland in the opening match; but once again on its home field Stade de Reims prevailed in the return match, posting a 3-0 win to make the finals against Real Madrid.

The championship game was set for Stuttgart, and a crowd of 80,000 was on hand for the match, which was completely dominated both in offense and defense by Real Madrid. Mateos and di Stefano scored for Real, which posted a 2-0 win, while the fullback combination of Marquitos and Zarrago completely shut off the opposing forwards. Upon its return home to Spain, Real Madrid was greeted by fans and civil servants and was honored at a special dinner hosted by Franco.

But how long could Real Madrid dominate the European Cup competition? In the 1959-60 competition, Real Madrid started by losing its first game to Jeunesse Esch of Luxembourg, 7-0 and 5-2; and in its next round it suffered a 3-2 defeat at the hands of Nice but bounced back to conquer the Frenchmen, 4-0, in the return match. A quirk of scheduling matched Real Madrid in the semifinals against its bitter rival Barcelona. Only a few weeks earlier the two teams had played a 2-2 draw in which one player from each team was ejected. Real had little trouble winning both games by identical 3-1 scores, however, to advance to the finals.

Eintracht Frankfurt won its first-round competition, when its scheduled foe, Kuopion Palloseura of Finland, withdrew after the scheduling had been completed. The West Germans then defeated Young Boys Berne, 4-1, and in the return the two teams played a 1-1 deadlock. Eintracht gained the semifinals with a 2-1 win over Wiener SK and a 1-1 deadlock in the return match. In the semifinals, the team shocked the highly rated Glasgow Rangers, 6-1 and 6-3, to gain a spot in the finals against Real Madrid, which now had Puskas in its lineup.

The final match was held before a crowd of 135,000 in Glasgow, and Real Madrid was above fault as it won, 7-3, with Puskas scoring four goals and di Stefano adding the other three. Stein scored twice and Kress once for Eintracht. Although they had won their fifth straight European Cup title, the Real Madrid players acted as if it were their first championship as they left the field. The Scots held numerous parties and made presentations to Real Madrid for two days after the championship win.

The following year, however, Real's winning streak finally ended. In the first round the club was sent to the sidelines by its old enemy Barcelona, which beat Real Madrid, 2-1, after the first game had ended in a 1-1 deadlock. Benfica beat Hearts of Scotland, 2-1 and 3-0; defeated Újpest Dozsa, 6-2, before losing the second match, 2-1; tore apart Aarhus FG of Denmark, 3-1 and 4-1; and took Rapid Vienna, 3-0, before tying the second match, 1-1, to advance to the finals. Barcelona, which had defeated Lierse SK of Belgium, 2-0 and 3-0, before beating Real Madrid, was also making its way to the championship game, beating Spartak Kralov of Czechoslovakia, 4-0, before playing a 1-1 tie. It took three matches in the semifinal-round for

Barcelona to advance to the finals against Benfica. Playing against SV Hamburg, it won, 1-0, lost, 2-1, and then won the deciding game, 1-0. The championship game was set for Berne, and a disappointing crowd of only 28,000 turned out to see the action. Benfica won the match, 3-2, getting goals from Aguas and Coluna and a gift goal from Barcelona goalie Ramallets, who accidentally put the ball into his own net. Kocsis and Czibor scored for Barcelona, but it was a case of too little too late as the championship trophy became the possession of the Portuguese Benfica club.

Real Madrid rebuilt its defense at it bid to return to the winner's circle the following season. Keeping such forwards as Gento, Puskas, and di Stefano, the team changed around the midfield, making it slightly more defense-oriented than it previously had been. Benfica, now with the services of Eusebio, a 19-year-old from Mozambique, opened defense of its title with a 5-1 victory over FK Austria in the second game after the first match had ended at 1-1. In its quarter-final-round play the team seemed well on its way out of the tournament after dropping the first game of the series to Nuremberg, 3-1. But Benfica then delighted a home crowd in Lisbon by winning the second game, 6-0, to make the finals against Real Madrid, which had defeated Vasas Budapest, 2-0 and 3-1, and ripped apart Odense BK 1913 of Denmark, 3-0 and 9-0, before engaging in a torrid series against the Italian powerhouse Juventus. In Turin, Real Madrid won its first match against the Italians, 1-0, but dropped the return game in Madrid by the same score. In the extra game, however, Real easily won, 3-1, and then disposed of Standard Liège of Belgium, 4-0 and 2-0.

A crowd of 65,000 in Amsterdam was treated to a wide-open display of aggressive soccer in the championship game, as Benfica won its second straight championship, 5-3. Puskas scored all three of Real Madrid's goals, while Eusebio scored twice and Aguas, Cavem and Coluna each scored once for Benfica. The following year, Benfica bid for a third straight crown as the team defeated Norrköping of Sweden, 5-1, in the second game after tying, 1-1, in the opening match. After beating Dukla Prague, 2-1, at home, Benfica went to Czechoslovakia and came away with a scoreless deadlock to make the semifinals against the Netherlands' Feyenoord. After tying the first game, 0-0, Benfica beat Feyenoord, 3-1, at home.

With such outstanding players as forward Altafini and halfback Trapattoni, AC Milan emerged on the scene with a bang, beating Luxembourg, 8-0 and 6-0; winning, 3-0, over Ipswich of England before losing the return game, 2-1; and taking Galatassaray of Turkey, 3-1 and 5-0, to gain a spot against Dundee in the semifinals. In the first game of the series, AC Milan won, 5-1, and Dundee's return 1-0 win meant nothing.

Famed Wembley Stadium was the scene of the 1962-63 championship match, which was played before a disappointing crowd of only 45,000. The game itself was not a disappointment, however, as with two goals by Altafini, the Italians defeated Benfica, 2-1. Eusebio scored for the losers.

Real Madrid and Inter-Milan emerged as the teams to beat for the 1963-64 championship, while AC Milan and Benfica found the going rough. Inter got past the preliminary round by winning, 1-0, over Everton after the two clubs played a scoreless deadlock in the first leg. Inter then defeated Monaco, 1-0 and 3-1, while Real Madrid ran over the Glasgow Rangers, 1-0 and 6-0. West Germany's Borussia Dortmund eliminated Benfica by beating the team, 5-0, after Benfica had won the initial game, 2-1. AC Milan topped Norrköping, 5-2, after the clubs had deadlocked the first game, 1-1. Meanwhile, Real had shown some explosive power against Bucharest Dynamo, winning 3-1 on the road and 5-3 at home. With 2-0 and 2-1 wins over Partizan Belgrade, Inter gained the semifinals; while Real Madrid eliminated AC Milan, 4-1, in Madrid before losing, 2-0, in Milan.

In the semifinals Borussia Dortmund was pitted against Inter-Milan, and the Italians won the second-leg game, 2-0, after the teams had played a 2-2 first-game tie. Real Madrid had a field day against Zurich, winning 2-1 and 6-0, to set the stage for the championship game, which was played before a crowd of 74,000 in Vienna. Inter was led by Spanish star Luis Suarez, Brazilian forward Jair, and Sandro Mazzola, son of the great Torino and Italian National Team star Valentino Mazzola, who had been killed in a plane crash along with the entire Torino team in 1949. Burnich and Facchetti were on defense, and Real Madrid still had Puskas and di Stefano. Based on two goals by Mazzola and a solo breakaway goal by Milani, Inter-Milan defeated Real Madrid, 3-1, whose only tally was scored by Felo. After the match, Mazzola wept, recalling that it had been his father's dream that a European Cup be played.

Bidding for a second consecutive title, Inter-Milan had little trouble getting past Dynamo Bucharest, 6-0 and 1-0, and taking the Glasgow Rangers, 3-2, on aggregate as the Italians won the first game, 3-1, and the Scots the second, 1-0, in the quarterfinals. After losing the opening game of the semifinals to Liverpool, 3-1, Inter-Milan defeated the great English team, 3-0, in Italy to make the finals. Benfica defeated Aris Bonnevoie of Luxembourg by scores of 5-1 both times; took La Chaux de Fonda, 5-0, in Lisbon after tying the first game at 1-1 in Switzerland; tore apart Real Madrid, 5-1, in Lisbon while losing, 2-1, in Madrid; and in the semifinals blanked Vasas Gyor of Hungary, 1-0 and 4-0 to make the finals. The tournament committee was sharply criticized for using a coin flip to determine the winner of the series between Liverpool and Cologne after the quarterfinals. The two teams had tied, 2-2, after playing two successive scoreless deadlocks, and Liverpool won the coin toss.

In the final round, Benfica was beaten, 1-0, on a goal by Brazilian-born Jair, but some members of the Italian press said that the referee had refused to make foul calls against the Italians because he feared for his safety. The Portuguese walked off the field with only a second-place finish to show for their efforts but with the respect of the entire soccer world. Such Benfica players as new forward Antonio Simoes, and midfielders Germano and Neto, drew praise from the European press. Inter-Milan halfback Bedin, the most important addition to the club, was also lauded for his play, in which he ran up and down the field at full speed for the entire 90 minutes of the game.

Real Madrid, now playing without di Stefano and Puskas, was not regarded as much of a title threat when the 1965-66 European Cup competition got underway. After losing to the Netherlands' Feyenoord, 2-1, in the Netherlands, however, Real surprised many with its over-whelming 5-0 victory in Madrid. The team then played a 2-2 deadlock with Kilmarnock on the Scots' home field and again proved masterful on its own home field by defeating Kilmarnock, 5-1. Real Madrid next played a listless match on the road in Belgium against Anderlecht and lost 1-0; but on their home field in Madrid, the Spanish ran rough-shod, winning, 4-2, even though they conceded the Belgians one of their tallies in the closing minutes on a disputed penalty shot.

Real Madrid was matched in the semifinals against defending champ Inter-Milan. The first match was in Madrid, and the Spanish won, 1-0. The Italian fans were confident that their team would be able to score enough goals in the return game at home to make the championship game, but Real held the Italians to a 1-1 tie and made the finals instead.

The ability of the Yugoslavian team Partizan Belgrade was really unknown, since the club had held only a few pretourney games and had held its practice sessions in virtual secrecy. Its first opponent in the 31-team event was the little-known Nantes club from France. Using a three-back formation, the Yugoslavians defeated the French, 2-0, in Belgrade and then battled in France to a 2-2 deadlock. Werder Bremen of West Germany was their next opponent, and in Belgrade the Yugoslavs put together a 3-0 victory that more than offset their 1-0 defeat in the following game. But it looked like the Yugoslavians were finished after they dropped the opening game of their series against Sparta Prague, 4–1. A three-goal first-half barrage in Belgrade and two early tallies in the second half, however, gave them a convincing 5–0 win that put them into the semifinals against Manchester United.

In the first game, held in Belgrade, the Yugoslavians had the English defenders and midfielders playing their type of game, and as a result they were able to capitalize on several costly errors to come away with a 2–0 victory. Manchester United, which in 1958 had seen many of its players and officials killed in a plane crash after a game in Belgrade against Red Star, bounced back in the second leg, winning 1–0. It was a prestige win for the English, but the final score wasn't enough to keep Partizan out of the finals.

Brussels was the scene of the championship game, and a crowd of 55,000 turned out to see if Real Madrid, without its great stars, could add another victory to its long list of honors. The fans were not disappointed. Amancio, the inside right, and Serena, the outside right, each scored one goal as the Spanish penetrated the weak Partizan left-side defense and sent blistering shots past Partizan goalie Soskic. The only consolation for the losing Yugoslavians was that they weren't blanked, as Vasovic scored for them in their 2–1 losing effort. The 1965–66 championship gave Real Madrid an impressive record of six championship titles and two runner-up awards in the 11 years the competition had been held.

The following year the famous Glasgow Celtic team emerged onto the scene. The Scots had had to get special permission from the Scottish Football Federation to drop some of their previously announced postseason scheduled games in order to compete in this tournament. Torpedo Moscow also joined in the action—the first time a club from the Soviet Union was competing. In the top first-round games, Inter-Milan eliminated the Soviets by winning the opening game in Milan, 1–0, and deadlocking the return match in Moscow, 0–0, while Celtic advanced with easy 2–0 and 3–0 wins over Zurich. Given a bye until the second round didn't help defending champion Real Madrid in its opening game against München 1860, as the West Germans won, 1–0. But on its home pitch, Real was a different club and posted a 3–1 victory. Meanwhile, Celtic made the quarterfinals by twice defeating Nantes by identical 3–1 scores, and Inter-Milan made the quarterfinals with 2–1 and 2–0 wins over Hungary's Vasas Budapest.

In the quarterfinal-round competition, Inter's defense was outstanding as the team recorded 1–0 and 2–0 shutouts over Real Madrid. Meanwhile, Celtic rebounded from an opening 1–0 defeat at the hands of Yugoslavia's Vojvodina to win the second-leg match, 2–0, and with it a spot in the semifinals.

136

Celtic's semifinal opponent was Dukla Prague, and after the Scots won the first match in Glasgow, 3-1, the two teams played a scoreless second-game deadlock, which put Celtic into the finals. After playing back-to-back 1-1 ties, Inter-Milan and CSKA Sofia played a rematch, which Inter won, 1-0, making the finals.

The championship game was played before a crowd of 56,000 in Lisbon, and the sponsors were a bit disappointed, as they had expected a crowd closer to 75,000 if Real Madrid had made it to this stage of the competition. Celtic got tallies from Gemmell and Chalmers, while holding Inter to only one goal—which was made on a penalty shot conversion by Mazzola. The championship belonged to Celtic, and there were reports that on the night of the championship game, some supporters of the Rangers, who are considered Celtic's arch enemies, even joined Celtic fans in celebrating the championship win.

A new and controversial scoring change was instituted for the 1967-68 tournament. It called for away goals to count double in the event that the teams were deadlocked in goal count at the end of their regular two-game series. Many felt that this would hamper the efforts of home teams who previously had gone out and pounded away at the opposition's nets without worrying about conceding a goal in return. In the first round the decision was invoked twice. Since Benfica had tied Ireland's Glentoran, 1-1, in the first game, which was held in Ireland and had then played a scoreless tie in Lisbon, Benfica was advanced to the next round. Manchester United, with such outstanding stars as George Best, Noby (Clown Prince) Stiles, and Bobby Charlton, advanced to the second round with a 4-0 win and a scoreless deadlock against the Hibernians Valletta of Malta.

In a second-round play, Celtic, the defending champion, sat on the sidelines following a 2-1 defeat at home to Dynamo Kiev and a 1-1 tie in Moscow. Manchester United played a scoreless deadlock with Sarajevo in Yugoslavia before winning at home, 2-1 to gain a spot in the quarterfinals. Dynamo Kiev's bubble burst, however, as the team dropped a 2-1 decision at home to Poland's Gornik Zabrze and then got a 1-1 draw in the rematch. Benfica also made the quarterfinals with a 2-0 win at home against France's St. Etienne before dropping a 1-0 decision in Paris. Real Madrid, which in the first round had tied Netherlands' Ajax in Amsterdam, 1-1, and had won the return game in Madrid, 2-1, got into the quarterfinals with a 2-2 tie and a 4-1 win over Hvidovre of Denmark.

The quarterfinal competition was well played. Manchester United ousted Gornik, 2-0, in the first game while losing only 1-0 in the return; Real Madrid won, 3-0, at home against Sparta Prague before losing, 2-1, in Czechoslovakia. Juventus was forced into an extra game against Eintracht Brunswick after losing, 3–2, and winning, 1–0; but the Italians won the replays, 1–0, to advance to the semifinals. Benfica beat Vasas Budapest in Lisbon, 3–0, after playing a 0–0 tie.

In the semifinals, Manchester United ousted Real Madrid, as the English won the first game at home, 1–0, and tied a wild second game, 3–3, in Madrid. In the other semifinal, Benfica beat Juventus, 2–0, in Lisbon, while the Italians won the second game by a scant 1–0 margin.

The championship game was set for Wembley, and a crowd of over 100,000 packed the stadium, rooting for Manchester to give England its first European Cup title. A goal by Bobby Charlton and one by Benfica's Graca were the only scores in regulation time; but in the 30-minute overtime session, goals by Charlton, Best, and Kidd gave England a 4–1 victory and set off a wild demonstration in the streets of London and in Manchester, where some hooligans took the opportunity to break in and loot stores.

The regulation stipulating that away goals count double cost Real Madrid another shot at the title during the 1968–69 tournament. The rebuilt Real team had humiliated the Irish Union Limassol team with back-to-back 6–0 victories. But in the second round, Real lost, 1–0, to Rapid Vienna while on the road and won 2–1 at home. Since the Austrians had scored once on the away goals, they were able to secure a spot in the quarterfinals instead of the Spanish. Manchester opened defense of its title with 3–1 and 7–1 wins over Ireland's Waterford; and Benfica topped Valur Reykjavik of Iceland, 8–1, in the second game after the first game had ended scoreless. After losing, 2–1, to Sweden's Malmö in the first game, AC Milan won the return match at home, 4–1, and then drew a bye, automatically going into the quarterfinals.

In the quarterfinals, the Italians were matched against Celtic, and when the Scots played a scoreless draw in Milan, the Italians were considered in trouble. They surprised many, however, by winning in Glasgow, 1–0 to make the semifinals. Manchester made it to the semifinals with a 3–0 win and a scoreless draw with Rapid Vienna, while Ajax of the Netherlands made it the hard way. The Dutch had lost, 3–1, to Benfica in Amsterdam but managed to beat the Portuguese, 3–1, in Lisbon; which set up a replay in which Ajax was victorious, 3–0. Spartak Trnava of Czechoslovakia eliminated AEK Athens, 2–1, and then played a 1–1 tie.

In the semifinals, AC Milan defeated Manchester United in Milan, 2–0, and the English won in England, 1–0. Because of an opening 3–0 win over Spartak Trnava, Ajax was able to overcome a subsequent 2–0 defeat in Czechoslovakia. A crowd of only 50,000 turned out in

Madrid to see the championship game between AC Milan and Ajax, whose lineup included the sensational young Johann Cruyff. The Italians tore apart the Dutch defense, as Prati scored three goals and Sormoni scored one for the winners. Ajax's lone tally in the 4-1 setback came on a penalty shot conversion by Basovic.

The following year saw the Dutch begin a four-year domination of the tournament, as Feyenoord won the title with a 2-1 overtime victory over Glasgow Celtic in a game played in Milan before 50,000. Feyenoord won its first-round series against the KR Reykjavik of Iceland with 12-0 and 4-0 decisions. In the second round, the Dutch team rallied from an opening 1-0 defeat by AC Milan to win the second game, 2-0. Vorwaerts Berlin of East Germany fell to the Dutch, 2-0, after winning the first game, 1-0; and in the semifinals Feyenoord beat Legia Warsaw, 2-0, in their second game after the teams had played a scoreless draw in the opening match of the series.

Celtic made it to the finals by first defeating Switzerland's FC Basel in a second-leg game, 2-0, after a scoreless first-game decision. The Scots then defeated Benfica on a coin toss after each team had won 3-0 decisions on its home grounds. In the quarterfinals, Celtic defeated Fiorentina, 3-0, at home and lost, 1-0, on the road to advance to the semifinals, where they defeated Leeds United of England, 1-0 and 2-1.

In the championship game the two teams were deadlocked, 1-1, at the end of regulation time, with Israel scoring for the Dutch and Gremmen scoring for the Scots. A goal in overtime by Kindvall, however, gave the Dutch the championship title.

The following season officials made still another change in the rules. In the event that teams were tied in total goals and in point value, instead of deciding a winner by holding a coin toss or an extra match, tournament officials decided that the two teams would each take five penalty shots, and the team that completed more would be declared the winner — a format that many preferred. Ajax made the championship round against Greece's Panathinaikos by first eliminating Nendori Tiranë of Albania, 2-2 and 2-0. Its next opponent was Basel, which it ousted, 3-0 and 2-1, before coming up against Celtic. In Amsterdam the Dutch won, 3-0, and Celtic's 1-0 return victory meant little. In the semifinals, the Dutch were defeated by Atletico Madrid, 1-0, in the first game in Madrid, but they came back strong to win at home, 3-0.

Meanwhile, the Greeks got past Luxembourg's Jeunesse Esch, 2-1 and 5-0, before beating Czechoslovakia's Slovan Bratislava, 3-0, at home and losing only 2-1 in the return game in Greece. In the quarterfinals, the Greeks tied England's Everton, 1-1, on the road and then played a scoreless tie at home, which gave them the decision on total goals since their one goal on the road counted twice. The situation was repeated when they played against Red Star Belgrade. They lost the first game in Belgrade, 4-1, but won at home, 4-0. That one goal on the road was enough to put them through to the finals at Wembley, where a crowd of 90,000 showed up for the title game.

Led by Cruyff on the left wing and Neeskens, who broke in from his midfield position, the Dutch used a fast-moving attack and dominated most of the match. After Van Kjik gave Ajax a 1-0 halftime lead, Kapsis made an accidental goal past his own goalie Economopoulos and gave Ajax a 2-0 win.

With newly acquired defender Krol giving goalkeeper Stuy excellent support, Ajax won its second consecutive title during the 1971-72 competition over a well-balanced Inter-Milan team. The Dutch successfully opened defense of their crown by beating Dynamo Dresden of East Germany in the Netherlands, 2-0, and then tying the team, 0-0, in East Germany. Next came 2-1 and 4-1 victories over a weak Marseilles club, followed by 2-1 and 1-0 wins over the English power Arsenal. In the semifinals, the Dutch were matched against Benfica, and it was one of the best-played semifinal series in Cup history. Ajax won the first game in the Netherlands, 1-0, and, despite great offensive pressure from the Portuguese in Lisbon, was able to tie the return game, 0-0, to gain a spot in the finals.

Inter's road to the title game started with a 4-1 home field win over AEK Athens, which more than offset the loss of the next game in Athens, 3-2. With a 4-2 win and the scoreless tie that followed, Inter was able to get past Borussia Mönchengladbach. Because of the rule stipulating that away goals counted double, the Italians disposed of Standard Liège in the quarterfinals. Although winning at home, 1-0, Inter lost in Belgium, 2-1, but the one goal it scored in defeat pushed the Italians into the semifinals. Here they were pitted against Glasgow Celtic and played two scoreless ties, which some reporters said helped set back the world standard of soccer for several years. By means of a 5-4 decision in penalty kicks Inter found itself in the finals against Ajax. Celtic was relegated to the sidelines, and its officials harshly criticized the way the entire tournament had been organized and run. The championship game was held in Rotterdam, and a capacity crowd of 67,000 roared its approval as the Dutch heroes blanked Inter, 2-0, with Cruyff tallying twice against the highly regarded Italian keeper Bordon.

Johnny Rep, a hard-charging midfielder who is equally adept at playing offense and defense, joined Ajax's lineup the following year. In first-round play, Ajax was awarded a bye, thus automatically gaining a spot in the second round against CSKA Sofia, whom they demolished, 3-1 and 3-0. Next came a matchup with Bayern-Münich. The Dutch won the first game in Amsterdam, 4-0, and dropped the return game, but only by a 2-1 score. In the semifinals, they were pitted against Real Madrid and scored 2-1 and 1-0 wins to advance to the finals against Juventus.

Juventus had made the finals by defeating Marseilles, 3-0, although the French had won the first game, 1-0. The Italians next earned back-to-back 1-0 wins over FC Magdeburg, which were followed by 0-0 and 2-2 deadlocks against Újpest Dozsa. Since Juventus had scored both its goals on the road, the Italians advanced to the semifinals against Derby County, whom they defeated, 3-1, in Turin and tied, 0-0, in England.

The Ajax players knew that Juventus had one of the strongest defensive sides in the game; Dino Zoff, the great keeper, was in goal; Morini was anchoring the four-man back defense; Altafini and Causio were in the midfield; and Bettega, Capello, and Anastasi were up front. But they were prepared for it. The finale drew a crowd of 93,500 to Belgrade, and the Dutch team won, 1-0, on a goal by Rep.

Ajax's bid for a fourth straight crown was crushed in its second-round series against CSKA Sofia, which beat the Dutch, 2-0, after losing the opening game by a score of only 1-0. Bayern-Münich began its bid for the title with a great deal of difficulty. The little-known Åtvidaberg Club from Sweden had not been given much chance to win after dropping the first game, 3-1, on the road; but before their hometown supporters, the Swedes came away with a 3-1 decision, which set up a penalty-shot contest immediately after the final whistle had sounded. How the West Germans were able to concentrate that day despite the loud noises reverberating across the stadium is still a mystery, but they defeated the Swedes on penalty shots, 4-3, and were advanced to the second round, where they were pitted against East Germany's Dynamo Dresden. Bayern won the first game of the series, 4-3, and then played a 3-3 tie to make it into the quarterfinal round against CSKA Sofia. The West Germans won the opener, 4-2, and lost the second game, 2-1. In the semifinals, they tied Újpest Dozsa, 1-1, in Hungary, but in West Germany it was another story as they recorded a 3-0 win.

Their opponent in the championship game, Atletico Madrid, certainly didn't appear to be championship material in its opening series against Galatasaray of Turkey. In the first game in Madrid neither team was able to score, but in Turkey the Spanish did win, 1-0, which put them into the next round against Dinamo Bucharest, whom they managed to defeat, 2-0, in Bucharest and tie, 2-2 at home. In the quarterfinals, they defeated Red Star Belgrade, 2-0, in Belgrade and tied, 0-0, in Madrid to advance to the semifinals against Celtic. In the opening game of the two-game series in Glasgow, neither team was able to tally; but in the return match in Madrid, Atletico won, 2-0, to advance to the championship game against Bayern-Münich.

On May 15, 1974, before a crowd of 65,000 in Brussels, a goal by Bayern's Schwarzenbeck offset a tally by Atletico's Luis, but there was no further scoring, even in the 30-minute overtime session. A replay was scheduled for two nights later, when again a crowd of 65,000 was on hand. The West German team—with Breitner, Schwarzenback, and Franz Beckenbauer (regarded by many as the most outstanding leader in the sport), Sepp Maier in goal, Hansen on defense, Roth in the midfield, and Gerd Müller and Hoeness on attack—was favored over the Spanish, whose chief players were goalie Reina, midfielder Luis, and forward Alberto. With two goals each by Müller and Hoeness, the West Germans romped off with a 4-0 win for their first championship title.

The following year the European Cup was hotly contested. Throughout the tourney, the referees had to take such strong action as flashing the yellow caution card and ejecting several players. Bayern-Münich received a first-round bye, and in the second round defeated Magdeburg, 3-2, on the strength of two goals by Müller. When Müller again scored twice in the second game to give Bayern a 2-1 win, the West Germans found themselves in the quarterfinals against Ararat Erevan of the Soviet Union. Bayern won the first match, 2-0, on its home grounds and then dropped the second game, 1-0, but made it into the semifinals on a 2-1 aggregate score. In the semifinals, it was matched against St. Etienne of France, and although the first game ended up a scoreless draw, the second match produced a 2-0 win for the West Germans and placed them into the finals against Leeds United of England.

In its first-round battle against Zurich, Leeds had won once, 4-1, and lost once, 2-1 to advance to the second round. In the second round the English topped Újpest Dozsa, 2-1 and 3-0 and beat Anderlecht of Belgium, 3-0 and 1-0. In the semifinals, they topped Barcelona, 2-1 and 1-0. A crowd of 50,000 was on hand in Paris for the finale between Bayern-Münich and Leeds, and the West Germans won their second straight European Cup title with an impressive 2-0 victory in which Roth and Müller scored, and Maier played brilliantly.

Bayern-Münich won its third straight European Cup title in 1976, when it defeated France's St. Etienne, 1-0, in the championship game held in Scotland's Hampden Park before a crowd of 85,000. The lone goal of the match came with 33 minutes left, as Franz Roth sent home a free kick, which resulted in a strong but futile protest by the French team.

In reaching the finals, Bayern had eliminated Real Madrid in the opening round by blanking the Spanish team, 2-0, following a bitter and often hectic scoreless first game. St. Etienne had ousted the Netherlands' PSV Eindhoven by a two-game, total-goal aggregate of 1-0, defeating the Dutch club, 1-0, in France after the opening game in the Netherlands ended up in a scoreless tie.

CUP-WINNERS' CUP

The second most important European club championship is the Cup-Winners' Cup, which is limited to teams that have won their nation's Cup championship. Since this tournament doesn't have the prestige of the European Cup, however, a team that qualifies for both tournaments will usually enter the European Cup tourney and relinquish the right to play in the Cup-Winners' Cup to its nation's second-place finisher. The tournament started in the 1960-61 season, and the initial championship was won by Fiorentina of Italy. The Italians were pitted in the two-game, total-goal finale against the Glasgow Rangers. Fiorentina made the finals by beating Dynamo Zagreb of Yugoslavia, 3-0, before losing the second-leg game, 2-1. The Rangers advanced with a 2-0 win and 1-1 deadlock against England's Wolverhampton Wanderers. The first game of the championship was played in Glasgow, and Milan scored two goals to give Fiorentina a 2-0 victory. In the second game, held in Florence, Fiorentina again won, 2-1, with Milan and Hamrin scoring for the winners and Scott tallying for the losing Rangers.

The following year the championship was given a one-game format like the European Cup, but it took two games to decide the title. Fiorentina, bidding for a second straight crown, made the final round with 2-0 and 1-0 wins over Újpest; while 1-0 and 4-0 wins by Atletico Madrid over Motor Jena of East Germany advanced the Spanish team into the championship round. The final, held in Glasgow, was a 1-1 draw, with Hamrin scoring for the Italians and Peiro for Atletico. A replay was held in Stuttgart, and goals by Jones, Mendonca, and Peiro along with Madinabrytia's great goaltending gave Atletico a convincing 3-0 championship win.

Tottenham Hotspurs of England thwarted Atletico Madrid's bid for a second crown the following year. Tottenham had beat OFK Belgrade, 2-1 and 3-1, to gain the finals; while Atletico had come back from an opening 2-1 defeat at the hands of Nuremberg for a 2-0 second-game win. In the finals in Rotterdam Jimmie Greaves and Dyson each scored two goals and White scored one as the English recorded a 5-1 win over Atletico Madrid, whose only goal came on a penalty shot conversion by Collar.

It took a replay to decide the winner of the 1963-64 championship title. In the semifinals, Hungary's MTK Budapest shocked Celtic by rallying for a 4-0 win and advancing to the finals after losing the opening game in Glasgow, 3-0. It took three games to decide the other semifinal. Lyon of France and Sporting Lisbon of Portugal tied, 0-0 and 1-1, but Sporting won the extra game, 1-0. In the championship game, held in Brussels, Lisbon got a big break when Hungarian fullback Dansky put a ball into his own goal, which enabled the Portuguese to tie the Hungarians, 3-3. The self-goal and two goals by Figueiredo offset Budapest's two goals by Sandor and solo tally by Kuti. Antwerp was the scene of the replay, and a goal by Mendez was the lone score of the match, as Sporting won the crown with a hard-fought 1-0 victory.

At Wembley on May 19, 1965, the West Ham United squad, captained by the world-famous Bobby Moore, played in the championship game against München 1860. The English had advanced to the finals with a 2-1 win and 1-1 tie against Real Zaragoza of Spain. It had taken München 1860 three games to make it into the finals. After losing to Torino, 2-0, the West Germans came back for a 3-1 win, which made a third game necessary. München won that game, 2-0, on goals by Sealey.

A fluke goal in overtime was all that Borussia Dortmund needed to defeat Liverpool, 2-1, in the championship game the following year. During the match, which was held in Glasgow, usually reliable defender Yeats put a ball past goalie Lawrence. Held had scored for Dortmund in regulation play and Hunt had scored for Liverpool. Liverpool had gained the finals by coming back with a 2-0 win after losing the first game to Celtic, 1-0; Dortmund had posted 2-1 and 3-1 wins over West Ham United to earn the championship round.

Because more and more nations were hosting cup tournaments in addition to their regular league championships, 33 teams entered the 1966-67 tournament. In the semifinals, Bayern-Münich defeated Standard Liège, 2-0 and 3-1, while the Rangers earned two consecutive 1-0 wins over Slavia Sofia. In the championship game, which was held in Nuremberg, the two teams battled through 90 minutes without scoring. In the overtime session, however, a goal by Roth gave Bayern-Münich a 1-0 win and the championship crown.

Bayern-Münich's bid for two straight crowns lasted until the semifinals the following year, where it was defeated, 2-0, by AC Milan in Italy and only managed a 0-0 tie in West Germany. In the other semifinal competition, SV Hamburg defeated Cardiff, 3-2, in Cardiff after the two clubs had deadlocked at 1-1 in West Germany. The championship game was played in Rotterdam, and two goals by Hamrin was all AC Milan needed to record a 2-0 win.

Basel, Switzerland, was the scene of the 1968-69 championship game between Czechoslovakia's Slovan Bratislava and Barcelona. Slovan had advanced to the final round with a 1-0 win at home after tying the first game, 1-1. Barcelona had tied Cologne 2-2 in West Germany; but on their home field in Barcelona, the Spanish ran wild with a 4-1 victory. In the title game, both teams abandoned defense, but Slovan took the title with a 3-2 victory, as tallies from Cvetler, Hrivnak, and Jan Capkovic offset Barcelona's goals by Zaldua and Rexach.

The future of the Tournament looked shaky the following year, when only 10,000 turned out in Vienna to see the title game between Manchester City and Poland's Gornik Zabrze. The English had advanced to the championship round with a 5-1 win on their home pitch after they were beaten, 1-0, in Germany by Schalke 0-4. After playing three consecutive ties with AC Roma, with scores of 1-1, 2-2, and 1-1, Gornik Zabrze called the toss of a coin correctly to advance to the finals. In the championship, a penalty shot conversion by Francis Lee and a solo goal by Young earned Manchester City a 2-1 win over the Poles, whose lone tally came off a shot by Ozlizlo.

During the 1970-71 games, there was an attempt to make the championship a two-game, total-goal series again. After a meeting, however, the idea was dropped, although it did take two games to decide the championship series in 1971. In the semifinals, Chelsea posted back-to-back 1-0 wins over Manchester City; while in the other contest, Real Madrid overcame a scoreless first-game deadlock to win its second game against PSV Eindhoven of the Netherlands, 2-1, and advance to the finals. Regulation time ended in the championship game with the score deadlocked at 1-1 on Chelsea's goal by Peter Osgood and Real Madrid's tally by Zoco, and overtime failed to produce additional goals. A replay was ordered to be played in Athens, the scene of the initial game, and in the rematch, Real got a goal by Fleitas but Chelsea got tallies by Dempsey and Osgood to post a 2-1 victory.

The 1971-72 tournament will always be remembered for demonstrating how the ugliness of some fans can cause hard feelings between nations and even ruin what could have been a great tournament. In the finals, the Glasgow Rangers, via a 1-1 deadlock and a 2-0 victory over Bayern-Münich, were pitted against Dynamo Moscow, which had defeated Dynamo Berlin on penalty shots after the two clubs had played two successive 1-1 deadlocks.

The championship game was held in Barcelona, and although there were only 35,000 fans on hand (most of whom were Scots), the noise throughout the game and the catcalls against referee Ortiz de Mendibi made the crowd seem much larger. Late in the game, with time running out, the Rangers forged ahead to a 3-2 lead, as Johnston scored twice and Stein scored once. (Estrekov and Makovikov had found the range for the Soviets.) Following a foul on the field, the fans poured over the barriers and attacked several Soviet players while joyfully carrying around Ranger players in a wild demonstration. Although there were only a couple of minutes remaining to play, the referee was unable to continue the match, and the game was abandoned with the final score reading Rangers, 3 and Dynamo Moscow, 2. The Soviets protested, arguing that the game should be replayed, but Cup officials overruled their protest and allowed the final score to stand. Because they had been unable to restrain their fans, however, the Rangers were banned from European competition for one season. The ugly outbreak left a sour taste in the mouths of many soccer fans throughout Europe, and after considering several proposals, and after much debate, tournament officials set down stringent rules of behavior for both players and fans.

But there was no peace among players and fans for the following tournament either, the finals of which were held in Salonika, Greece, before a restrained crowd of 45,000. Leeds United made the finals with a 1-0 win and a scoreless deadlock against Haaduk Splitt, while AC Milan topped Sparta Prague twice by identical 1-0 scores to advance to the championship round. Leeds fans were merely noisy, but late in the game Leeds players attacked Milan players and urged their fans to throw things at the officials, who the English players said were the real villains as the English fell, 1-0, to the Italians on a goal by Chiarugi. Later, Leeds officials were brought in for a hearing by English Football Association officials and were fined for not controlling their fans or players.

FC Magdeburg became the first East German European Cup-Winners' Cup champion on May 8, 1974, when it defeated AC Milan, 2-0, in a title game played before 5,000 fans. The East Germans won the match on a goal by Seguin and a self-goal, when Lanzi accidentally put the ball past his own goalie, Pizzaballa. In winning the title, the East Germans had also defeated Sporting Lisbon, 2-1, in the semi-finals in East Germany after the two teams had battled to a 1-1 draw in Lisbon. AC Milan qualified for the championship game via a 2-0 win over Borussia Mönchengladbach before losing the second game, 1-0.

In the finals of the 1974-75 competition, a small crowd of only 13,000 turned out in Basel to see Dynamo Kiev battle Ferencvaros. Dynamo had gained the final round by beating the Netherlands' PSV Eindhoven, 3-0, before losing the second-leg game, 2-1. Ferencvaros had taken Red Star Belgrade, 2-0, and then played a 2-2 deadlock in the return match for a spot in the championship game. From the outset of the match, the Soviets were by far the superior team. Playing a well-organized game in which they employed the total football concept introduced by the Netherlands in the 1974 World Cup, the Soviets defeated, 3-0, a Ferencvaros club weakened by injury and suspensions, as Onischenko, regarded by many as one of Europe's top forwards, scored twice and Blocklin, who also has received numerous press raves from European journalists, added the other tally in the championship win.

Anderlecht of Belgium captured the 1975-76 European Cup-Winners' Cup with a 4-2 victory over England's West Ham United in the championship match played in Brussels. In the semifinals, West Ham eliminated Eintracht Frankfurt of West Germany, 4-3, in the two-game, total-goal series. In the opening leg, held in Frankfurt, goals by Neuberger and Kraus overcame an early West Ham tally by Paddon to give the Germans a 2-1 victory. In the return match in England, however, West Ham piled up a 3-0 advantage on two goals by Trevor Brooking and one by Robson, while Beverungen averted a shutout for the Germans by scoring two minutes before the final whistle. In the other semifinal, Anderlecht blanked East Germany's Sachsenring Zwickau, 3-0 and 2-0. In the first game van der Elst scored twice and Rensenbrink once, while in the return match Rensenbrink and van der Elst each scored once to clinch the victory.

In the championship match, the English posted out to an early 1-0 lead on a goal by Pat Holland at the 28-minute mark; and they were able to maintain their advantage until early in the second half, when a poor defensive maneuver enabled Dutchman Rob Rensenbrink, playing for Anderlecht, to tie the score. Before the game was over, Rensenbrink added two more goals and van der Elst another. West Ham was able to counter only with a tally by Keith Robson in the 4-2 Belgian victory.

UNION EUROPEAN FOOTBALL
ASSOCIATION CUP (FAIRS CUP)

The third major European club championship tournament is the Union European Football Associations Cup, which was called the Inter-Cities Fairs Cup when it started in 1955. It took three years to determine the champion of the first tournament, and it was truly an Intercities competition, with various cities selecting all-star teams to represent them. But even before the tournament was completed with the title series in 1958, it became evident that the format desperately needed to be changed. In the initial tournament four groups had completed on a round-robin basis. With a 6-2 win and a 1-1 dead-lock, Barcelona won the Group A competition after Vienna withdrew. Birmingham City won the Group B competition over Inter-Milan, whose officials argued daily with AC Milan officials over the makeup of the team. Zagreb placed third in that bracket. In Group C, Cologne withdrew right before the first scheduled game, leaving only Leipzig and group-winner Lausanne. In Group D, London was the winner over Frankfurt and Basel.

In the semifinals, Birmingham City defeated Barcelona in the opening leg, 4-3; but the Spanish won the second game, 1-0, which made an extra game necessary. Barcelona won the extra game, 2-1. In the other semifinal, London bounced back from an opening 2-1 defeat in Lausanne to win the second match, 2-0, and a place in the championship game against Barcelona. In the opening game, held in London, the two clubs played a 2-2 deadlock; but in the return match in Barcelona it was no contest, as Barcelona ran off with an overwhelming 6-0 victory to take the championship.

After debating several alternatives to the original format, officials decided that they would duplicate the format of the European Cup and the European Cup-Winners' Cup and make the tournament strictly a club event rather than an all-star event. They did, however, keep the name, Fairs Cup. In 1960, after nearly two years of qualifying competition involving league champions or runners-up in either the Cup or regular standings, the first champion under the new format was crowned. Barcelona, which in the semifinals had defeated Belgrade, 2-1, after an initial 1-1 tie, was pitted against Birmingham City, which had twice defeated Union St. Giloise of Switzerland by 4-2 scores. In the title games following a scoreless deadlock, Barcelona won, 4-1, on its home grounds to take the title.

In the 1960-61 tournament 16 teams entered the competition. In the semifinals, the Hibernians of Scotland and AC Roma of Italy tied, 2-2 and 3-3, necessitating another match, which Roma won by an incredible 6-0 score to gain a spot in the championship match against Birmingham City, which had posted consecutive wins, 2-1 and 2-1, over Inter-Milan. After the two finalists played a 2-2 deadlock in Birmingham, the Italians won, 2-0, before a large crowd on their home pitch to capture the championship.

With a ruling that any of the top four league finishers in a nation would be eligible for Fairs Cup competition if they desired and were not bound by prior commitments to play in either the European Cup or the Cup-Winners' Cup, the tournament started to gain popularity. A total of 28 teams entered the next Fairs Cup competition, and the tourney officials announced that their insistence on going ahead with the event was now justified, despite earlier pressure by influential officials of top national federations. The championship was an all-Spanish affair, as Valencia and Barcelona gained the title round. Valencia had posted 3-0 and 7-3 semifinal victories over MTK Budapest; while Barcelona demolished Red Star Belgrade, 2-0 and 4-1, to set up the showdown. Valencia scored an impressive 6-2 opening win and clinched the crown with a lackluster 1-1 deadlock in the second game.

A total of 32 teams entered the 1962-63 tournament, and for the second straight year Valencia emerged as the champion. In semifinal-round competition, the Spanish took Roma, 3-0, in their first game and then lost the return game, 1-0, but still advanced to the finals on aggregate score. Their opponent in the title series was Dynamo Zagreb of Yugoslavia, which had posted 1-0 and 2-1 wins over Ferencvaros. In the final round, Valencia defeated the Yugoslavians, 2-1, in Belgrade and won the return match in Spain, 2-0.

The following year the format was changed to make the championship series a one-game affair, and Valencia came close to winning its third straight title. In the semifinals Valencia defeated Cologne, 4-1, which offset its 2-0 defeat in the second game. Meanwhile, Real Zaragoza of Spain met Liège of Belgium. Liège won the first match, 1-0, and the Spanish won the second, 2-1, making an extra match necessary to determine which club would go into the final round. Real Zaragoza won the extra game, 2-0. In the one-game championship, Valencia's bid for a third straight title went down the drain, as the team lost, 2-1.

The field for the 1964-65 tournament increased to 48 teams, and, despite extreme pressure, the tournament committee decided to continue to allow the championship to be determined by one game only. In the semifinals, each of the winners was forced to advance via a third-game replay. Juventus lost its first game, 3-1, to Atletico Madrid before bouncing back with a 3-1 victory, but in the replay Juventus again won by a 3-1 margin. Meanwhile, after losing its first game to Manchester United, 3-2, the strong Ferencvaros team from Hungary rebounded with a 1-0 win, which forced a replay. Ferencvaros won the replay, 2-1, and in the title game, played in Turin, the Hungarians shocked the Italians, 1-0. As the Juventus players left the field with their heads bowed, their fans shouted insults at them, claiming that the team had deserted them.

The following year the format was changed with the title series again made a two-game, total-goal series as virtually every national association had requested. In the semifinals, Barcelona and Chelsea exchanged 2-0 wins on their respective home grounds before Barcelona triumphed, 5-0, in the replay. In the other semifinal series, Real Zaragoza beat Leeds United in Spain, 1-0, before losing the return in England, 2-1. In the replay, the Spaniards won, 3-1, setting the stage once again for an all-Spanish championship series. Barcelona lost the opening game, 1-0, but came back with an impressive display of power to take the second game, 4-2, and win the championship.

With the field limited to 48 teams, the official name of the 1966-67 tournament was changed from just the Fairs Cup to the European Fairs Cup. This seemingly insignificant change was the result of months of debate between traditionalists and those who insisted that a change in name would give the tournament more prestige. In the semifinal round, Leeds United defeated Kilmarnock in England, 4-2, before playing a scoreless deadlock in Scotland to advance to the finals against Yugoslavia's Dynamo Zagreb, which had overcome an opening 3-0 defeat by West Germany's Eintracht Frankfurt to win, 4-0, on its home grounds. A 2-0 win and a scoreless second-leg game gave Dynamo Zagreb the championship title over the frustrated Leeds United team, which had been the prefinal favorite.

But Leeds was not to be denied the following year as it pushed into the championship round with a 1-1 tie and 1-0 win over Dundee. Its opponent in the final round was Hungary's Ferencvaros, which had made the finals by a 3-2 first-game win over Bologna and a 2-2 second-game tie. Leeds won the opening game of the championship series, 1-0, and when the two teams deadlocked at 0-0 in the second game, the title went to England.

The championship remained in England the 1968-69 season, when a total of 61 teams entered the competition. In the rugged semifinals, Újpest Dozsa scored impressive 4-1 and 4-0 wins over Turkey's Goztepe Izmir, which had been regarded as one of the real longshots before the competition started but proved to be a rugged squad. In their other semifinal, after playing an opening 0-0 tie in Scotland against the Glasgow Rangers, Newcastle United won the second game, 2-0. In the opening match of the finals, Moncur scored twice and Scott added another goal as the Newcastle team posted a 3-0 victory. In the second game in Budapest, instead of playing a defensive game as many had expected, the English came out attacking and won, 3-2, as Moncur, Arentoft, and Foggon scored for Newcastle and Bene and Gorocs scored for the Hungarians.

The field for the 1969-70 tournament increased to 64 teams, as more and more clubs began to feel that the competition had become a worthwhile tournament, rather than merely a competition for those who did not qualify for the other two European club events. Arsenal advanced to the finals with a 3-0 win over Ajax, before losing the second game, 1-0. Arsenal's opponent in the finale was Belgium's Anderlecht, which lost, 1-0, on its home field to Inter-Milan, but came back to shock the Italians in Milan, 2-0. The opening game of the two-match, total-goal title series was held in Belgium, and Anderlecht won, 3-1 with two goals by Mulder, and one by Devrindt, while Kennedy scored for Arsenal. In the second game, Kelly, Randford, and Sammels scored for Arsenal, securing a 3-0 win and the championship trophy on a 4-3 aggregate. Fans at historic Highbury went wild with joy.

The controversial policy of counting goals scored from home double in the event of a deadlock in aggregate scores was probably never more bitterly contested than in the 1970-71 season, when Leeds became the fourth straight English team to take the championship title. Leeds made the finals via a 1-0 win over Liverpool at home and a scoreless deadlock on the road. Meanwhile, after tying Cologne, 1-1, Juventus won the return match in Turin, 2-0, and made the title series. The opening leg of the final round was played in Turin, Juventus got goals by Bettega and Capello, while Leeds countered with goals by Madeley and Bates for a 2-2 deadlock. In the second match, which was held at the Leeds Field, Anastasi scored for Juventus, while Clarke scored for Leeds. Although each team scored and yielded three goals, the championship went to Leeds because the team had scored two goals on the road while Juventus scored only one road goal. The Italian Association protested the ruling, but it was a futile effort. The committee stuck to its original decision and would not alter the format despite increasing pressure from many of the nations that were backing the tournament.

Two English First-Division teams made the finals of the 1971-72 tournament. The Tottenham Hotspurs defeated AC Milan at home, 2-1, and tied the Italians, in Milan, 1-1, to make the finals; while the Wolverhampton Wanderers defeated Hungary's Ferencvaros, 2-1, after tying the Hungarians, 2-2. In the opening game of the title series, Chivers scored two goals to give Tottenham a 2-1 decision over Wolverhampton, whose goal was scored by McCalliog. In the return match, played on the Wanderers' home field, Tottenham played a primarily defensive game, prompting even its fans to boo its tactics. A goal by the Hotspurs' Mullery offset a tally by the Wolves' Wagstaffe to bring the final score to 1-1, which gave the Hotspurs the title on a 3-2 aggregate basis.

England maintained its domination of the championship the following year, with Liverpool emerging as the champion. In the semifinals, Liverpool defeated Tottenham, in Liverpool, 1-0, but lost the return match, 2-1. On the basis of the one goal it had scored on the road, however, Liverpool advanced to the finals to face Borussia Mönchengladbach, which had defeated FC Twente of the Netherlands, 3-0 and 2-1. The opening game of the championship finale was held in Liverpool, and the 41,169 fans on hand were treated to a wide-open display of offensive soccer as the English switched from their usual defensive tactics to long runs and passes down the field. Keegan scored twice and Lloyd once and, unable to counter the moves, the West Germans fell, 3-0. In the second game, 35,000 fans were on hand in West Germany to see Borussia Mönchengladbach win, 2-0, on two goals by Heynckes; but the English took the title on aggregate score.

England's domination of the tournament finally ended during the 1973-74 season. Tottenham advanced to the finals via 2-1 and 2-0 wins over Lokomotiv Leipzig, and Feyenoord made the finals by topping Stuttgart at home, 2-1, and playing a 2-2 tie on the road. The first game of the title series was played at White Hart Lane in England, and a lucky break enabled the English to tie the Dutch, 2-2. The Dutch had scored on goals by van Hanegem and De Jong, while fullback Mike England scored for Tottenham. Dutch fullback van Daele accidentally sent a ball into his own goal, however, to tie the count. A crowd of 68,000 turned up for the second game in Rotterdam, and the Dutch didn't disappoint their followers. They played a perfect game, cutting off the English attack at midfield and penetrating the reliable Tottenham defense to win, 2-0, on goals by Rijsbergen and Ressel.

In the 1974-75 tournament, Netherlands' Twente Enschede proved the surprise of the semifinals as it defeated Juventus, 3-1, at home and then posted a 1-0 victory in Turin to advance to the finals. Borussia Mönchengladbach defeated its bitter rival Cologne with 3-1 and 1-0 victories to make the championship round. The West Germans were heavily favored to take the championship, but after the two clubs fought to a bitter scoreless tie in the opening game in Düsseldorf, the oddsmakers figured that the swing had gone to the Dutch and established them as the choice to take the crown. Although the crowd was with them, however, the Dutch couldn't stop the assault of the West Germans, who powered in five goals—three by Heynckes and two (one on a penalty shot) by Simonsen—for an easy 5-1 victory over Twente Enschede, whose lone tally was scored by Drost.

Liverpool celebrated winning the English First-Division title by capturing the 1975-76 European Fairs Cup with a hard-fought series against Bruges of Belgium. In the semifinals, the English had eliminated Barcelona, 1-0, in Barcelona on a goal made by John Toshack with 13 minutes gone. In the return game, the two teams tied, 1-1, as Mike Thompson scored for England with five minutes gone in the second half and Rexach scored for Barcelona four minutes later.

Bruges made the finals by tying Hamburg, 1-1, in West Germany and then beating the West Germans, 1-0, in the return game in Belgium. In the opening game, Lambert scored three minutes into the second half, while Hamburg tied the count on a goal by Reimann with 14 minutes left to play. In the return match, Bruges won when West German player Kaltz accidentally put a ball into his own goal.

In the opening game of the finals, played in Liverpool, a 20-yard bullet shot by Raoul Lambert gave Bruges a 1-0 lead after just four minutes of action. Eight minutes later Julion Cools scored to give the visiting Belgians a 2-0 lead; but the Liverpool defense was tightened and the offense began to operate in high gear, as the English started pressing the goal. Their efforts were rewarded 14 minutes into the second half, when Ray Kennedy scored. Two minutes later Jimmy Case tied the score, and three minutes after that Kevin Keegan scored on a penalty shot to give Liverpool a 3-2 win. In the return match, with 11 minutes gone, Bruges' Lambert scored a penalty shot, but Keegan tied the game four minutes later, and the match ended a 1-1 tie. Because of its earlier win, the Liverpool team won the championship.

EUROPEAN NATIONS FOOTBALL CHAMPIONSHIP

Citing the need for a national-team tournament, members of the European Nations committee held various meetings during the late 1950s and devised the format for the European Nations Tournament, which was to be held two years after each World Cup and at least two years prior to the following World Cup. Because of the apprehension of several members, the field for the initial tourney was limited to 18 teams. Competition for the first tourney got underway in 1958, when the competing teams played first-round matches. After making the quarterfinals via 4-2 and 3-0 decisions over Poland, Spain withdrew because of conflicts with various club factions regarding a scheduled match against the Soviet Union. FIFA threatened to suspend Spain but later withdrew its threat after listening to the explanation of the Spanish Football Federation that it couldn't afford the costs and that there were problems within the federation and among club officials. In the semifinals, Yugoslavia defeated France, 5-4, in a wild game in Paris, while in Marseilles the Soviets blanked Czechoslovakia, 3-0. Czechoslovakia then defeated France, 2-0, in the battle for third place. The title game was played on July 10, 1960, in Paris, and an overtime goal by Ponedelnik gave the Soviet Union a 2-1 win over Yugoslavia for the championship. The Soviets, led by the masterful

Lev Yachin in goal, had tallied their first goal in regulation play on a score by Metreveli, but when Netto accidentally put a shot past Yachin while attempting to clear the ball downfield, the game was sent into overtime. The Soviets completely dominated the extra-time period, and only some skillful saves by Yugoslavian goalie Vidinic kept them at bay until Ponedelnik found the range for the winning tally.

The field for the following tournament jumped to 26 teams, but because of political problems, Greece pulled out prior to its scheduled first-round match against Albania, which sent the Albanians into the next round. In the semifinals, the USSR topped Denmark, 3-0, in Barcelona; while in Madrid, Spain took Hungary, 2-1, in a game involving fast-moving forward play and stiff defense. Two overtime tallies gave Hungary a 3-1 victory over Denmark in the fight for third place. The title game was held in 1964 in Madrid, and goals by Pereda and Marcellino gave the Spanish a 2-1 victory over the Soviets' lone tally that came on a 15-yard bullet drive by Khusainov past Spanish goalie Iribar.

With 31 teams entered at the start of the 1966-68 competition, the field was divided into eight qualifying brackets. In the quarterfinal round, Yugoslavia defeated England, 1-0, in Florence. In Naples the Soviets and the Italians played a scoreless deadlock. Extra time failed to resolve the game, and a coin was tossed to determine the winner. The Soviets argued against the coin toss even before the results were announced, but the Italians won the toss and found themselves in the title round against the Yugoslavians. A goal by Italy's Domenghini offset a tally by Yugoslavia's Dzajic and set up a replay to be played on the same field in Rome on June 10, two days after the original game. Italy won the replay, 2-0, on goals by Riva and Anastasi, to capture the championship. In the battle for third place, England defeated the USSR, 2-0.

The Soviet Union, Hungary, West Germany, and Belgium emerged as the semifinal contestants from an original field of 32 competing in the 1970-72 tournament. In Brussels, the Soviets made the championship round via a 1-0 win over the Hungarians; while West Germany topped Belgium, 2-1, in the other semifinal game, held in Antwerp. Before the championship game was played, Belgium, with its great goalie Piat, topped Hungary, 2-1, to win the third-place trophy. West Germany had no trouble disposing of the Soviets, 3-0, in the championship game, held in Brussels. Utilizing a fast-moving total-soccer concept in which their fullbacks came all the way upfield when the team was on attack, the West Germans won the match easily, with a goal by Gerd Müller in the first half and scores by Müller and Wimmer in the second half.

Penalty shooting decided the championship in the 1976 competition, and the Czechoslovakians proved better at taking penalty shots. They defeated defending champ West Germany by making all five of their penalty shots, while the West Germans could convert only three out of four attempts. After eliminating Yugoslavia with a 3-2 victory in the semifinals, the Czechs surged out to an early 1-0 lead on a goal by Suehaik with eight minutes gone. Four minutes later, to the delight of the crowd in Yugoslavia, they were ahead, 2-0, as Dobias found the range. The West Germans countered two minutes later as new international star Dieter Muellar, who had been instrumental in Germany's 3-2 overtime win over the Netherlands in the semifinals, found the range. With less than a minute left to play, Bonhof gave the West Germans a tying goal, which sent the game into a 30-minute overtime session in which neither team was able to score. In the penalty shooting, Massny, Nehoda, Ondrus, Jurcenik, and Panekika all put their shots into the net for the Czechs, but after Bonhof, Flohe, and Bongartz had scored their shots for the West Germans, Höness missed, which gave the Czechs the championship.

In the battle for third place the Netherlands, without Johann Cruyff (who, because of two earlier cautions, was not allowed to play), defeated Yugoslavia, 3-2, in overtime. The Netherlands took a 2-0 lead on goals by Geels and Kerckhoff before the Yugoslavians tied the score with goals by Katalinski and Dzajic. But with 13 minutes gone in the extra time, Geels scored again, and the Dutch took third place.

Limited Championships

European soccer authorities are also responsible for running two other limited championships. One is the tournament for under-23 teams, held at irregular intervals, in which players under the age of 23 are selected. It doesn't matter whether the players are members of their nation's national team; as long as they are under the age of 23, they are eligible to compete. Czechoslovakia was the winner of the first tournament, which was held between 1970 and 1972. Twenty-one nations entered the second competition, and even before the finals several of the semifinalists were extremely bitter. Hungary sent the Soviet Union to the sidelines after each team had posted 2-0 wins on its respective home grounds. The decision was determined on penalty shots, with the Hungarians outshooting the Soviets, 4-2. In the opening game between Poland and East Germany, the two teams battled to a scoreless tie. The return match, held in Poland, ended up a 2-2 draw, but East Germany was awarded a spot in the finals because of the double count for away-game goals. In the opening game of the championship series, East Germany defeated the Hungarians, 3-2, but in the return match on their own pitch, the Hungarians tore apart the East German defense to win, 4-0, and take the championship.

Under the jurisdiction of the European Union two UEFA Cups for amateurs have been held. In 1967 Austria topped Scotland, 2-1, to win the title, while three years later Spain defeated the Netherlands, 2-1, after the two clubs had battled to a 1-1 draw.

In 1948, England captured the first UEFA youth tourney, and since then the competition has been held 25 times and in various forms. England has had the most successful team, with six wins as of 1975. Among the other winners are Bulgaria, with three titles; and East Germany, Spain, and Italy, each of which has won twice.

Olympic Games

Europeans point with pride to the accomplishments of their teams in Olympic competition. Throughout the history of Olympic soccer play, the Europeans, whose amateur program is far better than that of the South Americans, have been the dominant force in the Olympic Games. One must remember, however, that in some eastern European nations a team competing in the World Cup and European Nations tournament one year can be found participating in the Olympic Games the next, only to resume playing against the professionals from other European nations in the next World Cup or European Nations Cup.

Great Britain won the first two Olympic soccer competitions by topping Denmark, 2-0, in London in 1908 and four years later in Stockholm, 4-2. Belgium took the 1920 competition in Antwerp; the trailing Czechoslovakians walked off the field, protesting that the fans were too rowdy and that the referee was favoring the Belgians. European dominance was broken in 1924, when Uruguay blanked Switzerland, 3-0. At the following Olympics in 1928, Uruguay won its second straight title with a 2-1 win that followed a 1-1 deadlock against Argentina. In the 1936 Olympics, Italy's 2-1 overtime win over Austria returned Europe to the winner's circle. Since the resumption of the Olympics after World War II, European teams have won each time. Sweden took Yugoslavia, 3-1, in London in 1948; Hungary topped Yugoslavia, 2-0, at Helsinki four years later; the Soviet Union edged Yugoslavia, 1-0, in 1956 in Melbourne; after three straight second-place finishes, Yugoslavia won the crown in Rome in 1960 with a 3-1 win over Denmark; Hungary beat Czechoslovakia, 2-1, in the finals of the 1964 Games in Tokyo; in 1968 Hungary blasted Bulgaria in Mexico City, 4-1; Poland edged past Hungary, 2-1, in 1972 in Munich; and East Germany beat Poland, 3-1, in 1976 in Montreal.

Super Cup

Because of several circumstances, the possibility of another Super Cup, matching the winner of the European Cup with the winner of the European Cup-Winners' Cup, is still very much up in the air. There are many teams throughout Europe willing to play again for the World Club Championship, in which the European Cup winner is pitted against the winner of a similar competition in South America. Although the history of this tournament has been rugged and the competition discontinued, there are some who say that a new format should be devised and the tournament restored as a regular yearly feature. In 1974, however, the Super Cup was held instead, with AC Milan of Italy battling Ajax of Holland. In the opening game, played in Milan, a goal by Chiarugi gave the Italians a 1-0 win; but in the return game in Amsterdam, Muldeer, Keizer, Neeskens, Rep, Gerrie Muhren, and Hann all scored solo tallies to give the Dutch an impressive 6-0 win.

In the 1975 Super Cup, Dynamo Kiev defeated Bayern-Münich, 1-0 and 2-0, which gave the Soviets tremendous prestige in the European soccer world. After losing the first game, 2-1, Anderlecht defeated Bayern-Münich, 4-1, in the second game to win the 1976 Super Cup.

EUROPEAN HONOR ROLL

European Cup

Year	Winner	Year	Winner
1956	Real Madrid (Spain)	1967	Celtic (Scotland)
1957	Real Madrid (Spain)	1968	Manchester United (England)
1958	Real Madrid (Spain)	1969	AC Milan (Italy)
1959	Real Madrid (Spain)	1970	Feyenoord (Netherlands)
1960	Real Madrid (Spain)	1971	Ajax (Netherlands)
1961	Benfica (Portugal)	1972	Ajax (Netherlands)
1962	Benfica (Portugal)	1973	Ajax (Netherlands)
1963	AC Milan (Italy)	1974	Bayern-Münich (West Germany)
1964	Inter-Milan (Italy)	1975	Bayern-Münich (West Germany)
1965	Inter-Milan (Italy)	1976	Bayern-Münich (West Germany)
1966	Real Madrid (Spain)		

European Cup-Winners' Cup

Year	Winner	Year	Winner
1961	Fiorentina (Italy)	1969	Slovan Bratislava (Czechoslovakia)
1962	Atletico Madrid (Spain)	1970	Manchester City (England)
1963	Tottenham Hotspurs (England)	1971	Chelsea (England)
1964	Sporting Lisbon (Portugal)	1972	Rangers (Scotland)
1965	West Ham United (England)	1973	AC Milan (Italy)
1966	Borussia Dortmund (W. Ger.)	1974	FC Magdeburg (East Germany)
1967	Bayern-Münich (West Germany)	1975	Dynamo Kiev (Soviet Union)
1968	AC Milan (Italy)	1976	Anderlecht (Belgium)

Fairs Cup

Year	Winner	Year	Winner
1958	Barcelona (Spain)	1963	Valencia (Spain)
1960	Barcelona (Spain)	1964	Real Zaragoza (Spain)
1961	AC Roma (Italy)	1965	Ferencvaros (Hungary)
1962	Valencia (Spain)	1966	Barcelona (Spain)

European Fairs Cup

Year	Winner	Year	Winner
1967	Dynamo Zagreb (Yugoslavia)	1970	Arsenal (England)
1968	Leeds United (England)	1971	Leeds United (England)
1969	Newcastle United (England)		

UEFA Cup

Year	Winner	Year	Winner
1972	Tottenham Hotspurs (England)	1975	Borussia Mönchengladbach
1973	Liverpool (England)		(West Germany)
1974	Feyenoord (Netherlands)	1976	Liverpool (England)

European Nations Football Championships

Year	Winner	Year	Winner
1960	Soviet Union	1972	West Germany
1964	Spain	1976	Czechoslovakia
1968	Italy		

Super Cup*

Year	Winner	Year	Winner
1974	Ajax (Netherlands)	1976	Anderlecht (Belgium)
1975	Dynamo Kiev (Soviet Union)		

*Between European Cup winners and European Cup-Winners' Cup champions.

CHAPTER 10

South American Championships

The *Copa Sudamericana* and the *Copa Libertadores* are the most sought-after international championships in South American soccer. The *Copa Sudamericana* involves the national teams of South American nations, while the *Copa Libertadores* is a club competition that pits the South American team that advances to the *Copa* Intercontinental championship (better known as the World Club Championship) against the winner of the European Cup.

COPA SUDAMERICANA

Like so many other events throughout South America, there have been bitter matches played on the field and hotly contested debates behind the scenes of the *Copa Sudamericana*. As a result, there never has been a firm schedule as in the European Cup, which is held every four years. Bitter arguments between the various national associations caused the tournament to be suspended, for example, from 1967 until 1975, when the organizers were finally able to persuade the conflicting nations to sit down to work out a format suitable to all the member nations in South America.

The *Copa Sudamericana* was a product of the South American Football Confederation from that group's inception in 1916 in the initial tournament—held in Buenos Aires—Brazil, Chile, and Uruguay joined host Argentina in the field of competing nations, and with two wins and a deadlock, the Uruguayans won the championship title. The following year the tournament was switched to Montevideo, and the Uruguayans swept all three of their matches to take their second straight crown. The Uruguayan star Romano was the leading goal-getter in the second tourney, scoring four times—once more than Uruguay's Oradin had been able to net the year earlier.

159

No tournament was played in 1918 because the organizers were unable to agree on a time and place. But in 1919 Brazil hosted the four-nation event and tied in points with Uruguay. The Brazilians won the playoff, 1-0, to take the title. With four goals, Brazil's Necco was the tournament's high scorer.

Beginning in 1920, the tournament was held uninterrupted for eight straight years. In that span, Uruguay took the crown four times, Argentina won the title three times, and Brazil won the crown once. In the 1922 tournament, Uruguay withdrew its team because of disorders and Brazil went on to defeat newcomer Paraguay, 3-1, in a special playoff. In 1929 Argentina again hosted the tournament and won the championship, but disputes among the participating nations, along with concentration on the World Cup, caused the tournament to be halted until 1935. Lima hosted the 1935 event, which Uruguay won. Two years later the event was played in Argentina, and in a playoff the Argentinians topped the Brazilians, 2-0, to win the title. Peru finally entered the winner's circle in 1939, when the tourney was again held in Peru.

Argentina won four of the next five tourneys held, taking the title in 1941, 1945, 1946, and 1947, while the powerful Uruguayan team took the crown in 1942. In 1949 Brazil won the crown, but four years lapsed before another tourney was held. In 1953 Paraguay rebounded from an opening-game defeat by Brazil to win the playoff against the Brazilians, 3-2, which compensated for a 7-0 playoff defeat Paraguay had suffered at the hands of Brazil in 1949.

In 1955 Argentina won the crown, followed by Uruguay and Argentina, respectively, the following two years. In 1959 two separate tournaments were held. Argentina won once at home and placed second to Uruguay in the other event, which was held in Ecuador. Bolivia hosted and won the 1963 Tournament, with Uruguay taking the 1967 championship at home in Montevideo.

It wasn't until 1975 that the tournament was resumed and this time it was well run and exciting. Brazil swept all four of its games to eliminate Argentina and Venezuela in Group One competition, while with three wins and one tie, Peru topped Chile and Bolivia to win Group Two. In Group Three, Colombia eliminated Paraguay and Ecuador.

Since it had been the last winner of the championship, Uruguay gained an automatic spot in the semifinals, drawing the ire of all the other competing nations, who felt that a team's success in 1967 should in no way reflect its reputation in 1975. In the opening semifinal series, Colombia blasted the Uruguayans, 3-0, but Uruguay took the return game, 1-0, which still allowed Colombia to make the finals. In the other semifinal, Peru shocked Brazil, 3-1, in Brazil, but in the second game, in Lima, the Brazilians came in with a stronger team and won, 2-0. Much to the dismay of fans, players, and national officials alike, a coin toss was held instead of a third match, and Peru won the coin toss to advance to the final round.

In the opening game of the finals in Bogotá, Colombia defeated Peru, 1-0, but won the second game, 2-0, in Lima. After a week of debate and threats by both clubs to refuse to play, a third game was held. Peru won the replay, in Caracas, 1-0, but then the rest of the South American competitors began flinging charges against one another, claiming that a nation that makes threats should be expelled. Others felt that a cochampionship should be declared. The confederation maintained the position it had held earlier, however, and awarded the trophy to Peru.

In the history of the tournament, two men have been able to score nine goals in one tournament. In 1957 Humberto D. Maschio of Argentina and J. Ambrossis of Uruguay each made nine scores. In 1959 Pelé was the leading scorer, with eight goals.

COPA LIBERTADORES

Disputes over policy have been a common part of the *Copa Libertadores* (or *Copa de los Libertadores*) tournament, which got underway in 1960. The original intention was to limit the competition to the champions of the various South American nations, but after many debates Uruguay threatened to pull out if the top two teams in each nation weren't placed in the field. Teams like Santos and many of the other Brazilian powerhouses decided to boycott the event for several years but eventually went along with the Uruguayans, who had Argentina's support. Rather than stay out of the event permanently, Santos and other Brazilian teams returned in 1973 and at least on the surface, harmony seemed to prevail. There are still many behind-the-scenes battles going on, however, and the national associations of several countries are unwilling to allow their teams to miss regular league matches in order to meet an obligation for a Cup game. The question of whether this tournament will ever work out to the expectations of its organizers continues to keep South American soccer fans guessing.

Uruguay's Penarol won the first two tournaments, held in 1960 and again the following year. In the first tournament, Penarol's Spencer led all scorers with seven goals, while during the following year Spencer, Cubilla, and Sasia each scored three goals for Penarol. The great Santos team then won the Cup the following two years, with Spencer and Santos' Coutinho each making six goals in 1962 to share scoring honors and Pelé leading all scorers with five goals in 1963. The great

Independiente team defeated Uruguay's Nacional to win the title in 1964 and the following year topped Penarol to take its second straight championship. With seven goals, Sanfilipo of the Bôca Juniors of Argentina led all scorers in the 1964 tournament; while during the following year, high-scoring honors were shared by C. Mora of Cerro Porteno from Uruguay and Independiente's M. Rodriguez, each of whom made six goals. In 1966 Penarol won the championship, while Pelé led all scorers with seven goals. In the 1967 championship, the Racing Club of Argentina took the title, even though Daniel Onega of Argentina's River Plate ran away with the scoring honors as he netted 15 goals. Estudiantes de la Plata captured the next three championships. High scorers during that time were Raffom of Racing, with 14 goals in 1968; Tupazinho of Brazil's Palmeiras in 1969 with 11 goals; and Isella of Chile's Universidad Católica, Iroldo of Colombia's Deportivo Cali, and Ferrero of Chile's Wanderers, each of whom scored seven goals in 1969. In 1970 Oscar Mas of River Plate and Bertochi of Liga Universitaria of Ecuador shared scoring honors with nine goals each. Nacional of Uruguay won the championship in 1971 as its great star Artime shared high-scoring honors with Penarol's Castronovo, each of whom scored 10 goals.

Independiente then took over domination of the championship tournament, winning the title four times in a row starting in 1972. In 1972, when the Argentinians defeated Universitario of Peru in the finals, São Paulo's great star Toninho became the high scorer, with seven goals. In 1973 Caszelly of Chile's Colo-Colo won top scoring honors with nine goals, but it wasn't enough to prevent his team from placing second to Independiente. São Paulo was the runner-up to Independiente in the 1974 tournament, with two São Paulo players, Terto and Rocha, tied for high-scoring honors with seven goals each. Union Española of Chile placed second to Independiente in the 1975 championship tournament, while the year's high scoring honors were shared by Morena of Penarol and Osvaldo Ramirez of Universitario of Peru, each of whom scored eight goals.

Featuring several members of the Brazilian National Team, Cruzeiro broke Independiente's winning streak by capturing the 1976 tournament in an exciting three-game series against Argentina's River Plate. The two teams split their first two matches, with the Brazilians winning in Brazil and the Argentinians winning in Argentina. The third and deciding match was played in Santiago, Chile, and Cruzeiro won the title by posting a 3–2 victory. During the tournament, Cruzeiro won a total of 10 games, tied two, and lost only one to claim the title contested among teams from Brazil, Argentina, Chile, Uruguay, Paraguay, Peru, Ecuador, Colombia, and Venezuela.

While many consider the *Copa Sudamericana* tournament to be in danger, the willingness of the various national associations to co-operate and even help defray the cost of several of the competing teams in the club championship is a good indication that the event will continue. The winner can no longer look forward to playing against the European Cup winner, however, but instead will face the winner of the CONCAF championship.

Another South American tournament that draws great interest is the South American Youth Tournament, which was first held in 1954, with Uruguay winning the first of three consecutive tournaments. The Uruguayans also won in 1958 and again six years later, when the third tournament was held. In 1967 Argentina took the crown, while in 1971 host Paraguay took the title, topping a field of nine nations. In 1974 Brazil was the champion; and Uruguay won in 1975 in an exciting game, although Colombia, Ecuador, Venezuela, and Paraguay did not compete for various reasons. Uruguay and Chile each finished with three wins and three ties for a total of nine points, and each ended up with a plus-six goal average as Uruguay scored nine goals and allowed three and Chile scored seven times and yielded only one tally. The two teams initially played a scoreless deadlock, and in the special playoff, the score was tied 1–1 after regulation time. Neither team was able to score in a 30-minute overtime session, so penalty shooting was held, with each team getting three kicks. Uruguay made all its kicks; while Chile could convert only one, giving Uruguay first place; Chile, second; Argentina, third; Peru, fourth; Brazil, fifth; and Bolivia, sixth.

There is a new tournament called the Atlantic Cup, which was first held in 1956. Contested mainly among Brazil, Argentina, Uruguay, and occasionally Paraguay, it was the idea of the Argentinian Federation, which wanted a South American competition for what it termed the "Atlantic" states. In 1956 Argentina and Brazil emerged as the cochampions, while in 1960 Argentina, Brazil, and Uruguay each won one game and tied another to share the title. In 1976 Brazil defeated Argentina, Paraguay, and Uruguay to take the crown alone.

Various other South American tournaments are held as special events on an irregular basis. Whenever a country's national association has an anniversary, for example, one can be sure that during the year there will be a major invitational tourney organized with great fanfare.

One of the biggest hopes for continuing South American championship tournaments was discussed in 1976, and although no firm commitment was made, the idea was endorsed by most of the members participating in the meeting in Chile. It called for establishing another major tourney similar to the *Copa Libertadores* in which only the third-place team in each nation would compete. A fourth-place team will have the opportunity of gaining a position in a tournament to be fashioned along the lines of the UEFA Cup. Although the motion was tabled, there is a strong indication that by 1980 there will indeed be three tournaments in South America to match the three big ones in Europe.

SOUTH AMERICAN HONOR ROLL

Copa Libertadores de America

Year	Winner	Year	Winner
1960	Penarol (Uruguay)	1969	Estudiantes de La Plata (Argentina)
1961	Penarol (Uruguay)	1970	Estudiantes de La Plata (Argentina)
1962	Santos (Brazil)	1971	Nacional (Uruguay)
1963	Santos (Brazil)	1972	Independiente (Argentina)
1964	Independiente (Argentina)	1973	Independiente (Argentina)
1965	Independiente (Argentina)	1974	Independiente (Argentina)
1966	Penarol (Uruguay)	1975	Independiente (Argentina)
1967	Racing Club (Argentina)	1976	Cruzeiro (Brazil)
1968	Estudiantes de la Plata (Argen.)		

Copa Sudamericana

Year	WJinner	Year	Winner
1916	Uruguay	1941	Argentina
1917	Uruguay	1942	Uruguay
1919	Brazil	1945	Argentina
1920	Uruguay	1946	Argentina
1921	Argentina	1947	Argentina
1922	Brazil	1949	Brazil
1923	Uruguay	1953	Paraguay
1924	Uruguay	1955	Argentina
1925	Argentina	1956	Uruguay
1926	Uruguay	1957	Argentina
1927	Argentina	1959*	Argentina
1929	Argentina	1959*	Uruguay
1935	Uruguay	1963	Bolivia
1937	Argentina	1967	Uruguay
1939	Peru	1975	Peru

* Two tournaments were held in 1959.

Copa del Atlantico

Year	Winner	Year	Winner
1956	Argentina and Brazil*	1976	Brazil
1960	Argentina, Brazil, and Uruguay**		

* Cochampions.
** Shared title.

164

CHAPTER 11

International Blood

The idea was a good one. Fans in soccer-mad Europe and in South America wanted a club championship that would show once and for all the comparative strength of club soccer on both continents. Would the more conservative Europeans prove dominant over the highly emotional South Americans?

In soccer quarters on both continents, plans were being drawn up as early as 1955 to have the European Cup winners face the winners of a newly planned tourney called the *Copa de los Libertadores,* which would crown a South American Cup winner. The plans were well devised and the intention was good, but the tourney proved to be a tremendous problem both to officials on both continents and to FIFA, which had to act on referee's reports and enforce expulsions for violence. As of early 1976, the tournament had been temporarily shelved; and the European powerhouses, unlike the top South American clubs, seemed intent on letting the tournament lie dormant. After all, they argued, they had suffered a great deal of physical abuse at the hands of players and fans alike in South America, and the danger just wasn't worth the excitement of competing against the South Americans.

The first tournament was held in 1960, with European Cup winner Real Madrid of Spain facing South American titlist Penarol of Uruguay. Before the tournament even got underway, there were disputes about the format. Some of the South American officials wanted the games to be a two-match, total-goal series while others wanted the winner to be determined by a best-of-three series. European officials wanted a one-game tournament to be played at a site determined by a coin flip. As the tournament continued over the years, disputes kept arising about whether the format should be changed or kept the same. Some even wanted to make it a three-of-five game series, and for a time some of the leading clubs on both continents threatened to boycott the tournament unless they received assurance that the officials really would be neutral. The disputes soured many fans, players, and club officials and hastened the eventual death of a tournament that had started out with good intentions.

In the initial tourney, the first match, which was held in Montevideo, ended up a scoreless deadlock. The Uruguayan defense — led by goalie Maidana and fullbacks Martinez, Aguerre, Piño, and Salvador — was able to contain the Real Madrid attack, which featured Puskas and di Stefano. When teams returned for the second game in Madrid, however, the Spaniards scored a 5-1 victory. Puskas scored twice and di Stefano, Herrera, and Gento each added solo tallies; but for Penarol only Borges was able to put a shot past goalie Dominguez.

It took three games to decide the 1961 championship between Penarol and Portugal's Benfica. In the opening game in Lisbon, a goal by Coluna gave Benfica a 1-0 win. In the second game, held in Montevideo, however, the Uruguayans won, 5-0, with Joya and Spencer each scoring twice and Sasia adding a penalty shot. Since the second game had been played in Uruguay, the third and deciding game was automatically played two days later at the same location. Sasia scored twice, once on a penalty shot, to give Penarol a 2-1 win over Benfica, whose lone goal came from Eusebio.

The following year was the year of Santos and Pelé. In the first game, played in Rio de Janeiro, Pelé scored twice and Coutinho, his brilliant teammate, scored once to give the Brazilians a 3-2 win over Benfica, whose two goals came from Santana. The return game was played in Lisbon, and Pelé scored three times and Pepe and Coutinho once, to topple Benfica, 5-2, as Santana and Eusebio scored for the Portuguese.

Tempers flared in 1963, when Santos and AC Milan met in a three-game series. In the opening game, played in Milan, Pelé scored twice; but AC Milan sent four shots past Santos' goalie Gilmar, Trapattoni and Mora each scoring once and Amarildo making two tallies. The return game was played in Rio, and goals by Altafini and Mora gave AC Milan a 2-0 halftime lead. But the Brazilians roared back with two goals by Pepe and solo tallies by Blmir and Lima to win, 4-2, despite the absence of Pelé who had been injured a few weeks earlier. Rio was the site of the third and deciding match, and a first-half penalty shot conversion by Dalmo earned Santos its second consecutive title by a 1-0 shutout over its Italian rivals. During the game, however, several fights broke out among players, and one player from each team was sent off the field.

For the following three years, there was relative peace among the competing clubs. Naturally, there were minor fracases on the field and an occasional fight in the stands, but there was no major violence.

In the 1964 tourney, Independiente of Argentina was pitted against Inter-Milan of Italy. A second-half goal by Rodriguez gave the Argentinians a 1-0 win in the opening match in Buenos Aires. In the second game, held in Milan, however, Sandro Mazzola and Corso scored first-half goals and the Italian defense withstood great second-half pressure to post a 2-0 victory, forcing a third and deciding game to be played in Madrid. Tournament officials were criticized for not allowing the deciding game to be played in Milan, but they wanted, they said, to hold the game in a neutral site. Corso scored a second-half goal, and Inter-Milan won, 1-0, to clinch the championship.

The same two rivals met the following year. The first game was played in Milan, and two goals by Mazzola and one by Peuro, along with some excellent goaltending by Sarti gave the Italians a 3-0 victory. If Sarti was great in Milan, however, he was superb in the second game, played in Buenos Aires. He turned back 21 shots as the two teams battled to a scoreless deadlock, which gave Inter its second straight crown.

Penarol gained revenge for its loss in the first World Club championship in 1966, when it again met Real Madrid.

Puskas and di Stefano had retired from Real Madrid, and the Uruguayans went all out, winning the first game in Montevideo as Spencer scored a goal in each half. In the second game, played in Madrid, a penalty shot by Rocha and a solo tally by Spencer gave Penarol another 2-0 win as Penarol goalie Mazurkiewicz proved himself one of the top keepers in the world.

Violence started to take over the tournament in 1967, when the Racing Club of Argentina was matched against Glasgow Celtic of Scotland. In the first game, held in Glasgow, several fist fights broke out as the Scottish team won, 1-0, on a second-half goal by McNeill. Fans were anxiously waiting for the return game in Buenos Aires, but as he took the field, Celtic goalie Ronnie Simpson was hit by a flying object and was knocked out of action, forcing Celtic to use substitute keeper Fallon. Fights continued to break out during the match, but when the final whistle was sounded, the Argentinians had a 2-1 victory. The action was so intense that four Celtic players and two Racing players were ejected from the game. The deciding goal was scored by Cardenas, after Raffo had scored for Racing and Gemmell got a penalty shot for Celtic. The suspended players were allowed to participate in the deciding game, much to the amazement of the fans, who had believed that they would be banned from the game. Again, the game was rough, but no more so than a typical international game, and Racing won, 1-0, on a second-half goal by Cardenas to take the championship.

The following year, 1968, Argentina's Estudiantes de la Plata played England's Manchester United, and in the opening game, held in Buenos Aires, Conigliaro's first half-goal gave the Argentinians a 1-0 victory. Manchester's Nobby Stiles was ejected for arguing over a linesman's call. In the return match in Manchester, several fights broke out, and when the game ended in a 1-1 deadlock, George Best and Estudiantes' Medina had been ejected for fighting. Manchester's goal was scored by Morgan in the second half, while Veron scored in the first half for the Argentinians. On the basis of one win and one tie, the title went to the Argentinians.

In 1969 officials decided to change the format of the tournament to a two-game, total-goal series to prevent a nation from claiming that it had a disadvantage by being forced to play the third and deciding game at the same place where the second game was played. The rivals in the 1969 tourney were AC Milan of Italy and Estudiantes. Sormani scored two goals and Combin, the Argentinian-born player, added another tally as AC Milan won the first game, 3-0, in Milan. In the return match in Buenos Aires, fights and violence broke out almost from the opening whistle, and Combin was attacked on one of his well-known drives toward the goal, breaking his leg. Estudiantes won the game, 2-1, on goals from Aguiree and Suarez (the Italian goal was scored by Rivera), and the title went to AC Milan on a 4-2 aggregate score. The entire Argentinian Football Federation was shocked by a decree of the president of Argentina, ordering lengthy suspensions for three Estudiantes players. Other violence went unpunished, however, and the bitter feelings between teams from the two continents continued to grow even when the clubs were engaging in otherwise meaningless international exhibition games.

In 1970 Estudiantes met Netherlands' Feyenoord, and if one year signaled the actual end of the competition, it was this one, although the competition continued for several more years. In the opening game, referees allowed vicious and intentional fouls by Estudiantes players to go unpunished, and it was something of a shock that the Dutch team, which had won the European Cup, was able to escape Buenos Aires with a 2-2 deadlock. The Argentinians had gone out to an early halftime lead on goals by Echecopar and Veron, but Kindvall scored for Feyenoord in the first half, and van Hanegem scored the tying goal late in the match. After his tying goal, van Hanegem was repeatedly fouled and was replaced in the lineup by Boskamp. In the European press, some of the strongest supporters of the tournament in the past announced that they had changed their minds and asked that the competition be discontinued. In the return match, played in Rotterdam, a second-half goal by van Deale, who came on as a late substitute for Moulijn, gave the Dutch a 1-0 victory. Only strong restraint on the part of many irate fans enabled the Argentinians to play their style of game. Few fouls were called as both clubs largely followed the rules of the game.

The treatment that its Dutch rivals had received the year before made Ajax, which had qualified by winning the European Cup over Greece's Panathinaikos, decline to play in the 1971 championship. Ajax gave its spot against Uruguay's Nacional to the Greeks, who agreed to play after the urging of several top civic leaders in Greece. In the first game, held in Athens, the two teams battled to a 1-1 deadlock, as in the second half Filakouris scored for the Greeks and Arime scored for the Uruguayans. The Greeks on occasion have been known to play in the rough style of South American soccer; but in the return game, played in Montevideo, two goals by Arime, one in each half, did them in, 2-1, as Filakouris scored the Greeks' lone tally in the second half.

Ajax had a change of heart in 1972 and agreed to play in the tournament, however, as fights broke out right from the starting whistle in the opening game played in Buenos Aires. The game ended up a 1-1 deadlock; but in the second game the Dutch, led by Johann Cruyff and aided by speedy play, won a 4-0 decision to take the title by a 4-1 aggregate two-game, total-goal score.

The Dutch were eligible to play the following year, but the players felt that it wasn't worth the risk and declined the invitation, giving their spot to Italy's Juventus, which had placed second to Ajax in the European Cup. The only reason the tournament was held at all was that the title was to be determined by a single game, which was to be played in Rome. The match was well played and free from dirty play and excessive fouling; and when the final whistle sounded, the Argentinians had posted a 1-0 win on a second-half goal by Bochini.

Bayern-Münich won the European Cup in 1974, but the West Germans followed Ajax's example and refused to play in the tournament. Their spot went to European Cup runner-up Atletico Madrid of Spain. In the opening game, which was played in Buenos Aires, Balbuena scored a first-half goal to give the Argentinians a 1-0 win, as late in the match goalie Perez saved two direct free kicks by the Spanish team. The second game was played in Madrid, however, and goals by Irureta in the first half and by Ayala, himself a former Argentinian star, carried Atletico Madrid to a 2-0 win and the aggregate victory by a 2-1 count. Atletico did make a major change in its lineup for the second game, replacing goalie Reina with Pocheco. The new goalie was outstanding, making several key saves early in the match as the Argentinians tried to stun their opponents with a quick goal.

But after this match, the tournament was a dead issue, as it became apparent that the European clubs were no longer interested. Early in 1976 a group representing the South American Confederation met with officials of the CONCAF and started working out arrangements for a new cup, to be contested between the South American titlist and the winner of the CONCAF Club tournament. How the proposed tournament will work out, however, is anyone's guess.

The Olympic soccer competition has led to almost as many behind-the-scenes fights as play on the field. Even before the 1976 Games got underway in Montreal, there was once again talk that soccer should be dropped from the program. Many nations, in which soccer is a legitimate amateur sport, want the soccer competition to continue, however. They argue that they uphold the stringent rules of the International Olympic Committee and send only their amateurs to the games. But they also point out that many of the eastern European and other nations send teams that have in the past qualified for the World Cup. Israel, for example, sent to Montreal all but three of the players from the Israeli team that attempted to win a spot in the 1974 World Cup. The eastern European nations—particularly the Soviet Union, East Germany, and Poland—have long been successful in international competition against the so-called professionals of the Netherlands, Brazil, and England. Yet when the three nations arrived in Montreal in 1976, their lineups looked very similar to the lineups they had had in the qualifying and even the final rounds of the 1974 World Cup.

The smaller nations argued that as intended, the competition should be limited to amateur players only. The three countries at whom they directed their ire, however, argued that since none of the players on their teams got paid for playing soccer, they were indeed amateurs. Before his retirement, the late Avery Brundage, head of the Olympic Committee, was put to the test many times, trying to settle the difficulties. With no success at the IOC level, many of the smaller nations decided that it didn't pay to send teams to even the Olympic trials, if when they got there, they would be facing the same players that their professionals would be playing against in professional tournaments.

To illustrate the hypocrisy in the soccer competition in the 1976 Olympic Games, it is useful to look at the Soviet Union, East Germany, and Poland, which won the 1972 Olympic soccer competition. The top team in the Soviet Union is Dynamo Kiev, which in 1975 won the European Cup-Winners' Cup. In this competition, the team beat every team it faced, and almost all its games were against clubs that considered themselves professional. Nonetheless, when it entered the Olympics, instead of picking players from some of the smaller and less successful clubs, the Soviet Olympic Committee decided to send the entire Dynamo Kiev team as the Soviet Olympic representatives. The committee argued that since no one gets paid in the Soviet Union for playing soccer, the players were actually amateurs. The English press, which criticized the act as a sham, however, pointed out that it is odd that a player like Oleg Blokhin, who was voted European Footballer of the Year, can live so comfortably, even by Western standards, without having any apparent means of income.

After winning the 1972 Olympic soccer title, Poland used essentially the same team to compete and gain third place in the 1974 World Cup competition. Then, because they said their players were amateurs, the Poles entered the same squad for the 1976 Olympic Games. East Germany, which in the 1974 World Cup was the one team to defeat eventual champion West Germany, likewise used the same squad in the 1976 Games that had played in the World Cup two years earlier.

So incensed did the other nations become, that Uruguay had an open fight on its hands when its committee decided that if its amateurs were to play against professionals, then it too should have the right to use its top players. The Uruguayans decided to withdraw from the competition, however, rather than undermine the meaning of the word *amateur,* and they ultimately gave their place to Cuba. In their withdrawal, the Uruguayans pointed out that the inability of the IOC to distinguish between amateurs and professionals in soccer had caused much criticism of the worthwhile aspects of soccer as a continuing sport.

For nations that want to make a legitimate attempt to use only amateur players as the terms are understood in the Western world, then the Olympic Games can be a valuable endeavor. But England has taken the position that in soccer there are really no amateurs on club levels, and so the English will not play in any Olympic soccer other than something that might be called an "open field," in which amateurs and professionals alike are eligible.

FIFA has been criticized for not helping to set up the true amateur-against-professional rules that are needed for Olympic competition. The worldwide ruling body of soccer has the power to oversee the IOC in any soccer decisions, but it has not acted; and as a result, many nations do not consider the Olympic soccer competition worthwhile. The pullout of the African nations at the 1976 Games also hindered the soccer program and added another bitter episode to the history of soccer at the Olympic Games.

Hungary has been the most successful team in Olympic soccer competition, winning three gold medals by taking the crown in 1952, 1964 and 1968 and winning the silver and bronze medals in 1972 and 1960, respectively. Great Britain, as mentioned before, is no longer an Olympic soccer competitor but won the gold medal in 1908 and again four years later. Uruguay is another two-time winner, having taken the championship in 1924 and again four years later. Yugoslavia, which also has often been criticized for using what Westerners consider professionals, topped three straight silver medal performances by capturing the gold medal in 1960. The Soviet Union won in 1956 and placed third in 1972; while Sweden won a gold medal in the 1948 Games and bronze medals in 1924 and 1952. Belgium won in 1920, Italy in 1936, and Poland in 1970.

Among the all-time top Olympic soccer performances, the 11 goals scored by Denmark's Sophus Nielsen in 1908, the nine tallies in 1928 by Taraconi, who was playing for the Argentinian Olympic Team, and the amazing 12 tallies recorded by Ferenc Bene of Hungary in the 1964 competition are particularly notable.

OLYMPIC CHART

Year	Gold	Silver	Bronze
1908	Great Britain	Denmark	Holland
1912	Great Britain	Denmark	Holland
1920	Belgium	Spain*	Holland
1924	Uruguay	Switzerland	Sweden
1928	Uruguay	Argentina	Italy
1932**			
1936	Italy	Austria	Norway
1948	Sweden	Yugoslavia	Denmark
1952	Hungary	Yugoslavia	Sweden
1956	Soviet Union	Yugoslavia	Bulgaria
1960	Yugoslavia	Denmark	Hungary
1964	Hungary	Czechoslovakia	East Germany
1968	Hungary	Bulgaria	Japan
1972	Poland	Hungary	East Germany
1976	East Germany	Poland	Soviet Union

*Czechoslovakia walked off during the final game and was disqualified, moving Spain to second place and Holland to third place.

**No soccer competition this year.

There have been several other smaller international club tournaments and small international contests on the national-team level. In the Seven Seas tournament, for example, merchant seamen on ships from all over the world schedule games when they are due in the same port city at the same time. Unfortunately, these games more often than not become wild brawls, despite the legitimate attempts of the organizers to maintain some semblance of order.

There is no end to the bitterness that international matches can generate, then, whether on the club, national, or even on the merchant-seaman level. But although the competition is often hindered by outbreaks on the field, there is still a feeling of satisfaction when one leaves the field a winner.

CHAPTER 12

Bitterness

In the history of soccer, both on a club level and in the international arena, there have been many bitter battles between rival teams and also among fans in attendance. Annual games like those involving Dundee and Dundee United in Scotland, Manchester City and Manchester United in England, Torino and Juventus and Lazio and Roma in Italy, the Bôca Juniors and River Plate in South America, Penarol and Nacional in Uruguay, Santos and the Corinthians in Brazil, and Hapoel Tel Aviv and Maccabi Tel-Aviv in Israel are hard fought and often violent. Matches between international teams are almost certain to lead to trouble, especially if an Italian team is pitted against a South American team.

But of all the rivalries, that between the two Glasgow teams, Celtic and the Rangers, stand out above all. During matches between the teams, short tempers and bitterness create danger for fans and players alike. It goes beyond just rivalry between clubs. The fans are deeply involved, and religion plays an important part in the controversy. The Rangers are a Protestant team, supported by the Orangemen; while Celtic, which was formed by a brother of St. Mongo's Academy, is backed by Roman Catholics. For years the two teams have been the dominant forces in Scottish soccer, and extra police and even fire brigades have been called in to prevent recurrence of violence when matches are played at either Ibrox park, home of the Rangers; Celtic Park, home of Celtic; or at Hampden Park, considered a neutral ground although frequented mostly by Celtic.

On April 17, 1909, a crowd attending the Scottish Cup replay between the Rangers and Celtic went wild in one of the biggest soccer riots in history. The background for that Bloody Sunday had been set a few days earlier, when Celtic managed to gain a 1–1 tie on a highly disputed goal as the referee allowed a goal by Celtic player Johnny Quinn to stand. Quinn had come charging in on Ranger goalie Harry Rennie with 12 minutes remaining, and in an attempt to avoid a collision, Rennie spun around with the ball in his hand. The Celtic team argued that the goalie took the ball over the goal line as he spun around. The referee agreed with them and ordered a goal to be recorded, which tied the score. With time running out, both teams walked off the field, and a replay was ordered. The replay took place before 60,000 fans at Hampden Park. The game was a bitter battle that ended after 90 minutes in another 1-1 tie, as several players started punching, kicking, and spitting at one another. Referee J. B. Stark blew his whistle, indicating that time had run out, and the Rangers left the field; but Celtic remained, believing that an overtime would be held. The referee walked over to the Celtic team and said that no provision had been made for overtime, and the fans started screaming at officials of the Scottish Football Association who were on hand to witness the game.

Suddenly, from over scattered barriers that separated the field of play from the stands, a few fans jumped onto the field. Within a few minutes, thousands of fans were pouring onto the field like a mob going wild. Police tried to stop the flood of fans, but they were kicked, stepped on, and punched. Some fans fought the police while others, spotting a Celtic or Ranger supporter, turned their rage on their opponents. Police began fighting back with their batons, but the rioters became intent on wrecking the stadium. Some ripped out the goalposts and tore the soccer nets to pieces while others ripped out chairs or broke up fences and used them as clubs to battle other fans and the police. Hundreds of people lay on the field, bloodied either by the police or by opposing fans. Mounted police officers and their horses were savagely beaten. Police were pulled off their mounts and then stepped on. Fed by pieces of broken seats, fencing, and by whiskey, fires broke out all over the field; and the fire brigade was called on to come in to put out the fires. When the firemen arrived on the scene, they too were beaten, and the mob literally tried to burn their uniforms and cut the fire hoses.

The battle raged for seven hours before order was restored, and several hundred victims of the outbreak were treated in hospitals. There were no immediate fatalities, but several deaths did occur later in the week as a result of injuries suffered in the melee. This incident was only a preview of things to come, however, as beatings of rival fans at the Celtic-Ranger games became a common occurrence.

On January 2, 1971, at Ibrox Stadium Celtic and the Rangers were engaged in a First-Division Scottish League game. As usual the game was hard fought, fans were rowdy, and tempers were short; and as is customary in games between these teams, fans were separated to prevent violence. But there are always those intent on starting trouble, who try to get a location in the other team's cheering section. With about three minutes left, Celtic broke a scoreless deadlock with a goal, and Ranger fans, believing their team had lost, started leaving their seats to avoid the postgame rush. Jubilant Celtic fans planned to stay after the game to savor their victory. Suddenly, with only a few seconds remaining, the Rangers tied the game. Ranger fans already near the exit gates heard the roar and came rushing back, crashing head-on into other spectators on their way out. The steel barrier on one of the stairways gave way, and fans tumbled down on top of one another, piling 30 feet high. Those in front of the collision were trampled, while others suffocated to death.

When the final casualty list was compiled, 66 fans were dead and 108 injured. It was the worst disaster in the history of English and Scottish soccer, surpassing even a 1903 calamity in which a section of seats (also at Ibrox) collapsed, killing 25 and injuring 517, and a disaster at Bolton when a barrier collapsed, killing 33 fans. If there ever was solidarity between members of Celtic and the Rangers, it was at Ibrox that afternoon in 1971, when players from both clubs helped pull people to safety. But later in the year, when they again faced one another, fans and players renewed their bitterness.

Whenever two South American teams are matched together in any sort of international competition, the feelings run high for weeks prior to the match. Such was the case in 1964, when Argentina and Peru met in a pre-Olympic qualifying match in Lima. From the starting whistle, players were battling one another, and referee A. Angel Pazone of Uruguay had his hands full trying to maintain some semblance of order. Several times he issued warnings to players to refrain from excessive body contact. With less than two minutes remaining and Argentina holding a 1–0 lead, the Peruvian fans exploded with joy as Enrique Lobaton scored the apparent tying goal. The referee disallowed the goal, however, claiming that Lobaton had fouled an Argentinian defender as he was scoring. Immediately two fans raced onto the field and started chasing the referee, who was led to the dressing room after calling the match off. Other fans joined in the attempt to get at the referee. As is often the case in critical South American games, the police were quick to lose their temper, and they started throwing tear gas grenades at the fans. Police dogs were also released, and the crowd turned toward the tunnel exits, which were still locked to prevent gate crashing. Thousands of fans poured into the tunnels, and those who were near the steel gates were crushed by the push of the others, as the police fired more and more tear gas grenades into the crowd.

Over 350 fans were trampled to death, many of them crushed against the gates. As gates were opened in other portions of the stadium, the fans banded into wild gangs and went on a rampage, burning automobiles, overturning a police bus, and destroying a restaurant near the stadium. Guards gathered near the palace and turned back an angry mob that was demanding that the game be declared a deadlock. The American-owned Goodyear plant near the stadium was stoned, and the government, under President Fernando Belaunde, declared martial law in effect for 30 days, urging fans to go home and stay indoors. There were reports that several players had been beaten by fans, and the Argentinians claimed that two of their players had been hit by police as well as by stones tossed at them by the angry Peruvian fans. The riot was quelled after hours of mayhem when police finally gained the upper hand.

But feelings run high everywhere in the world when a soccer game is at stake. In Dundee during games between the Dundee team and Dundee United, fans have attacked players and officials. In 1961 a fracas broke out when a last-minute goal was disallowed, and it took police six hours to stop the melee. It was a miracle that no one was killed. Fans are volatile even in Venezuela, where soccer is not so popular as elsewhere. A referee once abandoned a game because several fans went onto the field. The game was declared a forfeit, and the visiting team was awarded the decision. Irate fans attacked the referee on his way home and hung him upside-down by his feet for eight hours.

Juventus has several bitter enemies in Italy, most notably Torino and Roma. In 1969 Juventus fans turned their anger on opposing players twice within a two-month period. After a tie game, they clubbed two Torino players, and several fans wound up in the hospital as a result of beatings suffered at the hands of the police. But that was only a prelude to what happened on February 16, when referee Antonio Marchi awarded Roma a penalty shot in the closing minutes of the game, which enabled the Roma team to gain a 2–2 tie. Even before Roma forward Joaquin Peiro scored the tying goal, fans were making their way onto the pitch. As soon as the goal was recorded, the referee left the field, but fans chased him to the dressing room, where police prevented the fans from getting at him. A four-hour battle between fans and police erupted, however, and several fans got to the Roma bus, hitting players and spitting at Roma coach Helenio Herrera. Another fan aimed a pistol at some of the Roma players before police disarmed him. Fans then went on a rampage, burning automobiles and stoning a television station. There were many injuries but fortunately no fatalities.

In 1965 in Catania, Sicily, angry fans supporting Catania threw rubble on the field while the players were throwing punches at one another. The Torino team was leading the home team, 2–0, when the referee and linesmen decided to walk off the field because they were getting pelted with some of the objects thrown by the fans. Angered at their walkoff, fans started chasing the officials but were turned back by the police. They then set fire to the debris on the field and in the stands, and the fire spread to the clubhouse, where several players suffered from smoke inhalation.

Vienna was the scene of a riot when Benfica of Portugal played Rapid Vienna of Austria in the semifinals of the 1960–61 European Cup. The thousands of Austrian fans in attendance knew that only a miracle would enable their team to make the finals, since in the first match the Portuguese had won, 3–0. With 22 minutes left, the Rapid players started on a rampage, kicking and punching their Benfica rivals. Referee Leafe of England tried to restore order, but as the game drew to a close, the fouls became more vicious. The Benfica players started committing fouls and punching back, and suddenly the Rapid goalie came out of his nets and punched out a Benfica player. Seeing that the referee was helpless, several Rapid players and a few members of the Benfica team surrounded the referee and punched him and spat at him. As fans invaded the pitch to chase him, Leafe turned and raced to the dressing room. The fans then turned their anger on objects in the stadium, destroying benches, signs, lights, and concession stands. It took an armored police car to get Leafe out of the stadium; and after about two hours, the Benfica team was placed on a police bus and driven out of the city. In their anger, fans went into the streets and destroyed cars and broke windows for a one-mile radius around the stadium.

Randall's Island in New York was the scene of some bitter battles when the old International Soccer League was in existence. Fans attacked referees constantly, and because of poor police protection and lack of barriers, they were often able to roam the field and attack players and fans of the opposing team. In a 1962 game between Belenenses of Portugal and Panathinaikos of Greece, players were knocked down and stepped on by their opponents. Then the fans got into the action, attacking players from various clubs and beating police. With the police in pursuit, one Greek fan took a rolled-up newspaper, lit it, and raced around the field burning hedges. Prior to the 1974 World Cup, the Haitian National Team played an exhibition game in Randall's Island. The Haitian players were attacked by exiled Haitians, who demanded that they leave the field. During a match at Yankee Stadium between Cagliari of Italy and Cerro of Uruguay, referee Leo Goldstein was chased by a group of irate Italian fans, who were protesting some of his calls. He had to be rescued by police and suffered broken ribs that later required surgery. At Roosevelt Stadium in Jersey City, members of the Santos team were attacked by supporters of Bologna, and goalie Cejas was hit on the head by a fan wielding a chair.

One of the most bitter rivalries in New York soccer action is the Greek Derby game between the Greek-Americans and Hellenic. For six years, starting in 1969, only two of the 12 games played between the two clubs were completed. Referees have had to abandon the games because fans poured onto the small, unguarded fields and players openly punched and kicked the opposing players. A similar situation exists when Croatia plays against Dalmatinac in a game matching the opposite political factions of Yugoslavia now living in New York. The fans have threatened players, other fans, and officials with knives; and several games had to be suspended before even a half was played. Fights also erupt often when Inter-Giuliana, an Italian team, plays against the Greek-Americans. In 1973 in New York's Van Cortlandt Park, three men were stabbed and one shot after fans from two rival Armenian teams battled in the stands. The fight was an offshoot of fighting between players on the field and continual arguing with game officials.

There isn't a big city in the world where soccer is played on a major scale that has been free from violence. Referees are often forced to turn and run to save themselves, and because they fear the fans, there have been many cases in which officials have allowed illegal goals for the home team and disallowed apparently good goals by the visiting team.

It seems that the more intense the rivalry between clubs and nations, the more fans will take advantage of the situation and cause trouble. In England hooliganism has caused much trouble; and it is interesting to note that after battling among themselves, rival fans intent on destruction will often join forces as they go on a rampage.

In South America and in Mexico, where in the 1970s two referees were killed and others beaten by players, police protection is usually adequate to cope with a small outbreak. There is, however, no real barrier for a crowd on the rampage, and preventive steps must be taken before the violence erupts. There are stadiums in South America where a moat separates the playing field from the stands, but on occasion even this has proved inadequate to hold off a frenzied mob that attacks property, players, and officials.

Soccer is the sport of the people, and their moods vary with the degree of the rivalry. It is a sport where bitterness between opposing players often carries over to followers of the clubs. It is a sport where, sad to say, when someone yells, "Kill the ump," he may really mean it and go after the referee. But it's the great rivalries that make the sport so appealing to the crowds; even though there are times when fans attending a big game might be in danger, to followers of soccer the pleasures are worth the risk.

II. The Stars of the Game

CHAPTER 13

Pelé, the King

"In the kingdom of soccer, to whose territory all the states of the world belong, the only king is Pelé. Above his majesty only the spiritual power of Heaven can rule."

That's how a Brazilian journalist described Pelé after the greatest man ever to don a pair of soccer boots was visited on the playing field in Rio de Janeiro by Prince Phillip of England. For weeks negotiations had been going on between members of the British staff and their Brazilian counterparts. After the game, the English wanted Pelé to go up to the Box of Honor and greet Prince Phillip. The Brazilians, however, wanted the prince to come down onto the field to meet Pelé. Prince Phillip finally went down onto the field, and over 100,000 in Maracana Stadium roared their approval. After all, many felt, since Pelé was a king and Phillip only a prince, it was only proper.

Despite all the respect that he has gained, with the many visits he has had with heads of states and even with the pope, Pelé was not born a king nor even a prince. Named Edson Arantes de Nascimento, he was born into poverty on October 23, 1940, in the small village of Três Corações (Three Hearts) in the Brazilian state of Minas Gerais. His father, Dondinho, an obscure small-time soccer player and a physical instructor, could not even afford to put much bread on the table. Two years later Pelé's brother Zoca was born, and the two children shared the same crib, as one was considered enough for both. When Pelé was six, the family decided to move to Bauru, which is located in the Brazilian state of São Paulo. Dondinho had gotten a better offer to play soccer and also work part-time with the Bauru Atletico Club. A third child came into the family in 1943 — a sister named Maria Luci.

Just as American youngsters always want to own their own baseball gloves or to hold the American football in their hands and imitate great players like Joe Namath and O.J. Simpson, Pelé wanted a soccer ball of his own. But a ball was far beyond the financial means of the family; so Dondinho got Pelé (a nickname that had been given him by friends and a name he says that he hated, at first, fighting with the children who called him by it) a make-shift ball consisting of an old sock stuffed with rags. Even though it wasn't a real ball, to Pelé it was the start of a soccer career. He ran barefoot through the streets and in empty fields, kicking that sock around, lifting it over his head and heading and trapping it. He envisioned the sock as a real ball, he said many years later, and he imagined that he was playing before thousands of fans in one of the big stadiums. His aim was to become as good as his father, whom he once described as the greatest player in the world.

"My father gave to me his knowledge and understanding, and for that I will always be grateful," Pelé said in a 1966 interview in New York. "I only hope that I will one day be able to give to my children the same thing my father gave to me," and as he concluded there were tears in his eyes. Even as a child, the struggle to achieve perfection was sometimes overshadowed by his personal feelings. It has been said that Pelé is out to please everyone — a statement that will be confirmed by anyone who has gotten to know him.

Since there were no organized junior leagues for an eight-year-old to join, Pelé took to the streets to play street soccer. The players played barefoot, and the game was called *pedala*. If a youngster was lucky enough to find a discarded soccer ball, one almost cut to ribbons and out of shape, the children would play their game with that ball. But more often their ball was with a bag stuffed with rags. For three years, Pelé was the star of the team, which called itself Sete de Setembro. The team had no uniforms because it had no sponsor like American Pop Warner football or Little League baseball teams have. They wore their oldest clothes, because if they dared wear anything better, and got the clothes dirty, they would get a beating when they returned home. There were no real ground rules, and often fights would break out and players would be hurt while dribbling and shooting. Because Pelé was the star of the team, he got the most punishment from his opponents. Brother Zoca also played in some of the games, and some say that if Pelé had not become the greatest player in the history of the game, Zoca might have become an established star. Zoca was, in fact, once offered a contract to play pro soccer, but he did not want to try to duplicate his brother's feats and instead went to college. He became a lawyer and now heads the vast business empire of Pelé, besides directing the firm's public relations.

Even at age 10, it was already evident that Pelé was a far better player than the rest of the boys with whom he was playing. Pelé did not like school and would cut class to go out to the fields to practice soccer. He was finally caught by a truant officer; and when his father found out, Pelé received a beating that he says he has never forgotten. But after the beating, Pelé and his father sat down and talked; and Dondinho told Pelé that if he didn't want to stay in school, then he should go out and learn a trade. Pelé left school and went to work as an apprentice cobbler for $2 a month, part of which he gave to his father. The year before he became an apprentice, he also helped the family financially by going down to the railroad yards, picking peanuts off the ground, roasting them, and selling them to the people who were going to the theater. Originally, Pelé had hoped that the small amount of money he earned from the sale of the peanuts would be enough to buy a soccer ball, but the family needed the money more; so Pelé gave it to his mother, who to this day calls him not Edson or Pelé but Dico.

The work as an apprentice was long and often hard, but it also gave Pelé the chance to meet older players, who would spend their lunch hour practicing soccer. They didn't play in the fields but on the streets and in vacant lots. Often they would play a game against construction workers who were also on their lunch break. The field dimensions were whatever was available, and the goals consisted of two garbage cans or oil drums placed at each end of the "field." Since many construction workers had earned reputations as good amateur players and were often playing in these games, many of the established teams in Brazil would often send scouts to look them over. One such scout was Valdemar de Brito, who had been a top player for Brazil, and was on that nation's World Cup team in 1934. One afternoon, acting on a tip that some of the construction workers were pretty good prospects, de Brito wandered down to see one of the games. What he saw was not a player in his late teens or early 20s, but an 11-year-old who was making fools out of the older players as he dribbled, passed, and ran with perfection. Years later de Brito was asked about that experience. At a press conference held before the start of the 1958 World Cup, he said, "I saw then Pelé. I saw genius, and I knew that this youngster, with the proper training, could one day become the greatest player of all time."

De Brito kept an eye on the youngster for 45 minutes and then went over to him and had a short talk, because Pelé's boss at the cobbler shop would be angry if the youngster returned late from his lunch break. Pelé told him that he liked soccer and that he was the son of Dondinho. After work that night, Pelé joined his friends in another barefooted game, while de Brito went home to think about what he had witnessed that afternoon.

For the next three years, Pelé and de Brito were constant companions, as the former player worked with the youngster on every move in soccer. Often Pelé and de Brito disagreed and would argue. But despite the pressures of working and the pressures of Pelé's friends to

181

play with them, Pelé and de Brito built a strong relationship based on soccer. In 1953, at age 13, Pelé was asked to join a junior team formed by de Brito called Baquinho. The better youngsters in the area had been invited to join, and as their reward they got to have uniforms. Pelé later said that when he went home to his family that night, carrying his first uniform, he had tears in his eyes.

While playing without wages for Baquinho, Pelé also spent many hours in additional practice with de Brito and several of the club's first-team players. Although he soon left the team to go elsewhere, de Brito left his successor instructions to make sure that Pelé did certain things. By 1956 the name of Pelé was already starting to spread to other areas of Brazil. The youngster had been instrumental in leading Baquinho to three consecutive junior championships and was without a doubt the star of the team. De Brito felt that Pelé, though not yet 16, was ready to turn professional. He returned to Bauru and had a long talk with Pelé's family, finally persuading them that he should be allowed to bring Pelé to the Santos FC for a tryout. After a long discussion, the family finally agreed, and on June 8, 1956, Pelé and de Brito left for a train ride to Santos—a train ride that Pelé still remembers well. "It was the first time that I had ever been on a train ride, and I hated it," he recalled. "I became sick shortly after we left for Santos, and many times on the ride I asked de Brito to forget about the whole thing and take me home. He kept calming me down, but when we arrived in Santos, I was really sick."

But de Brito and Pelé went to the Santos training grounds for the tryout—a tryout attended by many of the Santos officials who had heard de Brito say that he was ready to present to them the boy who would one day become the greatest soccer player of all time. The officials had heard such predictions of greatness from many a scout in the past, but something told them that de Brito, who was, after all, a respected former player, might know what he was talking about. The rest of the Santos team was also on hand, anxious to see what made this kid Pelé so good. Once the tryout started, not only were the Santos officials shocked by the grace and skill of this youngster, but Santos players stopped practicing, and wandered over to watch from all over the field. For about 30 minutes, Pelé executed every move in the book and then trotted off the field. There was silence on the field because what the spectators had just seen this boy do was still sinking into their minds. De Brito went with Pelé to the locker room, where the youngster changed into his street clothes. The two of them then met with the directors of the Santos club, who offered Pelé his first contract. The salary would be about $5 a month plus room and board. Pelé first would be placed on one of the Santos junior teams, where he would be carefully watched and taught what, if anything, he lacked in his over-all game. The Santos junior team was involved in the championship game for the juvenile title, and the coach immediately put Pelé into the title game. The pressure was great and Pelé was selected to take a penalty shot, but he missed and the team lost the title game. Pelé was in tears after the game but was comforted by club officials, who had already taken a liking to the youngster.

As the junior season ended, Pelé was promoted to the main team but rode the bench, watching the older players perform. This is part of the training program of every major team throughout the world. Then on September 7, 1956, Santos played an exhibition game against a local São Paulo team called Corintians Santo André, and in the second half Pelé was inserted into the lineup as a substitute. The crowd cheered and Pelé responded with a goal, the first of 1,220 he was to score for either Santos, the Army team, or the Brazilian National Team. He played as a substitute until later in the year, when he was selected to start against the touring Swedish team AIK. By May of the following year, he was already a regular starter and was being placed at either the inside left position, at which he later became dominant; the outside right spot; or even the center forward position. He had scored 19 goals by this time and was selected to play on the combined Santos Vasco de Gama All-Star team, which was to play the popular Portuguese Belenenses club in an exhibition game. There was a large crowd on hand, and Pelé became the star of the game as he scored three goals.

Immediately it became apparent that Pelé was the man the Brazil-ians would be looking at as they made their national team selection for the following year's World Cup in Sweden. The people in charge of selecting players for the national side were enthusiastic about Pelé, and they decided to pick him for the squad that would play against the Argentinian National Team on July 7, 1957. Pelé was excited as he had finally seen his childhood dream fulfilled—being selected for the national team of Brazil. In the first half of the game, he sat on the bench, but then he was chosen as a substitute for the great Brazilian star Mazzola, who later played for the powerful Juventus team of Italy under the name of Altafini. When Pelé came into the game, he scored the lone goal for the Brazilians, as they dropped a 2-1 decision to Argentina. Three days later the two teams clashed again, and Pelé was in the starting lineup at the inside left position. He scored again, and this time Brazil won the match, 2-0. The crowds began to expect a great deal of him. They would harass him when he wasn't scoring and often jeer him. Such criticism was hard for a youngster not yet 17 to accept, and it hurt him emotionally.

In 1957 Santos played a game against visiting Juventus of Italy. Although he was not playing well, Pelé did manage to score a great goal as he dribbled the ball almost the entire length of the field around many defenders and then took the ball up to the penalty area, drawing out the keeper before sending a short shot into the goal. The crowd was no longer jeering but cheering, and Pelé ran over to the stands and leaped high in the air, his fists raised. This became Pelé's goal salute, and he continued this practice whenever he scored a goal.

The Brazilian National Team Board had to choose the 22-man squad that would be traveling to Sweden to play in the 1958 World Cup. There were many who felt that Pelé should not be selected because he was so young. Fans were begging to have Pelé picked, however; and as Pelé and the rest of Brazil waited, the selection committee finally decided — Pelé would go along as a full member of the Brazilian National Team. "To me all the work I had put in as a youngster and all the problems that I had to overcome now were worth it," he later said. "I didn't know what the future would be, but at least I did know that they had selected me for the team."

Being selected as a member of the team and playing in the World Cup were two different things, however. Pelé had suffered a knee injury, and as the World Cup got underway, he found himself sitting on the Brazilian bench during the opening game against Austria (which the Brazilians won, 3-0) and during a bitter scoreless deadlock with England. For the match against the Soviet Union, however, Pelé was in the starting lineup. He hit the post, and late in the game, with the score 1-0 in favor of Brazil, he got an assist on a goal by Vava. Because of the victory, Brazil gained a spot in the quarterfinal round against Wales. With Pelé getting the lone goal of the match, the game against Wales ended up a 1-0 victory for Brazil. "Although I have scored many goals in my career," Pelé said many years later, "the goal I scored against Wales still must rank as one of the most important and enjoyable goals I have ever scored."

In the semifinals, Brazil met France, and Pelé scored to move Brazil to the finals. In the championship game, he scored twice more, and Brazil won the title with a smashing 5-2 triumph over Sweden. The crowd roared as Pelé scored what has to be one of the most spectacular goals in World Cup competition. The ball came to Pelé, who had his back toward the goal. He chest-trapped the ball and let it roll down hiw stomach onto his foot. Then he flipped the ball over his head, and as he turned, with his other foot he kicked it home past a stunned Swedish goalie. Despite its biased view, the Swedish crowd roared, "Pelé! Pelé!" "It was one of the greatest gestures a foreign crowd has ever given me," he said later.

The following year Pelé spent time in the army, and a player called Coutinho came to Santos. Together they worked the wall pass (give-and-go) to perfection, and the crowds kept coming to see Santos and Pelé in action. Numerous invitations came for Santos to play abroad, and tours were arranged.

In 1960 several Italian teams offered Santos over a million dollars to buy Pelé. Almost immediately word spread about the offer, and fans started gathering outside the Santos office. The government killed the offer in a hurry, however, by declaring Pelé a national treasure that could not be sold to another nation. Several years later a director of Santos discussed the fears he had when fans were outside the office. "If we had sold him, I am sure the fans would have killed us," he said.

In 1961 Brazil was getting ready to defend its World Cup championship, and Santos was rolling along to its second straight São Paulo League championship crown. Some say that during a game that year in Maracana Stadium, Pelé scored a goal that will always be remembered in Brazilian soccer. In a match against Fluminense, Pelé went back to help his defense and intercepted a pass near the midfield line. He dribbled around and between many defenders, and finally drew the opposing goalie out of position. Instead of tapping the ball into the vacated net, however, he just dribbled the ball in. The crowd gave him a standing ovation that lasted over 10 minutes, and Pelé bowed to the crowd in appreciation.

As 1961 drew to a close, Pelé was putting in a lot of time not only with Santos but practicing for the Brazilian National Team. He was also becoming interested in the real estate business. An injury he suffered in the second game of the 1962 World Cup competition in Chile put him on the sidelines part of that year, but the King of Soccer sat on the bench, rooting his teammates home to their second consecutive World Cup title. Recovered from the injury, he returned to Santos and helped his team win not only the São Paulo League title for the third straight time, but also helped them capture the *Copa Libertadores,* the South American club championship.

In a two-game series for the Copa Intercontinentale Championship, Santos faced Benfica, since the Portuguese team had won the European Cup. The first game was held in Rio, and Pelé scored one of the goals in Santos' 3-2 victory. The return game in Lisbon was all Pelé's, however. By the end of the year, Pelé had accumulated 500 professional goals. The following year Santos once again took the South American crown and the São Paulo title; and in the World Club Championship, Santos turned back the challenge of AC Milan. A knee injury, however, kept Pelé out of the return match.

In 1964 Pelé saw more of his business partners and advisors than before, but also was seeing Rosemarie de Cholby, the daughter of a Santos merchant and a part-time municipal worker. Since Rosemarie insisted on keeping the courtship secret, the Black Pearl and the white woman were never seen together in public. Pelé continued to score goals during 1964, and in one game against Botafogo he hit the nets eight times as Santos recorded an 11–0 victory. After the game the press asked Pelé how he felt about the eight goals, and he said that he was sorry for the opposing goalie. Scoring that many goals against a weak team is not really enjoyable for any player.

In 1965 Pelé found the range for 101 goals in 65 games, which was his best average per game ever, although he had scored 110 goals in 83 games four years earlier. All Brazil was confident that Pelé would be able to lead the national team to its third straight World Cup title the following year. The tournament was in England, and Pelé was well received by the English. He became the victim of brutal fouling in the first two games against Bulgaria and Hungary, however, and was stepped on, punched, and thrown to the ground many times. He suffered a knee injury, and Brazil was sent into shock. People lined the streets outside crowded churches, praying for his recovery. Pelé indeed tried to play in the team's next game against Portugal, but he was in no shape to do it and had to leave the game. Brazil lost any chance of winning another World Cup, and a bitter Pelé declared that he would never play in another World Cup. Late in the year, he married Rosemarie, and the two set up housekeeping in a small home in Santos.

In 1967 Pelé's daughter Kelly Cristina was born, and the following year Pelé was besieged by offers to make television films, some of which he accepted, including one in which he played the part of a slave and another series in which he played a detective.

In November 1969, Pelé recorded his 1,000th goal, as all Brazil exploded with joy. The goal came on a penalty kick, and as the ball entered the net in the game against Vasco da Gama, Pelé raced toward the net and retrieved the ball. Before exploding in his famous goal salute, however, he took time to pat the goalie on the head.

"I realized at the time that I had just achieved a milestone," Pelé said. "But I also realized that for years to come people will tell the man I just scored against that they remembered seeing him give up the goal which gave me the 1,000th of my career. I know how he felt at the moment, and I hope I eased some of the pain he must have been experiencing."

Despite his vow never to play in another World Cup, Pelé did compete for the 1970 World Cup and performed as brilliantly as before, if not better, as he led Brazil to the championship in Mexico. The Mexicans loved him and Pelé could often be found with the youngsters outside the stadium. This was not a new experience for Pelé; a few years earlier he had become the goodwill ambassador of the game, making trips all over the world. The goodwill mission eventually took him to Mainland China and to Japan and even to Africa. Nigeria and Biafra actually declared a three-day ceasefire in their bitter civil war because Santos was playing an exhibition match. As soon as Santos left, the war resumed.

At the end of the year, Pelé became the father of a son named Edinho, and many who have seen the youngster control a soccer ball are sure that one day we will have another Pelé in our midst. Asked about this, however, Pelé says, "I will not make him become a soccer player. He must do that on his own. I will give him help if he wants it just like my father gave it to me."

In July 1971, Pelé played his final international game for Brazil. Over 135,000 fans turned out to see the game, which was played against Yugoslavia. Although it was just an exhibition game, the world wanted to see the farewell game, and the match was broadcast on free television or on closed-circuit telecasts throughout the United States and Canada. Pelé played the first half and came close to scoring; but as the half ended, he had not been able to add to his total of 96 goals in 110 international matches. Before the start of the second half, Pelé emerged from the dressing room, waved to the crowd and then ripped off his shirt and flung it around his head, taking the victory lap as the crowd broke into the song *"Obrigado, Pelé"* ("Thank You, Pelé"), which had become a big hit in Brazil. Others stood and yelled *"Fica! Fica!"* ("Stay! Stay!"). Pelé received several gifts and then made his way back to the dressing room, coming out dressed in a business suit to watch the end of the match from the president's box, where leading political and civic officials from all over Brazil were gathered.

He built up his vast business empire after his retirement, with rubber, plastics, real estate, and even a Café Pelé part of the venture. Pelé was able to spend more time with his family and devote more time to business; the fans still came to see Santos whenever he played. During 1971 Pelé and Santos made another trip to the United States. It was the fifth straight year they had come to the United States since 1966, when they drew a record 44,000 to Yankee Stadium and defeated Inter-Milan. Exhibition tours also took a great deal of Pelé's time, and on one occasion he was detained at the Rhodesian airport when found to be carrying several thousand dollars. It seems that he was to receive a certain amount for each exhibition game in which he played, while the team was to get a separate amount. Two years earlier he and his Santos teammates were jailed after the team had had a fight over a dispute with the referee about a Pelé goal that had been disallowed.

In 1972, with no obligations, he was playing loose and easy. He scored 50 goals, and the following year he hit the nets 52 times. Brazil would be defending its title in the World Cup in 1974, however, and the pressure for him to play for his nation once again began to mount. Even the president made an appeal, but Pelé kept saying no. One night shots were fired into a vacant room in the $600,000 home he and his family lived in. Pelé still said he would not play and went to the United States with Santos for several exhibition games. He and his teammates also went to the White House for a visit with President Nixon. (A few years earlier he had come out wrapped in a towel at Maracana to meet the late Senator Bob Kennedy.)

Early in 1974 Pelé announced that he would retire from soccer altogether later in the year. He attended the World Cup as a spectator and was greeted by such people as United States Secretary of State Henry Kissinger and other political dignitaries and heads of state. On September 22, on a penalty shot, he scored his 1,220th and last goal as a member of either Santos, Brazil, or any other Brazilian team. Then, before a packed house at the Santos stadium on October 2, 1974, he played his last game. When the match was over, he employed the same types of deceptive moves that he used to beat defenders in the field and, avoiding the press, he disappeared to meet his wife at their private ranch. Pelé was through with soccer — or so the soccer world thought.

But a former English journalist by the name of Clive Toye did not think so. Toye was the general manager of the New York Cosmos, owned by Warner Communications; and he felt that he had a chance to talk Pelé out of a permanent retirement from the game to wear the uniform of the Cosmos in the North American Soccer League. Toye, who had been criticized by the New York press for not landing George Best in early 1975, when it seemed that Best was ready to play for the Cosmos, had been after Pelé several times.

Actually, according to Toye, the first time he mentioned the Cosmos to Pelé was in 1971 during the team's initial 1971 season. Toye went to Kingston, Jamaica, where Santos was playing an exhibition game. He told Pelé about the Cosmos and about the seeds of soccer in America. During the 1974 World Cup, Toye met Pelé in Frankfurt and made an offer. Many members of the English press told Toye that he didn't have a chance of getting Pelé; but the groundwork had been laid, and an offer made for all to consider. A month before Pelé's final game with Santos, Pelé, Julio Mazzei, who is Pelé's personal trainer, adviser, and confidant, and Jose Xisto met with Toye at Kennedy Airport in New York. They talked for a while; then, Toye went one way and Pelé and his group the other way. After Pelé's final game for Santos, Toye went to São Paulo and Santos and held four separate meetings with Pelé, Mazzei, and Xisto. Nothing happened for another four months; but in February 1975, Mazzei came to New York and told Toye that Pelé might be ready to play again. The worldwide chase turned to Brussels, where a meeting lasting the better part of four days was held between Toye, Pelé, Mazzei, and Xisto. The deal looked close, and in April, Toye, accompanied by Cosmo vice-president Rafael de la Sierra and Warner financial adviser Jim Carradine, met Pelé, Mazzei, and Xisto in Rome. Pelé promised that he would have an answer for Toye in about a week. The New York press got hold of the story; but it started fizzling out, as Pelé turned down the offer, citing business and family reasons. Toye would not accept no for an answer, however, even though the Brazilian press, which had been criticizing Pelé for even considering the offer, was congratulating him for turning it down.

A great deal of Pelé's time was being spent with his brother Zoca, and from May 11 through 16, meetings were held in Santos, São Paulo, and Guarujá among Jay Emmett, executive-president of Warner Communications, Inc.; Neshuhi Ertegun, president of both the Cosmos and WEA International (a division of Warner Communications); de la Sierra; and Toye. From May 22 to 25, Toye, de la Sierra, and Carradine were in Brazil; and on May 28, Pelé flew to New York to see the Cosmos play an NASL game against Vancouver. He answered many questions and then left, while Xisto remained in New York for more talks. On June 3, word came that Pelé would come out of retirement to play for the Cosmos. The following week he was signed at a wild press conference at the swank 21 Club—a confab in which reporters and photographers were throwing punches at one another. At the conference, Pelé explained why he was coming to America, when he obviously could have come close to the estimated three-year $4.7 million pact playing for other countries. "I come here as a missionary. To help build the game in this country."

On June 15, at Randall's Island, Pelé played his first game for the Cosmos, an exhibition game against the Dallas Tornado, led by Kyle Rote, Jr. Over 500 foreign correspondents were on hand, there was live television coverage throughout the United States and Canada, and many foreign nations saw the game via their own TV outlets. Pelé immediately took charge, to the delight of the 21,278 present, setting up one goal in the second half and scoring the other himself as the two teams battled to a 2-2 deadlock. Pelé—the man who, according to coach Gordon Bradley, had asked jokingly if he was good enough to play for the team—and, to many, soccer had finally arrived in America. Although the Cosmos didn't even make the league playoffs for the remainder of the season, Pelé was the master, the man in demand.

When he was injured in a league game in Toronto and was ruled unfit to play in an exhibition two days later in St. Louis, the game was postponed. Fans in Boston almost tore him apart after he scored an apparent goal, forcing him to be wheeled from the field on a stretcher. Pelé had done for U.S. soccer what he had been doing for the game elsewhere for years—promoting it and excelling in it. After the season, he drew great crowds as the Cosmos played exhibition games in Europe and throughout the Caribbean. Meanwhile, he was spending time doing clinic work for Pepsi-Cola and promoting products, and he even met with President Ford. Pelé was the man of the hour and of the year, and his coming to the United States as a missionary did the trick as children who had never heard of soccer before came to see him perform his magic.

At the start of the 1976 preseason camp, Pelé was not present, having been delayed by a civil war attempt in Africa. But fortunately he was not injured, and the Cosmos breathed a sigh of relief. The beginning of the 1976 season was a bit disappointing to Pelé, as he and coach Ken Furphy obviously disagreed on tactics. Pelé soon was the victor, however, as Furphy was forced to "resign."

People in Italy named him *Il Re* (The King). In France he is known as *La Tulipe Noire* (The Black Tulip), while in Chile he is called *El Peligro* (The Dangerous One). What makes Pelé the player he is? Ask one of his friends, and you'll get a predictable answer. But ask Jao Saldanha, the former team manager of Brazil and a man who has never really been on good terms with Pelé why *Il Re* is the King, and he'll answer, "If you ask me who is the best fullback in Brazil, I will say Pelé. If you ask me who is the best wing halfback in Brazil, I will say Pelé. And if you ask me who is the best winger in the world, I will say Pelé. If you ask me who is the best goalkeeper, probably I would have to say Pelé. He is like no other player. He is to Brazilian football what Shakespeare is to English literature."

Of the 5'7" star, Professor Mazzei says, "Pelé could have been a genius in anything he attempted, whether sport or anything else. The great, great star, the genius whether he is a sportsman, a scientist, or a poet is at the bottom of a simple man. Greatness is simplicity, not complication, and that is what Pelé is."

His mother said, "Ever since Dico was born, he has strived to be the tops at whatever he set his mind on doing. That is why he is like he is."

And when once asked to describe his greatness, Pelé simply said, "What makes anyone like me is many things. My talent is the gift of God—I am what He made me."

190

CHAPTER 14

Tops in Europe

Pelé is generally regarded as the greatest soccer player ever in the world, but it is hard to say who the greatest player is in the history of European soccer. Maybe there really is no answer since, as the great Eusebio once said,

> It's impossible to call one man the greatest of all time. There have been many top players, and I'm sure that the future will bring even more top names, but to call one man the greatest is unfair. The requirements of an individual player have changed over the years with the changing systems, and the duties once called for may no longer be needed now. Then there is the reverse, where a certain player of say the 1930s wasn't required to be skilled in other areas of the game. There are no real criteria for deciding who's the best ever.

GOALKEEPERS

Three men—England's Gordon Banks, the Soviet Union's Lev Yachin and Italy's Dino Zoff—stand out as probably the top European goalkeepers of all time, although one can be assured that those who feel that Peter Bonetti or even Pat Jennings are the best will disagree.

Gordon Banks
Banks was often referred to as the man one could count on to shut out the opposition. Born in 1937, he played until an eye injury sustained in a car crash forced him to retire at the age of 35; although the way he had been playing before the injury had led many to believe that he could go on until his mid-40s. Before retiring from the game, Banks won 73 International Caps for England and was the man in the nets when the English won the 1966 World Cup. He was elected Footballer of the Year by the European press in 1972, only a few months before he was injured in a car crash; and although he attempted to make a

comeback, he decided that his vision impairment made it impossible for him to play the type of courageous game that he had played before. Banks broke into professional soccer at the age of 18 with Chesterfield, before being sold to Leicester City, where he played from 1959 to 1967. At the age of 22, he was picked as one of the goalies for the English National Team, playing four games his first year before taking over as the full-time keeper for the national team the following year. In a nation loaded with fine keepers, few goalies would come out as far as Banks in an attempt to stop breakaways. His leaping saves, in which he would go from one side of the net to the other, were a spectacle that all fans enjoyed, and he had the ability to make punch saves, often sending the ball to the midfield line when he connected. Because of his aggressive style, Banks was one of the most-fouled goalies; and many times he was helped off the ground, only to shake off the injury and the next moment come out again to cut off a breakaway.

In 1970 in Mexico City, he made a fabulous save on a header by Pelé, going fully lengthwise to the other end of the goal and tipping the ball over the bar. "I hated him for a brief moment as he made what I consider the greatest save I have ever seen," Pelé said later, as he sent a wire to Banks congratulating him on the play. Two years later in the FA League Cup final, Banks stopped a penalty shot by Geoff Hurst to give Stoke City, for whom Banks started playing late in 1967, the title. Banks was a hard worker and spent many hours practicing by having his teammates shoot crosses against him. In 1975 he was named to work with the English Youth Association. His experience with youngsters is certain to give England many great keepers in the future, but whether they can ever reach the heights that Banks did is a question that only time will answer.

Lev Yachin

Until 1970 Lev Yachin ruled the penalty area for his Moscow Dynamo Club, the Soviet National Team, and the Soviet Olympic Team. Anything that went into that area of the field was his, and he was not above going out head first in an effort to scoop up a loose ball. Standing 6'1", Yachin was not an immediate success at the beginning of his soccer career, however. He had always wanted to be a fighter; but his size and, some said, his lack of speed stopped him from accomplishing his goal. Yachin went to work in a factory and joined the factory's soccer team as a left winger. He didn't possess the skills the team's manager wanted, however, and since the team had no suitable goalie, he was offered a chance to play that position instead. "At first I felt disappointed because I wanted to be able to run and score goals," he said many years later, when he appeared in the United States as the manager of Dynamo Moscow. "But as things turned out, it was the greatest thing that ever happened to me. Probably I would not have stood in soccer on any important level if I hadn't been made to play goal."

It was also the most important position change ever made in Soviet soccer, because Yachin took to his new position with skill and determination. He received excellent coaching and started to attract the attention of several scouts, who watched youthful players on factory teams, looking for those with promise. Yachin dropped soccer for a year and tried his hand at hockey while in the Soviet army. He became a good hockey player while competing as a winger-goalie for Dynamo Moscow, but when he found that Dynamo's regular soccer goalie Alexei Khomich was thinking about retiring, he virtually begged Dynamo officials to give him a spot on one of their junior teams. They did so reluctantly, and in 1954 he led Dynamo Moscow to the Soviet championship. Two years later Yachin was a member of the Soviet Olympic Team, which won the title in the Melbourne Olympic Games.

For the remainder of his career, he played brilliantly, representing the USSR 78 times. He was in the nets when the Soviets captured the 1960 European Nations Cup, and three years later he was voted Footballer of the Year in Europe. In 1970 he decided that it was time to retire and devote his time to coaching. Late in 1970 over 100,000 fans jammed Lenin Stadium in Moscow for a special testimonial game in Yachin's honor, in which the Dynamo Moscow squad was matched against a team called the Rest of the World, which included Eusebio and Bobby Charlton. After making eight brilliant saves in the first half and with his Dynamo team leading, 2-0, Yachin played eight minutes of the second half before trotting off the field to a thunderous roar. Yachin was finished as a player, and even as soccer history continues to unfold, it remains unlikely that there will be many more goalies of his caliber.

Dino Zoff

Born in 1940, Dino Zoff has often been blamed for the poor performance of the Italian National Team. But opposing forwards almost unanimously regard him as one of the best keepers in the game. In Mariano del Friuli in Udine, Zoff started his career with the local team, before catching the eye of scouts from Napoli, who signed him in 1965. He was a member of the strong Napoli team nine years before going on to Juventus, where he was declared one of the untouchable stars so far as being sold again. Zoff has been a mainstay of the Italian National Team and was the cause of much fury when shortly before the start of the 1970 World Cup in Mexico City he was replaced as the starting keeper by Blabertosi, who was overcome by the North Ko-

193

reans. By the start of the 1974 World Cup elimination series, however, Zoff had regained his position as the starting keeper for Italy by posting 13 straight international shutouts, including a 2-0 victory over the Brazilian National Team. Zoff works hard at his position, and when he appeared in a series of games in the United States for the Italian National Team (a series in which he yielded three goals to England and four to Brazil), he talked about his future.

I would like to play until I'm close to 40 and then work with young goalies as a coach. I don't know if I want to take a position as coach of the bigger Italian teams, but working with youngsters on the level of our National Junior Team would give me a chance to pass on some of the knowledge that I have gained through the years. Being a goalkeeper is a strange thing. If you get a shutout, then not often is much said about you. But make a few mistakes and cost your team a game, and you're the first one to be blamed. At first this used to bother me, but as I have matured on the field I have also matured in being able to say after a game, even one in which I made a bad mistake, that at least I was out there trying my best.

Zoff has been the object of a lot of criticism, but much of it is unfair. He is one of the best keepers of all time and in 1973 placed second only to Johann Cruyff as European Footballer of the Year. As of 1976 he had been voted the top player in Italy on three different occasions. Zoff is a team leader and has been known to take aside younger players when they didn't do well and either comfort them if they had tried or yell at them if he felt that they hadn't put forth their best effort. "Wearing the uniform of any team, whether a small local club or the Italian National Team is an honor but also a responsibility, and if you can't play as hard as you are capable of, then don't wear the uniform," Zoff told a press gathering in New York before the start of the 1976 American Bicentennial Soccer Cup.

Peter Bonetti
When Peter Bonetti came to the United States in 1975 to play with the St. Louis Stars of the North American Soccer League, he had the reputation of being one of the best goalies in English history. Some said that next to Gordon Banks he was the best in Europe. Bonetti has played many fine games, but the game that he remembers probably more than any other was the 1970 World Cup match in Mexico City against West Germany. Bonetti had been the backup goalie behind Banks, and when Banks got sick from some food he had eaten the night before, Bonetti was given the chance to start, something he had done only six times in four years. England led, 2-0, but late in the match Bonetti foolishly allowed two goals and in the overtime he yielded the winning goal to the West Germans.

I went over to Sir Alf Ramsey, our coach, and told him that I was sorry. What else could I really say? I had some excuses, and some critics should be reminded that since injuring my knee a few months ago I hadn't been in goal except for two games. But I was the one everyone blamed, and it bothered me. We had 10 other players on the field. I was bitter then, but within a couple of years I got over it and just made the best of it.

Although Bonetti angered English fans with his performance that day, especially when he allowed the goal that tied the score by not leaping because he thought that the ball was already behind the net, on many occasions he made fans extremely proud that they had had the opportunity to see him play. Known as the Cat, Bonetti was born in Putney in 1941. At the age of 16, he quit school and after his mother wrote Chelsea coach Ted Drake a letter, he was given a tryout and was put on Chelsea's junior team. Drake admitted later that he had been impressed with Peter when he saw him play a schoolboy game. In 1959 he was promoted to the varsity team and signed a professional contract, but for the next six months he sat on the bench and played only in nonleague games. On April 2, 1960, however, he got his start in a game against Manchester City. Before leaving Chelsea at the end of the 1974–75 season, Bonetti played in over 500 games. Among his greatest successes were winning the English FA Cup in 1970 and taking the European Cup-Winners' Cup the following year, beating powerful Real Madrid of Spain. Bonetti achieved distinction by scoring over 100 shutouts in the years he was with Chelsea, a mark that won him the acclaim of the English press many times.

Pat Jennings

Pat Jennings didn't begin his athletic career as a soccer player. He won his first honors in the rugged Gaelic football competition, in which just about everything can and usually does happen. Being knocked down, having one's legs stepped on, and receiving an occasional punch in the mouth is an accepted part of Gaelic football and Jennings, born in Newry in Northern Ireland's County Down, enjoyed himself. As he recalled,

> My mom used to tell me that I should play soccer more and Gaelic football a little less. To make her happy at first, I would take my soccer boots and head for a practice field; but I never got there for the most part, since I would always find a Gaelic game going on, and I would play. Then finally I started to really get interested in soccer, and I was confident that I could be a good goalie because I feel that goalies should come out with no fear of being hurt. I never had any fear, and that is what I think caught the attention of some of the scouts who used to watch our schoolboy games.

He played his first season in the English First Division in 1964 after Tottenham purchased his contract from Watford. A year earlier Jennings had been a member of the Northern Irish team that was beaten by the English Youth Team at Wembley. With the Tottenham Hotspurs, he played a total of over 400 league games, winning the FA Cup in 1967, the League Cup in 1971 and 1973, and the UEFA Cup in 1972. In 1973 he was voted the English Footballer of the Year. Because of the great games he has played in goal, including many top performances for the Norther Ireland National Team, he has won the accolades of friend and foe alike. Jennings, who stands an even 6 feet tall, was highly acclaimed by Dave Clements, the player-manager of the Northern Ireland team. Talking about goalkeepers while he was with the Cosmos of the NASL in 1976, Clements mentioned Jennings. "Pat is an extremely hard worker, who exemplifies the courage of many a top goalie. He has outstanding hands and the ability to anticipate where a play is coming from. He's not easily faked out into committing himself too early like some other goalies, but he's ready to take the big gamble when he feels that is what is called for."

In 1967, Jennings fulfilled the dream of almost every goalkeeper in the world during the annual FA Charity Shield match with Manchester United, when he made a save and then sent a high booming kick downfield. Aided by a strong wind, the ball kept rising and then bounced just as opposing goalie Alex Stepney came out. Stepney misjudged the bounce, and the ball went into the goal, giving Jennings an unassisted goal, the first time a Tottenham keeper had ever scored.

"I felt both proud and embarrassed," Jennings told the reporters after the game. "I just know how I would have felt if it had been the other goalie putting the ball past me. It's something that you often dream of, but you never really expect to see a goalie score. That is why after the season was over I told them to make sure that they list me with their all-time scoring leaders. After all, a goalie scoring a goal is like a forward scoring 500 goals."

FORWARDS

No team can win unless it has the men who can put the ball into the other team's goals. Since organized soccer began some 100 years ago, there have been many outstanding goal-scorers, plus players with a skillful pass or dribble able to find another teammate free for an easy goal. Although there are many who would be quick to disagree, most people consider the top 10 European forwards to be, Sir Stanley Matthews, Johann Cruyff, Gerd Müller, George Best, Eusebio (who was born in Africa but starred in Portugal), Ferenc Puskas, Denis Law, Steve Bloomer, Dixie Dean, and Jimmy McGrony.

196

Sir Stanley Matthews

Sir Stanley is a legend in soccer and a man who was considered almost indestructible. He played until he was 50 years old, when he scored his last goal for Stoke City against Luton, and although he scored only 71 goals in 698 games, he was the man who often drew two and three defenders. He would force the defenders to come to him, and then, with a quick spin or a quick pass he would find a free teammate to put the ball into the opposition's net. At the start of his professional career with Stoke, Matthews was a scorer but soon found that he could serve his team far better by setting up the other forwards to put the ball into the net. From 1931, when he made his debut, until 1947, Stoke was Matthews's team. Then, despite great protest from fans, he was transferred to Blackpool, where he played until 1961. The following year he was once again in a Stoke City uniform and celebrated his return to "his" team, as he often called Stoke, by scoring 18 goals. It should be mentioned that the goal he scored in his final game of the 1962–63 season was his only one of the season. He attempted to play again the following year and did play in 19 games, but at age 49 he could not compete with the younger players. Nevertheless, a year later he was asked to play one final game for Stoke, which he did, to a packed house. Then, as many wept openly in the stands, Sir Stanley, who was knighted for his service to soccer, left the field and raced into the clubhouse, where his teammates later found him crying.

Winner of 54 International Caps, Sir Stanley also played in exhibition games for servicemen during World War II. After the war, he played in several Victory Games and donated his playing fee to charity. Many English soccer stars have been known to make news off the playing field, but that was not the case with Sir Stanley who publicly was always the model of decorum.

Johann Cruyff

A player who exemplifies the all-around ability of a top forward is Dutch star Johann Cruyff. Cruyff was a star almost from the time he put on his first pair of soccer boots, and his career has been both brilliant and controversial. Cruyff was a sensation in junior and schoolboy soccer, and in 1964 at the age of 17, he was signed by Ajax. Two years later he was named to the Dutch National Team and played his first game for it against Czechoslovakia. It was also his last game for one year. A Czechoslovakian defender had been continuously fouling him and Cruyff got angry and retaliated with a vicious foul of his own, besides a well-placed punch. That episode cost him a one-year suspension from international soccer. Since then Cruyff has matured a great deal, and many now look to him for leadership. Possessing phenomenal speed in addition to grace, Cruyff has managed to avoid serious

197

injury, eluding tackles as he sideswipes his opponents. Among his greatest assets are his ability to change the pace of his dribble quickly and his ability to cut and veer in different directions.

Before signing with Barcelona for an estimated million dollars, Cruyff was Ajax and Ajax was Cruyff. If Cruyff played well, then Ajax won; but when he was off form, missing easy shots and losing dribbles, Ajax lost. With Cruyff playing, Ajax won three straight European Cups, and in some of the games he was the Man of the Match. In the finals of the 1972 European Cup, for example, he scored two goals against Inter-Milan of Italy. Movie studios sought him for acting roles, and he was a frequent guest on talk shows throughout the Netherlands. Despite his success, however, he always refused to change his number from 14, a number worn usually by substitutes. His reason was simple: "That is the number I first wore when I joined Ajax, and I'll wear that number until I leave the team."

In September 1973, he did leave the team to join Barcelona, much to the chagrin of Dutch soccer fans, who were convinced that he was the best thing that ever happened to their nation in soccer. Under Spanish rules, he had to sit out a few games before finally suiting up. In his first game for Barcelona in the rugged Spanish League, he scored two goals, and the Barcelona fans saw for themselves just how good Cruyff is and why he has been named European Footballer of the Year three times.

Gerd Müller

Some call Gerd Müller a garbage collector. Others more affectionately refer to him as the King of the Penalty Box. But no matter how he does it, he scores goals, and because of his goal in the final of the 1974 World Cup his team beat Cruyff and the Dutch team, 2–1.

Born in 1945 just after the end of World War II, Gerhardt Müller was the fourth son of a family living in the Bavarian village of Zinsen. When he was 15, his father died and Müller, who had made a good name for himself in schoolboy soccer, was forced to quit school and go to work as a weaver. That year he joined the TSV 1861 Nördlingen team, and for two years he was the high scorer, hitting the nets for 46 goals. Soon the scouts of the big West German teams were coming to town on Sundays to see Müller play. On the recommendation of his coach, Conny Kraft, Müller signed with Nuremberg, Kraft's old team, but before the time to sign a more formal contract was past, Müller was swamped with offers from all the top clubs. He finally decided to play with Bayern-Münich. Not only is playing for the team the dream of many a German youngster but Bayern offered him the best deal possible. "If you ask me how come I score so many goals because I'm so short, have thick thighs and am heavy, I'll tell you what I tell everyone who asks me that question," Müller said before the start of the 1974 World Cup. "I just know where the ball is coming, and it's like a radar sense in me. I often, they say, smell out the ball and the goal at the same time."

In his first full season, he played only occasionally but still managed to score 15 goals in 33 games. The following season he was inserted into the lineup as a full starter and responded with 28 goals in just 32 games. The same year he also scored 19 nonleague goals, as Bayern won the West German Cup and the European Cup-Winners' Cup.

Helmut Schoen, manager of the West German National Team, was impressed and named Müller to the team in 1966. In his first game, he failed to score in a match against Turkey; but in his next game, against Albania, he hit the nets for four tallies, the first four-goal performance by a German player since 1942. Müller continued to make goals—in 1970 he was voted European Footballer of the Year after scoring 10 goals in the World Cup—but the constant fouling he was subjected to continued as well. Müller finally reacted against an unjustified foul against him in a "friendly" match that Bayern played against Universitario in Lima, Peru. The German Federation suspended him for two months, but the public outcry caused the federation to rescind the suspension in time for him to play the remainder of the season. With Müller chalking up goals in European Cup competition almost as fast as he did in league play, starting in 1974 Bayern-Münich won three straight Cup titles.

During the 1975 season, he averaged 0.90 goals per game. Although, as the 1976 season came to an end, he was not likely to hit the goal-a-game mark, he is without a doubt one of the greatest West German players, ranking with the great Uwe Seeler.

George Best

George Best is the Joe Namath of soccer. He makes more goals than most players when he is in the mood to, but he also creates more problems for his managers, himself, and even the police. He's known by many as the greatest dribbler in the game, and opponents consider him dangerous no matter where in the field he is playing. His curving, cannonlike shots will appear to go wide and then swerve in on the goalie. With two or three men guarding him, he'll fake them right out to one side, leaving them bumping into their teammates. Many feel that George Best could have been the greatest player of all time.

"If I wasn't so handsome and girls would not have chased me all over, then the soccer world would never have heard of Pelé," he told a Phoenix press conference before taking the field for the Los Angeles Aztecs. Although he later said that he was only kidding when he made that statement, one has to wonder if he didn't really mean it. Best has all the talent needed to become one of the top players in soccer, and that he accomplished his goal in some ways defies explanation. Never known to like training, Best would rather be dating women, drinking, or racing one of his fancy cars through London or Manchester. When he was in Manchester, he was surrounded by an entourage that helped him run his various businesses, which included a couple of discotheques and a clothing store.

Born in 1946 in Belfast, Northern Ireland, the son of a shipyard worker, Best started kicking around a soccer ball almost as soon as he could walk. He was an immediate star in one of the many young leagues, where players six years old are examined closely by experienced coaches. He played schoolboy soccer, where he was a member of the Northern Irish Schoolboy Team, and at the age of 15, Best was brought to Manchester United for a trial. Two days later he was homesick and returned to Belfast. His father talked him into returning, however, and Best was placed on Manchester United's reserved team. Two years later he had done so well that he was given the opportunity of playing with Manchester United. It surprised many that Manchester United even considered this skinny lad, who weighed just over 100 pounds. They felt that he was too fragile to play the hard-nosed soccer that the English First Division requires. Under the patient but often rough coach Matt Busby, however, Best started to develop into one of the most entertaining players in England. Making goals by firing cannonball shots or by dribbling the ball right past and sometimes between several defenders, then drawing out the goalie in order to go around him, Best was an overnight sensation. In 1966 he drew international acclaim when, disregarding the orders of Busby to play back a little more, he scored two quick goals against Benfica of Portugal in the opening 15 minutes of the quarterfinal round of the European Cup.

Many of his teammates resented him, however, not only for not listening to advice either on or off the field, but for the way he would occasionally hog the ball, trying to do everything by himself. Although he often had trouble with Busby, it wasn't until late 1971 that he started to crack under the pressure. He withdrew from an international match in Belfast when he was threatened with death if he showed up. The following January he skipped out of training for a week and then showed up to be interviewed by new coach Frank O'Farrell, who ordered him to leave his home and return to the team complex. He was fined and forfeited two weeks wages. Disgusted with the bad publicity he was receiving, Best went to work and played out the remainder of the season in fine fashion. But in early May, he didn't show up for his duties with Northern Ireland in the annual Home

International Championship, and a few weeks later he announced that he was through with soccer. "I am a physical and mental wreck," he explained. "I have been drinking too much because of the pressures particularly over the past few months."

The retirement lasted only a couple of months, however, until Busby, now club executive, convinced him to return. But on November 25, 1972, he skipped training and was again suspended. Told that he was on the transfer list, a secret meeting was held; but much to the dismay of several of his teammates, Best was told that if he worked himself into condition, he could indeed return to the lineup. He played in a couple of special games and then rejoined his old teammates to play 19 games and score four goals, although his thighs were heavier and his speed had slowed somewhat. But Best then left again, saying that he was once again through with professional soccer. At the end of the 1972-73 season, he made it clear that he might play again, but never in England; and the following year he picked up a lot of money by playing in South Africa and even in Australia.

The Cosmos persuaded him to come to New York. While in New York he told everyone that he was ready to play in the NASL. The Cosmos, who had not yet signed Pelé, believed him. Best was, they announced, going to be on their team for the start of the 1975 season. He returned to Manchester, and a deal was made for the Cosmos to purchase him; but the deal was never consummated, as Best informed the Cosmos through his lawyer that he was too tied up in business to come. The following year Best was declared a free agent, and at the start of the 1976 season he finally decided to play for the Los Angeles Aztecs after a long talk with Elton John, one of the team's owners. Best played well during his first year with the Aztecs but as he said, "Here, not too many people recognize me, and I have time to practice. That is something I didn't have time for in England."

What he did have time for in England was running around, bouts with the law, a breach-of-promise suit, and many other troubles. "Some people say that I have no feelings," Best said one day in a serious mood. "That's not true, you know; I'm not a machine. I have feelings just like everyone else. All I want is for people to be honest with me."

Eusebio
Born into poverty like Pelé, the man known as the European Pelé and the Black Panther of Mozambique is Eusebio da Silva Ferreira, known throughout the soccer world simply as Eusebio. His family lived in Lourenço Marques, the capital of then-Portuguese East Africa, and in 1947, when Eusebio was five, his father died. He began his career play-

ing junior soccer barefooted because his mother couldn't afford to buy him even a pair of used shoes. When he was 11, he found an old boot that had been discarded by a member of the Sporting Club Lourenço Marques. Finding that the boot was too tight, Eusebio placed it around the outside of his right foot and tightened the laces. Eventually he was invited to try out for the club's junior team, and since he was in excellent shape from running, playing basketball, and high jumping, he was able to outrun several of the established stars. At the age of 17, he was offered a contract with the club he had so often watched. In America often a player persuaded to sign a professional contract gets a huge bonus. What was Eusebio's bonus? "I got a new pair of soccer shoes, the first ones I had ever gotten. To me this was worth more than money. I cried for hours as I walked around the streets with my new shoes shining," Eusebio said.

Some might say that the new boots had steel in them, for Eusebio had a powerful kick without shoes. With his new shoes, however, he sent shots at goalies that would knock them backward. In his initial game, he scored three goals, and by the end of the season his reputation had spread to Lisbon. Two clubs—Sporting Club Lisbon and Benfica—immediately showed interest. The owners of his East African team felt an obligation to Sporting Club Lisbon since that was the club that had actually been responsible for forming the East African club Eusebio was playing with. Eusebio accepted the offer from Benfica, however. But when he arrived at Lisbon, he found that he was not going to be allowed to play until the Portuguese Federation made a final decision about which team he should play for. For seven months he waited for the decision; finally Benfica won.

On May 23, 1961, he played his first game for Benfica and scored three goals against Atletico. He then went on to play in a World Club Championship game against Santos and scored. Probably his greatest acclaim came during the 1966 World Cup, when he led all scorers with nine goals as Portugal placed third behind England and West Germany. Immediately he was proclaimed the new Pelé. When Benfica came to the United States for a match with Santos (which it eventually lost, 4-0, Eusebio was asked if he considered himself the new King of Soccer. "There is only one King of Soccer," he replied. "That's Pelé. If I can ever be good enough to be the man next in line to him, I will be very proud."

Eusebio finally stopped playing with Benfica after a disagreement over wages, and in 1975 he came to the United States to play in the NASL with the Boston Minutemen, who also had signed his former Benfica teammate Antonio Simoes, regarded by many as one of the finest all-around forwards in Portugal. The Minutemen sold Simoes and him the following year, Eusebio to Toronto and Simoes to San Jose.

But no matter how many goals he scored and how many accolades he received, there are few players in the game (with the possible exception of Pelé) who have received as much punishment as Eusebio. Defenders are unable to contain him, and they use brutal force to try. Eusebio has overcome knee surgery and many injuries to see his name written into the record books; he was named Footballer of the Year in Europe once and Portugal's top player five times.

Ferenc Puskas

Few men have been able to match the success both as a player and coach that Ferenc Puskas attained during his long and brilliant career. Like so many great players, Puskas was born into poverty in his Kispest, Hungary, home. The son of a mediocre soccer player, Puskas was born in 1926, and since he was the second son of the family, he was given the nickname Ocsi (Kid Brother). He always hated the name, and many an opponent would get his goat by calling him that, in an effort to unnerve him. So poor was the family that they could only purchase one pair of shoes. Ferenc was given the right foot and warned not to scuff it, so whenever he was fortunate enough to get near a soccer ball, or even a rag-filled stocking, he would boot the object with his bare left foot. Many years later he said that this was the reason he developed what was probably the strongest left-footed kick in the history of soccer. When he was 15, Puskas joined a local soccer team; and the short, stocky youngster, now with his own pair of soccer boots, was trained not only by his coach but by his father, who saw that the boy did indeed have a good future if he trained hard, lost a few pounds, and listened to instructions.

Puskas eventually was chosen to play for the Hungarian National Youth Team and then was invited to join the Kispest team, where he won wide acclaim. At age 17 he was selected for the full Hungarian National Team and became a steady fixture in the lineup for the following 11 years. He remained with Kispest after the team's name was changed to Honved, and soon the Hungarian style of soccer became the classic of Europe, with its fast-moving attack, its sharp dribbling, and frequent solo runs. The star of the team was Puskas, who played for Hungary 84 times, including two games against England in 1953, in which the Hungarians first ripped the English, 6-3, at Wembley and then butchered the stern English defense, 7-1, in the return match in Budapest later that same year.

In 1956 Puskas, who for the past five years had been the leading scorer in his nation, was on tour with Honved when the Russians took over Hungary. Puskas and a couple of his teammates decided that they would not return to Hungary but would instead seek political asylum. At the age of 30, after playing only occasional exhibition games for a year, Puskas was finally allowed to join the world-famous Real Madrid team in Spain, where he teamed with Alfredo di Stefano to make the Spanish team the best club in Europe. A rule permitting a player who had attained political asylum to play on the national team of his new nation was passed by the Spanish Football Association and approved by FIFA, and immediately Puskas was selected for the Spanish National Team. The only problem that he faced was di Stefano, who had to personally approve all players joining Real Madrid. The year before there had been stories circulating that Puskas had been killed in the Hungarian uprising. Di Stefano had openly expressed shock at the loss of the great player, however, so when Puskas asked to join Real Madrid, di Stefano welcomed him. In the five years he played with Real, he led the Spanish League four times in scoring and easily could have made it five straight. He was tied with di Stefano at 26 goals each when the team played its last game of the regular season in 1961-62. Both players had scored a goal in the first half, and with time running out, Puskas broke through the defense and drew the opposing goalkeeper out of position. He started to shoot at the open net, but at the last minute he passed the ball back to di Stefano, who put the ball into the net to win the scoring title. As the final whistle sounded, di Stefano openly kissed and hugged Puskas. As Puskas explained after the game, "It was deserving that I give him the chance after winning the title so many times as the leading scorer."

In his 84 appearances for Hungary, he scored 85 goals and added another three for Spain before finally retiring as player to accept the task of building the Panathinaikos team of Greece into a European power. In 1971 he led the Greek team to the finals of the European Cup, losing to Ajax of the Netherlands, 2-0.

Denis Law
Many people feel that if Denis Law had not been the victim of so much fouling and the object of beatings even from his teammates in dressing room fights, he could well have been one of the all-time greatest scorers in England. During his long career, he was able to score over 225 goals. But Law let his feelings be known and no matter how big an opponent was, if he fouled Law, then he was in for a battle both on and off the field. Law had been known to challenge an opponent to meet him after the match, despite warnings that he would suffer a beating. Sometimes his opponent would not show up, so Law would go looking for him. Born in 1940 in Aberdeen, Scotland, the son of a trawlerman, Law went to England to play for Huddersfield Town, where he played

for three full seasons until he was sold to Manchester City. Matt Busby, at the helm of rival Manchester United, had been impressed by the man whom he called a will-o'-the-wisp, but he could only offer $30,000 and when Manchester City came up with a better offer, Huddersfield sold him to Busby's rivals. While at Huddersfield, Law was selected during the 1958-59 campaign for the Scottish National Team, a place he held regularly until the conclusion of the 1974 World Cup.

Law played with Manchester City for two years, but after seeing him play, the Italian Torino team offered him a spot, which he took. He scored for Torino but also got himself into trouble with teammates and had a fight in a night spot with an Italian photographer. A year later he was purchased by Manchester United for a fee close to a half-million dollars, and under the guidance of Busby, he established himself as a great star. For 11 years he played with United; but when offered a free transfer, he decided to go back to Manchester City, where he scored a goal that relegated United to the Second Division.

After that game, Law sent a message to United, saying that he was sorry he had to be the man to do it to them, but "if I hadn't taken the shot, I would have hated myself, for I knew that the ball would go into the goal." Those who have known Law throughout his career swear that if any man on his team in the same situation had passed up the shot, Law would have been the first to fight him when they reached their dressing room after the conclusion of the game. Law played a hard game and kept opposing goalies guessing about whether he would head the ball, kick it to the side, or dribble right around them. He was an exciting player and gained the respect of many top coaches from rival teams throughout his playing days.

Steve Bloomer

To look at the career of Steve Bloomer, it is necessary to turn the calendar back to 1892, when at age 17 he made his debut in professional soccer for Derby County and scored his first goal. Before he retired from the game following the 1913-14 season, Bloomer scored 352 goals in 600 league matches besides 28 goals in the 23 international matches he played for England. Derby fans, who were accustomed to seeing some strange-looking players turn up for tryout games, laughed when Bloomer made his first appearance. He was thin, pale and actually looked sick. The first game he played for Derby changed their minds, however, and throughout his career the man who was often called The Ghost played like a giant. When he ended his playing career, he accepted a job as a coach in Germany, but when World War I broke out he was imprisoned, and he set up the first prison-camp soccer league.

An English writer once wrote of Bloomer, "There has never been a player more deceptive in his appearance. He might have been slender of build, but there was steel in his arms and legs." And there was also cleverness in the way he would move, always knowing where both the opposing defenders and his teammates were. If anyone had ever bothered counting assists, the record might have shown that for every goal Bloomer scored, he helped set up two others. Steve Bloomer's name will always live in English soccer history.

Dixie Dean

Born William Ralph Dean but known to his friends as Dixie, Mr. Dean, as he is also referred to, was one of the men who benefited most from the change in the offside rule in 1925 that stipulated that it was necessary to have only two defenders, instead of three, between a player and the goal when receiving a pass. In the 1923–24 season, Dean, who had been born in Birkenhead in 1907, made his English Football League debut with the Tranmere Rovers. As a youngster he had shown great promise, and for the equivalent of about 10 American cents a week, Dixie was signed on. The first year he played only in two or three league games and a few practice matches; but the following season, still under the old offside rule, he scored 27 goals in 27 games before he was sold to Everton at the end of the season. He first played with the English National Team in 1926, scoring 12 goals in five games, while the following year he hit the nets for Everton 60 times in only 39 games.

Opponents found him almost impossible to stop as he would side-swipe them with his brilliant dribbling and send cannonlike shots into the goal from every angle within 20 yards. His head shot was regarded as the hardest in England, and often he would practice toughening his head by banging it on a punching bag. In spite of heavy leg muscles, he had great leaping power, and when he ended his career in 1939 with Notts County, the record showed that in 437 league games he had scored 379 goals while scoring 18 times in 16 international appearances. It was a sad scene in 1964 when players from Liverpool and Everton played a charity match for Dixie, who was destitute; but Dean, who later became a tremendously popular speaker, said after the match, "I today got more out of the game pleasurewise than I put into it." No one interested in soccer history would agree with his statement, however, because for years Dean gave English soccer fans some of their greatest enjoyment.

Jimmy McGrory

When Jimmy McGrory was coaching Glasgow Celtic from 1945 to 1965, he would often criticize one of the team's forwards for not looking for goal chances. And the players listened to him, because McGrory was one of the greatest scorers in European soccer history. When he first joined Scotland's Celtic at age 17 after starring for the St. Roch junior team, the team couldn't find a steady spot in the lineup for him, so they loaned him to Clydebank for the 1923-24 season. After he scored 13 goals, however, he was returned to Celtic and was in the lineup for 408 games in which he scored 410 goals, better than a goal-a-game average over a 15-year span. He was like a hunter as he went looking for the anticipated rebound. He would cut into a seemingly open spot to receive a totally unexpected pass and then with one quick fake and a strong boot he would add another goal to his long list. He was, many feel unfairly, often overlooked as a member of the Scottish National Team, but in the seven games he played for Scotland, he scored six goals. When a Glasgow paper asked him to explain his great goal-scoring ability he said, "There was no secret about my success as a center forward. I played my heart out for the club and was always afraid of being dropped from the squad." During McGrory's years with the team, Celtic had a man who truly can be called one of the greatest forwards in the history of soccer not only in Scotland but in all of Europe.

Honorable Mention
In addition to the above 10 forwards, there are others who deserve mention. **Florian Albert** was named European Footballer of the year in 1967 and had it not been for injuries, he might well have been able to play past the beginning of 1974, when he retired at age 33. He played 75 times for his native Hungary and while playing for Ferencvaros, he was the leading scorer in Hungary for three seasons.

Josef Bican played 19 times for the Austrian National Team and 14 times for Czechoslovakia. When he retired in 1952 at age 39, he had scored over 500 goals with such teams as Hertha, SK Rapid, Admira, SK Slovia, and Vitkovice and with both Austrian and Czechoslovakian national teams. He never had a hard shot, but his curving shots gave goalkeepers nightmares.

Franz Binder scored 1,006 goals in 756 games between 1930 and 1950, but many of his goals came in meaningless exhibition games against factory workers and junior teams. He played for both the Austrian and German National Teams besides with such clubs as Sturm 19, St. Pölten, and Rapid Vienna. When he retired in 1950 at age 39, he became manager of Rapid and led the team to numerous victories.

Hughie Gallacher made 19 international appearances for his native Scotland, and many feel that he was one of the greatest of all Scotish forwards. Standing only 5'6", he leaped higher than defenders six inches taller and was a deadly shot, scoring 387 goals in league competition with such clubs as Airdrieonians, Newcastle United, Chelsea, and Derby. At age 54 he committed suicide.

Lopez Francisco Gento, known as Paco, won 43 European Caps for his native Spain and was a member of Real Madrid's six victorious European Cup teams. Watching him play was an impressive sight. Although he was rather heavy, weighing 190 pounds, he was still one of the fastest left wingers in the game.

Sandor Kocsis was a teammate of Puskas on the Hungarian National Team, and, like Puskas, he defected after the Hungarian uprising in 1956 and played with Barcelona. He led the Hungarian League by scoring three times and scored an additional 75 goals for the Hungarian National Team. He could score equally well with either foot and was also very deceptive. Puskas has praised Kocsis as "one of the best."

Ladislav Kubala won International Caps for Hungary, Czechoslovakia and Spain and was named to the Swiss National Team. In 1969 at age 42, he managed the Spanish National Team. He could play any position on the front line well.

Tommy Lawton came along at the end of Dixie Dean's career to continue the scoring pace for both Everton and the English National Team. In 390 league games, he scored 231 goals; while in 23 matches for the English National Team, he scored 22 goals. Deception and fast play were his trademarks.

Nils Liedholm was a star in his native Sweden, where he played many times for that nation's national team. One year after playing in the 1948 Olympic Games, in which Sweden won the gold medal, he went to play for Italy's AC-Milan and became one of the team's top scorers.

Waldimir Lubanski ended his successful career because of knee problems when he was only 27 years old. But while he was playing for Poland, he was one of the best, sending balls into the net with his head as often as with his feet. A deceptive dribbler, Lubanski could usually be spotted by the two opposing defenders who invariably followed him around the field.

Silvio Piola was a deadly center forward, equally good in the air and on the ground. He played with the Italian National Team 34 times, and the total would have been much higher if World War II hadn't interfered. Piola played with such prestigious clubs as Lazio, Torino, and Juventus; and when he retired in 1951, he had scored over 360 goals, setting an Italian record.

Uwe Seeler played for the West German National Team from 1954 to 1970, winning a total of 72 International Caps. A chunky center forward, he scored a total of 760 goals, most of them with Hamburg, before retiring in 1972.

Branco Zebec was a great left winger before turning his skills to defense, but he still goes down in the record books as one of the most prolific scorers in Yugoslavian soccer history. He played 65 times for Yugoslavia, and on a club level he performed for Partizan and Red Star Belgrade.

Luigi Riva, who played for Cagliari and the Italian National Team, had the knack of accelerating past the fastest defender. Possessing a strong left foot, Riva was considered by many to be the darling of Italian soccer fans. He had outstanding ball control and was able to resume playing after several severe knee injuries.

Giovanni Rivera starred for both AC Milan and the Italian National Team for many years. A small, hard-nosed forward who could also play halfback, Giovanni caused many problems to his coaches with his temper, but when asked how he could stand the abusive fouls of defenders, he said, "The temper I have on the field in fighting back is the same temper as I have off the field. They are my trademarks, and I don't care who likes them or who doesn't like them. That's me and the way I am."

Sandro Mazzola was only six when the 1949 plane crash killed the entire Torino team, including his father Valentino. His mother didn't want Sandro to follow in his father's footsteps but under the often-secret training of his uncle, Sandro became good enough to try out with Inter-Milan. He eventually starred for Inter-Milan, and the Italian National Team. He played for Italy 71 times and was one of the few players who never displayed the hot-headed attitude Italian players characteristically show toward their national team coaches. At the end of the 1975 season, he announced that he was limiting his soccer playing and would start devoting more time to helping young-sters through a series of clinics.

Jimmy Greaves was just 31 when he ended his 14-year career, but in those 14 years, he thrilled the soccer world and devastated both opposing defenders and goalkeepers with deceptive moves in which he would fake them one way and then go in the opposite direction. At age 15, two years before breaking into professional soccer, Greaves scored 114 goals in 54 games in youth soccer and was signed by Chelsea, where he scored 132 goals in 169 games. He had a short stay (10 games) with AC Milan but couldn't stand Italy and returned home to England to play with Tottenham before going to West Ham United. In 517 league games, he scored 357 goals and made 57 appearances with the English National Team, tallying 44 goals.

MIDFIELDERS

The top three midfielders — that vital link between the defense and the front line — seem to be Gunter Netzer, Bobby Charlton, and Alan Ball, although Billy Bremmer also merits mention.

Gunter Netzer

Considered by many to be a real rebel, Gunter Netzer is what a halfback is supposed to be. A fierce defensive player when the occasion calls for it, Netzer is also a deadly scorer when the opportunity arises to attack. Throughout his long career, he has had a history of fighting with managers and teammates alike; and Netzer will never win a popularity poll with players. But with the fans it's another case, as he has drawn crowds even after he left his native West Germany to play for Real Madrid.

Born in 1944, Netzer began playing schoolboy soccer when he was 10 and appeared twice for West Germany's National Schoolboy Club. In 1963 he was signed to play for IFC Mönchengladbach, and two years later made his first appearance for the West German National Team. Many people blamed him for West Germany's 1-0 defeat at the hands of England in 1966, however; and bowing to the pressure, manager Helmut Schoen, who didn't respect him much anyway, dropped him from the national side. Two years later Netzer was back in good graces but then was quickly back in the doghouse. After being fouled during a match in Chile, he kicked the player who had committed the foul and was sent off the field. He openly criticized Schoen for not letting him play enough, and some fans begged for his appearance on the national team while others backed the national team manager. Although he was still playing for Mönchengladbach and he was having great seasons, the word was out. Opposing players knew that to get him out of the action, all they had to do was mark him closely and he would fight both mentally and physically and often get kicked out of the game.

With vast business interests, Netzer was making enough money, and in 1972 at age 27, he decided that he was through with West German soccer and went to Real Madrid. Schoen was incensed at Netzer's desertion, but Netzer said he didn't care what Schoen believed — it was his life and he was doing what he felt was best for him. Schoen didn't pick him for the 1974 World Cup, and Netzer has told close friends that he really cared but was too proud to beg for a spot on the team. Summing up his career once, he said, "Football has been great for me, but there's more to life than playing the game. I like living."

Bobby Charlton

The most sought-after schoolboy star in English soccer history is Bobby Charlton, the same player who won a record 106 International Caps for his native England. Charlton was discovered by Joe Armstrong at 14 years old, when he was ripping apart the opposition from his midfield position with East Northumberland Schoolboys in Newcastle. Before Joe had a chance to report his findings, however, every club in England had been directed to sign Bobby Charlton. But Armstrong's determination paid off. A few minutes after he got the youngster over to Manchester United's offices, Charlton was under agreement to play for United. The team's boss Matt Busby handled the difficult negotiations since the younger Charlton had been accompanied to the office by his father, a tough business negotiator. "As long as I live I will never regret the decision to sign for Manchester United," Charlton has said repeatedly on banquet circuits, where he has certainly become the best-liked English player.

Busby didn't want to rush his new find into major-league action, and for the next two years kept him in a central league and on United's youth teams. Then at age 17, Bobby was put on the main team, and in his debut he scored two goals against a team called Charlton Athletic. The two goals didn't impress Busby, however, who told the press that Bobby still had a lot to learn about the game. Busby let the youngster ride the bench until he felt that the time was right and then inserted him into the starting lineup. For the next 17 years, Bobby Charlton was a Manchester United and English National Team hero. He played 606 games for United and won the title of European Footballer of the Year in 1966.

In 1973 he played his final League game to accolades that poured in from everywhere. Pelé paid tribute to him, and Uwe Seeler called him the best midfielder he had ever faced. All the praise gave one the feeling that with the retirement of Charlton an era had ended. What made Charlton so good? There are many reasons, but probably the major one was his dedication to the sport. As he said, "For me I always trained hard and played hard but clean. Of course, there were times when I would make a foul some say was uncalled for, but if I ever did it with the intention of hurting someone, I wouldn't have stayed in the game I love."

Alan Ball

When Alan Ball first started playing professional soccer, the opposing players would look at him and laugh. He was only 5'6", weighed less than 125 pounds, and would cry after he lost a game. At the start of the 1975-76 season, Ball still cried after a defeat, and he still didn't resemble a full-time professional soccer star, but Alan Ball was a star both on the field and off, devoting much energy to helping youngsters get the proper start in soccer. The first team to take a chance on Ball, who once admitted that his father forced him to play professional soccer, was Blackpool, which sold him to Everton after four seasons. Five years later Everton transferred him to Arsenal.

Ball's involvement in football started under his father's guidance when the youngster was only four. At first his career seemed to be heading the same way as his father's, a man who never made it to the top. At age 14 he tried out for the Lancashire Boys but was taken off the field after only 20 minutes because it was felt that he was too small. But his father kept pressuring him; and a year later he tried out with Bolton, which also rejected him because of his size. Lesser men would have quit, but Ball respected his father's wishes and kept working out. At age 17 he was finally signed by Blackpool.

Asked to defend his insistence that his son be a pro soccer player, the elder Ball once said in an interview; "Now I feel more guilty about what I was doing to him then than I felt guilty in those days. Maybe I should have let him go into something that he wanted to do. But when I look at him and see what he has accomplished, I am proud not for myself but for him. Alan is a wonderful son."

With his deceptive style of play and his ability to bounce back off the turf after being tackled, Ball has won 71 International Caps and played in over 400 league games. He is also one of the best-loved players, although if necessary he will resort to retaliation against an opponent who is roughing him up. "If he knocks me down legally, then I don't complain, but if he does it illegally more than once, then I will react on my own," Ball explained after he was ejected from an international youth game when he was 18, and he has maintained that policy throughout his long and brilliant career.

212

Billy Bremmer

Another great European halfback is Billy Bremmer, considered one of the best ball-control artists from the midfield area. Bremmer was capped 86 times by his native Scotland and played one of his best seasons in 1975 before he and three other players were banned from the Scottish National Team for becoming involved in a brawl in a Danish restaurant regarding payment of a bill. But although he was often cautioned for some hard fouls, on the field Bremmer was the man to whom both Scotland and his English team Leeds United always looked for either slowing or speeding up the pace of a game. Standing only 5'6", Bremmer never backed off from an opponent and if fouled, instead of retaliating, he would often execute deft moves to make the man who had fouled him look like a fool as Bremmer headed for the goal area.

When angry, however, Bremmer would argue with referees and even punch opponents, and he drew many fines from both the English FA and his Leeds team. Some members of the Leeds management even wanted him to go to another club. He has been paid many compliments from friend and foe alike, however, and after Bremmer was named English Footballer of the Year in 1970, English National Team manager Don Revie said, "It is a constant mystery to all of us how he has been able to survive in the game. I think that more than anything else it is his dedication and character which has [sic] carried him through. He is a skipper [captain] with perfection unlike most others, and although there are times when I have had to manage against him, I still will always respect the man for what he has done for the game." Before his suspension from the Scottish team, Bremmer had played for his nation 86 times, while with Leeds he had performed in over 500 games.

Honorable Mention

Josef Bozsik is one of several European midfielders also worthy of note. He was a Hungarian wing half who would organize the team's attack or defense with just one quick glance at the opposition's formation. Between 1947 and 1962, he played for his native Hungary in over 100 international games and was one of the key men responsible for leading the Honved team to its numerous titles. He was, interestingly enough, also a member of the Hungarian National Assembly.

John Charles is one of the most gifted players ever to come out of Wales. The center halfback scored over 250 goals in England and in Italy, where he joined Juventus after beginning his career with Leeds United. After Juventus, he went back to Leeds and then back to Italy to play for Roma before ending up his career with Cardiff City. He was selected 38 times to play for the Welsh National Team.

Mario Coluna, when playing for the touring Benfica club in 1966, displayed to American soccer fans why he was one of the top midfielders in the game. Quick to change his pace to fool defenders, Coluna was one of the key players in Benfica's success in the 1961 and 1962 European championships. He played 73 times for the Portuguese National Team and finished his career with Lyon in France.

Duncan Edwards was only 21 in 1958 when he was killed in a plane crash along with several teammates from Manchester United. But despite his youth, he had already established himself as a top player, making his debut for the English National Team when he was only 18. He was a great ball handler and often completely undermined the opposing team's defense with his accurate passing.

Gerhardt Hanappi retired in 1964 at age 35, but while an active player was one of the best midfielders in the game. Hanappi was the top defensive player in a game if plans called for the halfback to go back, and he was a great goal scorer if the midfield was on attack. At the time of his retirement, he had been capped 96 times in his native Austria, where he starred for both Wacker and Rapid Vienna.

Josef Masopust won the title of European Footballer of the Year in 1962 at age 31. Throughout his career, in which he won 63 International Caps for Czechoslovakia, Masopust was an attacking wing half with outstanding balance. He was able to shake off tackles and keep coming in on goal. Although he played for Union Teplice, Dukla Prague, and in many all-star games in Czechoslovakia, he ended his career in Belgium.

Vicky Mees had the ability to anticipate the opposition's plays from his halfback position and is one of the most respected players in Belgian football history. He was capped by Belgium 68 times and missed only a few games in the 20 years he was with Antwerp.

Igor Netto was the man in the center of the powerful midfield of the Soviet National Team, with whom he won 57 International Cups. He was a member of the gold medal Soviet Olympic team in 1956 and two years later helped the Soviets win the European Nations Cup. He won five titles with Spartak Moscow, for whom he played 367 games.

Gyorgy Orth started playing professional soccer with the MTK team of Hungary when he was 15 years old. Because of a severe leg injury, he was forced to wind up his career when he was only 27; but while he was active, he would interweave with the other halfbacks and could play both sides equally well in addition to attacking from the center half position. He was selected for the Hungarian National Team 17 times and was injured when he was tackled by an opponent who stepped on and broke both his legs.

Valeri Voronin was 21 when he won his first cap for the Soviet Union as a brilliant midfield attacking wing. In nine years while playing for Torpedo Moscow, he won 69 caps for the Soviet Union and captained both Torpedo and the Soviet National Team on numerous occasions. With much still to offer, he was injured in a car crash in 1969 at age 30 but worked hard to come back. He succeeded, but the man who twice was voted the top player in the Soviet Union, called it quits after a few games, saying that if he couldn't play the way he felt he should, then it was time to leave the game for good. It was a sad day when he went to Lenin Stadium for his farewell, and over 100,000 fans turned out to pay him homage. Not only was Voronin in tears, but many spectators wept openly in tribute to the man they had come to love so much.

Billy Wright was only 5'8" but was a giant in English football history, having played 105 games, in 90 of which he also served as the captain of the national team. He began his career with the Wolverhampton Wanderers and ended his soccer affiliation as manager of Arsenal. The short, fat, blond man was a believer in physical soccer but often said, "If I have to foul a man, I won't do it in order to get the ball." He played in 490 league games, and in 1952 at age 28 he was named English Footballer of the Year.

DEFENDERS

Defenders are probably the most unsung heroes of the soccer scene, and although many goalies have been lauded for making a great save or not allowing the opposition a score, fans have been slow to react when a defender pulls the ball off the goal line. Among the greatest European defenders throughout the years have been such players as Bobby Moore, Franz Beckenbauer, and Giacinto Facchetti.

Bobby Moore
"Bobby Moore is my representative on the field. He is responsible for seeing that the plans we have worked on are carried out." Sir Alf Ramsey made this statement before England took the Wembley pitch for the 1966 World Cup championship game against West Germany.

During the match, Moore certainly fulfilled his duties admirably; and after the overtime game had ended and England ruled the soccer world, Moore stepped up to the Royal Box and accepted the Jules Rimet Championship Trophy from Queen Elizabeth II.

Many people consider Moore the greatest defender in the history of soccer. Unlike many other defenders who, if unable to stop a player legally will resort to violence to get the ball away and stop the play, Moore is known as the gentleman player. He is endowed with talent, anticipation, and a fierce desire that causes him to rise early in the morning to practice, a habit he has continued even after becoming a member of the NASL's San Antonio Thunder in 1976. Moore practices hard whether in the midfield spot or as a strict defender, and with sheer work and dedication he has become probably the greatest defender of all time.

Pelé battled Moore many times while Moore was a member of the English National Team and Pelé was starring for Brazil. As he described him, "To me he is the ideal defender who cannot be fooled by anyone. I know that Bobby makes a mental note of everything you do against him and if you revert the next time to the same tactics, he's going to stop you — not by fouling but with his great technique. To me he is the greatest gentleman I have ever encountered on the soccer field. . . ."

Born in East London in 1941, Moore, like many other youngsters, got his start in soccer playing in the schoolyards. For a time it looked like the bigger English clubs would ignore him as they picked some of his teammates and opponents for trials but not him. Then came a call from West Ham United for a tryout. West Ham was impressed but wanted him to get more experience; so Moore was put on one of the team's farm clubs, where he also represented the English National Youth Team 18 times. In 1958 he signed on as a member of the West Ham team and made his international debut as a member of the English Under-23 team. His first full cap for England came at age 21 while England was playing Peru in Lima. Since then he has won 111 caps and has been team captain on many occasions.

After playing a record 545 times for West Ham, he accepted the dual role of player-manager for Fulham and led that team into the finals of the English FA Cup against his old team, West Ham United. Fulham lost but not because of Moore, who despite his age raced all over the penalty area covering loose West Ham players.

Before the start of the 1970 World Cup in Mexico, the English National Team was visiting Bogotá when Moore was arrested and charged with stealing a bracelet from a department store. The entire soccer world was shocked, and although Moore was later cleared of the charges, his bitterness was evident when he said, "I am innocent. I don't know why they picked on me." The reason they picked on Moore was evident, however. His opponents wanted to upset him emotionally so he would not play well in the World Cup. Fortunately, they were not able to accomplish their goal, as Moore did play well even though England did not win the title.

Franz Beckenbauer

"As Beckenbauer goes, so goes West Germany" best describes the immense importance of Franz Beckenbauer, who is a close second to Bobby Moore as the all-time defensive hero of European soccer. Beckenbauer, called Herr General Franz by many, was born in 1945 and developed in German Youth soccer, becoming one of the most sought-after youngsters. After playing the center-half position, Beckenbauer became the modern-day attacking back, which won him numerous honors. In 1965 he won his first full International Cap for West Germany, and 11 years later he had accumulated 83 caps. Why is Beckenbauer the man who gets credit for a West German victory but also is blamed when the team loses? Perhaps the 1974 World Cup title game in which West Germany defeated the Netherlands, 2-1, can best illustrate the reason.

The Dutch were dominating the action in that game with their attack, and the West Germans were constantly having to race backward to defend. Beckenbauer was the free safety back, after taking the ball away from such players as Johann Cruyff and Johann Neeskens, he started coming up on the attack. The tide turned, and the West Germans carried the game to their Dutch opponents. The game plan hadn't called for these tactics, but when Beckenbauer started his aggressive ball carrying, manager Schoen was not angry. Beckenbauer had perceived the situation and carried out a change in tactics that he felt would be effective. Once again, as he had proven throughout his career both with the West German National Team and with Bayern-München, he was right.

"Winning that World Cup was for me the high spot of my career," Beckenbauer said, and he once admitted that he was disturbed that Bayern-München, his team, had even considered an offer of $750,000 from AC Milan for his services in 1966. With Beckenbauer playing the free safety back, Bayern began a run of three straight European Cup titles in 1974, and he was a key man in the title games just as he had been for the past 10 years.

Some say that he plays the game like a great chess master, to which he once said, "I play the game to win, but if I lose I accept defeat and plan for the next game which I will be playing in. Soccer is a sport and not the end of the world. It is something I enjoy doing and the game has been good for me." It is this attitude that has made Beckenbauer one of the best-loved and, of course, one of the most successful players of all time.

Giancinto Facchetti

It was indeed a sad sight to see the Brazilian forwards beat Giancinto Facchetti time and again when the Italian National Team met the Brazilians at the Yale Bowl in the American Bicentennial Soccer Cup in 1976. Obviously Facchetti was feeling his age and the pressure.

Throughout a long career, during which he became the most-capped player in Italian soccer history, Facchetti, with his speed and determination, always had been the defender given the task of taking on not one but often two of the top opponents. Deadly in the air with his 5'11" frame, Facchetti joined Inter-Milan in 1960 when he was 18 years old and became one of the very best players of all time. He won his first full International Cap in 1963 against Turkey, and in the years that have followed, he has won 75 more.

So popular has he been that for fear of having its offices destroyed by irate fans, Inter has been forced to turn down many lucrative bids for his services from other Italian clubs. Facchetti has often been called indestructible, but at this he laughs. "Just look at my body after a rough match, and then say that I don't feel pain. You can't tell me that I or any other player doesn't feel the pain both physically or mentally. I have never learned how to accept defeat graciously. It was hard for me to accept defeat when I played in school soccer, and it has been hard for me to accept defeat throughout my days with Inter-Milan and with the Italian National Team." Better than any others, those words probably best sum up Facchetti's fierce desire for success. He is a tiger against the opposition and one of the most feared defenders in the game.

"I love playing soccer for Inter," has been his pat answer to those who ask him why he keeps on going strong. "When the day comes when I no longer am able to do the job, I will hang up my boots."

Honorable Mention

There have been many other top defenders in the history of European soccer whose fans might well claim that they are the best.

Jimmy Armfield, for example, was captain of the English National Team 14 of the 43 times he represented England, and he played a total of 568 league games for Blackpool from 1954 to 1971. Armfield was an attacking defender. He overlapped with the halfbacks and would take the ball down the wing. As soon as he shot or lost the ball, however, he would head back and usually be able to join the other defenders to stop a counterattack. In 1971 he became manager of the Bolton Wanderers.

Orvar Bergmark broke into Sweden's first division when he was only 17 and represented the Swedish National Team 94 times. Some of his greatest games, however, were played while a center back with Roma in the Italian First Division. After ending his playing career, he became manager of the Swedish National Team in 1971. He held that position for two years before he was replaced, but many feel that Sweden's ability to gain a spot in the 1974 World Cup was the result of groundwork laid by Bergmark.

Jackie Charlton was a steady fixture for Leeds United and England's National Team for 20 years. Unlike his brother Bobby, he was not an immediate success in the game as a schoolboy; hence, he enjoyed being with his friends, many of whom were not cut out to be soccer stars. Nevertheless, when Leeds offered him a tryout, he went along and ended up signing with the team. He played a total of 629 games and was named to England's National Team, where he competed 35 times, including the 1966 World Cup championship game against West Germany at Wembley. In 1973 Charlton, who had many run-ins not only with opposing players but also with his own managers and teammates, took the job as coach of Middlesburg and led the team to the Second Division title.

Roger Marchie was one of the dominant figures in French soccer from the time he first broke into the game at age 17 with Reims. A fierce tackler who often got into brawls with opposing players, Marchie played for the French National Team 63 times before retiring in 1959 from the Racing Club at age 35.

Ladislav Novak was a man who positioned himself where he felt the play was coming, and a forward who entered into his area quickly found that Novak was a fierce tackler and it was impossible to go around him. With a defensive header, he could send the ball toward the midfield line. He starred with Dukla Prague and represented the Czechoslovakian National Team 75 times, playing in three World Cup competitions before retiring at age 34. He was later named coach of the Czechoslovakian National Team.

Sir Alf Ramsey, best known for his skill as a manager, must still be mentioned as one of the best defenders in the history of English soccer. In only nine years of league soccer, Ramsey, who was knighted by the queen, played with Southampton and Tottenham Hotspurs and represented England in 32 international games. He was a fast thinker and a great reader of the game. Nicknamed the General, Ramsey was considered by many to be one of the best players and coaches in the game. In 1966 he led England to the World Cup championship. After England failed to gain a spot in the 1974 World Cup, however, he was relieved of his duties as coach and many expressed the feeling that the game has passed Ramsey by. Sir Alf, with great dignity, never responded to his critics.

Puck van Heel was one of the heroes of Dutch soccer immediately after World War I, and he played for the Dutch National Team 64 times, making his first appearance at age 21. Van Heel was a creative wing back, who would often come up a few yards, wait for a defender to try to get him, and then quickly flick the ball back to the goalie as he broke up the middle. Throughout his career, he played with the ever-powerful Feyenoord FC.

Ray Wilson, at age 31, was a member of the winning English World Cup team in 1966, but he never showed his age. He was very quick and one of the most creative defenders in English soccer history, playing for his nation 63 times. While he had played for such teams as Huddersfield Town, Oldham Athletic, and Bradford City, it was at Everton that he made his successful tactics work, captaining the team to the FA Cup in 1966. In all he played in 405 league games and 63 games for England; and at age 34, slowed by injuries, he hung up his boots.

All these players may some day be overshadowed by others, who may be starting to kick the ball around or playing in little league or in schoolboy soccer. But even after others come along, these men will remain among the most respected players in European soccer history.

CHAPTER 15

South America's Best

In the history of South American soccer, there have been many top forwards, halfbacks, and defenders, but in the area of goalkeeping an absence of talent has been evident. Three goalkeepers—Gilmar of Brazil, Ladislas Mazurkiewicz of Uruguay, and Pedro Zape of Colombia—have excelled, however, while two other goalies—Gatti of Argentina and Cejas, an Argentinian who starred in Brazil—also deserve special mention.

GOALKEEPERS

Gilmar

Unlike many other Brazilian goalies, Gilmar had the ability to handle the cross—a play in which a high pass is sent in front of the goal in order for a teammate to head it past the goalie—even though he was unfamiliar with it. Many of Brazil's top scorers make goals with sharp dribbling and passes. The European style of play, however, often calls for the ball to be crossed. As a result, Brazilian goalies were considered out of their class when it came to handling such a maneuver. Gilmar, born in 1930, proved them wrong.

"If you are not familiar with a type of play, then you study movies and work in practice with other members of your team in an effort to get ready for a match in which a European opponent will be attempting to beat you on a cross. I felt that this talk about us not being able to handle crosses was absolutely wrong," Gilmar said, when he came to the United States in 1966 for an exhibition series against European teams Inter-Milan, Benfica of Portugal, and AEK of Greece.

A product of the vast junior system in South America, in which top-flight youngsters are trained and then allowed to take part in workouts with the main team they are under contract to, Gilmar, who was born dos Santos Meves, came to the attention of Brazilian National

Team selectors when he was only 16 and playing with a junior club run by Jaguaquara. For the next 10 years, he slowly developed to where he was regarded as the best in Brazil, a distinction that most great goalies in Brazil had been unable to attain until they reached age 30. In 1954 Brazil had been disappointed with its goalie Castilho, who yielded four goals to Hungary in the quarterfinals. The following year the selectors decided to give the job to Gilmar, who made several trips to Europe over the following three years to watch the style of play he would be facing in the 1958 World Cup in Sweden.

The long trips and practice sessions paid off in a big way, as Gilmar came up with shutouts against Austria, England, and the USSR in the opening round, and then blanked Wales in the quarterfinals. In the seven games he played, he allowed only four goals. Four years later in Chile, he was even sharper, coming out without hesitation to pull a corner kick or a cross out of the air. When the tournament was over, Brazil was again the winner. Gilmar had allowed five goals in six games, but he was also credited with 73 saves. Four years later, in England, at age 36, Gilmar was a bit heavier and a lot slower. Brazil was eliminated in the opening round, and he yielded six goals in three games.

During his career, he appeared for the Brazilian National Team 100 times and yielded 95 goals. Out of all his international performances as goalie, Gilmar walked off the field a loser only 14 times. He also scored impressive international club victories, winning the World Club championship for Santos and for the Corinthians.

Ladislas Mazurkiewicz

Some claim that from 1961 to 1967, Ladislas Mazurkiewicz was the best goalkeeper in South America. He performed brilliantly for the Uruguayan National Team, and for Atletico Mineiros and Penarol. Of Polish parentage, Mazurkiewicz was a product of the youth development program. Although he was in a nation where foreign influence is often scorned, he was able to overcome obstacles and eventually develop into a dynamic, high-leaping, and quick-diving keeper. As Pelé, whom he faced many times, described the Uruguayan keeper, "No matter what move you tried to put on him, and although you felt that you had completely fooled him, you could rest assured that somehow he would get himself back into some position to give him a better-than-even chance to come up with the save. The stop of a shot he made against me in the 1970 World Cup was a classic example of a goalie maintaining his balance and position although at first being faked out of position."

While he was with Penarol, at the age of only 21, Mazurkiewicz scored a shutout over Real Madrid in one of the 1960 World Club championship games—a feat that was even more remarkable in light of the final statistics, which showed that he had stopped 17 shots. Because Uruguayan soccer salaries are small and because many other teams in South America desired his services, Mazurkiewicz was sold to the Brazilian club Atletico Mineiros.

Pedro Zape

While in school, Pedro Zape, who was born in 1951 in Colombia, participated more in track and field than in soccer. But after leaving school at age 16, he joined one of the Millonarios' junior teams and with his grace and agility soon became one of the club's highly regarded junior goalies. His first assignment was as the backup keeper, but eventually he took over as the regular starter. When the famous Pelé-led Santos team toured Colombia, a game was arranged between Santos and Millonarios, Zape was assigned as starting goalie.

"I am not ashamed to admit that I was scared out of my mind," Zape later remarked.

> Here we were a pretty good team but still by no means equal to what Santos was with all their stars. The game started and immediately Santos put on the pressure and Pepe put a shot past me. I figured that this was going to be a runaway for them. Then we scored, and late in the first half they came back with another goal to go ahead, 2-1. Pelé came in on me all alone as he beat a couple of our defenders and let loose with a bullet drive, which I was able to punch out from the left corner. He got the rebound and put it low to the right and I dived and caught it. The crowd roared, and Pelé came running to me. I figured that he was going to hit me, but instead he patted me on the back. In the second half, we scored and gained a tie, and after the game Pelé and I talked. He offered me many compliments, and of course I was like in a dream world.

A year later at Yankee Stadium, Santos again played Millonarios. In the game, which ended as a 2-2 tie, Pelé again failed to score against Zape. For 1½ minutes in the second half, the large crowd stood in disbelief as Zape stopped back-to-back shots by Lima, Pepe, and Pelé and then booted the ball almost 75 yards down the field. After the game, Pelé again complimented Zape, and he predicted that the Colombian national keeper would one day be the best of all South American goalies. Indeed, in 1975 with Zape in the nets, Colombia was able to place second in the South American Championship tournament.

Gatti

The main reason Gatti of Argentina's Bôca Juniors never achieved the international recognition that his backers feel he deserves is his wild, often reckless type of play, and his showmanship. But those who have followed his career will testify that underneath the theatricality Gatti is a sincere person, dedicated to the game but also fun-loving on and off the field. In a game between Bôca and River Plate, for example, Gatti was supposed to be in the nets for Bôca. When the time came for the Bôca team to take the field, Gatti was nowhere to be found. Then suddenly, with one of his hangers-on blowing a trumpet, out raced Gatti—dressed in a full tuxedo. Only the referee's insistence made him return to the locker room and change into a regular uniform; and Gatti was bitter, telling the reporters who had raced to the dressing room after him that as far as he was concerned, so long as he wore the proper boots, he should be able to play no matter how he was dressed. His antics have included making a tip-over-the-bar save and then hoisting himself up to sit on the crossbar. Once, during a game against the Santos team, after making a save on a difficult shot by Pelé, he slammed the ball full force against the goal post, caught it on a fly, and then boomed the ball downfield. He has also been known to come out to midfield in an attempt to stop an opposing forward, make a legal tackle, and then head back for the goal.

Cejas
Cejas was a great success with River Plate and a few other Argentinian teams before he came to Santos, where he developed into one of the best keepers in Brazil. Because of arguments with Argentinian officials, however, he was dropped from the 1974 World Cup team and fell out of favor with the national association. Like Gatti he is a fun-loving person; on occasion he could be seen giving Pelé advice on how to play goal.

Leao of Brazil, Miguel Sandoro of Independiente, and Chile's Adolfo Nef of the Colo-Colo club are South American goalies who will be worth watching in the future.

FORWARDS

Alfredo di Stefano
Although some of his greatest moments on the soccer field took place while he was playing in Europe, Alfredo di Stefano, who was born in Argentina, also achieved distinction on the fields of South America. Born on July 4, 1926, in Buenos Aires, di Stefano was introduced to soccer by his father, who in addition to being a bus conductor was a fairly good amateur center forward.

His father was a stern teacher when it came to giving the youngster soccer lessons. "I was right-footed, so my father didn't let me play unless I would shoot the ball with my left foot," he once related at a press conference when asked why he had one of the most powerful left-footed shots in the history of soccer. When he was 15 years old, his mother insisted that soccer was not the way for Alfredo to make a decent living, and she demanded that he become a farmer. His father decided, however, that his child was not made to work in the cattle fields; and the youngster joined the district team, Barrancas, which during 1940 remained unbeaten for 43 games. Veteran River Plate manager Lubrowski discovered the 17-year-old di Stefano while watching a junior game and signed him with River Plate as an amateur. So powerful was the River Plate organization that many of its amateur players were substitutes for regular substitutes and although working out with the team, never saw any action. Di Stefano got a break, however, when officials of the Huracan team saw him practice and took him from River Plate on a one-year loan. This pleased both the River Plate Club and di Stefano, because he started working his way into the regular lineup. One year with Huracan was all River Plate would allow, however; the team recalled him, and he signed a professional contract. Playing the center-half position, but often in front of some of the team's forwards, di Stefano was with River Plate for three seasons; and in 1947 he led the Argentinian League in scoring with 27 goals as the team copped the league crown. In 1949, after playing seven international games for Argentina, he and many other top players from his nation joined the Los Millonarios club of Colombia. "They kept asking me why I was leaving them," he explained years later, "and I told them that no one in his right mind turns down 15 times as much money as River Plate had been paying me. I didn't care what the fans or the officials thought. I had myself to worry about, and the offer was one that would have been almost impossible to turn down."

For 30 months he played with Millonarios, and the team ran away from the rest of the Colombian League, capturing two titles and finishing as the runner-up the other season. In September 1973, he got restless, however, and this time he headed for Real Madrid. At age 27, he said, he felt that he could achieve greater recognition and status in Europe than in South America. His fame did indeed spread rapidly throughout Europe and eventually di Stefano became the man the fans came to see.

When Real Madrid first signed di Stefano, protests from virtually every other club in Spain made headline news. Barcelona claimed that it had been promised his contract by Millonarios, and for months the dispute, one of the worst ever in the Spanish League, kept growing until the president of the Colombian team declared that he had promised di Stefano to Real Madrid after the Spaniards had seen him

225

on one of their many South American tours a couple of years earlier. With Real Madrid, di Stefano was the master of the team, winning the European Footballer of the Year award in 1957 and again two years later. In 1958 he helped Real begin a run of five straight European Cup titles. In all, he played 510 games for Real Madrid and scored 428 goals.

Di Stefano was, however, a difficult person. He was a loner, and his teammates and managers alike found him hard to reach. When Puskas joined Real Madrid, di Stefano rarely spoke to him. When Brazilian star Didi came onto the scene, di Stefano openly criticized him as unable to fit in with Real Madrid's style of play. Some people consider di Stefano's unfriendliness a façade and a shield against the invasion of his privacy. Others, however, have attributed it to conceit.

In 1964 at age 38 he went to Spanish League team Español, where in 81 games he was able to score only 19 goals. Two years later, at age 40, he called it quits.

Although finished as a player, di Stefano was far from finished in soccer. In 1968 he returned to Argentina and joined the technical staff of the Bôca Juniors. His main duty was to look for promising players; and he was so successful in this venture that one year later he took over as coach of the team, slowly molding it into one of the most entertaining clubs in South America. Di Stefano had always hated defensive systems such as the 4-3-3 (see chapter 20) and made Bôca an attacking team, sending six men into the attack at all times, with two additional midfielders coming up as soon as their teammates reached the other team's penalty area. Di Stefano was no pleasure to play for, and many a top-name player, showing age, quickly found himself off the team. Occasionally club officials threatened to keep a player over di Stefano's objections. But the wild man from Argentina, as some called him, would slam his fist on the desk and walk out unless his demands were met. At the end of the season, Bôca tied its final game on the road with River Plate and won the championship. Di Stefano was offered a new contract; but instead he headed back to Spain, where his wife and six children lived, and signed to coach Valencia. After leading the team to the league title, he held an open press conference and shocked all those attending when he said, "The credit is not mine. The players only carried out my instructions, but they did the work. They had great determination and enthusiasm, and I played not so big a role in their success." Alfredo di Stefano had certainly changed.

Carlos Alberto

Carlos Alberto was another great South American halfback. Born in Guanabara in 1944, he was an outstanding youth player before signing a professional contract with Flamengo when he was 17. Two years later, at age 19, he played his first full international match for Brazil and was a steady member of the Brazilian National Team until its 1970 World Cup win. His remarkable play in the 1970 World Cup was particularly astonishing considering that for six months before the competition he had been out of action with a serious leg injury that threatened to end his career.

Alberto, who joined Santos when he was 22, was often a problem to the heads of the Brazilian National Team; and in 1966 he was not included on the World Cup team for disciplinary reasons that were never really disclosed. "Let's just say that there were many things that led up to their action. I still say that they considered me guilty before I had a chance to explain my side of the story," he said in an interview late that year.

Zito
Many people feel that Zito, whose real name was Jose Elki de Miranda, was one of the most versatile halfbacks in the history of Brazilian soccer. When he first broke in with Taubaté, he did so as a fullback; but after only a few games, the 17-year-old was moved to the front line. Over the next two years, he played eight different field positions before he finally moved on to Santos in 1951 at age 19. With Santos he played as a wing half and became one of the very best with unmatched speed, deception, and passing and tackling abilities. Zito was with Santos until his retirement in 1967, and during that time he played a total of 706 games and won 53 International Caps for the Brazilians. In the 1958 World Cup competition, Zito played the right halfback spot and set up two of the goals made in their victory by his teammates. Four years later, he came roaring in from the right side, sped to the other side to take a pass, and scored one of the goals in the title game in which Brazil defeated Czechoslovakia, 3-1.

"They didn't bother watching me and I had a free area to roam into," Zito later explained. "I would have to have been crazy not to move into the opening. My teammates knew where I was going, since I had practiced that move only a few weeks earlier; but the opposition didn't pay any attention, so that is where I went. It feels great to score a goal in a World Cup final because then you know that everyone else in soccer knows that you are one of the few who have achieved that honor."

Clodoaldo
Another great South American halfback was Clodoaldo. Born in Aracaju, Brazil, he was orphaned shortly before his sixth birthday. As a

child he played street ball and skipped school, and his guardians never paid much attention to the way he was living. A Santos official spotted him when he was 15 years old, playing with a tennis ball against the wall of a stadium. The official went over and talked to him, and he was placed on one of Santos' junior teams. When he was 17, he was brought up to the varsity. He won his first International Cap in 1969 as Brazil defeated England in Rio de Janeiro, 2-1, and he continued to win caps until early 1974, when he was dropped from the national team. People still talk about his goal against Uruguay in the semifinals of the 1970 World Cup in Mexico. He took the ball near his own penalty box, leaped over a defender who was attempting a sliding tackle, and crossed the midfield line by dribbling around two defenders. He then sent a 20-yard pass to Tostao and, running full speed, he received a return pass, trapped the ball, and fired it into the back of the Uruguayan net.

"I will always remember that goal because it came with no planning at all. My teammates didn't know what I was doing, and neither, to tell you the truth, did I. I just kept coming and Tostao spotted me, and I made the perfect trap and boomed the ball home. It was certainly the most enjoyable goal of my career," he later said.

Honorable Mention

Pelé is, without question, the greatest forward in the history of soccer, but many other South American forwards have played brilliantly as well. Some of the men whose fans consider them second only to Pelé are Friedenreich, Garrincha, Labruna, Leonidas, Tostao, Rocha, Brindisi, Cubilla, Cubillas, Gallardo, Jairzinho, Rivelino, Munante and Pastoroza.

Artur Friedenreich broke into professional soccer with the Germania club in Brazil in 1910 and won his first International Cap for that nation four years later when he was 22 years old. In the days when scoring was more difficult because the old offside rule was in effect, Friedenreich was the most prolific scorer in the game, recording 1,329 tallies in just over 1,450 games. He was the man opposing goalies feared most because of his fierce drives with either foot, his great headers, and his powerful half-volley shots.

Garrincha, born in 1933 as Manoel Francisco dos Santos, was known as the Little Bird. Few men in the history of the game have been able to duplicate his speed or his ability to pass the ball perfectly while going as fast as he could. In 1972, at age 39, he retired from the game because of injuries to his right knee, but while he was active, he played

60 times for the Brazilian National Team. He was a member of the Brazilian World Cup champion teams in 1958 and 1962; and during his long career he played with Pau Grande, Botafogo, Corinthians, Flamengo, Bangu, Portuguesa Santista, and Olaria. The most remarkable part of the Little Bird's career was that at age five he could hardly walk because of a badly deformed left leg. Through rehabilitation and hard work, however, he went on to become one of the greatest forwards in South American soccer history.

Angel Labruna was born in 1918, and few men have been able to duplicate the grace, agility, and ball control that this Argentinian star had. For 19 years, until he was 41, he played for River Plate and scored 489 goals for the team, many of them strictly on his own as he would roam his area picking up loose balls, diving to intercept clearances, and driving in rebounds.

During his career, he also played with such teams as Platense, Green Cross and the Rampla Juniors, and at age 40 he won the last of his 36 International Caps for his nation.

Da Silva Leonidas played for 10 different Brazilian clubs during his lengthy career. From the time he joined Havanesa in 1929, at age 16, he played as a center forward. He won the first of his caps in 1932 and played for Brazil 23 times. In the 1938 World Cup, he was the leading scorer, with eight goals. His greatest league seasons were spent with Vasco Da Gama, Botafogo, and Flamengo. In 1950, at age 37, he retired and began coaching in the junior program, which was becoming popular in Brazil.

Tostao, born in 1947 as Eduardo Gonçalves Andrade, was only 26 when he was forced to retire because of a detached retina. Only three years earlier he had amazed the experts when he was able to play for the victorious Brazilian World Cup Team after surgery for the condition. While playing with both Cruzeiro and Vasco da Gama as a center forward, he used the quick, deceptive moves necessary for playing that position well. In the all-too-brief time that he appeared on the soccer scene, he made the most of his chances, certainly making him one of the outstanding forwards in the history of South American soccer.

Pedro Rocha began his career in 1959 at age 16 with Penarol, in his native Uruguay. Three years later he was selected as one of the forwards for the Uruguayan World Cup team. Standing 5'11", he was an agile and graceful performer with a deadly header and a powerful kick with either foot. In 1966 he scored a crucial goal against Real Madrid, and as a result, Penarol won the World Club championship. In late 1970, he was sold to São Paulo FC of Brazil.

Miguel Brindisi was born in 1951 in Buenos Aires, and although he played top junior soccer, he said that he had no intention of playing professional soccer until he was 19. Along came the strong Huracan club, however, which signed him at age 18, despite a late appeal to the youngster's parents by the rival River Plate team. He became a member of the Argentinian National Team when he was 20, at which time River Plate again sought to purchase him, offering Huracan $250,000. Huracan turned down the offer for the fleet-footed forward and in 1973 sold him instead to France's Valenciennes. The Argentinian Football Federation held up the sale for nearly six months but finally allowed the purchase and transfer to go through.

Luis Cubilla was born in 1953 and had a stormy career, shifting from club to club after he signed his first pro contract when just 16. He ended up with Penarol and devastated the team's opponents. In Penarol's 1961 World Club victory over Benfica, he scored two goals in his team's 5-0 win. He won his first International Cap in 1961, and by the beginning of the 1976 season he had won 43 caps. His over-the head scissor kick is one of the best in the world, and he can shoot balls into the net from seemingly impossible angles. In 1968 he was sold to Nacional and retained his past form, leading that club to many important victories.

Teofilio Cubillas is regarded as practically a god in his native Peru. Born near Lima in 1951, the son of a peasant, he signed with Alianza, where he displayed grace and confidence as he raced unafraid toward the goal. So popular was he in the European tour Peru made in 1972, that the club received offers from 27 clubs for his services. The Peruvian government, however, declared that he could not be sold. "The decision of the government not to allow me to be sold made me feel very good," he said later that year. "I felt then that they really wanted me."

Alberto Gallardo, one of Cubilla's teammates, was born in 1954. At age 17, he signed with Alianza and won his first cap when he was just 19. He is a strong winger, able to play right past defenders, and in just eight years, he had already established himself as one of the greatest South American forwards.

Jairzinho, born Jasir Ventura Filho in Brazil in 1946, is probably one of the greatest goal-finishers in the history of South American soccer. His cannonlike kicks, following long rushes down the wing, have made him the kind of powerful all-around forward that every team so desperately needs. But throughout his career, he has habitually baited officials, and, as a result, early in 1975 he drew a six-month suspension while playing in Europe. He made his first international appearance for Brazil in 1964 and scored a goal against Portugal. He was playing the left wing spot with Botafogo and doing well in it at the time; but when he was switched to the other side of the field, he really came into his own, with devastating power and flawless ball control.

Rivelino was 32 in 1976, when he led Brazil to the championship in the American Bicentennial Soccer Cup. For years he has been the mainstay of the Brazilian National Team and he has performed brilliantly with the Corinthians. His swerving free kick is the deadliest in the game, and his sharp passing, shooting, and dribbling make him a triple threat to opponents.

Juan Munante joined the Universitario Club of Peru when he was 17 years old and two years later won his first International Cap. A clever ball-control artist, he proved his skill on the Peruvian National Team in 1975, when that nation won the South American title. He has been rated one of the best forwards in the history of his nation, and his most outstanding trait is his ability to change direction often, leaving his opponents behind.

Omar Jose Pastoroza, once called a wild man, was an average player in junior soccer; but after he was signed by Independiente at age 17, he matured into the tough, no-nonsense forward needed in Argentina's rugged style of play. A tough competitor, he won his first cap in 1969, when he was 19. In 1972 he was one of the men responsible for stopping the Mini-World Cup in Brazil, when he became angered at a defender for constantly fouling him. A fight ensued, and 18 players became involved. When the referee finally regained control, Pastoroza was sent from the field, drawing a two-month suspension. As a result of the suspension and punishment imposed on him by the Argentinian Federation, he was dropped from the World Cup Team in 1974; but after Argentina's poor performance, he was put back in the lineup, where, it appears certain he will remain for many years to come.

DEFENDERS

Djalma Santos, Gerson, Hector Chumpitaz, and Brito have been the top four defenders in South American soccer. These four men all played the attacking style of soccer and on many occasions scored vital goals that affected the outcome of the games.

Djalma Santos

Djalma Santos was a powerful right fullback with a deadly downfield kick, and one of the most reliable penalty shooters in all of his native Brazil. Born the son of impoverished parents, he lost his father when he was just 10 years old. Several backers took him under their wings and signed him with the Portuguesa de Desortos club when he was just 16; but Santos was not ready to assume the duties of a full-time starter and would often ride the bench during his early days. He spent the better part of two seasons playing only in practice and exhibition games. His big break came when he was sold to the fine Palmeiras club, where he immediately worked his way into the starting lineup. His hard tackling invariably pleased the crowds, and in 1952 at age 23, he won his first International Cap for Brazil. By the time he ended his career with the Atletico Paranaense club late in 1969, he had accumulated 100 caps.

"Soccer made the difference for me between becoming a nobody and a somebody," he wrote in the Brazilian sports journal. "With so many good youngsters coming into the game at the time I did, I was just fortunate that there was someone who took an interest in me not only as a player but as a person. Winning the World Cup titles in 1958 and again in 1962 are thrills that are hard to explain. Unless you are able to achieve them, then you cannot know the feeling. Soccer gave me many friends, and I hope that one day I will be able to offer to the people of Brazil something in return for all the glory they gave me."

Santos did have much to offer, however. He spent many hours in the junior coaching movement, teaching youngsters the basics of defending against top players.

Gerson

It was only fitting that one of the goals the Brazilians scored in their 4-1 win over Italy in the 1970 World Cup final came from Nuñes de Oliveira Gerson. Throughout his career Gerson, who was considered an unorthodox defender, amazed fans and often angered coaches. One of his favorite plays was to come downfield, send a shot in on goal, and then come in for his own rebound instead of retreating as the play called for.

When Gerson wasn't coming up on the attack and following his own instinct, he was a hard-nosed defender who was also one of the most accurate passers in the game from a range of 30 to 50 yards. Often he would cut down toward the wing spot and pass to a teammate he spotted on the far other side of the field near the opposing team's penalty area. The Gerson pass was a trademark of many a Brazilian National Team, and there are many who said that Gerson could pass better than any fullback in the history of soccer—better even than many English defenders, who traditionally were experts in this pattern of play. During his club career, he played for Canto do Rio, Flamengo, Botafogo, São Paulo, and finally for Fluminese; and he played on the Brazilian National Team 84 times. In 1973 he retired from the game because of a broken ankle and became the coach of several leading junior teams in Brazil. Despite the frequent arguments he had with his coaches, he is recognized as one of the best defenders in Brazilian soccer history.

Hector Chumpitaz
Hector Chumpitaz of Peru was a reckless player who would sometimes drive his teammates and opposition crazy with his unorthodox style of play. Standing only 5'5", he had great spring in his legs as a result of high-jumping in high school; and this enabled him to jump high above much taller opponents. Many coaches in the junior movement in Peru were unwilling to take a chance on a fullback who was so short, and for a long time it seemed that none of the big teams in the nation would be willing to sign him. In 1963 Chumpitaz, then 17, was signed by the powerful Universitario Club, but for two months it looked like he would never break into the lineup because of his stubborn attitude. The team's coach wanted to switch him to halfback but Chumpitaz fought the move. He eventually won his point, however, and went into the game as a substitute. In his first effort with Universitario, he scored a spectacular goal, heading away a pass in his own goal area, trapping the ball, and then taking it all the way downfield past six defenders before firing a 12-yarder into the far right corner of the net. His direct free kick had an uncanny swerve to it, often twisting into the corner of the net at the last possible moment. He was also a master at finding the slightest opening in the other team's defensive wall and sending a shot between several men into the net. In 1964, at age 18, he made his debut with the Peruvian National Team, and over the next 10 years was picked to represent his nation 56 times.

Brito
Maria de Brito, who was born in Ilho de Governador in the state of Guanabara, in Brazil, was not a player easily beaten. In 1970, when

he was 30 years old, many of the teams Brazil was to play in the World Cup in Mexico figured that their greatest chance for success was to work on this old man of the defensive unit. That, however, proved to be their greatest mistake, because Brito demonstrated to the soccer world how an orthodox fullback is supposed to play.

Throughout his career, Brito was a tough player. His tackles were swift and clean, and his ability to roam the entire backfield area often enabled the team's other fullbacks to come upfield on attack. In covering distance, he was not one of the fastest defenders in the game, but like a chess master he was able to pivot swiftly and cover loose men by getting there before his opponent did. As a youngster, Brito wanted to play halfback, but his slowness forced his junior coach at Flamengo to put him in the backfield; and eventually he developed into one of the best backfielders in the nation, winning a total of 54 caps before calling it quits at the end of the 1973 season. From playing he joined the coaching ranks, and at the start of the 1976 season he was also in charge of the top scouting program run by Flamengo. He is a popular speaker, and he also spends a great deal of time working to rehabilitate children.

"I have no financial worries," he once explained, "but I do worry about some of the children who will give up on themselves unless they get help. I know that soccer taught me not to give up. If some of my earlier coaches had not worked with me so hard, I might have given up my dream."

All these players are among the best in South American history, and although there are undoubtedly fans who will disagree, the achievements of these men should be recognized and respected.

CHAPTER 16

United States Stars

Although soccer has been relatively slow to catch on in the United States, there *have* been American soccer stars. When Pelé came to America in 1975 and signed with the New York Cosmos, a reporter at a press conference held in Boston asked him who would be the first truly great soccer star in America. Without hesitation, Pelé replied, "I don't know who it will be, but as you should know, the United States has had a few good goalies over the years, and I see that here in Boston you have a pretty fair one [Shep Messing], and I've seen one or two others around the league who are Americans and who can handle themselves pretty well in the goalie department."

GOALKEEPERS

The two goalies who emerged on the professional scene in the early 1970s can play with most clubs throughout the world. They are Shep Messing, born and raised in the New York area; and Bob Rigby, who was born in Pennsylvania. It was sheer chance that both ended up with the Cosmos in 1976.

Stan Chesney
Long before Messing and Rigby ever dreamed of playing professional soccer, however, another goalie made his name in American soccer. His name was Stan Chesney, and at 6'4", he commanded the attention of opposing forwards as he ventured out of the penalty area and challenged them in any battle for a loose ball. After playing an exhibition game against him, many top European clubs tried to get him to come to their country.

Chesney was an all-around athlete who once tried out for the old Boston Braves of the National Baseball League. During the late 1930s and early 1940s, he also played basketball and football pretty well, but his first love was soccer.

One of Chesney's closest friends was Phil Fox, a man generally regarded as the top soccer referee in the game at the time and a man who later went on to become a top official in the early days of the National Basketball Association. As Fox described Chesney,

> Stan was a clever and exciting goalie who, despite his large size, was very agile. He would be able to handle all the high shots to either corner; and when a team would attempt to send low drives into one of the corners, it seemed that Stan was able to get there in time to make a diving save. He also had a strong downfield punt, and there were few opposing forwards who would try to dribble around him. His size frightened them away. I remember that the New York Americans, whom he had been playing for at the time, had just played an exhibition game against a team from Scotland, and after the game the coach of the Scottish team came over and asked Stan if he wanted to play in Scotland. Stan said he would think about it; and the owners of the New York team were eager to make the sale, not only because of the money they would get, but because of the prestige they would gain by being able to sell an American goalie to a club in a nation as strong in soccer as Scotland was.

But when three different clubs in Scotland made offers, Chesney himself decided that he didn't want to leave the country and the bids were rejected. To me, I feel that in the days when a goalie would receive almost no protection from a referee, Chesney was the type of man who could not only take care of himself but also was the perfect type of goalkeeper.

Shep Messing

Shep Messing is one of the top goalkeeper's in the game today, despite his reputation as an eccentric. As a child, Messing played a pretty good game of baseball and football, but in high school he started playing soccer. He wasn't much good at any of the field positions, so he started practicing as a goalie. He attended New York University, where he won All-American honors, but after several disputes with the coaches and occasional blowups with teachers, he transferred to Harvard, where he again won All-American soccer honors, becoming one of the few college players in history to achieve the distinction of earning All-American awards at two schools.

Messing was selected to play with Harvard in the NCAA finals in Miami in 1972 and walked off with the Most Valuable Player Award. After the college season was over, he was selected to play with the U.S. team in the 1972 Olympics in Munich; but after a brief flurry with team officials, many of whom he felt were overlooking eastern players in favor of those from St. Louis and from the West Coast, he was left to ride the bench.

But if there were louder complaints than Messing's, they came from some of the teams he competed against in pre-Olympic trials in the Caribbean and North American areas. In a game against Jamaica, for example, the United States held a 1–0 lead late in the game when a penalty shot was called against the Americans, giving the Jamaicans an ideal opportunity to tie the score. Suddenly, as the crowd roared, Messing called time just before the shooter was set to boot the ball. He raced out to his opponent, pulled down his own shorts, and then ripped the shirt of his opponent as well as pulling down the man's pants slightly. The referee could have ejected Messing from the game for such an action but instead just cautioned him. The unnerved shooter booted the ball wide of the net, giving the United States the victory and the eventual spot in the Munich Games. It was just one example of Messing madness; another time he showed up to a semi-professional game, carrying his large pet snake in a box.

One of the things that makes Messing a top-flight goalie is his balance, which he is able to maintain despite the oncoming charges of many a forward. Various European clubs have offered him a chance to play abroad and with the help of his father, an attorney, he has evaluated all of the offers.

In 1973 the now-defunct Olympique de Montreal team of the NASL drafted Messing, but before he could sign with the team, he was rescued by the Cosmos, who were seeking a local boy to man their nets. Messing played in only one game his first season, but the following year he won the starting spot after a bitter battle with Poland's Jerry Sularz. Messing and the Cosmo brass were never on the best of terms, however. He wanted to play every game, but the Cosmos felt that some of his actions off the field were too much for them to cope with. The last straw came when Messing posed in the nude for the centerfold of a magazine. The Cosmo officials released him, and after the start of the 1975 season, he was signed by the Boston Minutemen. Messing was named the starting goalie in the Minutemen's fifth game of the season and went on to record six shutouts, 140 saves, and a league-leading 0.93 goals-against average. At the start of the 1976 season, Messing was again the top goalie, but financial troubles were plaguing the Minutemen. When Bob Rigby of the Cosmos broke his collarbone and was sent out for the remainder of the season, Messing received a phone call he never believed he would get and returned to play for the New Yorkers. The first match he played in was against the Rochester Lancers, and he posted a shutout and completed the season as a member of the Cosmos.

In a serious mood, a mood that now dominates his personality most of the time, Messing reflected,

No matter what level you are playing at, goalkeeping requires an extraordinary amount of intensity and concentration. Being in the headlines, posting the lowest goals-against average, or the night life reputation doesn't mean anything unless I do the job in the goal. I just love to play this game because of the pressure. I say let that come first and the other things later.

The 6-foot, 170-pounder, who was born in late 1949, has held the position of physical education teacher and soccer coach for a leading high school on Long Island and has been responsible for starting many youngsters on the right track in soccer.

I look at the opportunities that youngsters are now getting as they start in soccer [he said] and I can't help but wonder how many potentially good goalies were denied the opportunity of developing their game because at the time they were getting interested in the sport there was no one there to help them along the way to becoming a pretty good player. That is why I want to give to the young players of our day the chance to develop with some help.

Bob Rigby

Bob Rigby has gained a worldwide reputation with his skillful goalkeeping in international competition. As Vladimir Agopove, coach of the Moscow Red Army team commented in 1974 after the Soviets had met Rigby's Philadelphia Atoms in an indoor soccer game, "This Rigby clearly is the most brilliant American soccer player I have seen. He is talented and he is exciting. He is good enough to play soccer at any international level."

What Agopove said has been reiterated often by Rigby's fellow Americans, fans and players alike.

Rigby loves playing goal, but it wasn't always that way. He remembers when he wanted to be a forward or to play any position on the field other than goalie. His coach insisted that he play goal, however, and it was one of the most rewarding changes made in American Soccer.

As Rigby said,

I wasn't that big for a basketball player and I didn't particularly like football; so when several of my friends asked me to play soccer while I was in the sixth grade at Ridley High School, I decided that I didn't have anything to lose. The coach started me out as a midfielder, but I guess I didn't do that well and then I was moved to goal. I didn't enjoy it at first, but then I began to realize that there was more to being a goalie than just catching the ball. I could always catch the ball, I guess because I had played basketball.

From high school, Rigby moved to the popular soccer-oriented school of East Stroudsburg State College in Pennsylvania's Pocono Mountains. After winning All-American honors twice in a row, he was selected to play for the East in the first annual College Soccer Senior Bowl. Rigby was outstanding in the game, turning back several dangerous threats by the opposition; and he so impressed the scouts on hand that in 1973, when the Philadelphia Atoms was formed and Al Miller, a successful college coach at Hartwick, was named the coach of the new franchise, Rigby was the number-one collegiate draft choice. In his first season, he virtually rewrote the record books of the NASL as he posted an incredible 0.62 goals-against average, and the Atoms won the league championship in their initial season. During the season, Rigby posted six shutouts.

One of the reasons he was so quick to adjust to the rugged NASL competition was the hard work he had put in during the previous two summers when, along with several other college players, he traveled to England to work out with some of the better smaller teams in a series of clinics. Tony Field, who later joined Rigby as a member of the Cosmos, recalls the time he first encountered him.

> I was running some clinics with Southport, and a group of American college players came to us and worked out with us. Right from the start I realized that Rigby was more than just an average goalkeeper. He had the potential then to become a fine keeper. True enough, he was rough around the edges, but the makings were there, and he kept working hard. I followed his career even before I came to America, and I can honestly say that I wasn't surprised how he developed in just a couple of years.

Rigby was selected for the NASL All-Star team in his first season, and although his goals-against average rose to 1.10 in 1974, he still commanded the respect of opposing forwards. He was then picked for the U.S. National Team and earned the admiration of thousands of fans for his performance against the Italians, making 28 saves in the United States' 0-0 deadlock in Rome. Rigby put on a brilliant performance, coming out of his nets to stop numerous breakaways, diving to either side to cut off twisting shots, and leaping high over the bar to grab high drives. In December 1974, he was invited as a guest instructor to a training camp in England run by English National Team goalie Ray Clemance. The following year Rigby had a fine season although his average went up to 1.60, but the Atoms were having defensive problems and Rigby cannot be blamed for the team's failure to win either the league title or a divisional crown. At the end of the 1975 season his reputation had earned him a chance to play in the Superstars competition, and Rigby, who spent many hours practicing and building up the upper part of his torso, made a great bid to pull off the title, finishing fourth behind Kyle Rote, Jr. By the time of the competition, he had also become financially secure, as the Cosmos purchased him from the Atoms.

Gene Olaf
Another goalie worthy of mention is Gene Olaf, who during the 1940s and early 1950s guarded the nets for the famous Brooklyn Hispaño club. Olaf was probably one of the best line goalies in the game, rarely coming out of his nets but able to go to either corner with equal effectiveness. Excellent at stopping penalty shots, he would pretend to go one way and then, as the player touched the ball, swerve to the other side of the net, making the save more often than not. After retiring from soccer, Olaf joined the New Jersey State Troopers and became head of the organization.

The man who replaced him in the Hispaño nets was radio-TV broadcaster Scott Morrison, who remembers working with him.

Gene, no matter how much team pressure was being put on him, never panicked. I remember seeing him play a game against a touring English team. They must have fired 45 shots against him, and Gene handled all but one. After the game, he was visited by the manager of the other team and was offered a contract but said that he didn't want to leave the United States. I feel that he definitely must be one of the top keepers in the history of American soccer, and if he had played in Europe, he would also have received great recognition. As far as line goalies are concerned, I don't think there ever was an American keeper to match him either before he played or after he retired as an active player. After giving up the game to go into law enforcement, he spent a great deal of time in the junior leagues in New Jersey, teaching youngsters how to play goal.

FORWARDS

Freddie Shields
In the late 1930s and early 1940s, the Scots Americans were one of the dominant teams in U.S. soccer, and opposing forwards were driven crazy by the fullback play of Freddie Zibrowski Shields, a graduate of Panzer College. Shields would roam the defensive areas as a free safety, hustling from one side of the pitch to the other, and it was almost impossible to dribble around him. His goal kicks covered three-quarters of the length of the field, and he was selected many times to play on the U.S. National Team. When asked once why he didn't stay put in the backfield as other fullbacks at the time did, Shields replied, "I get bored staying in one spot, and I know that I have as much speed as the other team's forwards, and I can also cover a great deal of room going sideways."

Harry Keough

Another great fullback was Harry Keough, who later coached St. Louis University's great teams of the 1960s and 1970s to NCAA championships. Keough played with the Simpkins team of St. Louis and was an attacking fullback who would venture up either of the sidelines and then attack with a powerful kick and a strong shot with his head. He was a member of the U.S. World Cup team and made many trips abroad. Not only did he become familiar with the various styles of play employed around the world, but he gained insight into top-flight coaching and made St. Louis University's Billikens the most dominant collegiate team in U.S. soccer history.

MIDFIELDERS

Over the years, the United States has had several top midfielders. Men like Johnny Althouse, Charles Altemose, Billy Gonsalves, Walter Bahr, and Phil Slone were the equals of many top foreign players. These five players were sought by foreign clubs but chose to stay in the United States, and they continually devoted time to promoting the game both at the college level and in the junior movement.

Johnny Althouse

Johnny Althouse emerged on the scene in the early 1930s, fresh out of Grover Cleveland High School in New York City. A dominating speedster who had learned the game from top foreign instructors at the school and played in the limited junior movement at the time, he was one of the heroes of the U.S. team that competed in the 1936 Olympic Games in Germany. Many call his performance one of the greatest games ever played by a midfielder, as the United States dropped a heartbreaking 1-0 decision to Italy. A constructive halfback, he never yielded ground in the vital midfield area. He often tackled opponents and came right up from a sliding tackle to race past an oncoming defender. Althouse will be remembered by many for the way he could head a ball, bouncing it off his head like a cannonball. Throughout his amateur career, he scored many important goals in top-flight competition.

Charles Altemose

Charles Altemose was a distinguished collegiate player at powerful Muhlenberg College in Allentown before he went on to prominence with the Philadelphia Germans—one of the better teams in the nation during the early 1940s. More than an attacking halfback, Altemose was the type of player who could fall back quickly on defense and then strike from a counterattacking position, often heading the ball to himself several times as he drew out his opponents. With a swift pivot, he would then be gone to midfield, where he would direct one of his accurate passes to a waiting forward for a sudden score. Although no official statistics were ever kept of the number of assists that he made, some old-timers guess that the number would be around 500.

Billy Gonsalves

Billy Gonsalves has been called by many the greatest American player of all time; but this would not be a fair judgment since, as Pelé himself said, no one should be called "the greatest" because different positions require different patterns of play and separate tactics. During the late 1920s and early 1930s, many people called Gonsalves the Babe Ruth of American soccer. He was raised in the Portuguese community of Fall River, Massachusetts, and because of his upbringing, his soccer style often resembled that of some of the top players in Portugal. In his early days as a forward, he was awkward; but once out of the high school, he developed rapidly. Playing in a strong amateur league, which many felt was actually a semiprofessional league, he developed an exciting style of play and was capable of running nonstop for the full 90-minute game. From Fall River he came to New York, where he joined the Brooklyn Hispaños, at the time the best club in the eastern United States. Under his leadership, many a local junior player was introduced to the game; although at the time, the only juniors playing soccer were youngsters whose parents had either played in one of the many amateur leagues in New York or had just come from Europe and wanted their children to carry on the soccer skills that they had been taught by their parents.

While playing for the Brooklyn team, Gonsalves was often invited to play with the various all-star teams that hosted touring foreign teams, and three times he accompanied the New York All-Star team to Europe and Latin America. Gonsalves's main task was to play a lone-man position between the other two halfbacks and the three defenders, and he did this with perfection. If the play called for him to go outside to cover one of the wings, he would do so without hesitation; when spotting a man free before the fullbacks, he would quickly go to challenge him, make a hard shoulder tackle, and usually take the ball away as soon as he touched it.

> I have seen many a top player in my time [said Phil Fox]. I did not see Billy in his prime, but even at the twilight of his career he was still a domineering force as he would be the man his team looked for and also the man who would be the leader both on and off the field. If he felt his team was moving too quickly, he would slow the pace; but whenever he did slow the pace, he was still able to size up a situation and react quickly should the

other team gain control of the field of play. His ability also to hasten the pace of the game when the situation called for this type of action would see him at his best as he would work the give-and-go and often be the first man upfield, even ahead of the regular forwards on his team. He had a powerful kick which he could connect with from some 30 or 40 yards out, but also the gentlest of taps, which would drive a goalie crazy should Billy be in the position of receiving a feed-through pass near the other team's goal. Billy may not have been the greatest of all U.S. players, but he certainly was one of the most exciting halfbacks ever to play the game in the United States. He was admitted to various all-star teams, and throughout his playing career and later his work with the junior development, he was a true credit to the world's most popular sport.

Walter Bahr

Some people feel that Walter Bahr was one of the top halfbacks not only in the United States but in the world. He played a strong role for the United States in its incredible 1-0 victory in the 1950 World Cup against England, as he was the man who stayed close to the great English stars. His play in that game was an inspiration to many who got to know him after his playing days were over. Admitted to the U.S. Soccer Hall of Fame in 1976, Bahr was responsible for turning Penn State into a collegiate soccer power. His players were among the best-conditioned college soccer players; and as coach of the Nittany Lions, he aided in the development of many top players such as his own son Chris, who played with the Philadelphia Atoms. Bahr has made numerous appearances at clinics, where he has often spoken about conditioning.

Before a team even starts kicking the ball around and getting set plays formed, it is essential that each and every player on the squad be in the best physical condition possible, since this is the basic fundamental of becoming even a fair player. Too often coaches ignore this one basic requirement, and as a result no matter what types of plays they are able to get their men to execute, they have failed to get from each individual player his maximum performance. I have always stressed the physical conditioning aspect of soccer, and it goes back to my early days as a player. I was instructed, often against my own wishes, to continue a strong physical fitness program, and it certainly paid off in the long run. One of the reasons we were able to beat the English in 1950 in Brazil was that we were able to keep running throughout the full match. Otherwise, I am sure they would have run right past us. To me this was the greatest thrill I have ever experienced in soccer—a thrill that sent shivers through me when the referee sounded the final whistle and we, to the amazement of the entire soccer world, had done the impossible of beating the great English team.

Phil Slone

Phil Slone came out of St. John's University in New York—a school never known for developing top soccer players. But with hard work, a solid understanding of the game, and the fearless, adventurous spirit of a roaming midfielder, he became one of the greatest halfbacks in the history of U.S. soccer. When the great original Hakoah Vienna team settled in the United States in the late 1930s, it was short a few top players, and the team searched frantically for American stars in order to maintain the prestige the team had enjoyed while in Europe. Phil Slone had been doing quite well in semiprofessional soccer, and he was given a tryout under the careful eyes of some of the greatest names in the Hakoah management. He impressed everyone with his long runs down the wing, his sharp long-passing, and his ability to tackle hard but clean; and he was signed. Hakoah's prestige continued to grow, so did Slone's, and his playing enabled his team to win countless exhibition games and various tournaments. Slone was the son of American parents who at first were opposed to their son's participation in the "alien" game of soccer, but the youngster continued to practice hard and rewarded his followers with many fine performances on both the local and international levels.

Joe Gaetjens

Joe Gaetjens's name will live long in American soccer history, because it was he who scored the goal that gave the United States its 1-0 win over in England in the 1950 World Cup. Along with such players as Arnold Oliver, Charlie Ernst, George Nenechk, Jimmy Wilson, Razzo Carroll, Kyle Rote, Jr., and Al Trost, he will be recalled years from now as a top forward.

Born in Haiti, Gaetjens played amateur soccer in the New York area and was a devastating force in games played on makeshift fields in Central Park and rocky pitches throughout the city. As was the case with many top foreign players, Gaetjens never signed a professional contract abroad, but when he was 17 he signed his first pact in the United States. A popular crowd pleaser with his brilliant running, dribbling, and passing, Gaetjens was selected for the U.S. team when only 19 and immediately was placed in one of the three front positions the Americans were utilizing at the time. The story of Joe Gaetjens did not have a happy ending, however. In the late 1960s, he returned to his native Haiti and was never seen again. According to some reports, he had been arrested as a traitor, while other stories reported that he had been executed for trying to start a revolt against dictator François (Papa Doc) Duvalier.

A committee was formed to locate him or at least determine what had happened to him, but its efforts were fruitless. The Cosmos even played a charity game to raise money to search for him, but still no one knows or is sure if Gaetjens is alive or dead. Many a defender who played against his skillful moves found it hard to accept that Joe would never be seen again and Kurt Lamm, executive secretary of the USSF, said,

> I know that for years we have been trying to locate him. I think it would have been truly fitting that Joe would have been on hand to see our group run the American Bicentennial Soccer Cup. I played with and against him, and I can honestly say that there were few men in soccer who could match his determination. I remember one particular game when he was tackled three times enroute to the goal, but he kept his balance and even got off the ground with the ball firmly in his possession and went in to score a goal. His play was of the utmost. Although often fouled, he never displayed a temper, and instead of trying to fight the foe who had fouled him, would make him look foolish with a tricky maneuver on the next play. He was like a man who had eyes in back of his head, and his short passes with any part of his body were like the soccer textbook come alive.

Arnold Oliver

From his first international appearance for the United States in 1929 until his retirement as a player, Arnold Oliver was one of the best forwards in soccer and became one of the most capped players in the United States. A skillful center forward with a strong head shot and a deadly half-volley shot, Oliver, who was born in New Bedford, Massachusetts, was one of the stars of the American Soccer League, a league he joined when he was 24 years old. In his early days at New Bedford, he was the outstanding high school player three years in a row before leading the New Bedford Defenders to the National Amateur Cup Championship in 1926. After playing with such teams as Hartford, J and P Costa, New Bedford-Providence, and the powerful Fall River aggregation, he turned to coaching in New Bedford and at the Institute of North Dartmouth, Massachusetts, where he compiled an 80 percent winning record. In 1969 he was elected to the U.S. Soccer Hall of Fame for his playing and coaching achievements. During his playing career, he never stopped pounding away until the ball was in the net.

One event in his career is particularly well known. The New Bedford Defenders were engaged in a bitter struggle against a New York-based all-star team in a special challenge match, and with 15 seconds left, Oliver scored the lone goal of the match. He raced into the goal after the ball had already entered the nets, and in a joyous moment of triumph, he booted the ball against the back of the nets no less than five times as the whistle sounded ending the contest. "It was a rare show of emotion for me," he said at a press conference following the match. "Many thought until then that I had no feelings. Not everyone who scores a goal has to jump up and down all over the field, but to score a goal at a time like this did strange things to me."

Charlie Ernst

Charlie Ernst won the top goal-scoring award of the American Soccer League in 1937 and 1940, while playing with the Baltimore SC. A hard-driving forward who could control the ball through a maze of traffic, Ernst was a hard worker during a match, often controlling the action of the front line with his change-of-pace dribbling, his give-and-go passes, and his sharp boots. He was still an active player at age 37, and when asked the reasons for his success, he said, "To me the challenge of trying to beat a smart defender is one of the best feelings I have. If you are able to get around a defender who is not skilled, then you might score many goals but inside you still have a somewhat empty feeling. Give me a good defense to get around, and I'll be at my best."

George Nenechk

George Nenechk came out of collegiate soccer at Temple University as an inside left, but while playing for many years in the eastern leagues during the 1930s, he developed into a strong center forward. Because of his agility, he was able to move all over the front line, accepting the challenge of the opposition and making the proper moves. While at Temple, he was the top player in the country for two straight years, but while making the adjustment to the center forward position, he had some anxious moments as he could no longer rely on his speed alone. Speed was the critical factor at that time; but he soon found, to his displeasure, that there were many defenders able to match him step for step. Many coaches would have told him to forget about being a pro player, but the men behind him at such clubs as Brookhattan let him work his way slowly into their plans, and he rewarded them with key goals many, many times.

Jimmy Wilson

Jimmy Wilson was another top forward in the early 1930s, and his style of play for the powerful Bethlehem Steel Company team was responsible for many victories over visiting foreign teams. As Phil Fox recalled, "To see Wilson match his skills against some of the top defensive players who would come over to this country with their invading teams was a pleasure and proof that an American-born player could succeed in the sport."

Razzo Carroll

Razzo Carroll, who starred in the late 1930s and early 1940s with such teams as the New York Americans and Brookhattan, had one of the hardest shots in the game. He had a devastating though seemingly careless style of play, and he was able to go right between two and three defenders, which made him one of the most feared competitors in the game.

246

Kyle Rote, Jr.

Kyle Rote, Jr., seemed to have been destined to follow in his father's footsteps and be a top American football player. While attending high school in Dallas, he continually won honors not only in football but also in baseball and basketball. Almost every major football college sought him and he selected Oklahoma State. Before enrolling, however, he went to England, where he became fascinated with the game of soccer—a sport that at the time was alien to Texas. After an injury at Oklahoma State for which he was forced to undergo knee surgery, he decided to leave the school and enroll at the University of the South in Sewanee, Tennessee. No athletic scholarship was involved, and Rote went out for soccer. For the next three years, he starred on the team and attracted the attention of the NASL's Dallas Tornado. Many criticized the club as just out for publicity when it drafted Rote in the annual collegiate soccer draft, and indeed, the well-built youngster, who once played soccer to get him ready for football, was not an instant success, riding the bench and just watching. But in 1973 he became a Tornado regular and set a fast pace, winning the scoring title with 10 goals and 10 assists. He became Rookie of the Year and was selected for the U.S. National Team. A rugged forward who is not afraid of making contact with a defender, Rote became an inspiration to the thousands of youngsters throughout America just learning the basics of the game. At the start of the 1976 season, he once again had to fight his way into the starting lineup, but the same determination that carried him to consecutive victories in the Superstars competition in 1975 and 1976 saw him once again placed in the starting lineup.

Rote has had a continuing interest in education and as evidence of this, he began theological studies in 1973, which he hopes will one day carry him into the ministry. "I feel that sports is only one part of life, and I feel that I have a great deal to eventually be able to offer to youngsters and others," he said.

Al Trost

Another top forward is Al Trost, who is equally able to hold down a leading midfield position. Born the youngest of six sons in 1949, Trost started to become a legend in the St. Louis area soon after learning the game when he was only five years old. St. Louis has always been considered a strong soccer area, but Trost soon became the best of the many players who later joined NASL's St. Louis Stars. Through his experiences in the game at Holy Rosary School, at St. Englebert, at St. Philip Neri, with a local amateur team, and then finally with the powerful Billikens of St. Louis University, Trost developed into one of the most feared and respected players on the American soccer scene. The Billikens voted him their most valuable player three times, and

1. Steve Ralbovsky of the Skyhawks slips the ball under this late-diving goalkeeper. Timing is essential for goalkeeper technique.

2. Kyle Rote, Jr. of the Dallas Tornado successfully passes the ball as Ramon Moraldo of the Aztecs attempts a sliding tackle.

3. George Best successfully foils a tackle as Aztec teammate Bobby MacAlinden rushes in to assist.

4. Obstacles come when you least expect them, as this Los Angeles Aztecs player discovers, about to tumble over a San Diego Jaws player.

5. Denis Law of Scotland.

6. Gerd Müller of West Germany.

7. Johann Cruyff of the Netherlands.

8. Sandro Mazzola of Italy.

9. George Best attempts to divert his opponent in order to carry the ball around the other team's player.

10. John Mason of the Los Angeles Aztecs attempts to intercept a ball being carried by a Tampa Bay Rowdies player.

11. Rivelino of Brazil.

12. Jairzinho of Brazil.

13. Gunter Netzer of West Germany.

14. George Best in action.

15. Benny Binshtock of the American Soccer League's Los Angeles Skyhawks executes a tackle.

16. Kyle Rote, Jr. of the Dallas Tornado tries to move in on the ball, which is being carried by an Aztecs player.

17. Gianni Rivera of Italy.

18. George Best.

19. Eusebio.

20. The great Pelé.

21. *Kick with the Outside of the Foot.* Balance and followthrough are important.

22. *Instep Volley Kick.* The player is balanced and has his eyes on the ball. His knee is lifted, and his leg swings from the knee to kick the ball before it hits the ground.

23. *Trap with the Inside of the Foot.* As the ball approaches, the player withdraws his foot, and the ball is cushioned against the inside of the foot.

24. *Instep Kick.* The player first swings his leg back at the knee and then forward to the ball. Note that the nonkicking foot is kept near the ball.

25. *Chest Trap*. Again, balance is important in this maneuver. The player keeps his eyes on the ball and his body beneath it.

26. *Thigh Trap*. This move requires good concentration and balance. The player drops his thigh just before impact.

27. *Sole Trap*. Keeping his eyes on the ball, the player places his foot lightly on the ball as it hits the ground.

28. *Trap with the Outside of the Foot*. As the ball strikes the ground, the player turns the outside of his foot inward to control the ball's fall to the ground.

29. *Sliding Tackle*.

    a. The defender (left) gets his leg in front of the attacker,

    b. and slides the ball from the attacker.

    c. Falling position. The ball is out of play.

30. *Catching a High Ball*. The goalkeeper concentrates on the ball, preparing to extend his arms and dive to meet it.

31. *Punch Save*. The goalkeeper meets the ball at the highest point of its flight and punches it with a tightly closed fist.

32. *Catch*. With his hands around the ball, the goalkeeper pulls the ball securely into his chest.

33. *Diving Save*. With his body extended, the goalkeeper reaches for the ball.

34. *Shoulder Charge.* Both players are within playing distance of the ball. They lean their bodies and shoulders toward each other in a challenge for the ball.

35. *Frontal Tackle.* As they approach the ball, the players prepare to tackle the ball with their insteps. Balance and strength are the key qualities required for this play.

36. *Side-Block Tackle.* The players must maintain their balance and lock their knees to execute this tackle successfully, and they must always be ready to make a second effort.

37. *Throw-in*. Pelé prepares to make a throw-in.

38. *Header*. The player jumps to head the ball keeping his eyes on it.

39. *The Wall*. The number of players in the wall depends on the angle. The goalie defends one post. Note that there is no space between the players' legs that a ball could slip through.

40. *Scissor Kick*. Pelé executes the scissor kick.

twice he won the Bob Hermann Award, given to the top collegiate player in the nation. In addition to playing for the Stars, in 1974, he also started to coach the McCluen North High School team, and in his third season, he led them to the Missouri state championship. He is extremely enthusiastic about the sport—just days after his son Timothy was born he went out and bought him a uniform—and his pleasant manners and perceptive analyses of the game make him a sought-after speaker. When once asked about his career, he said, "The thing about soccer is that it takes many, many hours of teamwork. Knowing when to hold onto the ball and when to pass it is the key to success. A player who understands that is over the hump. You must be quick off the mark and have reflexes, agility, and flexibility." And indeed, speed and finesse have marked his game throughout his career.

Who will the next American soccer star be? Just look at some of the youngsters now starting to kick around the soccer ball. Maybe one of them will someday make a name in American soccer history.

III. The Duties of the Participants

CHAPTER 17

The Field of Battle

The battlefield for soccer can vary greatly from city to city or from nation to nation. This variance is curtailed somewhat, however, when an international match is to be played. Unless a field meets specific requirements of FIFA, it cannot be used for big international games. The markings on all fields must be similar, and they must be marked clearly not only to aid the officials but also to prevent the arguments that often result when an official cannot interpret the markings plainly. Usually the field is marked with lime, but on some artificial surfaces the markings are painted directly onto the artificial turf.

In most leagues throughout the world, except for nonsanctioned leagues, which can use any dimensions they desire since they are not members of FIFA, the length of the field may vary from a minimum of 100 yards to a maximum of 130 yards. The width of the pitch, as a field is often called, can run from between 50 and 100 yards. FIFA requires, however, that all international matches be played on fields between 110 and 120 yards in length, unless special permission is grated. Because of this regulation, several stadiums in England were ruled out as possible sites for the 1960 World Cup, and a couple of those used had to have seats removed in order to comply with FIFA's requirements. In an international game, the rule is the field must also measure between 70 and 80 yards in width, although there have also been occasions when FIFA allowed a narrower measurement. Longer dimensions have never been allowed, however. With the exception of the North American Soccer League, which in 1973 introduced its blue-line concept for offside (see chapter 4), the offside line everywhere in the world is drawn widthwise directly in the center of the field, breaking the pitch into two equal halves. Not less than one yard off to each side from the points where this halfline meets the touch or side lines, flags are usually placed to indicate to fans, players, and officials that the offside infraction occurs at this point.

THE FIELD OF PLAY

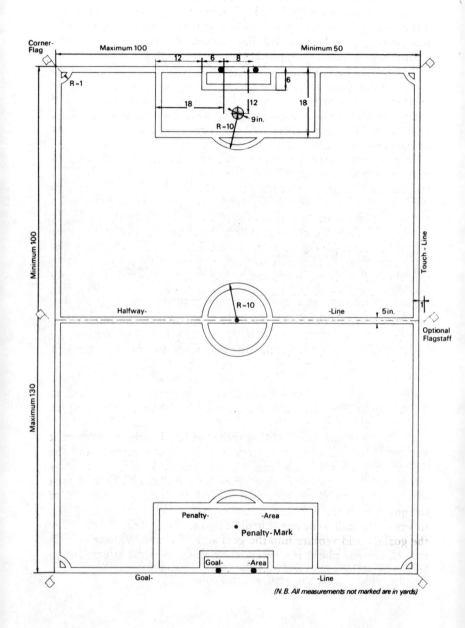

(N.B. All measurements not marked are in yards)

The North American Soccer League received approval from FIFA to utilize a different offside rule. The NASL rule stipulates that a player is not considered offside until he is within 35 yards of his opponents' goal, rather than midfield. Thirty-five yards from each goal, a line is drawn across the field. This blue-line concept, similar to hockey, is the area up to which a player can go without being deemed offside. But once he goes beyond that line toward his opponent's goal, the traditional offside rule is applied.

The four corners formed where the touch lines and the goal lines meet are the spots where corner kicks will be taken from, which are awarded to the attacking team when the defensive team puts the ball out of bounds over its own goal line. Flags on poles five feet high stand next to the four corner spots, and the corners themselves are marked with a one-yard semiarc pattern. Under the rules of the game, a player taking the corner kick cannot touch the ball again until either a teammate or an opponent, who is required to stand at least 10 yards away, touches the ball first. It does not matter how the defending team puts the ball over its own goal line, but it does matter where the ball crossed the line. The corner kick is always taken nearest the side where the defense put the ball over the goal line. If a goalie tips the ball over the bar to his right, for example, then the corner kick is taken from that side of the field. Referees are instructed to take careful note of which side the ball went out when indicating that a corner kick has been awarded. In some of the stadiums in the NASL and the American Soccer League, the plan of the field makes it more advantageous to take the corner kick from one side than from the other because there is more room to run up to the ball before kicking it. This means that the referee must make sure that the offensive team does not take the kick from the side it prefers if in reality the ball should be cornered from the other side. As in every other sport, a player is always looking for an edge, and since a corner kick, if taken properly, can often lead to a goal, the referee and the linesmen must be aware of exactly where the ball went over the goal line.

In the event that the attacking team last touches the ball before it goes over the goal line, then a corner kick is not awarded, and the defending team will get a goal kick. A goal kick can be taken by the goalie, but it is more often taken by a fullback. The goal area measures 6 yards by 20 yards, and the ball is placed in either half of the goal area if the ball went straight over the net, or the half closest to where the ball went out if it didn't go straight. At one time, only the goalie could venture into the goal area, but now, so long as he is not offside, any player is allowed inside this area while attempting to kick or head the ball past the goalie.

On a goal kick, no player may touch the ball until after it has traveled out of the penalty area. There is no restriction to prevent a fullback or a goalie from tapping the ball out of the penalty area and then receiving a return pass in order to punt the ball, but some teams today station a player just outside the area in case the goalie or fullback attempts such a maneuver.

The area outside the goal area, measuring 18 yards out from each goal line and extending widthwise 44 yards, is called the penalty area. This is the only area in which the goalie is allowed to use his hands, and outside this area, the goalie is treated like any other player. If the defending team commits a flagrant foul in this area, a penalty kick will be awarded the other team, and the penalty shooter will have only the goalie to bypass in order to score a goal. Outside of the penalty area, however, the same type of foul will result only in a direct free kick, in which the defense is allowed to position itself between the shooter and the goalie. There have been many occasions when a referee has been severely criticized and at times even beaten by fans and players alike for placing the ball outside the penalty area when it was obvious to all that the foul was committed by the defense inside its own penalty area. Many forwards, when fouled just outside of the penalty area, will dive into the area, hoping to draw a penalty kick. Usually this is to no avail, however. If the referee is upfield when the foul is committed, he will depend on the linesman who is following the play. If the linesman points his flag to a spot outside the penalty area, then a direct free kick is awarded, not a penalty kick, and the defensive player who committed the foul invariably will breathe a sigh of relief (see chapter 19).

When a penalty kick is awarded, however, a field marking plays an important part. Twelve yards out from the center of the goal is a mark indicating the spot from which the penalty kick is to be taken. The referee can simply place the ball on this penalty spot marking, but more often he will pace the 12 yards out from the goal line himself to make sure that the marking is actually at the required distance. If there has been heavy traffic in the penalty area during the game, the markings may have been erased or smudged to where it is not exactly clear where the spot should be.

During a penalty kick, only the shooter, who is 12 yards out, and the goalie, who is on the goal line, are allowed inside the penalty area, and the goalie may not move until the ball has been touched. All the other players must stand outside both the penalty area and the 10-yard semicircle that is marked on the field. The centermost part of this arc is directly in line both with the penalty spot and the place where the goalie will be standing. After the ball has traveled the distance of its circumference, these restrictions no longer apply.

Except in leagues with young players, for whom a different size goal may be necessary, all goals in soccer are a standard size regardless of where the game is played. A standard goal's inside measurement is eight yards wide and eight feet high, supported by posts at each end and joined on top by a crossbar. For most competitions, it must have a net, which can be made of either nylon or hemp. Because the net moves when the ball hits it, it prevents controversy about whether a goal was actually scored. Most posts and crossbars are wooden, but metal, although dangerous, is sometimes utilized as well.

Another important marking on the field is the circle around the exact center point of the field. The circle is 20 yards in diameter, with a 10-yard semicircle on each side of the field. During kickoffs, which are held at the start of the game, at the start of the second half, and whenever a goal has been scored, no player from the opposition is allowed to cross into the circle until the ball has been put into play by the team making the kickoff. After the ball moves the distance of its circumference, it is considered in play. The player making the kickoff cannot touch the ball again until someone else touches it first. There is no restriction on how many players from the team making the kickoff can be inside the circle, but the defense is required to be at least 10 yards away from the spot of the kickoff, and in the event that rain has washed away the marking, the referee must be alert to see that the defending team doesn't come closer.

In some cases, a marking known as the substitute box can be used, although it is not required by FIFA. Several tournaments are held around the world, however, which require that a substitute about to enter the game stand in a box near the center of the field. This is supposed to make the referees notice the potential substitute, but many feel it is just another marking to confuse the spectators.

Many fields in North America are used for American football besides soccer. When the markings are painted on the field, it becomes very confusing, as there are too many lines on the field. Usually the markings for each game are painted in different colors to differentiate them, but it remains confusing nonetheless. When the touch lines for soccer extend beyond the side lines for football, it is especially difficult and has caused many teams to claim that a ball went over the touch line when in reality it went over the football side line and was within bounds. It has also caused players taking throw-ins to go to the football side line instead of the touch line. When American stadiums are built strictly for soccer, this confusion may be resolved, but until then American soccer fans will have to make do with what they have.

When the day comes, however, soccer fans should be more than content to have a few soccer fields resembling the Maracana Stadium in Rio de Janeiro that can seat 200,000; Azteca Stadium in Mexico

City, with a capacity of 120,000; any of the three stadiums in Spain, such as Santiago Bernabeu in Madrid with a capacity of 125,000; Manzarares, also in Madrid, which holds 100,000 fans; or the Campo Nuevo in Barcelona with a capacity of 100,000. Other great soccer stadiums include the Buenos Aires stadium, where games draw 100,000 or more; the Wembley pitch in England, with its crowds of slightly over 100,000; Hampden Park and Ibrox in Glasgow; the Lenin Stadium in Moscow with a capacity of 102,000; Crvena Zvezda in Belgrade, Yugoslavia, which seats 95,000; the Polish stadiums — X Anniversary in Warsaw and Stadium Slaski in Chorzów; the beautiful Olympisch Stadium in Amsterdam; the 90,000-capacity Stadio Olimpico in Rome; the Stadio Comunale San Siro in Milan, with a capacity of 79,000; the Stadio S. Paolo in Napoli; the 80,000-capacity Nepstadion Budapest in Hungary; the Olypiastadion in Berlin; the Sportforum in Leipzig, East Germany; the 70,000-capacity Centenary Stadium in Brussels; and the 72,000-capacity Wiener Stadium in Vienna.

Many Americans believe that soon they too will have a soccer stadium of their own, and if the game continues to progress in America as it has in the past few years, that dream could well become a reality by the 1980s.

CHAPTER 18

The Officials

In no other sport does the referee have as much power as he has in soccer. Although he has two assistants, known as linesmen, he can ignore them when he chooses to, and if he feels one of them is not doing a proper job, he can even order the linesman off the field. He has the power to stop a game if he feels that the fans or players have become unruly and are threatening the successful completion of the contest. He has been the brunt of many an assault from fans and players alike; in recent years several referees around the world have been badly beaten, one was kicked to death, and two others were maimed by irate players and fans. The referee decides whether to allow a goal to stand regardless of what a linesman has indicated, and he has the option of ignoring the appeals of players to confer with the linesman to get a clearer interpretation of what the linesman's flag-waving means. The referee keeps the official time of the match, despite the fact that throughout the world there are many modern scoreboards that indicate the time, and he can add extra time to the match if he decides a team is stalling out the clock. He can also order players to leave the field if they commit violent fouls or if they repeat offenses—a penalty that not only leaves the team a man or more short, but that will lead to possible fines for the players and even suspension from further games.

The referee must take control of the match immediately by calling all obvious fouls, or else he is in for a rough time. If a team sees that the referee is letting violence go unpunished, the playing field will soon resemble a battleground. The referee can also order a trainer not to come onto the field when a player is injured if he feels that the injury is not serious enough or that it would interfere with the other team's advantage at that moment. At the start of the second half, the referee comes onto the field and orders the halftime entertainment off so play can resume. The rules of FIFA declare that the referee is the boss of the match, and sometimes, even though he has not taken specific action during a match, the report that he submits after each game to either the league or the national federation can lead to fines, suspensions, or other punishment for both teams and individual players. The referee is also responsible for checking the player passes of each team, which are issued by each league to ensure that the player whose picture is on the pass really is the man playing. If a player does not have his pass, he cannot play, no matter how much he or his team protests. The referee makes notes of all players he ejects or warns with the issuance of a yellow card. These names are then handed in to the league office.

If a referee becomes ill or injured during a match and cannot continue, then the senior linesman steps in. The senior linesman is the person holding the red flag to signal corner kicks, goal kicks, throw-ins and, although he isn't always listened to, offside violations. His duties are similar to those of the other linesman, who stands on the opposite touch line and indicates these plays, sometimes with a yellow flag.

On occasion the linesmen also signal the referee by a predetermined motion that a play should be allowed to continue even though an obvious foul has been committed. This is known as the advantage rule, and it stipulates that if a team that has been fouled against maintains control of the ball after the foul and is on its way toward the other team's goal, then the referee can opt not to blow his whistle. All too often a player, seeing that the referee will invoke the advantage rule and not blow his whistle, will resort to unnecessary fouls in order to slow down the game and realign his defense.

The referee and the linesmen both can call a throw-in violation, and often, having missed a foul throw-in, the referee will stop play as soon as he notices that one of the linesmen has his flag up. Occasionally a linesman will signal that a team put the ball over the touch line by pointing his flag in the opposite direction from the way the offending team's play was going. The referee many times overrules the linesman, however, and indicates that the throw-in should not go to the team that the linesman has indicated. Although it is not always enforced, sometimes the referee will also blow his whistle and order a throw-in to be retaken by a team if, in his judgment, the player taking the throw-in moved too far from the original spot where the ball went out of bounds.

The linesmen have often been jeered and even beaten when they have held up their flags to signal an offside violation. As mentioned before, an offside call goes against the attacking team when one of the attacking players precedes the ball into the other team's half of the field and there aren't at least two defenders between him and the goal at the time.

The senior linesman often also keeps a watch on the time of the game; and a few minutes before time is to run out, he usually motions the referee. This usually acts as a signal for the referee to look at his watch.

Often a linesman will have to indicate the exact location of a foul so the ball is not "accidentally" moved ahead to gain a territorial advantage. The referee must make sure that there are at least 10 yards between the player taking the free kick and the closest opponent, and on penalty shots, the referee makes sure that the goalkeeper does not move before the shot is taken.

A referee also has the power to award the match to the visiting team if the home team does not supply a proper ball for playing. This ruling is not enforced during many junior games, but the referee has the right to enforce it if he sees fit. A referee must also check to see that the goal nets are securely fastened before the start of the game and again before the resumption of play in the second half, and he must make sure that the field is properly marked. The referee is not required to allow a substitute into the game until it becomes legal for him to enter the game, and he will usually check the player's pass to make sure that the player whose picture is on the pass is indeed the man entering the game. The referee can also order a game abandoned if he feels that weather conditions make it too dangerous to continue, as is often the case on artificial surfaces.

The referee can also abandon the game if he is attacked by fans, and when this happens, he will usually award the game to the visiting team, since it is the responsibility of the home team to control the fans. If a referee abandons a game, the league or national federation usually follows his recommendation either to have the game replayed in its entirety, resumed from the point it was stopped, or forfeited to a specific team, especially if the game is one in which a Cup or championship is at stake.

The referee, who at times may seem petty, can also order a team to change its uniforms if he feels that they are too similar to those of the opponents. He must also make sure that the goalie wears a jersey completely different from either his field teammates or from the opposing team. Even though a referee can often be wrong, the league will most likely uphold his decision. During a game in Yankee Stadium between the Cosmos and Boston in 1976, however, the referee allowed a Boston player who was not on the original list of penalty shooters to take a shot and when the shot hit the bar, he ordered another player, who was on the original list, to retake the kick, which he made. Boston beat the New Yorkers, and the Cosmos successfully appealed the referee's action.

Because there is so much continuous action during a soccer match, there have been suggestions about and even a few experiments with two referees, one in each half of the field. The referees themselves, however, have voiced strong objections to such a change, and it looks like for years to come there will continue to be one referee and two linesmen against whom the fans will vent their anger.

CHAPTER 19

Why a Foul?

For every foul called in a soccer match, a kick of some kind is awarded to the team that has been fouled against. The two most frequently awarded kicks are the direct free kick and the indirect free kick; a penalty kick is awarded if a direct free kick foul occurs within the penalty area. A referee can award an indirect free kick inside the penalty area against the defending team, however, if he feels that the foul itself was not flagrant and that it is not necessary to punish the team that committed the foul severely.

If the attacking team is fouled intentionally or if the opposition commits a hand-ball infraction that the referee feels is deliberate, then a penalty kick is awarded. The ball is placed at a mark 12 yards from the goalie, and the other players who stand around a semicircle that is 10 yards in circumference cannot enter the penalty area until the ball has been touched; but once the ball is kicked and rolls the distance of its circumference, it is in play, and the battle for the rebound begins. When penalty shooting is being used to settle a deadlocked game, however, the rules are slightly different. Then the ball cannot be touched by *any* player once it is either touched, saved by the goalie, or hits the post.

During penalty shots, the goalkeeper cannot move until the shooter takes the shot. If he does move and makes the save, the referee should award the kicker another chance to make the goal. If the goalkeeper moves before the kick is taken and the ball is sent into the goal, however, then the goal stands. The retaking of a penalty shot has led to many a riot, as sometimes the goalie moved so slightly that most of the fans were unable to see the move. But since the referee and the linesmen were on the field, they were better able to see the move.

A direct free kick can be awarded for nine different types of fouls. An indirect free kick is awarded for five other fouls or violations. The direct free kick is so named because the ball can go directly into the goal from a player's kick. With the indirect free kick, however, the ball must first touch either a teammate, an opponent, or even the goalie before a goal can be scored. A direct free kick is awarded to a team whenever an opponent commits the following nine fouls:

1. Kicking or attempting to kick an opponent. (The key word here is "attempting," since the referee can usually spot intention even if the foul itself was never really committed.)
2. Tripping an opponent (which really means throwing oneself into his path or attempting to make him fail by using one's legs or by stooping behind or in front of him).
3. Jumping at an opposing player.
4. Charging into an opponent in a flagrant, violent, or dangerous manner.
5. Charging an opponent from behind if he is not obstructing one's path. (This violation is often called when two players are leaping for a loose high ball and one player attempts to gain an advantage by practically climbing on his opponent's back.)
6. Striking or attempting to strike an opponent.
7. Holding an opponent with any part of one's arm or hand.
8. Pushing an opponent with any part of one's arm or hand.
9. Using one's arm or hand to touch the ball, advance it, slow it down, or propel it in any direction (except for the goalie while he is in his own penalty area or the player who has been awarded a throw-in once the ball has passed over one of the touch lines).

When any of these fouls are committed by the defending team inside the penalty area, the attacking team is awarded a penalty kick, so if the only way to stop an opponent is to foul him, it is best for a player to make sure that he does it outside the penalty area.

The five fouls that result in an indirect free kick are more complicated and the referee and linesmen must be aware of the infraction or they will find the fans and player in an uproar.

Briefly, the five fouls are:

1. Playing in a manner that the referee considers dangerous. An example of this would be if the attacking player attempted to kick the ball out of the hands of the goalie. If the violating player also made contact with the goalkeeper, the referee would have the option of awarding a direct kick.
2. Using a shoulder or legal charge (see chapter 22) when the ball is not within playing distance.
3. Intentionally obstructing an opponent when not playing the ball. (This rule is often difficult to interpret, but the key is determining that the player charged with the foul did so with intention of cutting off the play. Often, when the foul is committed inside the

penalty area, the referee will, instead of a penalty shot, award an indirect free kick if, in his opinion, the foul was not committed deliberately.)

4. Charging into the goalkeeper when the goalie is holding the ball either inside or outside the penalty area.

5. If the goalie takes more than four steps while holding, bouncing, or throwing the ball and catching it without releasing it to another player or indulges in tactics that the referee feels are designed solely to hold up the game and give his team an unfair advantage.

When a player is sent off the field, he may be allowed back into the game if he has been ordered off for playing with what the referee considers dangerous or broken equipment and no substitution is made. He may not, however, return to the field until the referee waves him into action; and before waving him in, the referee will usually examine the new equipment to make sure that it conforms to the requirements of the game. A player may also be ordered off the field to receive medical treatment and allowed back as long as no substitution was made for him.

Even when a foul calls for awarding the indirect free kick, the referee can caution the fouling player with the yellow card and mark down his name, or he can give him the red card. Both the yellow and the red cards are kept in the referee's pocket, but the red card means that the player is out of the game. Most leagues require a player who has been ejected to sit out a suspension ranging from one to three games. In the North American Soccer League, the suspension usually is for one game, usually the next road game that the team plays in. The reason, NASL officials say, is that they don't want the player's home fans penalized by not having him in action on his own field. Some referees have been critical of this, however, and have urged the league to have a player sit out the very next game, whether at home or away.

Fouls are indeed serious offenses in soccer, but in light of this it is surprising that during the 1975 and 1976 seasons, sometimes as many as 40 or even 50 fouls were called in one game.

CHAPTER 20

Formations and Patterns

From the 1-10 to the M or W to the 2-3-5 and up through the 4-3-3, the 4-2-4 and the 4-4-2,* soccer teams throughout the world have been devising new formations for beating their opponents. What formations will be used in the future may well defy the imagination, but one can rest assured that any team that comes up with a new formation and fools its opponents will be successful.

Soccer tacticians are always working on new ways to get the most out of their men; undoubtedly even today plans are being worked out in the minds of coaches and on the drawing boards and blackboards of many a club throughout the world. Many ideas may at first sound foolish; but often if one looks at a plan in its proper perspective, it becomes clear that if executed properly, the new formation just might work and help the team planning the move to become a dominant force in soccer.

To dream up a new soccer formation is not so easy as it sounds. After all, it took many years for American football patterns to change from the T and the Single Wing to the A and whatever else may be invented today. Soccer is, above all, a team game, and it takes practice to work a plan to its best adantage. For example, Helmut Schoen, the coach of the great West German team that won the European Nations Cup in 1972 and the World Cup two years later, briefly used a formation called the double winger pattern of play during one key game, but he admitted after the completion of the World Cup,

> I feel the plays from this formation will eventually work, but with the great pressure put on my team, I certainly felt that this was not the time or the place to go fully into a tactical change. Putting a completely new formation into a game is not done overnight. It takes long months of practice, and unless you can work on making the change while at the same time beefing up the type of play you have been working on for the past few years, avoid it for the time being. As Rome wasn't built in a day, neither is a completely new type of team pattern in soccer.

*Formations are named with the defenders first, the halfbacks second, and the forwards last.

Although some of the old patterns of play may seem amusing today, they were the systems that brought the most teams the most success. A system of play that was used in England during the middle of the 19th century called for one goalie and 10 attackers when one's team had the ball. The goalie would punt the ball as far downfield as possible, and every one of his teammates would race in at the opposing goalie in an effort to score a goal. When the opposing goalie made a save, the team would then hurry back in an effort to help out its goalie. Often the game was nothing more than a foot race between the 20 field players, while the two goalies stood in their goals. This system of play may seem funny, but it was successful not only in England but wherever soccer was played in those days.

When the first great pattern change took place, immediately the traditionalists were quick to argue against it. But some of the teams in England felt that having 10 men suddenly come bearing down while one's teammates were trying to reverse direction to come back and help was just too much for a goalkeeper to cope with, so after careful planning a new concept was introduced. Now, when a team had the ball on attack, its goalie had company—one man who stayed back to help in the event that the ball was suddenly reversed. The goalie and defender had little to do while the team was on attack, and often the two would stand and talk over the weather or anything else they found interesting. The man selected as the defender was usually the slowest and biggest man on the team, and he did not like the task assigned to him at all. But since he wanted to remain on the team, he usually kept quiet about it, at least in public.

Several more changes in the game also took place, but the most important one came about around 1905, when some teams began to use a second defender. The game still featured almost exclusively running, shooting, and then reversing-field techniques once the other team got the ball.

THE 2-3-5 FORMATION

When the offside rule was changed so that a forward needed to have only two opponents instead of three between him and the goal when he got the ball, the 2-3-5 (or W or M) formation was devised. Even today some of the older college coaches go back to it, and youngsters often learn this type of formation because it is considered the least complicated one to teach. The formation was successful for a long time, and by examining it in light of today's variations, one can see why it was so popular.

The 2-3-5 formation called for two defenders to be placed about 15 yards upfield of the goalie, one to the left about midway between the touch line and the goalie and one to the right in the same position. In front of the defenders were three midfielders, one in the center around the midfield line, and the others four, five, or sometimes seven yards to either side of him. Next came the offensive unit with the center forward (the man in the middle) flanked by an inside left and an inside right who positioned themselves about 10 yards to either side of him. On the far right and left sides, aligned with the center forward and the inside right and left, were the outside right and left or wingers, as they were sometimes called. The plays almost always revolved around the center forward, and he was actually like the captain, calling the moves for his men to follow.

W System

Some teams decided that there was not enough variety in this type of play and adopted the W formation, in which the placement of the five forwards looked exactly like the letter W from their goalie's point of view. In the W system, the center forward was on the edge of or sometimes even slightly within the penalty area. The outside right and outside left were parallel to him on the far sides of the field. The inside forwards were about five to eight yards in back of the penalty area with their position calling for them to be directly on the perimeter of the 18-by-24-yard area inside the penalty area at the required distance. There were numerous advantages to the formation, and teams were unable to defend against it. On attack there was great passing potential between the midfielders and the forward line because there was a lot of open space within which to manipulate. The main task of the center forward in this system was to get the ball and, since he was within good shooting range, to fire the ball as hard as he could at the opposing goalie. The inside forwards were like the quarterbacks of the play and would move the ball to either side in an effort to draw out the defense. The inside forwards would try to draw out the opposition and then try to hit the center forward with an accurate and open pass so that he could take a hard shot on goal. The biggest advantage of the W pattern of play was that because of the setup of the forwards, there was a great deal of attacking space. Often the players executed plays in which the inside men and outside men reversed position. This would confuse the opposition's defense, eventually leaving an unguarded forward who could almost solo in on the goalkeeper before the opposition spotted him and tried, belatedly, to stop him.

To counter this system of play, the defense tried many different tactics, but the best way was generally considered to be covering (or

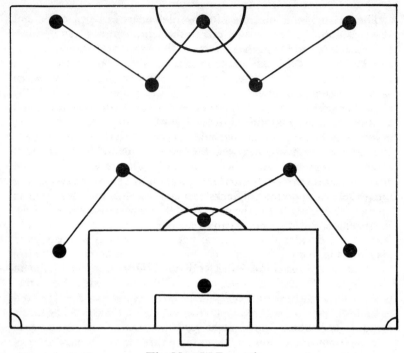

The M or W Formation

marking) each man on the front line, besides putting an extra defender in the middle of the formation to stop the passes to the center forward. The extra defender would be expected to cover not only the center forward but also any of the other four forwards who had managed to overcome their own defenders. With every man on the front line covered, it was hard to complete passes, and the system began to fail. It was replaced, however, by the M or inverted W system, which produced many opportunities for goals.

M System
Under the M pattern of play, the two inside forwards were positioned inside the penalty area about 15 yards away from the goal and about 10 yards apart. The center forward would station himself about eight to 10 yards outside the center of the goal area, and the outside forwards would stand parallel to but about 15 yards away from him and about 10 yards away from the inside forwards. Their goalie would see the five forwards deployed in an M formation, while the opposing goalkeeper would see it as a W formation.

264

The advantages to this type of formation were numerous. The team was better able to control the vital midfield area since there were three forwards able to help out the three midfielders, who functioned as they had in the W formation. The M formation was employed by most coaches from the late 1930s until the 1960s, since it also gave the attackers the ability to fall back and aid the defense whenever it became necessary. The M formation did have some real drawbacks, however, that caused fewer goals to be scored because there were only two men near the opposition's goal; and unless the other three forwards were able to hit them with accurate passes, the ball would often be picked off by the defense.

What teams were really attempting to do through the M system was force the two opposing fullbacks to make careless mistakes deep in their own territory, but as the play of defenders became more exacting, the success of the M system began to decline.

THE 4-2-4 FORMATION

It was another five to seven years, however, before the next new system came into use. Called the 4-2-4, it was drastically different from the M, and today it has numerous variations. Although the inventors of this system actually intended for it to stress defense more than offense, it had almost completely opposite effect, as teams now found that while on attack they were able to have six men in scoring position and while on defense they could have seven and eight men back. While using the 4-2-4 system on the attack, the four front men and the two halfbacks work out such plays as the give-and-go and the lateral side pass, and then a midfielder suddenly thrusts deep near the opponent's goal. On the move upfield there is also the advantage that one of the fullbacks (usually one of the wing backs or in some cases even the center back, who is playing in front of the sweeper) can come upfield and either keep on going or interchange with one of the halfbacks, taking over his duties and freeing him for the attack. Because of the dual role of the midfielders in this system, a team must have the talent to put it into effective use.

On defense either the two midfielders can both fall back and make the defense almost a six-man force, or one man can join the fullback line, freeing the other midfielder to stop any opposing forwards who have been able to penetrate the defense. On occasion the two midfielders must also join in the defense against free kicks. Since they are well back of any of their own team's front-line action, they must quickly cut downfield in anticipation of a backward pass from one of

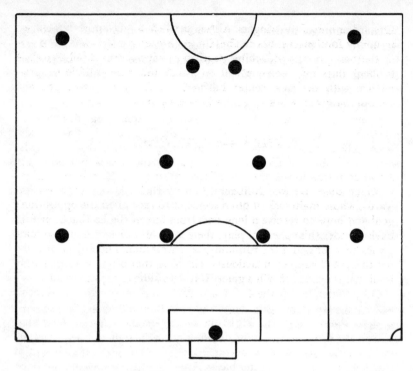

The 4–2–4 Formation

the front forwards, who will try to split and deceive the opposing defense. The backward pass is one of the best ways to draw out a clogged defense and open up an area for a team.

The 3–3–4 Pattern

One of the many variations of the 4-2-4 system is the seldom-used, but highly efficient (once it is perfected), 3-3-4 pattern in which a third halfback is added and one defender dropped. Many coaches, especially those who came to the NASL from England, are unwilling to utilize this style because they are afraid of not having at least four defenders back at all times. Unlike the 4-2-4, in which two midfielders link the defense with the offense, the 3-3-4 utilizes three linkmen; and one of them, usually the center half, is always behind the other two in order to have greater mobility to fall back to help the defensive trio if the other team should intercept the ball. When he gets the ball, the center half has the option of sending the pass slightly ahead to one of the other midfielders or shooting the ball down the center to the center forward or one of the wingers. Although the 3-3-4 is not yet recognized by many foreign coaches in the United States and Canada, it is one of the best plays for teaching youngsters what soccer is all about. A fullback does not come upfield on attack unless he is able to interchange with the new center halfback—a deceptive move effective against many of the best-organized defenses in soccer today.

THE 4–4–2 FORMATION

Another formation is the sometimes-utilized 4-4-2 style of a play, in which there are four fullbacks, four midfielders, and only two forwards, whose main task, it often seems, is to race in on the opposition's goal and hope to receive a long pass from one of the halfbacks or fullbacks. Under this system of play, there is no offensive buildup, so some critics have termed it the run-and-pray formation. The Europeans who use the 4-4-2 support it zealously, claiming that often one breakaway is all that is needed to win a game, if it is possible to capitalize on it.

Other defenders of the 4-4-2 are quick to point out that under this system of play there is the option of switching into other formations, such as the 4-2-1-3, which is one of the newer playing techniques. There are, however, certain drawbacks to the 4-4-2. For example, the team's attack is apt to become clogged in the center, since two of the four defenders are center backs. The two midfielders are positioned slightly off center; and the center forward, or striker, and the lone man backing up the three forwards all play primarily in the center of the field. In addition, the opposing team can easily take one of its center backs off the play and use him to challenge the attackers in the midfield area.

THE DOUBLE-WING FORMATION

The double-wing formation mentioned earlier, in which two wings are lined up on each side of the field, still needs a great deal of refinement, but the idea is feasible. With the defense having more men back most of the time, the four forwards are well covered. But if one forward is left on the far left side of the field, if the center forward plays not only in the center of the field but as a pivot similar to basketball, and if the right side of the field is overloaded with two wingers, the defense will not only have to shift its game plan around, but will become confused, with three defenders sometimes coming over to stop the two wingers. With a short pass to the center forward or, if he is playing slightly back, the striker, one of the wings can cut in for a return pass while

267

the other wing keeps his defender busy by feinting a run deep into either the goal area or the right side of the penalty area. Another advantage of this pattern is that the striker will have less traffic in the penalty area when he makes his move, and if he gets an accurate pass, he will be able to make a clear shot on goal.

The double wing system also offers the attacking team a way of attaining even greater penetration, since the defense not only will have to shift to counter two wingers but at the same time will have to make sure that one of the opposing halfbacks doesn't float over to the side of the field where the two wingers are. Often the only way a team can prevent the halfback from coming in and making it a three-wing frontal attack is to pull two of its own halfbacks over to that side of the field. With the confusion that this causes, the man on the far side of the field, who until this maneuver was virtually out of the play, can cut in toward the penalty area and either take a cross or act as a low pivot; the striker now actually becomes a high pivot. Some of these moves may sound like they belong in a basketball formation, but pivotal play, too often forgotten by many clubs, is a very important aspect of modern soccer.

FORMATION VARIATIONS

At first glance, the next formation, which might be called the 3-2-1, might seem a little strange, and since only a few nonprofessional clubs have utilized it, one is entitled to initial skepticism. The formation calls for three defenders spread out equally in front of their own goal, with the left back covering the left side; the right back, the right side; and the centerback, the middle of the penalty area. There are two halfbacks, one on the far right and one on the far left; and in front of them is a center man, who can't be called either a halfback or a forward. He is the player to whom the fullbacks make their initial passes. He then either turns around and feeds the pass to one of the wing halfs, who has come up to join the attack, or he sends a short pass to the striker, who is 5 to 10 yards behind the other four forwards. The striker now can pivot and make a move toward the goal, take a hard shot, or pass to either the two forwards on the right or the two on the left. After passing the ball, the striker then moves toward the goal. The opposing team's defense will invariably commit itself and leave one of the four forwards free either to dribble, pass, or take a shot. Often the most successful play coming out of this type of formation is a double or even triple wall pass, in which several forwards execute the give-and-go, moving the ball quickly and often beating the over-worked defenders.

The 4-2-2-2 Style

In 1976, after his team had earlier in the season been hard pressed to defeat the Cosmos, 3-1, in overtime, coach Bill Foulkes of the Chicago Sting worked out another system of play for the team's return game later in the year. Foulkes, considered a great tactician, decided that since the Cosmos were a team that needed room to operate when on offense but were slow on defense, he should concentrate his efforts around the midfield; so he sent the Sting onto the field employing a 4-2-2-2 style of play. The Cosmos were helpless against the play in which there were four fullbacks, two regular midfielders, two deep forwards, and two men who played between the midfielders and forwards. Under this system, there could be as many as five or six men up on the attack and eight men on defense to clog up the lanes of play. The Sting won that game, 4-1, completely dominating the midfield by winning almost every battle for a loose ball and being able to take the ball away from the Cosmos forwards when they started to cross the midfield line. The 4-2-2-2 requires that the two regular midfielders be able to run laterally and that the two men behind the forwards can both carry the ball downfield and race backward should an opponent intercept the ball.

Changing Styles

Different teams use different systems to guard against a free kick or a corner kick, but so far as the actual team pattern is concerned, the main thing a new player or novice coach should remember is that what is good today may not be adequate tomorrow, as ever-changing systems of play call for innovations and new ideas. Something else that should always be remembered is that during the game a team must be able to change its tactics if the ones it began the game with aren't working.

A hundred years from now the entire style of system play will have changed drastically as new ideas that at first seemed funny, become standard. Changing one's style to fit the situation while at the same time making new ideas work is what the game is all about, and the inability to do this is one of the reasons why some teams suddenly find that the style they used a year ago is no longer successful.

One day there may well be a system in which a goalie, two backs, and two left midfielders play interchangeably, while the remaining players are positioned so that there is one fullback on the right, two men linking the midfielders, and three forwards—possibly two on one side and one on the other, leaving the center lane clear for some innovative moves. There is no end to man's imagination, and the challenge of beating one's opponent with something new will continue to inspire new strategies for years to come.

CHAPTER 21

Guarding the Nets

The modern concept of total soccer has changed the overall responsibilities of the goalie, the man who guards the nets and tries to stop opposing shots from going in to the goal for scores against his team. There was a time, many years ago, when clubs seeking a goalie would look for the biggest man with the most skill. They figured that once the ball came to him, he would be able to punt it, much as a punter in American football does. It never occurred to them that almost as soon as the ball was punted upfield, it was returned once again toward the same goal. The main task of the goalie was to make the save, almost always by catching the ball, and then get rid of it. During the late 1950s, however, someone looked into the rule book and discovered that once the goalkeeper catches the ball, he is not required to punt it; he has the option of throwing or rolling the ball to one of his teammates. When clubs in several nations began to protest this rule, claiming that what was done in the past was legal and what was being tried now was not cricket, FIFA set down a ruling blasting the critics of the throw or the roll downfield, and goalies throughout the world suddenly decided that the roll and the throw were preferable.

Whipping a ball downfield to a teammate is a safer way to assure that he will maintain control of the ball than kicking the ball downfield and having him battle an opponent for possession of it. Today goalies who can't toss the ball accurately for long distances are being shunned not only by professional clubs but also by many amateur teams. There are some exceptions, like George Barnett of the NASL's Minnesota Kicks, who will kick the ball eight times out of 10, especially on the shortened field at Metropolitan Stadium in Bloomington, home of the Kicks. His punts electrify the crowd, but even though he has been seen to punt the ball more than 70 yards, it doesn't take the opposing defense long to get wise to his tactics and put an extra man back to intercept the punt and prevent the Kicks' forwards from breaking in for a sudden shot on goal.

There are many ways a goalkeeper can make a save; on occasion he may even head a ball upfield. The goalie can use his hands anywhere within the penalty area, but if he uses his hands outside of it, the other team will be awarded a direct free kick.

The key to good goalkeeping is anticipation. The goalie must read the play and often guess where the forward will fire the ball, or whether the forward will fake the shot and try to pass the ball off to another forward for a clearer shot on goal.

The surest and best way to make a save is to catch the ball, but depending on the path and speed of the ball, the way the goalie catches it can vary greatly. If the ball is high, for example, then a goalie must use one set of techniques; catching a ball either at chest level or on a low-line drive creates different problems for the keeper.

The most basic requirement for catching a ball that all coaches teach is that the goalie must never take his eyes off the ball, even if there is traffic in the area or an oncoming forward. Shep Messing, the former U.S. National Team goalie and a man who represented this country in the Olympic Games before starring in the NASL with the New York Cosmos and the Boston Minutemen, has spent many hours with youngsters on his native Long Island, teaching them how to catch a shot. "If a youngster can catch the ball, he's on his way to becoming a goalie," says Messing, who believes that when they get the proper experience U.S. goalies will be among the best in the world. The Brazilian National Federation, feeling that its goalies do not see enough crosses during the regular season, has spent numerous hours having players cross the ball over in practice so that the goalie will be exposed to a shot that he is certain to see in international competition.

At first sight, catching a high lob or shot looks easy, but more goalies are injured making this type of save than any other. After the goalie has carefully followed the flight of the ball and even figured the wind factors that affect it, he must make sure when catching the ball with both his hands that he clutches it to his body to cushion its impact. The high ball will often give a goalie trouble because after deciding to leave the nets to catch the ball, he will frequently change his mind in mid-stream, enabling a smart opposing forward to lob the ball over his head into the nets.

A rainy day presents additional problems, since the wet ball can easily slip out of the goalie's hands. After making the catch, the goalie should step slightly sideways, since there is certain to be traffic in the area, and the risk of injury is great. His body acts as a backup to prevent the ball from going into the net. If he is catching a ball at or below chest level, a goalie should also make sure that he doesn't stand upright immediately afterward since the odds are great that a player will come in for a possible rebound.

While a member of the Bermuda National Team, Sam Nusum, the veteran NASL goalie, lost three of his teeth when he was hit by a charging opponent. A few years earlier, his teammate, scurrying back to help him by kicking the ball clear if it rebounded off his chest, banged into him and cut Nusum's mouth badly.

Making the catch on a high shot requires almost the same initial moves as a driving layup in basketball. The leg not used to start the jumping movement should be bent at the knee, so it will enable the goalie not only to get good balance on the ground but if necessary can also be used to push an oncharging opponent away to prevent a collision. Once he has decided to leap, the goalie must also get his hands ready for the catch by bringing his arms up and spreading his fingers out. After the catch is made, and hopefully there is no rebound, the goalie should make sure that he wraps both hands around the ball and quickly brings it into his stomach. The goalie is now in complete legal possession of the ball, and if an opponent knocks him down and the ball goes loose into the net, the goal will be disallowed and a foul called against the man who hit him.

To catch a shot coming at waist or chest height, a goalie should hold his arms in front of his body with his elbows close at his sides. In making the chest-high save, he should lean forward to soften the impact of the ball. Once the catch is made, he should quickly pull the ball into his stomach and put both hands over it to prevent it from slipping out and giving the opposition a chance for a rebound shot. The same holds true for a save at waist height.

Saving a shot that comes in toward one's knees or even lower is more difficult. There are several schools of thought on this, but most of the top goalies in the NASL, such as Toronto's Paolo Cimpiel, bend from the waist, keeping their legs straight and pointing their hands downward with the fingers spread out. Again, the basket-type catch is the best one to use in this type of save, and there should be no hesitation; immediately after making the catch, the goalie should pull the ball upward into his stomach.

The diving save is most difficult and often electrifies the crowd. A goalie should not attempt this type of save if it is at all possible for him to catch the ball in another position, even on his knees. The timing for making the diving save must be perfect, because if the goalie dives to the side too soon, the ball will go into the net after he has passed the line of the shot. If he dives too late, the ball will slip off his fingers or even go under him. To make the save successfully, the goalie must propel himself sideways, using one arm to catch the ball and the other arm used to cushion his fall. As soon as he catches the ball, he must clutch it to his stomach, and he should also curl himself around the ball to prevent it from slipping out.

Making a save on ground balls is far more difficult than it might first appear. How a ball rolls depends on the playing surface. A ball coming from the side of Yankee Stadium covered by the dirt infield, for example, will roll smoothly until it suddenly hits a clump of dirt, when it will bounce awkwardly. On artificial surfaces, the ball tends to skip along the ground, and it is most difficult to judge on which bounce to make the save. There are two ways to best field the ground shot. Some goalies claim that kneeling with one leg and planting the other leg on the field is the best because this enables them to hold their palms upward—the easiest way to catch the ball—and the leg planted firmly on the ground acts as a deterrent against a rebound. Other goalies, however, prefer to kneel with both legs, using their body as a cushion and catching the ball by turning their palms toward the path of the ball. To say one style is more correct than another is foolish, however, since top goalies use both techniques effectively.

What happens if a goalie is unable to catch a ball because it is just too far away? There are three different things one might do, depending on where the shot is coming from and where the goalie wants to send the ball. When the ball is too high to catch, a goalie should tip the ball back over the bar so that the ball will not go into the upper part of the goal. This is also advisable when the ball is coming in high and there is a great deal of activity around the goalie. The goalie tips the ball over the bar by leaping much as he might when he is going for the high catch, but he must get his hands under the ball, and his palms should be facing the goal. He should lift the ball to give it the height needed for tipping it over the bar. Although it is best to tip the ball over the bar using both hands, there invariably will be situations in which the goalie can get only one of his hands under the ball. By flicking the ball again with his wrist and fingers, he will be able to get sufficient lift for tipping the ball.

Inexperienced goalies often make the mistake of coming out of the nets too far and then trying to tip the ball upward instead of catching it. The danger in this is that the lift will be insufficient and the ball will end up in the goal. At times tipping the ball to the sides is also necessary, since occasionally a goalie will be unable to get the ball, even with a diving save. When tipping the ball to the sides, the goalie must make sure to give the ball further momentum by pushing his fingers hard against it and turning his hands in the direction where he wants it to go. Although a goalie who tips the ball over his own net or to the side of the net will reward the opposing team with a corner kick, it's much safer than giving the team a rebound shot or even a goal.

Another save that requires a great deal of practice is the punch save. It also requires accurate anticipation since there will be traffic in the area when the goalie attempts it, and just punching the ball out with both fists is not enough unless he knows where the ball is likely to go. Gordon Banks, the great former goalie of the English National Team, was able to perfect his punch saves so that the ball would often go 30 yards upfield out of danger.

The goalie should make the punch save with his hands coming straight out from in front of his shoulders. Occasionally the ball can also be punched with only one hand, but it is much safer to execute this maneuver with both fists. The punch save is made, not surprisingly, by punching the ball with the fists; and although it isn't recommended, it is only fair to mention that many goalies who use the one-fisted punch save use the other fist as a weapon to ward off oncoming forwards.

How a goalie reacts when trying to stop a breakaway—a move in which an attacker gets past the defense, leaving the goalie with no help—is often one way of separating the men from the boys. A goalie coming out to stop the breakaway must make sure not only that he gets possession of the ball or kicks it out of danger, but also that he avoids possible injury. When a keeper decides to come out toward an oncharging forward, he must make sure that he times his dive so that he is able to get as much of his body as possible in front of the shot. Keeping this in mind, after making contact with the shooter, the goalie must immediately lie on top of the ball, using his hands to curl it into his body. Cutting down the angle of the shot is also important, since a smart forward will at times come dribbling toward the goalie and then fire the shot once the goalie commits himself into the widest opening in the net. Knowing one's opponent plays a big role here, and that is why many top teams throughout the world watch game films of their opponents. If a forward shoots more with one foot than the other, for example, then on a breakaway the goalie must be able to prevent him from shooting with the foot he prefers to use.

Sometimes a good goalie will stop a strong forward on a breakaway, only to have the impact of the ball free the ball for a rebound. In these cases, the goalie would be wise to flick the ball out of bounds when he makes the initial contact. And although it sounds simpler than it really is, the sliding tackle with both feet will often move the ball either out of danger or upfield. The goalie can also stop the breakaway by not committing himself until the forward starts his shot. The great Italian goalie Dino Zoff will come out to an oncharging forward but will not roll or toss himself at the opponent unless absolutely necessary. Instead he will come out straight and throw his hands upward in an attempt to punch or flip the ball away.

Perhaps the most difficult thing to teach a young goalie is not to come too far out of the nets, because a smart forward with a soft lob shot will be able to send the ball over his head and into the back of the net for a goal. On a breakaway, the goalie must also know the traffic situation inside the area, because often he will come out on a breakaway only to have the forward flip or pass the ball to a teammate. On a two-man breakaway, the best policy for the goalie is to stay in the center of the net and make his move only at the last minute to stop the man he figures will be most likely to take the shot against him. It is important for him to use a head feint here because with a series of moves, he can make the forward commit himself. It is very difficult for a goalkeeper to stop a breakaway, but when he does, the crowd usually goes wild.

It is essential for a goalie to learn how to prevent a direct or even an indirect free kick from resulting in a goal. The defenders on a team and, under the concept of total soccer sometimes even the forwards, must form a wall between the man making the kick and the goal. It is up to the goalkeeper to set up the wall as he wants it. Some teams use four or five men in the wall, while the great Italian team AC Milan has been known to put as many as seven men in the wall. The goalie's main job in this situation is to cover any space in the wall left unguarded. Watching for the shot that will come from either the open spot or over the wall of players should be his main concern. Of course, throughout the history of soccer, there have been top forwards with the ability to curve a ball around the wall, and the goalie must watch for this also. On a high direct free shot, tipping the ball over the bar is the best solution, because if the goalie attempts to punch the ball out when he is unable to catch it cleanly, the great congestion in the area will make it as possible for the offense to make a rebound shot as for one of the defenders to clear the ball upfield. On an indirect free kick, the goalie must keep an eye not only on the inevitable open spot in the wall but also on the forward, who is almost certain to break through the wall and try to head the ball past him.

Playing goal against a corner kick is another chore that distinguishes the good goalies from the average ones. On a corner kick, the goalie should position himself near the far post of the goal, about two-thirds of the way across the goal mouth. One or more of his defenders should take the other side, but when the ball comes and the goalie has a chance to leap across the goal mouth to either catch the ball or punch it, it's his job to clear his men out of the way. Many times a man taking a corner shot will kick the ball so that it comes out 12 or 15 yards in front of the goal. On this type of kick, the goalie must decide in a split second where the ball is going and how many men are in his way. He must also decide whether to grab the ball or punch it, and he must make sure with a signal that his teammates know that he is coming out to handle the corner kick or the cross. Goalies should work on the play with their teammates, a great deal of understanding between them.

After stopping a penalty shot, many a top goalie will be quick to mention that he was lucky. Luck indeed plays a major role in stopping a penalty shot, but a goalie can reduce the odds that a penalty kick will be scored against him if he is observant and knows the opponent who is taking the penalty kick. Over the years, there have been many top forwards or sometimes fullbacks who kick the ball in a certain manner. Knowing this, the goalie can figure that a particular player will usually make the shot in the same way and take steps to stop it. Shep Messing has an excellent average against stopping penalty shots, and he keeps a list with him detailing how certain shooters in the league try to convert penalty shots. The best way for a goalie to stop a penalty shot is to try to fool the shooter by leaning one way and then diving the other way as the shot is taken. When the Cosmos played an exhibition game against Team Japan in Hawaii during a 1976 preseason tour, they saw a new way to stop a penalty kick. Although it isn't likely to be widely adopted, it is an interesting and amusing strategy to consider. As required, the goalie positioned himself in the center of the goal area, leaning one way, but when the shot was taken, he cartwheeled across the net to kick out the shot!

Many teams require that their goalies make the goal kicks, while other teams have one of their fullbacks perform the task. The goal kick, which is awarded to a team when the other team puts the ball over the goal line, is a stationary kick, and the ball must be booted well upfield to clear the opposing team's men, who will be waiting for a short kick that they can pound right back. Kicking the ball to the side of the field on a goal kick rather than straight up the middle is the most effective strategy. Increasing numbers of coaches are having their fullbacks make this type of goal kick, however, because they have more powerful kicks for hitting a stationary ball. In these cases, the goalie is usually in position in case the kick is short and is intercepted.

Most of the goalie's efforts are directed at saving the ball. But once he has caught it, he has to get rid of it. It is important for him to get rid of the ball as quickly as possible, because if they are allowed the time, the defenders will be able to ready themselves for interception and another drive toward the goal. Under international rules, the goalie is allowed to take four steps before releasing the ball. If he desires, he can take one or two steps and roll the ball, which does not count as a step, or he can dribble the ball around his penalty area. But no matter what the sequence is, the goalie will be charged with a foul and the other team awarded a kick if he takes more than four steps before releasing the ball. The advantage of dribbling the ball is that if the goalie makes the save near his own goal mouth, he then can dribble it all the way up to the edge of the penalty area, which is 18 yards from the goal line itself. If a goalie does dribble the ball, however, and he should do so only if no opponent is trying to intercept the dribble, he gives the opposing team the opportunity to get set to intercept either his punt, toss, or roll when he does release the ball.

Punting the ball was the old way a goalie got rid of the ball, but as mentioned before, the opposition more often than not was able to intercept the punt and start another move on the goal. Punting the ball is usually done with three or more steps, just as in American football, but it can also be accomplished with as few as one or two steps. The goalie holds the ball in the hand opposite from the leg he is going to use to punt the ball; then he drops the ball and steps into the kick as it is dropping, like a drop kick in football. The ball usually travels quite a distance with this type of release, but the goalie must almost immediately get back into the proper position to guard against the possible return of the ball.

Many coaches now insist that the goalie throw the ball to a teammate. This can be accomplished in various ways. One technique is the whip throw, in which the goalie spots a teammate he wants to receive the ball and throws the ball in a manner similar to a sidearm baseball throw or, in extreme cases, a discus throw. Another way to toss the ball to a teammate is the overhead method, which resembles the type of throw used in javelin competition. Great teamwork is always necessary; as soon as he gets the ball and starts his throw, the goalie should know where his teammates will be to receive it. If the goalie spots a free teammate not too far away, he can also roll the ball to that player, much as a bowler does when delivering his shot.

Under today's concept of total soccer, with an accurate roll, throw, or short kick, the goalie can get his team started on the attack. In recent years, coaches have been using the goalie's release for this purpose more than previously. In the NASL during the 1976 season, although they never were officially credited with an assist on the play, several goalies made long throws to a teammate, who then passed to a free forward for a shot on goal that resulted in a score.

Bob Rigby, the star keeper for the New York Cosmos and for the Team America contingent that competed in the 1976 American Bicentennial Soccer Cup competition against Brazil, Italy, and England, was originally put in as a goalie by his high school coach because the coach felt that Rigby had the hands to be a good keeper but not the foot skill needed to play the field positions. Whatever the coach saw then, it is unlikely that he realized that Rigby's anticipation and ability to get a counterattack going would prove valuable in future years. Rigby has one of the best releases in the game, and before he got hurt in mid-1976, the Cosmos were taking advantage of his releases to start attacks on their opponents' goal. The goalie who can not only release the ball properly and without hesitation but can demonstrate agility as well is the modern prototype keeper, and clubs spend great amounts of money to attain such players.

CHAPTER 22

Defensive Play

The opposing forward comes in on the goalie. Just inside the penalty area, one of the team's defenders gets the ball away from him and kicks the ball downfield with all his power. The crowd roars its approval; the fullback has stopped the attack and sent the ball upfield for a possible counterattack by his own team, just as he is supposed to. This was the scene throughout the soccer world from the 1920s until the late 1960s. Fullbacks weren't supposed to do anything but clear the ball once they stopped an opposing forward.

In the 1970s, however, all this changed. A fullback like U.S. National Team member Bob Smith of the New York Cosmos, for example, takes the ball away from an opposing forward. He dribbles the ball to the side and then comes upfield with the ball if the opportunity is there. Otherwise he can pass to a teammate. But he's still coming right past the midfield line, up to the penalty box area, and taking a hard shot as he receives a pass from Pelé or Giorgio Chinaglia. The role of the fullback, or defender, in the modern concept of total soccer has certainly changed, and some of the all-time greatest fullbacks, who had the power to take balls away from their opponents often by sheer force, would never have made it in today's game. The fullback must not only have the skill of a forward, but he must also play aggressively on attack and defense and have the more traditional skills of tackling a ball away from an opponent, combining all this with all the skills a midfielder needs to be good at his position.

A fullback must have tremendous stamina, as he will often find himself downfield on the attack one minute and running full speed backward a minute later to get in position to stop the other team's scoring drive. The fullback must protect his goalie in addition to often bombarding the opposition's netkeeper, since that is what total soccer is all about. And since most of the teams in today's game utilize four fullbacks, all the men must be able to work together in covering the free men and the open spaces. If by accident a fullback uses his hands

278

to touch a ball, he will leave the gate wide open for a goal by the opposition. Fullback is one of the most difficult positions in the game and one that can never be taken for granted. If a team has a strong forward line and a weak defense, it most certainly is not a championship club.

DEFENSIVE MANEUVERS

Tackles

A fullback can take the ball away from an opposing forward in a number of ways. If he can't intercept the other team's pass, then he must use one of numerous tackling methods. Tackling an opponent in soccer isn't the same as tackling in American football. In the latter, the player wraps his arms around his opponent's waist, or even head, and throws him to the ground. But if a soccer player did that, he would not only be charged with a foul but could even draw the yellow caution card and in some cases the red card, meaning he was out of the game and his team would have to play shorthanded.

The five basic tackles are the frontal, back, side, sliding, and shoulder charge, and a defender must be proficient enough in all to counter the moves of the opposing forwards. But in addition to executing tackles properly, the defender must be able to execute feints in an effort to make the forward believe that he is going to attempt to get the ball away from him with a specific move. Only after long hours practicing the feints, often by looking at himself in a mirror, will he gain any measure of success and become a valuable asset to his team.

Frontal Tackle. The beginner should first learn the basics of executing the frontal tackle. To accomplish this maneuver, the fullback must jar his opponent slightly, but legally, with his shoulder by leaning into him as the two men come together. To prevent the opponent from getting around him, the fullback must maintain perfect balance by bending both knees into the play. By putting his shoulder into the charge, he will be able to knock his opponent off balance and force him to back away from the ball. As soon as he is able, the fullback should get his foot under the ball and lift it quickly to prevent the opponent from regaining control. To force the ball free, the fullback should push his opponent with his tackling leg at the same time he uses his shoulder. In the frontal tackle, it is best to use the inside of the foot, with the ankle held rigidly. The body weight should be placed over the ball. When a fullback has executed all of these body movements, then to get the ball away he must swing his tackling leg in and push the ball away from the man who has possession of it. The most frequent mistake that players learning the frontal tackle make is that they are often too anxious and lunge at the ball too soon. This warns the dribbler of what the defender is planning, and with a quick pullback of the ball, the forward can not only dribble off in another direction but he will usually leave the fullback on the ground since when the defender starts the tackle, he will be falling against air.

If the opponent is running downfield ahead of the defense, the frontal tackle cannot be executed. One of the most efficient tackling methods in this situation, however, is the side-block tackle, which is used by such defenders as Charlie Aitken, who joined the Cosmos after playing with England's Aston Villa. To execute the tackle, the fullback must first get his tackling leg in front of the ball. This not only slows down the opponent's dribble but, even more important, it can jar the ball loose from his possession, giving the defender the opportunity to take the ball away cleanly with a quick pivot of his tackling leg. As soon as the fullback completes his pivot, he should use a shoulder charge, because the opponent is no longer in complete control of the ball, and the object is to keep him off balance while the defender remains steady to take the loose ball back on attack.

The same principle applies when the defender is behind his opponent and unable to catch him. If, however, a fullback sticks his non-tackling leg in front of an opponent and trips him, and at the time does not have his tackling leg in a position to gain control of the ball, he will be charged with a foul and the other team will be awarded a free kick. Many times the fans will scream that an opponent has tackled their man and tripped him in the process, but if the tackle is legal, it is not a foul.

Sliding Tackle. The sliding tackle—whether executed with one foot, as most Europeans prefer, or with two feet, as the South Americans favor—should be avoided if it is possible to tackle in any other way. The sliding tackle has left more forwards wide open for a clear path to the goal than any other maneuver, because the defender who tried this tackle was left lying flat on the ground after the forward spotted what he was attempting to do and either slowed down or moved to the side to avoid him. In making this type of tackle, the defender must veer slightly away from his opponent and keep his tackling leg well behind the other leg. As he starts the tackle, he should bend his inside leg since that is the leg that will be carrying the most weight, and otherwise the chance for injury is great. The fullback should maintain his balance as he starts the tackle and should hold one hand on his inside leg. If he is attempting a two-footed sliding tackle, then he must bend both legs, because they will be coming into contact with the man who has the ball. It is a beautiful play when it works, but a fullback is destined to look foolish if he fails to accomplish what he set out to do.

Scissor Kicks

Unlike the forward who might occasionally attempt to score with the scissor kick, the fullback or defender executes this play not to entertain the crowd but to stop a ball from getting past him if he hasn't the time or the room to stop the ball or the opponent in any other way. When it is attempted inside the penalty area, there is great danger because if the official feels that the defender has interfered and made contact with the man controlling the ball, he could easily charge him with a foul. To execute the scissor kick, a player should pull his toes back and hit the ball with the top of his foot at about the time it comes to him waist-high. This angle sends the ball backward, where it usually covers great distance because of the powerful followthrough. Again the player should lean his body backward to ensure greater movement. The scissor kick is recommended except when there is heavy activity in the area, because in this case a foul will often be charged for dangerous play.

Headers

Forwards and midfielders aren't the only players on a team who must know how to head a ball.* One of the most accurate ways to clear a ball upfield and out of danger is with one's head, and that is why all major teams require their fullbacks to join the other players for heading drills. One of the ways a fullback can aid his goalie is by heading the ball to him. But there is also great danger in this type of play, because if the goalie is unaware that the fullback plans to head the ball to him or if the header is too powerful or spins too much, then the fullback might make a self-goal, since he will put the ball into his own team's net.

In the finals of the 1976 European Nations Cup, the great West German National Team gave Czechoslovakia one of its goals when one of the West German fullbacks headed the ball with too much spin to keeper Sepp Maier, who could only deflect the ball to the right, where a Czechoslovakian forward was waiting to kick home the rebound for a goal.

The fullback must be able to head the ball back, in which he bends his body backward and strikes the ball with the uppermost portion of his forehead. He should use this maneuver only after making sure that no opposing forward is charging in and that his own goalie is in a perfect position to be ready for such a maneuver.

In trying to head a ball back to his own goalie while facing him, the

*See chapter 24.

fullback must be sure to get the ball high enough and with as little spin as possible so that the goalie will be able to catch the header. He should, therefore, try not to flick his head because a flick of the head will spin the ball, which is undesirable since the object is not to score but just to clear the ball to the goalie. Often when the pressure is mounting, a fullback may attempt to clear the ball over his own goal line. Although this gives the opposition a corner kick, at the same time it eases some of the pressure for a few valuable seconds so a team can regroup its entire defense.

The two basic steps that a fullback must remember while making this type of header is that when attempting to clear the ball over his own goal line, he should flick his head high enough to get the ball to carry over the goal, and he should send the ball far enough to the side to prevent it from going into one of the corners of the net for a self-goal. The defender should also head the ball wide and as far away from the goal as possible.

When he feels that he should head the ball to one of his teammates, he should make sure that he avoids heading it to a teammate who is surrounded by opposing players. He should pick out another fullback or even a halfback and head the ball swiftly to him so that the teammate is able to get the ball under control quickly. Until a fullback masters the technique of defensive heading, he will be far from a complete defender.

Kick Defenses

Fullbacks also play an important role when the other team has been awarded either a corner kick or a direct free kick from just outside the penalty area.

Corner Kick. As soon as the referee signals for the opposition to take a corner kick, the fullbacks must be ready to defend. If the corner kick is to be taken from left of the goalie, the right fullback must run over to the goal area and position himself about five yards ahead and to the goalie's right, cutting down the opening where many good corner kickers aim. The two center fullbacks or the center back and the sweeper should plant themselves on the edge of the penalty area and at the center of the goalkeeper's position. The left fullback in this case should go out about 10 yards from the man who is taking the corner kick.

Since many teams use a short corner kick, which is actually nothing more than a pass from the corner kick spot, it is often the left fullback's responsibility to cover any loose offensive men who might come in for the short corner and then cross the ball. Interchanging positions are vital in defending against a corner kick. If the center backs are being crowded by three or four opponents, for example, the fullbacks on either side of the goalie must be aware that a set play may have been worked out and that one of the uncovered forwards might even dribble the ball for a clear shot on the goal. Only by working together for long hours can the defense learn who must cover whom or what area and what to do once the ball comes into the goal area.

Often the man guarding the near post, the goalpost nearest to where the corner kick is to be taken, will head the ball right over the goal line. This player must also make sure when the goalie calls for the ball (either by yelling to him or by prearranged signal), that he steps aside and lets the goalkeeper catch the corner kick. The fullback at this position must also make sure that he blocks one of the forwards out of the play, without committing a foul. Once the corner kick has been lofted or lined (shot at waist level) inside the goal area, the man at the near post should immediately get back as close to the goal line as possible. If the goalie is unable to catch or punch the ball out, this player must make sure to head the ball off the goal line or kick it as far downfield as possible to give his defense more time to organize itself against the next attack by the opposition. Defending against corner kicks is a vital part of the game, and that is why great defenders are among the highest-paid players in the world.

Direct Free Kick—The Wall. If the opposing team is awarded a direct free kick, in which the ball can go into the goal for a tally without first touching anyone else, the fullbacks play the most important part in the defensive wall. They must follow the instructions of the goalie as to who and how many will form the wall; often there will be three fullbacks, two halfbacks, and even a forward or two, but that is up to the goalkeeper. Everyone in the wall must know what to do in the event the ball comes directly at him. The man attempting the shot may try to fool the defense with a short lob over the head of the wall instead of a bulletlike kick, for example. The defense must try to head out such a lob shot, and if a man starts to break through the wall, it is up to the defense to keep him from sliding through to where the ball is being passed. Once the direct kick or the lob pass is taken, the wall immediately must disband and a tight man-to-man or zone coverage should be put into effect.

Indirect Free Kick—The Wall. For an indirect free kick, the defense must try to figure out to whom the shooter will be passing, because the ball must touch another player before a goal can be scored. Many teams position one of their men alongside the man taking the indirect free kick. The defense must keep a close eye on this man, as one of the favorite offensive plays is to have the man taking the indirect free kick shuffle a pass to his side, where the other man receives it and then fires the ball toward the goal. The defensive wall must space itself to cover the players alongside the man taking the indirect free kick, making sure that there are no holes in the wall for the receiver to shoot at once he gets the ball.

Throw-ins

Guarding Against. Guarding against a throw-in from anywhere within 30 yards of the goal is also important, even if the throw-in is not of the long-range variety. The defenders must cover every man in the area around the throw-in. Many teams have been fooled by a short throw-in; while they were covering all the open men, they forgot about the man who was making the throw-in. This man would simply throw the ball to his nearest teammate and then step onto the field, finding himself wide open and unmarked for a return pass. To prevent this, the defense should assign one man to cover the man who is taking the throw-in. The defense should also make sure that there is a man near the goal once the throw-in has been made. This will prevent the man receiving the throw-in from quickly crossing the ball into the goal area.

Often a crowd will roar its disapproval when a fullback intercepts a pass by the opposition and seeing that a pass upfield is not wise, passes the ball back to his own goalie. If executed correctly, however, this is one of the most effective plays in defensive soccer. But when he makes this play, the fullback should be aware of exactly where his keeper is at all times and make sure that the pass is neither too slow to be intercepted by an oncharging forward nor so hard that it gets past his keeper. It should be rolled accurately so the goalie is not forced to make a difficult save. The ball should come to the goalie so that he can pick it up without anyone around him and then release it either by a throw or a punt. As soon as the ball is sent back to the goalie, the man who sent it to him must then get in a position to receive the pass if that is the game plan.

Making Them. The fullback is often called upon to make a throw-in, and unless he executes this maneuver perfectly, the opposing team will often intercept the ball. When making a throw-in, a fullback should make sure that the man to whom he is throwing the ball is in the clear. When he throws the ball in to the goalie, he should also make sure that the keeper is either wide open to receive the throw-in or that there are no opponents between himself and the goalie at the time of the throw-in. Otherwise, the player who intercepts the throw-in may suddenly fire a shot at the goalie. As a rule of thumb, a fullback should try to spot a teammate free and away from his own goal when he makes the throw-in.

Zone and Man-to-Man Defense

There are two major defensive tactics in soccer—the man-to-man defense and the zone defense—and often during a game the fullbacks will switch from one to the other if one system isn't working. In a man-to-man defense, each of the fullbacks has a specific opponent to cover. The zone defensive system is much harder to use, and is often used in combination with the man-to-man system. Under the zone setup, each man is assigned an area rather than a player to cover. The one weakness in this system is that if the attacking team overloads one zone, a single player might find himself overwhelmed. If this occurs, then other fullbacks must immediately break from their zones and come into the overloaded area to help out. Not all four fullbacks should move to the troubled zone, however. One of the men guarding the other side of the field should stay there in case the three attackers see that they are being matched by three defenders and try to find the open winger on the other side of the field. It takes a great deal of insight to know when to come out of the zone and when to cover the attackers on an individual basis.

Offside Trap

A good defensive unit should also be able to execute the offside trap, in which the attackers are allowed to work the ball around while the defenders slowly move upfield, leaving an attacker alone inside the goal area. According to the rules, this is an offside violation, but there is always the danger that the referee or linesman will not notice that the defenders have moved away and will allow a goal to stand.

Open-Space Pass

The fullback is also required to master the open-space pass. If he is able to execute this type of pass from around the edge of his own penalty area, then he will force the opposition to send a man into that area in an attempt to get the ball. If he is open, he will then be able to come in for a return pass and go downfield for a possible goal. There have been many cases, however, in which the fullback taking the ball upfield has been intercepted and a goal scored against his team because of a foulup by the other fullbacks on his team. That is why every fullback must know where to go when one of the other fullbacks takes the ball upfield. If the left fullback, for example, takes the ball upfield, then the right fullback should move slightly toward the center. One of the two center backs should remain where he was while the other center back assumes the previous position of the left fullback.

Fullbacks play a vital role in both the defensive and offensive setup of a team, and they must have skill, guts, and determination. They are the players who often make the difference between the success and failure of a team, and they will become even more important in the future as the total football concept continues to develop.

CHAPTER 23

Men in the Middle

No matter what formation a team plays, the men in the middle— known either as halfbacks, midfielders, or linkmen— are the ones who must tie the defense with the offense. The history of the game is filled with accounts of men who have excelled in this position. During the 1976 North American Soccer League season, fans were treated to the performances of such top midfielders as former English World Cup captain Bobby Moore, who was playing with the San Antonio Thunder; Dave Clements of Northern Ireland and Everton; besides two of Pelé's former Santos teammates—Ramon Mifflin, who has also excelled for the Peruvian National Team, and Nelsi Morais—both of whom joined Pelé with the New York Cosmos.

EXPECTATIONS OF HALFBACKS

The duties of the midfielders vary greatly. Some teams want their midfielders to come up on attack only when they're pounding away at the opposition's goal, while other teams, primarily those influenced by the English style of play, want their halfbacks to fall back immediately and aid the defense whenever the other team gets the ball. Still other teams want their halfbacks to challenge for the ball at midfield, while others allow the other team to get control of the ball and then have their linkmen step back and challenge only about 35 yards from their own goal. There have been many debates about what system of play halfbacks should utilize, but under the trend toward total football, the idea is developing that at least two of the midfielders should be more devoted to the attacking style of play than to defensive tactics. Under the old M or W formations, when each team utilized two fullbacks and three halfbacks along with their five forwards, the midfielders were seldom found deep in the opponent's territory. But with today's system of play, a team may use either the 4-2-4 or 4-3-3 style, and the halfback has more offensive liberty than in the past. It's simply a matter of numbers, since it is hard for a team using only three or four forwards to penetrate the other team's area if the defense is using the same system of play. Under a system of play resembling a 4-4-2 setup, which some coaches used in the NASL campaign during late 1975 and early 1976, halfbacks are especially important. Under this setup, unless the halfback is able to go on the attack at every opportunity, the chances that one's team will score a goal are almost nonexistent.

Endurance
Although all the players on a team must be in top physical condition, it is the halfbacks who lack of this conditioning who will be noticed most by both fans and the opposition alike. A forward and a fullback must be able to run top speed, but they do have moments of rest on the field when the play is in the opposition's end of the field or in their own, depending on their position. There is no rest for the halfback, however, who runs an estimated 10 miles during a game. He should be the most exhausted player after a game, or he may not have played as well as he should have.

Multifunctional Man
The halfbacks are the men who help set not only the offensive pattern of their team in motion but the defensive patterns as well and must be able to execute every play in the game. They must be among the best on their team at tackling, be able to pass accurately to set up goals, be able to take long throw-ins, and do just about everything that a full-back or forward does. The scoring statistics of any major league game, whether in North America, Europe, South America, Asia, or Africa, will reveal that the halfbacks get their share of goals, shots on goals, and assists. The halfback is usually charged with more fouls than the fullbacks, but at the same time he also draws his share of fouls by the opposing team. Because of the constant pressure that he is under during the game, the halfback also comes up with his share of injuries.

The Skipper
As soon as the game gets underway, the halfback must establish himself on either offense or defense. If the other team eventually scores a goal, he is the man who will be criticized for allowing the play to reach his end of the field. He is also the man who can control the tempo of the game. He is called the "skipper" in soccer, even though some teams don't select a captain from among the halfbacks. His jobs are many and they start as soon as the referee blows his whistle to

indicate that the game is about to begin. Being a halfback is not easy, and many top forwards who were made midfielders in their later days have found the transition almost impossible to make.

Even before the kickoff is made, the halfback must survey the opposition's setup. If his team is to take the kickoff, he must see how the opposition's fullbacks and midfielders are setting up. If his team is not making the kickoff, he must make a quick estimation of where the other team's inside and outside forwards and halfbacks will be coming as soon as the initial contact has been made with the ball.

Once the ball has traveled the distance of its circumference, it is considered in play. More often than not the halfback will get a pass back from one of his forwards, who has either made the kickoff himself or received a short pass from the man who took the kickoff. The halfback must then decide whether he will boot the ball upfield (usually to the side) or if he will dribble the ball while his forwards are racing downfield, in an effort to draw the other team's defenders over to him and create more room for his forwards. He must make the decision knowing that if he does dribble and loses the ball, then the other team will have fewer defenders to contend with.

Once the halfback who gets the pass back from the opening kickoff is challenged, he must also determine if he can get around the defender challenging him, if it would be better to send a short pass cross-field to one of his team's other halfbacks, or if he should attempt to find one of his team's free forwards and start executing the wall pass, or the give-and-go. Once the plan is made to start the wall pass, there is no turning back, since the forward getting the ball will wait only a split second before returning the ball to the halfback.

Pelé played mainly a halfback role with the Cosmos when first joining the team in 1975, and along with Manoel Maria, he executed the wall pass perfectly. Maria would take the kickoff and dribble about 15 or 20 yards inside the other team's territory. He would then release a quick pass to Pelé, who in turn would either make a short dribble of his own and then pass the ball back to the oncoming Maria for a shot on goal or in some cases immediately execute the heel pass—flicking the ball back to Maria with the heel of his foot. In these cases, Maria would have to put on extra speed to be in position to receive the return pass, since the entire play was completed in less than a half a second.

A halfback must be able to vary the type of play he will execute upon receiving the ball from the kickoff. If he is unable to do this, then the opponents will learn in a very short time exactly what type of play to expect from him and will intercept the ball and be on their way downfield in a counterattack.

Halfbacks are also called on to make rapid decisions regarding the team's style of play. If the halfback feels that his team is wasting numerous opportunities by not moving the ball quickly or in a certain manner, it is his job to control the pace himself with speedy, sharp passes. If, on the other hand, he feels that the defense is slow in reaching and that he will be able to accomplish much more by slowing down the pace of the game, then by all means he should slow down the flow of play by working the short, slow pass with the other halfbacks in order to spread out the opposing defense and find obvious weaknesses.

Passing and Dribbling

The great halfbacks of the game have also been great passers, for both short and long distance. If the halfback is dribbling and sees that he is going to have trouble avoiding an oncoming opponent, for example, he must try to upset the other team's defensive tactics by lobbing a high pass into the goal area with the expectation that one of his forwards or fellow halfbacks will be there to receive the ball and head it past the goalie. He must also have the ability to pass the ball down the wings, which will draw out the opposition's center back and leave the middle of the goal area less congested so that one of his teammates can get in for a clear shot on goal.

On dribbling the ball, most halfbacks prefer to take the ball down one of the wings, as they feel that if they are intercepted, their fullbacks will have a much better chance to set up a defensive pattern than if the dribble is intercepted in the center of the field. No matter where he plans to dribble the ball, however, the fullback must have mastered all the techniques of dribbling that the forwards on his team have.

Challenging the Dribbler

When the other team is making the kickoff, the defensive duties of the halfback are many and include anticipation. When the opposition takes the kickoff, a team will usually send three forwards up to try to stop the play before it gets started effectively. If they are successful in intercepting the ball, however, then they will have generated their own attack, and the halfback will be expected to come upfield as fast as possible to aid in the concentrated drive on the goal. But if the opposition has successfully brought the ball toward the other team's goal and the three forwards are left hanging downfield, the defending team will now be considerably outnumbered, and it is often the halfback's duty to go out and challenge the ball carrier by trying to tackle the ball away from him. It is here that differences between various teams become apparent. Some coaches will be happy to have the halfback challenge the dribbler. Others, however, may decide that he should retreat and allow the opposition to gain control of the midfield. This will make his team weaker in the middle, but by having the halfback to help the fullbacks, the team will, in turn, be stronger against a concentrated offensive thrust by the opponent.

If the opposing team is starting to make a drive upfield off the kickoff, the halfback must try to force the opposition to the side, away from the center. This will not only alleviate the congestion around the penalty area but will also slow down the attack enough to give the defending fullbacks the opportunity to position themselves to handle the attack from wherever it might be coming. Often a halfback will not be successful in getting the ball away from an opponent by a tackle and consequently must play the attacker man-on-man and try to slow down the progress of the play. When the attacking team sends a wave of five or six men off the kickoff toward the goal, sometimes a desperate attempt at a tackle will result in a foul, but if the foul was committed far from the defender's goal, then it was a move necessary for slowing down the attacking team.

Fouling
A deliberate foul is not recommended as a means of hurting an opponent, and to our knowledge few, if any, of the leading European or South American teams play with the direct intention of injuring someone. A slight push off the ball or a grab at a player's shirt is recommended, however, for getting the referee to whistle a foul and delay the ball from being put in play again. At times such a foul may be the only solution to the dilemma that a team is in if it is unable to intercept the ball or kick it over the touch line.

Tackling
Often the best opposing forward will be guarded not by a fullback but by the halfback who is the best at tackling and who has the agility to avoid being tripped out of the play. He must maintain his balance, and by doing so, he continually challenges the top forward until his teammates have the opportunity to come and help him out.

Taking Corner Kicks
Halfbacks also figure prominently when their team is either taking or defending against a corner kick. Utilizing the 4-3-3 system of play, if the cross off the corner is made in his direction, the halfback in front of the goal will get the opportunity to head the ball into the net. The man nearest the goalie will attempt to outjump the goalie, who will come for the cross, and if the ball is too far across the goal area, he should immediately race sideways to get the ball either with his head

290

or with a quick chest trap and put the ball down to his feet and kick it either to a teammate who is in the clear or into the goal. The man at the edge of the penalty area should pick up any rebounds that might come out and, even more important, intercept any clearing passes or kicks from an opposing defender. While their team has the ball, the halfbacks can often be effective decoys by moving before the corner kick has been taken, forcing the opposition to change its defensive structure to cover them. This at times will leave one of the forwards clear in front of the goal.

Defending Corner Kicks

When the other team is awarded a corner kick, the halfbacks naturally must assume other duties. If a corner kick is to be taken from the right of the goalie, the right halfback must guard the area at the right side of the net some 10 or 12 yards out. The opposing team's center forward or striker will be coming in from around that area, and the halfback must guard him one-on-one. The left halfback should position himself about five or six yards slightly to the goalie's left and, along with his team's other defenders, must be prepared to head the ball out of danger. Under the 4-3-3 system, the center half should remain in front of his defenders. If a short corner kick is taken, he must move quickly to whichever side of the field the ball is in to help his teammates there. He sometimes is also responsible for covering the man who has taken the corner kick, since after executing it the kicker will race into the goal area to pick up a loose rebound if he has the opportunity. If the center halfback is able to gain possession of the ball, then his best bet is either to kick the ball upfield out of danger or start dribbling toward the side of the field. In guarding against the corner kick, halfbacks must know exactly where their teammates are positioned and should be prepared to kick the ball firmly over the touch line if they feel they are unable to get the ball upfield or dribble it.

Defending Throw-ins

On throw-ins the halfbacks also play a vital role both when they are making the throw-in and when the opposition is executing the maneuver. During a throw-in by the opposition in the midfield area, the defensive halfback must guard the men flooding into the middle of the field. If the man the halfback is assigned to guard does get the ball, then before he is able to turn upfield, the halfback should quickly try to get the ball by a sliding tackle. It is much better and much safer to let the opponent have another throw-in than to let him turn and get past, leaving the halfback out of the play and as a result putting added pressure on the defense. Anticipation is critical in guarding against a throw-in as is full knowledge of the opponent. Most opposing midfielders, for example, who will be taking the throw-in for their own team around the middle of the field, will try to throw the ball either ahead to one of their wingers or backward to one of their fullbacks, who in turn will either dribble down the wing, send a long pass to one of his team's wingers, or kick the ball toward the goal area. If the halfback is unable to intercept the throw-in or tackle the opponent, he should make the opponent rush his kick so that his men don't have time to get into the proper position to receive the pass.

Making Throw-ins
Just as the halfback guards against the other team's throw-ins, however, he must be able to judge where to make the best throw-in from the middle of the field. A throw-in going to a marked man will usually be intercepted, for example, and the halfback will not only have lost the possibility of gaining control of the ball, but since he is out of bounds at the time of the throw-in, the opposing team will be on its way toward the goal while his team is in effect one man short. On a throw-in in the middle of the field, the halfback should try to spot a man able to get away from his defender and hit him with a sharp throw-in. If the halfback makes the throw-in behind a defender, then if he is close enough, he should make sure to cut into that area of the field to receive a possible return pass. The halfback making the throw-in can thus start good offensive play, and he must not waste the opportunity.

Handling Goal Kicks
When a team makes a goal kick (awarded when the opposition sends the ball over the goal line), then more likely than not the halfback will move to a spot where he can prevent a possible return of the kick, should it be short or wild. If he is able to stop the opposition's interception, it is best not to hesitate in getting rid of the ball. Halfbacks should also be ready to receive passes from their fullbacks or goalie, depending on who is taking the goal kick.

Handling Free Kicks
The halfbacks also play an important role in making and defending against free kicks. Often a halfback will play in the defensive wall his team sets up against a direct free kick. Here he will be called on to make all the moves of a fullback, and no matter how hard the kick comes at him, he must not duck or else there will be a hole in the wall and the ball could sail into the goal. The halfback should not try any fancy maneuvers but should head the ball either upfield or to the touch

line. On offense the halfback may often be called on to take the kick, and here he must be powerful and accurate at the same time. But if another player on his team is taking the free kick, the halfback should position himself where he will be able to work himself free for a rebound as well as where he can break through the wall if the play calls for the man taking the direct free kick to lob the ball over the heads of the wall men.

Open-space Passing

Halfbacks will also be called on to make the open-space pass, and a well-executed open-space pass is one of the most effective ways to take the pressure off closely guarded teammates. Defenders tend to rush to wherever it appears that a pass will end up in the other team's possession. But the intention behind the open-space pass is just that. In other words, the ball is heading for what appears to be an open space, but when it actually gets there, it will be met by a teammate of the man who passed it. The defense will have committed itself in haste to that area, possibly leaving the man who made the pass virtually unmarked to receive a quick return pass and be on his way downfield for a possible goal. Many goals are set up in this manner, but only a complete understanding of the play will make it work.

Unsung Heroes

The halfback once was considered just a man to help either the defense or the offense when needed, but that concept changed with the 4-2-4 and 4-3-3 systems of play. Those teams that have only two halfbacks in their formation, such as the ones utilizing the 4-2-4, must make sure that the halfbacks work a triangular shape of attack—with their striker while going forward, and with the center back while going backward. This style of play is often used in such nations as Poland and Czechoslovakia, both of which were successful in the mid-1970s. The halfback with stamina, dribbling, and passing skills; the ability to spot and then exploit the openings; and the great gift of anticipation is becoming more and more important to teams no matter what type of pattern of play they use.

Halfbacks have been called the unselfish players on the soccer team because they often have to change their own style of play to help one of their teammates. Of course, that is why halfbacks do more work, both physically and mentally, than any other player, and consequently we must not criticize them for the mistakes they sometimes make.

Some say that by the early 1980s, the halfback will be the dominant player in soccer everywhere in the world. Indeed, a halfback who can put the ball into the goal with any regularity, besides defending and attacking, will soon be the highest-paid player on the team.

CHAPTER 24

Forward Play

There was a time not too long ago when each team presented a lineup consisting of five forwards whose only job was to score goals. Today a man who can do little else but score goals is almost worthless to teams that use the total football concept of play.

MULTIFACETED SCORERS

Because of the new role of the forwards, their tasks today are much more complicated than in the 1960s. Not only must they score to keep their team winning and the fans coming to see their games, but they must also be able to defend against breakaways and then come back and help their defensive teammates clear balls away from the goal, aid in stopping corner kicks, and get into the wall setup to stop opposing team's free kicks. The forward who is unable to run for the full 90 minutes is no longer the forward who gets the highest ratings in the game.

Probably no one is better able to demonstrate the new duties of a forward than the great Pelé, who one minute can be found in the defensive wall, the next minute coming back to clear a corner kick from the opposing team, and then with a sudden burst of speed be on his way downfield either with or without the ball, getting into a position to score.

The total concept of football calls for the forward to be all over the field, and many times he will be on defense when the other team is pressing until he himself intercepts a pass. During the 1976 North American Soccer League and American Soccer League campaigns, forwards were in several key instances credited with stopping opposing forwards deep in their territory. With their skillful passing, they were also responsible for setting up numerous goals that were scored by the halfbacks.

Men like Pelé and Eusebio have been able to adjust to the new style of soccer, but many others have had more trouble. Not only must today's "complete" forward be able to play defense, but when it comes to getting the ball into the net or setting up a play in which one of his teammates finished with a goal, he must often use a combination of shots, passing, and dribbling.

Kicking

Kicking a ball is an art. Just because a punter in football can send the ball downfield for a long distance doesn't mean he will make a good soccer player. It takes far greater skill to drive a ball into the back of the net from 15 to 20 yards out than it does to make a long punt. The three greatest kick "weapons" a scorer has are the instep kick, the kick with the inside of the foot, and the kick with the outside of the foot. If he is able to utilize any of these three kicks and add a little swerve to the ball when he kicks it, a forward has a better chance of scoring a goal than the man who shoots what is called a flat shot, with no curve to the ball.

Rivelino took over the curving shot after the great Pelé left Brazilian soccer. When Rivelino sends a shot toward the opposing team's defensive wall, the ball angles sharply around the outside man in the wall, and the opposing goalie goes crazy as he first leans one way and then the other in an effort to catch the ball. If he is able to get his hands on the ball, the curving is often so pronounced that he won't be able to hold onto it, and the ball will slip onto the waiting feet of a forward who is running in for a rebound shot and an easy goal.

One of the main things that both youngsters and many pros often forget is not to kill the shot when they are five or even 10 yards from the net on the rebound. A simple nudge of the ball will send it home more often than not, especially since the goalie is usually unable to recover from the initial contact with the ball in sufficient time to make a save.

The Instep Kick. One of the main advantages of the instep kick is that the ball usually goes straight to where it is aimed. It often takes a great deal of practice to execute this kick well, but shots in professional games that wind up in the goal or force the opposing keeper to make a save have more likely than not been kicked with the player's instep. The kick looks simpler than it really is. To a layman, the ball often looks like it has been booted with the player's toes. But the player actually strikes the ball with the laced part of his boot.

In executing the instep kick properly, there are certain elements that a player must remember. The basic rule is that the toes must be kept downward, otherwise the ball will hit the ground too quickly or be chipped (lifted high in the air), providing little chance of scoring a goal. The player executing the kick should flex his knees, much as he would if he were running at full speed. In addition on all instep shots, much of the shot's power comes from the important follow-through. In the followthrough, the knee continues as if it were swinging through the center of the ball while the arms swing back in the opposite direction. This enables the player not only to get the maximum power on his shot but also to maintain his balance in the event that the ball becomes loose and a rebound opportunity arises.

The Outside Kick. Another important shot that a successful forward should master is the kick with the outside of the foot. Although it is not so powerful as the instep kick, it still serves a valuable purpose. Many players will use this type of kick only rarely for a clean shot on goal, but numerous goals have been scored with it. The kick is used mainly for passing to a player cutting down one's side. It is made with the outside of the foot and, if executed properly, usually produces an accurate pass. It is often used in the wall pass.

Before the Cosmos procured Italian forward Giorgio Chinaglia in 1976, Pelé and his former Santos teammate Ramon Mifflin utilized this type of passing very effectively. Pelé would go down toward the penalty area and then while faking a drive on goal would quickly kick the ball to Mifflin, who would draw the defenders. Pelé would continue right on toward the opposing goalie for a return pass from Ramon and a shot on goal. Ideally the player making the kick should stand 90 degrees from where he wants the ball to go and push the ball across with a swift motion of his leg.

A clever forward can also use this kick to feint effectively. In a game against the Los Angeles Aztecs, Pelé pushed the ball to his side with this pass and then swerved around to catch the ball perfectly with the inside of his foot, which completely fooled the opposing goalie, who thought that he could take his eyes off Pelé because he had seen him pass with the outside of his foot.

The Inside Kick. The kick with the inside of the foot is the one coaches first teach young players. It is the simplest one to learn, but it must be perfected before a player can consider himself an accomplished forward. At a FIFA coaching clinic held in West Germany in 1973, the coach was shocked to find that many coaches neglected to teach their players how to get use out of this type of kick effectively. The ball is kicked with the instep of the foot and provides varying power and accuracy. The instep of the foot is one of the strongest parts of the foot and the ball will not swerve when hit naturally, bound down, nor chip upward if the player remembers to kick the ball at a right angle to his body.

The Chip Kick. To many observers, the basic chip kick may seem to be just a simple loft. The kick is executed by using the lower part of the instep. One of the most appealing plays executed by many South American teams is the chip kick that clears the head of the defender and then rolls only a few feet before stopping dead. In the play, often used by a prearranged signal, one man will chip the ball upward and two of his teammates will rush to the spot where the ball is going. If a teammate gets there before a defender, he should either fire a rapid shot on goal or move the ball away from traffic. The defender will be forced to turn around or race backward to reach the ball. The chip shot or pass is also one of the best ways to set up a teammate for a head shot on goal, since the ball won't swerve before it contacts the player.

The Swerve or Banana Kick. The swerve kick, sometimes referred to as the banana kick, is one of the most difficult to master. To swerve the ball properly from right to left with the right foot, the player must hit the right side of the ball with a portion of his instep and toes, and his ankle must be turned outward. To swerve the ball from left to right, the player must have his instep around the left side of the ball. The swerve is used most effectively on corner kicks and can make a goalie commit himself before he normally would on a straight kick. A swerving ball can also end up in the far corner of the net, if the goalie is pushed backward as he attempts to grab the ball out of the air. If the swerve kick is going to the side of the goal, then the goalie must decide in a split second whether or not he will take the gamble and leave his nets to attempt to either catch or punch the ball out toward the midfield.

A low swerving kick, something done best by such players as George Best of the Los Angeles Aztecs and Rodney Marsh of the Tampa Bay Rowdies, is also an effective weapon, as a player can often trap the ball and boot it home. Many teams have started to utilize a predetermined plan in which a player will loft the ball off a corner either toward or away from the goal one time and, the next time he gets it, hit it low so that one of his teammates in the goal area will be in a position to trap the ball and score because the goalie will usually have already committed himself to coming out of the nets. Another advantage of the banana kick is that when the ball bounces, it spins in a slightly different direction from the way it was flying before it hit the ground. Even if he can get his hands on it, the goalie usually will be unable to hold onto it and prevent a rebound.

The Scissor Kick. Although it might excite the fans and sometimes lead to a goal, the scissor kick for all practical purposes is nothing more than a show maneuver and if not executed perfectly can lead to an injury. Even if the player is successful in executing this type of kick, there is a good chance that the referee will not only disallow a goal scored this way but will call a foul, because if a player makes a scissor kick with defenders around him, he could easily injure an opponent. To accomplish the scissor kick, which was made famous by Puskas, the player has to have his back to where he intends the ball to go. In the beginning sequence of the kick, the player leans away from the ball with both feet off the ground. With his hands stretched out to give him balance, he then boots the ball in midair with the kicking leg stretched straight out almost directly toward where he is trying to send the ball. The other foot or landing foot, as it is called, remains down. With the ball heading in the desired direction, the player then extends his landing foot slightly ahead of him toward the area in which he desires to land. He drops his hands to his sides with the palms down to cushion his fall and avoid injury and bends his landing leg so that his toes actually make contact with the ground first, all the time keeping the kicking foot in the direction from which he had started the kick. It is not easy to control this kick, and it takes a great deal of practice. If a player wants the ball to go over his right shoulder, then he must make the scissor kick with his left foot, and vice versa. In executing the scissor kick, the player must strike the ball when it is over his body, and when striking the ball, he must hit it with the top of his foot with the toes flexed.

Volley Kicks. Two other maneuvers a forward should learn are the volley and half-volley kicks, which can be used either for shots on goal or for accurate passes. The half-volley is more difficult than the volley, but when it is performed perfectly, it can lead to a goal or at least a shot on goal that is difficult for a keeper to stop. The half-volley kick is executed by kicking the ball when it rebounds off the field's surface. A player can kick the ball at any height he desires, but for maximum force, he should strike at it where he feels most comfortable. In this type of kick, the player should lean his head and body slightly forward to maintain the perfect balance that is needed.

The full-volley kick differs from the half-volley in that the ball is kicked before it touches the surface of the field. Again, perfect balance must be maintained and the kicking leg should be on a level with the ball as it comes at the player. Many foreign players in the North American Soccer League have had trouble because they have been forced to rely more on the full-volley kick than the half-volley. They have found it difficult to control the half-volley on the artificial turf because of the unpredictable bounces that the ball will sometimes take. But although it is better in such cases to use a full-volley kick, there is the danger that some players will stretch too far in attempting to reach the ball and will pull a muscle, as Pelé did in 1975.

Trapping

Another skill that a good forward must master is trapping a ball in order to get a good shot on goal or to take off dribbling. By making a clean trap, a player has the advantage of knowing what he is going to do with the ball, and he gains that all-important split-second edge over the defender who must either get back in the proper position to stop the shot or attempt to take the ball away. The history of the game is filled with the names of men who electrified crowds with the way they would trap the ball. Pelé, who stresses trapping in the many clinics he conducts around the world, has been able to get away from more than three defenders through a clean trap, leaving them behind as he dribbled toward the goal.

Every part of the foot can be used to trap a ball, but a chest trap, a thigh trap, and even a head trap can fool the opposition and lead to a shot on goal. But no matter what type of trap a player attempts, one basic technique must be used: it is called the relaxation and withdrawal procedure, and it is as important to follow this as it is for a goalie to follow the rules for making saves. It involves simply placing one's foot gently on the ball and then withdrawing it to make the next move. Another important rule is to keep one's eyes on the ball, since the ball will often be swerving or bouncing wildly when a trap is attempted.

The Sole Trap. The most basic of all traps is the sole trap, and is, obviously, made with the sole of the foot. As the ball makes contact with the sole, the player crouches slightly forward with most of his weight on the nontrapping foot and bends the knee of his trapping leg. When contact is made, the leg must be relaxed and the foot drawn back slightly to cushion the impact of the ball. The ball stops once it makes contact with the sole, and the control of the ball is maintained by pushing the sole slightly back onto the top of the ball. From this position a player can either manipulate the ball to where he can kick it with the inside or outside of his foot, or he can push it slightly to his side and begin dribbling.

The Inside Trap. Forming the proper angle is essential for trapping with the inside of the foot—the trap that most professional players use. The player attempting this type of trap must first make sure that the nontrapping leg is placed slightly ahead of the leg he will use to do the trapping and stand with his knees bent slightly. The trapping leg should be held so that it forms a cushioning angle straight down between the ground and the inside of the foot. To execute the trap, the ankle, foot, and leg should be drawn back and downward to absorb the impact of the ball.

The Outside Trap. Trapping with the outside of the foot is very effective, because it can often facilitate either a solid kick or a quick pass. It is, however, not easy to master, and most players will avoid using it if a trap can be executed with another part of the body. What makes this particular trap so difficult is that if the player executing it does not balance himself perfectly, there is danger of a fall and even an injury. The trapping angle is formed by the ground and the outside of the foot, and the trapping leg must cross over the nontrapping leg. When stopping the ball, the player must remember to sweep his leg forward, which enables the ball to be positioned for the next move, whether a shot, a dribble, or a pass. The options available to a player who executes this trap successfully are numerous, and although it is difficult, every forward should master trapping with the outside of the foot.

The Thigh Trap. Many times players attempting to make a thigh trap lose complete control of the ball, which is then taken away by an opponent. Usually the main reason that the ball bounced wildly away from the player attempting to make the trap was that he forgot the basic ingredients for executing the trap—making sure to place the thigh at a right angle to the body and relaxing the thigh once it makes contact with the ball to prevent the ball from bouncing away. After the ball strikes, the thigh should be withdrawn. Because of its difficulty, many coaches recommend that the thigh trap be used only when no other is possible.

The Chest Trap. With practice, by using the area between the base of the neck and the sternum, one can execute the chest trap, one of the most efficient traps when a player knows in advance what he wants to do with the ball. Relaxation again is the single most important element in this maneuver. If a player doesn't relax when he receives the ball, the ball will rebound off his chest and either roll away or be intercepted by an opponent. The player's chest should be in line with the oncoming ball, and his hands must be at his sides, completely clear of his chest, or else he will be charged with a hand-ball infraction. When a player makes a chest trap, he can let the ball slide down to his feet for a powerful kick on goal or a sharp pass.

Dribbling

Although every player on the team must be able to dribble the ball, the forwards must be particularly adept at it since they are often forced to dribble while closely guarded and have less space in which to operate. That is why a good dribbler must be accomplished at feinting. With a quick, simple head movement, great dribblers like George Best, Pelé, and Antonio Simoes are able to fool defenders into going the wrong way while trying to intercept the ball. The recommended way to execute the head feint is to stand close to one's opponent without giving him a chance to take the ball away with a tackle. Making a series of gestures with his head and the body, a player should make the defender think he is heading in one direction, and once the defender commits himself, the player should move in the opposite direction. While dribbling in close quarters, it is not wise to continue in one direction, because the opposing defender will be able to position himself so that the player will run into him and either lose the ball or be charged with a foul for bumping into him. The best way to dribble is to use both the inside of the foot, which is a difficult technique for the opponent to defend against, and the outside of the foot, which allows an alert player to pass the ball quickly if he is stopped.

A good dribbler will never allow the ball to get so far away from him that he is forced to change his pace, but he will establish a change of pace deliberately. By quickly slowing down from a full-speed run down the wing or through the penalty area and simply placing his foot over the ball, for example, he can cause the opponent who is after him to lose his balance and thus clear himself for either a good shot on goal or an accurate pass. The dribble play often results in the wall pass. Pelé, for example, will run at full speed with the ball seemingly tied to his shoes; then he'll stop and send a pass to a teammate, who in a split second returns the pass so Pelé can get a shot and score.

Executing Headers

It is essential that every forward master the head shot since there will always be passes too high for him to kick. A good header usually changes the direction of the ball quickly, making it difficult for an opposing goalkeeper to make a save. No matter what type of head shot a player tries to make, the most important thing for him to remember is to fight the natural tendency to close his eyes when the ball is coming at him. When making the different types of head shots, a player should strike the ball with his head, not let the ball strike his head. In other words, the player should make contact with the ball, not the ball with him. He should hit the ball with his forehead, because that is the flattest and hardest part of the head and the part least likely to be injured. In executing the perfect header, the feet, neck, legs, and trunk of the body must work in perfect harmony. When his head makes contact with the ball, the player should lunge forward with his upper torso and bend at the waist, letting his legs form the powerful base for the execution of the shot. With this technique, a player will be able to make the header while standing flat on the ground. If he is forced to leap upward to make contact with the ball, however, then the power is gone from his legs and feet and has to come from his neck and trunk.

Changing the direction of the ball with a header is an effective way to score goals. If the ball is coming from the right side and a player wants to have the header go to the left, when his head contacts the ball, he must turn his trunk, neck, and head to change the direction of the ball's flight. Sometimes a player will want to head a ball downward. To accomplish this, he should strike the ball from a higher position and keep his chin tucked into his neck, moving his trunk forward. To head the ball upward, he should reverse the maneuver, hitting the ball below. To execute a diving header, the player should propel himself either straight ahead or to the side, thrusting his trunk out fully and keeping his hands at his sides with the palms aiming forward in a manner similar to starting a dive in swimming. A player should not attempt a diving header when an opponent is next to him since an injury can easily result, and he can be cited for a foul if he bumps into the opponent.

The Deflection Header. Another header that is sometimes used is the deflection header. Because the player executing the maneuver positions himself with his back to the goalkeeper, this shot can often surprise an opposing keeper. During the nationally televised 1976 game between the New York Cosmos and the Tampa Bay Rowdies, Derek Smethurst used the play to score a goal against Cosmos goalie Kurt Kuykendall. Smethurst received a pass from the side, and with a sharp movement of his neck, he was able to deflect the ball backward with great spin, fooling the goalkeeper. The deflection header can also be used effectively if the player leaps upward and glances the ball off the back of his head but this will hurt and should be avoided.

Making Throw-ins
Like other members of the team, the forward gets a chance to use his hands when he takes a throw-in. When a player kicks the ball over the side lines, the play is awarded to the opposing team. When made from anywhere within 20 yards from the end line a throw-in can be almost as effective as a corner kick, and many teams designate one man to take the throw-ins from this area, since he will be able to throw the ball into the goal area to set up one of his teammates for either

a header or a goal shot. Certain rules must be followed when making the throw-in to assure that it is legal. If the rules are not observed, the other team will be awarded the throw-in and the first team will lose the opportunity to score or maintain possession of the ball.

A player must have both hands on the ball while throwing it in, and he must throw it over his head with a followthrough, although the extent of the followthrough doesn't matter. He must also keep both feet on the ground until after the ball has been thrown in. The player is not allowed to cross over the touch line until after the ball has been delivered, and he must face the field so everyone can observe the throw-in. Proper execution of the throw-in is essential and only rarely is an illegal throw-in called during professional league games in the United States and Canada.

The Standing Throw-in. There are two types of throw-ins—the standing throw-in and the running throw-in. For the standing throw-in, the player must first assume a comfortable position, with his legs spread apart about shoulder width. The player can either keep his feet parallel or put one leg in front of the other. His fingers should be spread apart on both sides of the ball, and he should hold the ball about chest height and bend his knees forward in the direction in which he is going to throw the ball. While leaning his trunk back, he should raise the ball over his head with both hands facing downward toward the neck. He should then straighten his knees with his body following the knees in a forward motion, and his arms should follow his body, as he flicks the ball with his hands. For a long throw-in a player must use more body whip than for a short one.

The Running Throw-in. The running throw-in can be an effective weapon, and to execute it, a player must remember that the same rules apply as for the standing throw-in. When the ball is finally released, it is best for the player to have one foot in front of the other, since this will provide better balance and cause the ball to go farther. The back foot should then move parallel to the front foot, because this will enable the player to balance himself, and he won't be cited for not having both feet touching the ground. The followthrough in the running throw-in is much greater than in the standing throw-in, and one can use either his sole or his toes as a brake to stop the run.

Although forwards are usually considered the main scorers on a team, every player on the team would be wise to learn how to score. Shooting, passing, heading, dribbling, and throw-ins all can lead to goals and an accomplished forward, and anyone calling himself an accomplished player, should master these techniques.

CHAPTER 25

What's the Future?

The future of soccer is a subject that has produced many hours of debate among fans in North America, Europe, and South America as well. Pelé's signing by the New York Cosmos in 1975 was viewed by many as the turning point in the game both in the United States and Canada. Many others, however, felt that Pelé alone wouldn't be able to assure a successful future for soccer in North America.

Meanwhile, as enthusiastic followers of the game talked about the true emergence of the sport in North America, many fans in Europe were sending danger signals across the Atlantic as they openly expressed fear that the game was starting to lose its appeal in many European nations. Fans in South America expressed both optimism and despair for the future of the game there. Several nations that had long been successful in international soccer were starting to feel an economic pinch, and fans also feared that the exodus of many top South American soccer stars was going to take its toll not only on the field but at the gate.

When Pelé signed his lucrative contract with the New York Cosmos, he said that he did so as a mission. He felt that he could help the game develop here and give the United States and Canada the respect they never had in international soccer circles. No one can dispute that his arrival aroused more interest in soccer in the United States, but toward the end of his first season, there were already some discouraging signs. For example, although Washington, D.C., set a one-game NASL attendance record of over 35,000 fans when it hosted Pelé and the Cosmos at RFK Stadium, in its following home game attendance was down to the team's regular season average of around 3,000. The same was true in other cities, and Pelé's appearance with the Cosmos against Toronto in Toronto was said to have saved the franchise, enabling it to pay off past-due bills.

As the 1976 NASL season began, many people wondered if it would indeed be the year the sport finally turned the corner here. During the year, attendance was up 20 percent and a limited three-year TV pact was signed, but to many the future of soccer in the United States remains uncertain. Many people feel that despite all the foreign stars that are brought in, the game won't make it here as a full professional sport because foreign players won't get the children out to play the sport. The old National Professional Soccer League was formed in 1967 along with the United Soccer Association found that foreign players alone could not make the sport a success here. They also found that without a national television contract they would be unable to pay the bills.

Critics of American soccer argue that until the United States gets both a strong national team and a strong national soccer body to oversee the sport, the game will go nowhere here. The NASL heard these same comments several years before Pelé joined the Cosmos and attempted to stock some of its clubs with a fair number of collegiate players. The draft never accomplished what it was intended to do, however, as players drafted high often were dropped immediately, or, if they were selected to join the club, they found themselves on the bench. It got so bad that two of the teams even told the American players, who were needed to fill out the roster, not to report to practice. Some feel that this is the reason the league put an immediate limit on how many foreigners could play with each club instead of requiring American and Canadian players to be added to the roster each year. This quota system had been used in several European nations, including Spain and Italy, and seemed to ease the hard feelins that many natives had because of the wholesale importation of foreigners into their leading soccer clubs.

In 1976 the NASL and the United States Soccer Federation, the ruling body of American soccer, decided to host the American Bicentennial Soccer Cup. The national teams of England, Brazil, and Italy were invited to play a round-robin tournament in various American cities, and the field was completed by a squad called Team America. Many at first believed that Team America would be comprised of native American players. But fearful of poor attendance when that team played, the USSF decided that Team America would include foreign players who were participating in the North American Soccer League. Many critics protested that the USSF had sold the Americans out. They argued that a team with the likes of Pelé, George Best, and other foreigners could hardly be called Team America. But despite the indignation, the USSF went ahead with its plans and lost many loyal American players, who were needed to give America a solid team for future international competition. The USSF's decision was particularly bad, because 1976 also marked the beginning of the United

States' bid to gain a spot in the 1978 World Cup in Argentina. Critics argued that the experience the American players would have gained playing against Italy, England, and Brazil would have helped them be better prepared for their upcoming World Cup qualifying matches against Mexico and Canada.

But it was no surprise to those who have fought futilely for a strong U.S. National Team that the USSF ignored the interests of the American players. There have been many farces in the past, and players returning from foreign tours or games often relate astonishing accounts of incompetence. For example, when the entire United States team arrived in Bermuda the night before a game, the coach called the players into his room. Since he had not met most of them before, he asked them to raise their hands when he called their names. The first player replied that he played left wing and was shocked to hear the coach ask him, "Can you play defense?" As funny or as sad as his question might seem, this has repeatedly been the case as far as getting the United States National Team ready for an important international game.

In the successful soccer nations, the national team is usually selected almost a year before their World Cup qualifying rounds, and they are then kept together for several months of training and again assembled for two-week periods each month for the next six months. About a month before the scheduled game, the team is once more brought together in a regular training camp and stays together until their games are finished. A leading member of the USSF was once asked why the United States doesn't have a strong national team that can go into an international battle fully prepared. He replied, "The U.S. is too big to have a strong team selected that would stay together, and it's also very expensive."

The USSF has been called a closed body unwilling to take criticism, and hundreds of articles have been written about its failure to at least help get this country on the soccer map. With less than six months before the start of the 1976 qualifying matches for the World Cup, however, the U.S. National Team had still not been selected and no full-time coach had been hired, although the situation eventually was remedied.

Many feel that with its wholesale importation of players, the NASL has actually hurt the growth of soccer on a domestic level in this country. When Atlanta was a member of the NASL, for example, soccer started to become popular there. Youngsters received proper coaching and were permitted to use the many recreational facilities previously reserved strictly for American football. But many people in the city also had a strange feeling. Game after game, parents watched the Atlanta franchise take the field composed almost entirely of foreign-born players. How could an American boy go onto his local field, critics argued, and say that he was duplicating the moves of Boy Boy Moutang of Africa, for example? Although soccer continued to grow on the sandlot and junior level in Atlanta, fans ultimately stayed away from the games played by the professional team. Atlanta dropped out of the league as its stockholders (many of whom had also invested in the Braves baseball team) saw that they were hitting their heads against a wall.

St. Louis, on the other hand, promoted the idea of American players, and even though the franchise still loses money (as does almost every franchise in the league), the team is starting to gain acceptance. At one point late in the 1975 campaign, the team fielded an entire squad of Americans.

One of the biggest draws in the league during the 1975 season was the Portland Timber but they had only a few Americans on their roster. Before the start of the 1976 season, they were informed that they would have to follow league regulations and carry at least six Americans or Canadians on their 16-man roster. They went overseas and signed 10 foreign players, most of them English, and then invited numerous Americans to try out for the remaining six spots. A reporter asked the club's manager what would happen if during these tryouts he found that there were eight or nine good American players to sign. The answer was a classic example of poor public relations: the manager said that since he already had 10 foreign players under contract, he would be able to sign only six Americans.

The same anti-American bias is true of many of the other clubs in the league and in the rival American Soccer League, which in 1975 hired former basketball great Bob Cousy as its commissioner. The American Soccer League, which started in the middle 1930s and didn't expand to the West Coast until the start of the 1976 season, refused to limit the number of foreigners each club could sign.

Soccer purists are also quick to criticize the NASL for confusing the fans with its controversial offside rule (see chapter 17). Since FIFA, which is responsible for the international rules, has not gone along with the NASL offside regulation, American players in the NASL are faced with a serious problem when they engage in international competition. They must realign their style of game, which adds pressure onto their problems of being untrained.

Several years after it was formed, the NASL adopted a new scoring system that, it was felt, would give the American fans added excitement. After they realized that fans here would not tolerate the 0–0 games that European soccer fans might consider exciting, NASL officials replaced the internationally accepted scoring system of two points for a win, one point for a deadlock, and no points for a defeat, with a system in which a team would get six points for a victory and an additional point for each goal scored, up to three per game. A losing team would also be awarded one point for each goal it scored, up to three per game. So that no game would end in a deadlock, the league also instituted a tie-breaking procedure. If the two teams were tied after a 90-minute regulation time, then there would be a 15-minute sudden-death overtime session. In the event that neither team scored, a penalty shooting contest would be held, with each team taking five shots. If the game was still deadlocked, teams would alternately take penalty shots until one converted and the other missed.

The American Soccer League, for some reason, also decided to change its scoring system to award five points for a win with an additional point, up to three per game, for each goal the team scores. The losing team would also be awarded one point for each goal scored, up to three per game. The league also decided, however, that if the game was still tied after regulation time, there would be a sudden-death overtime session, but if still deadlocked, the game would be declared a tie with each team getting three points on top of one point per goal, up to three. It angers soccer purists that the internationally accepted scoring system has been pushed aside by both the NASL and the ASL.

Although there are currently many factors detrimental to the growth of soccer in North America, there are a number of positive aspects as well. In the suburbs of any major city in the United States, there will be hundreds of youngsters kicking around a soccer ball. They are the future of the game. But the youngsters' involvement in the game wouldn't be enough for the future of professional soccer in North America if it weren't for the interest of the parents. Many towns have established coaching clinics in which USSF-licensed coaches conduct lessons in the game. The referees have also realized that there aren't enough young referees and are currently setting up clinics for parents and club officials who want to help out their programs by officiating. The job is ambitious, but it is necessary to promote the growth of soccer in this country.

The future of the sport in the United States also rests with the colleges, which have increased their soccer participation over the last 10 years. Once only major schools located in major cities fielded soccer teams; but as the cost of fielding a football team has increased to where some can hardly afford it, soccer has filled the vacuum. The colleges have had to fight hard to get favorable rulings by the USSF, and they have succeeded; but the colleges may soon try to get a new national group formed. As one critic of the USSF said in 1974, "The organization has outlived its purpose."

In all probability, soccer will continue to grow in the United States, but it remains to be seen if this country will ever be able to take its place alongside some of the current giants of the game. Clearly FIFA and the rest of the soccer world would like nothing better than to see the United States climb the soccer ladder. Holding a World Cup in America appears to be a long way off, but when it does come about, FIFA, which derives substantial revenue from the tournament, will be able to count on receiving a lot of money, since an event of this magnitude in soccer has never been held in the United States.

Money appears to be the major problem plaguing soccer in many European nations. The financial crisis ruined several clubs in England, and many other clubs were forced to seek new backers. Owning a club in the prestige-laden English First Division was once considered a sure way to make money, and a team would do everything it could in order to avoid relegation to the Second Division. In 1975 and again the following year, however, many First Division clubs found that they couldn't meet the salary demands of their top players and started releasing them to play with other First Division or even Second Division clubs. Although at first this seemed to solve the financial problems of the troubled teams, they soon found that their fans were abandoning them. After selling some of its top players and refusing to buy other players to replace aged veterans, Sheffield United dropped from fifth place into the Second Division, and a certain financial crisis faces the team until it is able to climb into the top division once again.

Scotland's powerful clubs, finding that they drew good crowds in games against other top clubs, decided in 1976 to experiment with a Premier Division consisting of the 10 top finishers from the year before. The result was higher attendance and income for those clubs taking part in the new division, but a bigger loss than before for the other clubs. Several English First Division clubs wanted to try a similar arrangement for their 1976-77 season, but the English Football Association vetoed the idea because it was felt that the arrangement would increase financial failures and cause franchises to fold.

Spain seems to have solved some of its financial problems by allowing clubs to bring in top foreign players. Late in 1976, however, those interested in developing Spanish talent expressed a strong desire to limit the transfer of foreign players. Italy, also plagued with the loss of team revenue, has stood by its rule banning foreign players unless there are exceptional circumstances. The West German Football Association is also investigating the possibility of starting a premier division, but West Germany is one of the few European nations where the future of soccer does not look bleak.

During its 1975 and 1976 seasons, the North American Soccer League experimented on a limited basis with indoor soccer because it was believed that Americans wanted to see lots of goals scored, and the smaller field and rebounds off the sideboards produce more goals. But even though the goals came, the fans didn't, and except for the championship round for which many free tickets were given out, the venture was not successful financially.

When a Toronto-based promoter tried to form an International World Football (Soccer) League with teams in England, France, Germany, and Canada, he found that FIFA feels that it has the power to rule the game. West Germany was receptive to the idea at first, but once the novelty wore off, few fans came to the games.

South America is in a state of turmoil regarding its soccer future. The players have been complaining for many years about low wages, and during 1975 and 1976 there were player strikes in Argentina, Chile, and Uruguay. A team from Peru refused to take the field for an international game until the owner paid the players' back wages. Uruguay is probably worse off than most South American countries because its players are leaving en masse.

In an effort to appease some of its discontented players, Chile recently adopted the English Football Association's transfer fee regulation. The rule permits a player to transfer to another club if his wages are not paid or renegotiated at the end of his contract. If a player does sign with another club, then his previous team gets a fixed amount of money, depending on the player's past experience and his projected value to his new club, based on past performance. Argentinians are turning out in large numbers for soccer games, but the same is not true in Bolivia and Chile. Even in Brazil, where soccer is the king of sports, there has been a decline in attendance. Some of the financially troubled clubs have had to either sell their top players in an effort to meet the bills, or borrow in an effort to purchase top players from other teams, hoping new stars will bring in the fans.

In Japan, however, there has been a soccer boom. Attendance is up over 200,000 from the mid-1960s, and the team owners are making a profit. Naturally, the caliber of play has improved as well, and foreign teams, knowing that they will not be cheated, come to Japan to play games, thus bringing out more fans. Soccer is also becoming increasingly popular in Africa, and countries like Zaire, Zambia, and Ghana are now drawing more fans than ever before. But as their players become more famous, the foreign offers for their services flow more rapidly into their club's offices and there is danger that the top players will leave. The future of soccer in Australia, Iran (which has just built a new stadium), and Egypt also seems to be brighter than it was at the beginning of the 1970s. It appears that some nations are going to have to change their policies regarding players and others are going to have to find new ways of attracting fans if soccer is to remain the world's most popular sport.

Glossary

Understanding the terms used in soccer will surely heighten the enjoyment of fans everywhere. Here are the most common terms that one can expect to hear at soccer games. This list is by no means complete, for almost every day some terms are introduced that one day may become part of the accepted language of soccer.

Advantage rule   When the referee does not call a foul or an offside violation because, in his judgment, it would create an advantage for the offending team and a disadvantage for the team that was fouled.

Attacking team   The team in possession of the ball.

Backs   The halfbacks and fullbacks, also called midfielders and defenders.

Ball in play   The ball is continuously in play so long as it is in the field of play. It is out of play only when completely over the side line or goal line. The ball is the key, not the player.

Blanked   Shutout.

Breakaway   A maneuver in which an attacker breaks through the defense and approaches the goal alone for a shot on goal.

Bye   When there is an uneven number of teams, one team is selected to skip its initial game and then joins the winners of the first round in the next round.

Center   See Cross.

Charge   To use any part of the upper shoulder against an opponent to make him lose his balance. If a player uses his hands or any part of his arms (with the exception of the shoulders) to push an opponent, he will be charged with pushing, and the offended team will be given a free kick.

Clearing Moving the ball away from one's own goal. Goalies, defenders, and any other players back to help out the defense clear the ball away from the area around their own goal. A goalie can accomplish this by either punting the ball or by throwing it downfield to either side. Fullbacks and other defenders clear the ball away and out of danger by booting it, often backward, downfield. If they have a chance and are in the clear, defenders can also decide to dribble the ball away from the danger zone.

Corner kick A direct free kick given the offensive team when the defense sends the ball over its own goal line. It is kicked from the corner of the field nearest the spot where the ball went over the goal line. Any player on the offensive team may take the corner kick.

Cover To guard an opponent by remaining near him.

Cross A kick across the field to a spot out of the goalkeeper's reach and in front of the goalpost. It is usually associated with the wings. The wing and inside forward on the opposite side of the field are expected to meet the cross and head it at the goal.

Dangerous play An infraction that is called by the referee when a player does something that is likely to cause injury, such as bringing the foot up above shoulder level or putting one's head down to head in a low ball. The team that did not commit this foul is awarded an indirect free kick from the point of infraction.

Decoy play or move A play or move made to draw an opponent away from the ball and to open up a space so a teammate can move in.

Defender A player who primarily assists the goalie in protecting goal.

Defending team The team trying to gain possession of the ball.

Direct free kick A free kick from which a goal can be scored directly by the kicker, usually awarded for any personal foul.

Draw Any act that attracts an opponent toward a player. Usually executed when a player dribbles to pull a man to him in order to free a teammate for a pass.

Dribbling Advancing the ball by using the feet while keeping the ball within one stride and under complete control.

Drop ball A way to restart the game when the ball has not gone over the end line or side line and a free kick has not been awarded. The referee restarts the game by dropping the ball at the place where play was suspended. A drop ball is called when (1) play was suspended for injury to player or official, (2) the ball lodged between two players and the situation could cause injury, (3) interference by spectators caused the game to be stopped, (4) when the ball burst, etc.

312

Duration of game   Two halves of 45 minutes each. Halftime is 5, 10, or 15 minutes by consent of referee.

End line   The boundary line marking the ends of the field (also called goal line).

Field   The number of teams entered in a competition.

Field of play   An arena with the following specifications:

length: minimum 100 yards (90 meters); maximum 130 yards (100 meters).

width: minimum 50 yards (45 meters); maximum 100 yards (90 meters).

marking: distinctive lines on the field not more than 5 inches wide; also a flag on a post not less than 5 feet high placed in each corner.

goal: posts (or uprights) and crossbar 8 yards wide and 8 feet high (inside measurements).

goal area: marked 6 yards beyond uprights and extending 6 yards into the field.

penalty area: marked 18 yards to the side of each goalpost and 18 yards into the field.

penalty spot: marked 12 yards from the center of the goal in the penalty area.

corner area: a 1-yard arc marked in the field of play at each corner.

goalposts: 8 yards apart (inside measurement) on goal line, joined by a horizontal crossbar 8 feet from the ground (inside measurement). The width and depth of the crossbar and goalposts shall not exceed 5 inches (5 cm) and both should be the same.

offside line: in NASL play the offside line is placed 35 yards from the end line at each end of the field. In other jurisdictions, the center line is the offside line.

Formations   A strategic arrangement of players on the field. Examples:

4-3-3: the formation most used today (goalkeeper, four defenders, three midfielders, three forwards).

4-2-4: an alternative to a 4-3-3 (goalkeeper, four defenders, two midfielders, and four forwards).

Forward   A player whose primary responsibility is to set up and score goals.

Give-and-go   See Wall Pass.

Goal   A goal is scored when the whole of the ball has passed over the goal line inside the posts, provided it has not been thrown, carried, or propelled by hand or arm except in the case of the defending goalkeeper who is within his own penalty area. A defending goalie may

313

step over the goal line while holding the ball but unless the ball was completely over the line, it is not a goal. See also Field of play.

Goal area Indicated by lines marked 6 yards from each goalpost, 6 yards into the field, and joined by a line parallel to the goal line. Actual goal area is 6 x 20 yards. In this area, the goalkeeper cannot be charged if he is jumping or running for the ball. He can be charged, however, if his feet are on the ground and he holds the ball or obstructs an opponent. The goal kick must be made within this area. See also Field of play.

Goalkeeper The last line of defense. The only player allowed to use his hands, and that limited to the penalty area.

Goal kick An indirect free kick taken by the defensive team. The ball is kicked from the front corner of the goal area on the side where the ball was last played by an offensive player and it went over the goal (end) line.

Goal line The boundary lines at the ends of the field (end line).

Halfback See Midfielder.

Half-volley A ball that is kicked the instant after it touches the ground.

Hand or hand ball A violation in which a player intentionally touches the ball with any part of the arms or hands.

Heading A method of scoring, passing, and controlling the ball with the head. The proper use of the head is to make contact with the ball with the forehead. If contact is made beyond the average hairline, it will result in a headache; if contact is made below the forehead, it will cause a black eye, bloody nose, or worse.

Holding Obstructing a player's movement with hands or arms.

Indirect free kick A free kick from which a goal cannot be scored directly by the kicker. The ball must be touched first by another player. This free kick is usually awarded for any technical foul.

Kickoff A soccer game is started, or restarted after a goal has been scored or at the beginning of the second half, by placing the ball, in a stationary position, on the center spot in the middle of the field. The referee signals the start of play by blowing his whistle. The ball is kicked and must make one full revolution in a forward direction, before any player can touch it, and the kicker may not play it a second time until it has been played or touched by another player. On a kickoff, *all* players must be in their own half of the field and opponents can be no closer than 10 yards; hence there is the center circle 10 yards from the center spot. A goal shall not be scored from a kickoff.

Kick to a spot, kick into space Kicking the ball to a logical open or uncovered spot on the field where a teammate expecting the kick can move in to receive the ball.

Lead pass A pass made ahead of the intended receiver so that he can pick up the ball and continue on without reducing his running speed.

Linesmen Two men assigned as assistants to the referee. The referee may choose to ignore the linesmen's signals, or he may consult with the linesmen.

Linkman Usually another name for a midfielder or halfback.

Loft or lob A high, slow kick usually over the heads of the defense.

Loop League.

Loose Free, or unmarked.

Man-to-man marking Covering and guarding a player so closely that it becomes difficult for the opposing player to receive a pass or get into position to receive the ball.

Midfielder A player who is both an offensive and defensive player, whose primary responsibility is to link the forwards and defense and support both.

Obstruct or obstruction To hamper the movement of an opponent by remaining in the path he wishes to travel.

Offside A player is offside if he is nearer his opponents' goal line than the ball, *at the moment the ball is played* to him unless:
1. he is within that part of the field before the 35-yard-line in NASL play (the rest of the world uses the midfield line as the offside line);
2. two of his opponents are nearer to their own goal line than he is;
3. the ball last touched an opponent or was last played by him;
4. he receives the ball directly from a goal kick, a throw-in, or when it was dropped by the referee.

NOTE: a player in an offside position shall not be penalized unless, in the opinion of the referee, he is interfering with the play or an opponent, or is seeking an advantage by being in an offside position. The penalty for an offside violation is an indirect free kick from the point of the violation.

NOTE: The offside infraction shall not be judged at the moment the player in question receives the ball, but at the moment when the ball is passed to him by a member of his own side.

Offside trap A means of making the offense move away from the goal by placing the offense in an offside position. Usually it means the defenders move upfield, drawing the offensive forwards with them so that they cannot get a pass without being offside.

Overlap   The attacking play of a defender going past his team to attack, usually out of the defense.

Overtime   See Tie-breaking.

Penalty arc   The marking outside the penalty area that indicates 10 yards from the penalty spot, for when a penalty kick is taken. The penalty arc is not part of the penalty area.

Penalty area   That portion of the field bounded by lines drawn at right angles to the goal line, 18 yards out from each goal post (total 44 yards) and 18 yards into the playing field. This area has four purposes:

1. If any of the nine offenses calling for the award of a direct kick is committed in this area by a defending player, a penalty kick from the 12-yard spot is awarded instead.
2. This area is where the goalie can handle the ball.
3. It indicates the distance the ball must travel before being touched by a second player when played from a goal kick or a free kick awarded to the defending team within the area.
4. When a penalty kick is being taken, all players except the kicker and the defending goalie must stand outside the penalty area and be 10 yards from the ball. See also Field of play.

Penalty kick   A kick taken from the 12-yard spot in front of the goal in the penalty area. A penalty kick is awarded to the attacking side for any of the nine penalty fouls committed by the defending team. Also called a *spot kick*.

Place kick   A kick at a stationary ball placed on the ground.

Punt   A kick executed by the goalie by dropping it from his hands and kicking it before it hits the ground.

Riding a ball   Also called *cushioning a ball*. A way of reducing the impact of a ball coming at a player and bringing it under control by using the head, the feet, or the body. Accomplished by relaxing the part of the body where the ball hits.

Running off the ball   When a player moves into an open space, ready to receive a pass from a teammate who has the ball, or possibly draw a defender with him in order to leave a gap in the defense.

Save   Stopping a shot on goal; preventing a score executed by the goalkeeper.

Scoring chance   An opportunity to take a shot on goal.

Screen   Obstructing an opponent's view of the ball.

Side   A team.

Sudden death   Playing after regulation time until one team scores a goal.

316

Side line   The boundary line on the long sides of the field. Also called *touch line*.

Skied   A ball kicked unnecessarily high in the air.

Spot kick   See Penalty kick.

Stalemate   When two players face each other, and each waits for the other to make a move.

Stop   Usually a catch or deflection by the goalkeeper, preventing a score. Can also refer to a difficult deflection or elimination of a scoring threat by a defender.

Striker   A center forward position with the major responsibility for scoring goals and maintaining pressure on the defense. The striker usually stays as far upfield as possible without being offside, waiting for passes to be fed to him.

Strong foot   The foot with which a player is most proficient.

Sweeper   A defender whose job is to pick up loose balls coming through the defense and start his team on the offense.

Tackle or tackling   An attempt to kick the ball away from an opponent to make him lose control of it, cause him to hurry a pass, or prevent him from getting a set play in motion.

Throw-in   When the ball goes over the touch (or side) line, either on the ground or in the air, the team last playing the ball before it went out loses control and a player from the other team puts the ball back in play. The player must hold the ball in both hands, face the field of play, and keep part of each foot on or outside the touch line, bringing the ball over the head with both hands. The player making the throw-in may not play the ball again until it has been touched by another player.

Tie-breaking   Both the North American and the American Soccer League have adopted tie-breaking procedures. In the NASL, the teams play a 15-minute sudden-death overtime session. If neither team scores, then each team is awarded five penalty shots to be taken on an alternate basis. The winner is determined by the result of the penalty shooting. If after five shots each, the teams are still deadlocked, then alternate shots are taken until one team converts and one misses. In the ASL, the teams play a 20-minute sudden-death overtime, but if the score is still deadlocked, then the game is considered a draw. In many major international championships, a 30-minute overtime session is played; and no matter how many goals are scored, the entire 30-minute session must be completed. In other tournaments, if the overtime produces no winner, then penalty shooting is started; while in still other tournaments, a replay is ordered.

Touch line   See Side line.

Trap   Bringing a ball, usually a high ball, under complete control.

Volley   Kicking a ball before it touches the ground.

Wall   A defensive move on a free kick from outside the penalty area. The defenders stand in a line in front of the ball, at least 10 yards away, to force the kicker either to chip the ball over their heads or to kick it to the sides. The goalkeeper is in the open portion of the goal. The wall cuts down the angle that the goalie needs to defend against. A member of the attacking team may try to get into the wall and drop to the ground as the ball is kicked in order to create a gap.

Wall pass   A pass to a teammate, followed by a return pass that the first player picks up on the other side of an opponent (also called give-and-go).

Weak foot   The foot with which a player has the least skill.

Wing backs   The defenders playing nearest the side lines.

Wing forwards   The attackers or forwards who position themselves nearest the side lines.

Zone defender   A player who guards a specific area of the field rather than specific opposing players.

Appendix

LAW I.—THE FIELD OF PLAY

(1) **Dimensions.** The field of play shall be rectangular, its length being not more than 130 yards nor less than 100 yards and its breadth not more than 100 yards nor less than 50 yards. (In International Matches the length shall be not more than 120 yards nor less than 110 yards and the breadth not more than 80 yards nor less than 70 yards.) The length shall in all cases exceed the breadth.

(2) **Marking.** The field of play shall be marked with distinctive lines, not more than 5 inches in width, not by a V-shaped rut, in accordance with the plan, the longer boundary lines being called the touch-lines and the shorter the goal-lines. A flag on a post not less than 5 ft. high and having a non-pointed top, shall be placed at each corner; a similar flag-post may be placed opposite the halfway line on each side of the field of play, not less than 1 yard outside the touch-line. A halfway-line shall be marked out across the field of play. The centre of the field of play shall be indicated by a suitable mark and a circle with a 10 yards radius shall be marked around it.

(3) **The Goal-Area.** At each end of the field of play two lines shall be drawn at right-angles to the goal-line, 6 yards from each goal-post. These shall extend into the field of play for a distance of 6 yards and shall be joined by a line drawn parallel with the goal-line. Each of the spaces enclosed by these lines and the goal-line shall be called a goal-area.

(4) **The Penalty-Area.** At each end of the field of play two lines shall be drawn at right-angles to the goal-line, 18 yards from each goal-post. These shall extend into the field of play for a distance of 18 yards and shall be joined by a line drawn parallel with the goal-line. Each of the spaces enclosed by these lines and the goal-line shall be called a penalty-area. A suitable mark shall be made within each penalty-area, 12 yards from the mid-point of the goal-line, measured along an undrawn line at right-angles thereto. These shall be the penalty-kick marks. From each penalty-kick mark an arc of a circle, having a radius of 10 yards, shall be drawn outside the penalty-area.

(5) **The Corner-Area.** From each corner-flag post a quarter circle, having a radius of 1 yard, shall be drawn inside the field of play.

(6) **The Goals.** The goals shall be placed on the centre of each goal-line and shall consist of two upright posts, equidistant from the corner-flags and 8 yards apart (inside measurement), joined by a horizontal cross-bar the lower edge of which shall be 8 ft. from the ground. The width and depth of the goal-posts and the width and depth of the cross-bars shall not exceed 5 inches (12 cm). The goal-posts and the cross-bars shall have the same width.

Nets may be attached to the posts, cross-bars and ground behind the goals.* They should be appropriately supported and be so placed as to allow the goal-keeper ample room.

LAW II.—THE BALL

The ball shall be spherical; the outer casing shall be of leather or other approved materials. No material shall be used in its construction which might prove dangerous to the players.

The circumference of the ball shall not be more than 28 in. and not less than 27 in. The weight of the ball at the start of the game shall not be more than 16 oz. nor less than 14 oz. The pressure shall be equal to one atmosphere, which equals 15 lb./sq. in. ($= 1$ kg/cm^2) at sea level. The ball shall not be changed during the game unless authorized by the Referee.

LAW III.—NUMBER OF PLAYERS

(1) A match shall be played by two teams, each consisting of not more than eleven players, one of whom shall be the goalkeeper.

(2) Substitutes may be used in any match played under the rules of a competition, subject to the following conditions:

  (a) that the authority of the international association(s) or national association(s) concerned, has been obtained,

  (b) that, subject to the restriction contained in the following paragraph (c) the rules of a competition shall state how many, if any, substitutes may be used, and

  (c) that a team shall not be permitted to use more than two substitutes in any match.

---

*Goal nets. The use of nets made of hemp, jute or nylon is permitted. The nylon strings may, however, not be thinner than those made of hemp or jute.

(3) Substitutes may be used in any other match, provided that the two teams concerned reach agreement on a maximum number, not exceeding five, and that the terms of such agreement are intimated to the Referee, before the match. If the Referee is not informed, or if the teams fail to reach agreement, no more than two substitutes shall be permitted.

(4) Any of the other players may change places with the goalkeeper, provided that the Referee is informed before the change is made, and provided also, that the change is made during a stoppage in the game.

(5) When a goalkeeper or any other player is to be replaced by a substitute, the following conditions shall be observed:
- (a) the Referee shall be informed of the proposed substitution, before it is made,
- (b) the substitute shall not enter the field of play until the player he is replacing has left, and then only after having received a signal from the Referee,
- (c) he shall enter the field during a stoppage in the game, and at the half-way line.

Punishment:

(a) Play shall not be stopped for an infringement of paragraph 4. The players concerned shall be cautioned immediately after the ball goes out of play.

(b) For any other infringement of this law, the player concerned shall be cautioned, and if the game is stopped by the Referee, to administer the caution, it shall be re-started by an indirect free-kick, to be taken by a player of the opposing team, from the place where the ball was, when play was stopped.

LAW IV.—PLAYERS' EQUIPMENT

(1) A player shall not wear anything which is dangerous to another player.

(2) Footwear (boots or shoes) must conform to the following standard:
- (a) Bars shall be made of leather or rubber and shall be transverse and flat, not less than half an inch in width and shall extend the total width of the sole and be rounded at the corners.
- (b) Studs which are independently mounted on the sole and are replaceable shall be made of leather, rubber, aluminum, plastic or similar material and shall be solid. With the exception of that part of the stud forming the base, which shall

not protrude from the sole more than one quarter of an inch, studs shall be round in plan and not less than half an inch in diameter. Where studs are tapered, the minimum diameter of any section of the stud must not be less than half an inch. Where metal seating for the screw type is used, this seating must be embedded in the sole of the footwear and any attachment screw shall be part of the stud. Other than the metal seating for the screw type of stud, no metal plates even though covered with leather or rubber shall be worn, neither studs which are threaded to allow them to be screwed on to a base screw that is fixed by nails or otherwise to the soles of footwear, nor studs which, apart from the base, have any form of protruding edge rim or relief marking or ornament, should be allowed.

(c) Studs which are moulded as an integral part of the sole and are not replaceable shall be made of rubber, plastic, polyurethene or similar soft materials. Provided that there are no fewer than ten studs on the sole, they shall have a minimum diameter of three eighths of an inch (10 mm.). In all other respects they shall conform to the general requirement of this Law.

(d) Combined bars and studs may be worn, provided the whole conforms to the general requirements of this Law. Neither bars nor studs on the soles shall project more than three-quarters of an inch. If nails are used they shall be driven in flush with the surface.

(3) The goalkeeper shall wear colors which distinguish him from the other players and from the referee.

Punishment: For any infringement of this Law, the player at fault shall be sent off the field of play to adjust his equipment and he shall not return without first reporting to the Referee, who shall satisfy himself that the player's equipment is in order; the player shall only re-enter the game at a moment when the ball has ceased to be in play.

LAW V.—REFEREES

A Referee shall be appointed to officiate in each game. His authority and the exercise of the powers granted to him by the Laws of the Game commence as soon as he enters the field of play.

His power of penalising shall extend to offences committed when play has been temporarily suspended, or when the ball is out of play. His decision on points of fact connected with the play shall be final, so far as the result of the game is concerned. He shall:

322

(a) Enforce the Laws.

(b) Refrain from penalising in cases where he is satisfied that, by doing so, he would be giving an advantage to the offending team.

(c) Keep a record of the game; act as timekeeper and allow the full or agreed time, adding thereto all time lost through accident or other cause.

(d) Have discretionary power to stop the game for any infringement of the Laws and to suspend or terminate the game whenever, by reason of the elements, interference by spectators, or other cause, he deems such stoppage necessary. In such a case he shall submit a detailed report to the competent authority, within the stipulated time, and in accordance with the provisions set up by the National Association under whose jurisdiction the match was played. Reports will be deemed to be made when received in the ordinary course of post.

(e) From the time he enters the field of play, caution any player guilty of misconduct or ungentlemanly behaviour and, if he persists, suspend him from further participation in the game. In such cases the Referee shall send the name of the offender to the competent authority, within the stipulated time, and in accordance with the provisions set up by the National Association under whose jurisdiction the match was played. Reports will be deemed to be made when received in the ordinary course of post.

(f) Allow no person other than the players and linesmen to enter the field of play without his permission.

(g) Stop the game if, in his opinion, a player has been seriously injured; have the player removed as soon as possible from the field of play, and immediately resume the game. If a player is slightly injured, the game shall not be stopped until the ball has ceased to be in play. A player who is able to go to the touch or goal-line for attention of any kind, shall not be treated on the field of play.

(h) Send off the field of play, any player who, in his opinion, is guilty of violent conduct, serious foul play, or the use of foul or abusive language.

(i) Signal for recommencement of the game after all stoppages.

(j) Decide that the ball provided for a match meets with the requirements of Law II.

LAW VI.—LINESMEN

Two Linesmen shall be appointed, whose duty (subject to the decision of the Referee) shall be to indicate when the ball is out of play and which side is entitled to the corner-kick, goal-kick or throw-in. They shall also assist the Referee to control the game in accordance with the

Laws. In the event of undue interference or improper conduct by a Linesman, the Referee shall dispense with his services and arrange for a substitute to be appointed. (The matter shall be reported by the Referee to the competent authority.) The Linesmen should be equipped with flags by the Club on whose ground the match is played.

LAW VII.—DURATION OF THE GAME

The duration of the game shall be two equal periods of 45 minutes, unless otherwise mutually agreed upon, subject to the following: (a) Allowance shall be made in either period for all time lost through accident or other cause, the amount of which shall be a matter for the discretion of the Referee; (b) Time shall be extended to permit a penalty-kick being taken at or after the expiration of the normal period in either half.

At half-time the interval shall not exceed five minutes except by consent of the Referee.

LAW VIII.—THE START OF PLAY

(a) **At the beginning of the game,** choice of ends and the kick-off shall be decided by the toss of a coin. The team winning the toss shall have the option of choice of ends or the kick-off. The Referee having given a signal, the game shall be started by a player taking a place-kick (i.e., a kick at the ball while it is stationary on the ground in the centre of the field of play) into his opponents' half of the field of play. Every player shall be in his own half of the field and every player of the team opposing that of the kicker shall remain not less than 10 yards from the ball until it is kicked-off; it shall not be deemed in play until it has traveled the distance of its own circumference. The kicker shall not play the ball a second time until it has been touched or played by another player.

(b) **After a goal has scored,** the game shall be restarted in like manner by a player of the team losing the goal.

(c) **After half-time;** when restarting after half-time, ends shall be changed and the kick-off shall be taken by a player of the opposite team to that of the player who started the game.

Punishment. For any infringement of this Law, the kick-off shall be retaken, except in the case of the kicker playing the ball again before it has been touched or played by another player; for this offence, an indirect free-kick shall be taken by a player of the opposing team from the place where the infringement occurred. A goal shall not be scored direct from a kick-off.

(d) **After any other temporary suspension;** when restarting the game after a temporary suspension of play from any cause not mentioned elsewhere in these Laws, provided that immediately prior to the suspension the ball has not passed over the touch or goal-lines, the Referee shall drop the ball at the place where it was when play was suspended and it shall be deemed in play when it has touched the ground; if, however, it goes over the touch or goal-lines after it has been dropped by the Referee, but before it is touched by a player, the Referee shall again drop it. A player shall not play the ball until it has touched the ground. If this section of the Law is not complied with the Referee shall again drop the ball.

LAW IX.—BALL IN AND OUT OF PLAY

The ball is out of play:

(a) When it has wholly crossed the goal-line or touch-line, whether on the ground or in the air.

(b) When the game has been stopped by the Referee.

The ball is in play at all other times from the start of the match to the finish including:

(a) If it rebounds from a goal-post, cross-bar or corner-flag post into the field of play.

(b) If it rebounds off either the Referee or Linesmen when they are in the field of play.

(c) In the event of a supposed infringement of the Laws, until a decision is given.

LAW X.—METHOD OF SCORING

Except as otherwise provided by these Laws, a goal is scored when the whole of the ball has passed over the goal-line, between the goal-posts and under the cross-bar, provided it has not been thrown, carried or intentionally propelled by hand or arm, by a player of the attacking side, except in the case of a goalkeeper, who is within his own penalty-area.

The team scoring the greater number of goals during a game shall be the winner; if no goals, or an equal number of goals are scored, the game shall be termed a "draw."

LAW XI.—OFF-SIDE

A player is off-side if he is nearer his opponents' goal-line than the ball **at the moment the ball is played unless:**

(a) He is in his own half of the field of play.

(b) There are two of his opponents nearer to their own goal-line than he is.

(c) The ball last touched an opponent or was last played by him.

(d) He receives the ball direct from a goal-kick, a corner-kick, a throw-in, or when it was dropped by the Referee.

Punishment. For an infringement of this Law, an indirect free-kick shall be taken by a player of the opposing team from the place where the infringement occurred.

A player in an off-side position shall not be penalised unless, in the opinion of the Referee, he is interfering with the play or with an opponent, or is seeking to gain an advantage by being in an offside position.

LAW XII.—FOULS AND MISCONDUCT

A player who intentionally commits any of the following nine offenses:

(a) Kicks or attempts to kick an opponent;

(b) Trips an opponent, i.e., throwing or attempting to throw him by the use of the legs or by stooping in front of or behind him;

(c) Jumps at an opponent;

(d) Charges an opponent in a violent or dangerous manner;

(e) Charges an opponent from behind unless the latter be obstructing;

(f) Strikes or attempts to strike an opponent;

(g) Holds an opponent;

(h) Pushes an opponent;

(i) Handles the ball, i.e., carries, strikes or propels the ball with his hand or arm. (This does not apply to the goalkeeper within his own penalty-area);

shall be penalised by the award of a **direct free-kick** to be taken by the opposing side from the place where the offense occurred.

Should a player of the defending side intentionally commit one of the above nine offenses within the penalty-area he shall be penalized by a **penalty-kick.**

A penalty-kick can be awarded irrespective of the position of the ball, if in play, at the time an offense within the penalty-area is committed.

A player committing any of the five following offenses:

(1) Playing in a manner considered by the Referee to be dangerous, e.g., attempting to kick the ball while held by the goalkeeper;

(2) Charging fairly, i.e., with the shoulder, when the ball is not within playing distance of the players concerned and they are definitely not trying to play it;

(3) When not playing the ball, intentionally obstructing an opponent, i.e., running between the opponent and the ball, or interposing the body so as to form an obstacle to an opponent;

(4) Charging the goalkeeper except when he
    (a) is holding the ball;
    (b) is obstructing an opponent;
    (c) has passed outside his goal-area;

(5) When playing as goalkeeper,
    (a) takes more than 4 steps whilst holding, bouncing or throwing the ball in the air and catching it again without releasing it so that it is played by another player, or
    (b) indulges in tactics which, in the opinion of the Referee, are designed merely to hold up the game and thus waste time and so give an unfair advantage to his own team

shall be penalised by the award of an **indirect free-kick** to be taken by the opposing side from the place where the infringement occurred.

A player shall be **cautioned** if:

(j) he enters or re-enters the field of play to join or rejoin his team after the game has commenced, or leaves the field of play during the progress of the game (except through accident) without, in either case, first having received a signal from the Referee showing him that he may do so. If the Referee stops the game to administer the caution the game shall be restarted by an indirect free-kick taken by a player of the opposing team from the place where the offending player was when the referee stopped the game. If, however, the offending player has committed a more serious offense he shall be penalized according to that section of the law he infringed;

(k) he persistently infringes the Laws of the Game;

(l) he shows by word or action, dissent from any decision given by the Referee;

(m) he is guilty of ungentlemanly conduct.

For any of these last three offenses, in addition to the caution, an **indirect free-kick** shall also be awarded to the opposing side from the place where the offense occurred unless a more serious infringement of the Laws of the Game was committed.

A player shall be **sent off** the field of play, if:

(n) in the opinion of the Referee he is guilty of violent conduct or serious foul play;

(o) he uses foul or abusive language;

(p) he persists in misconduct after having received a caution.

If play be stopped by reason of a player being ordered from the field for an offense without a separate breach of the Law having been committed, the game shall be resumed by an **indirect free-kick** awarded to the opposing side from the place where the infringement occurred.

LAW XIII.—FREE-KICK

Free-kicks shall be classified under two headings: "Direct" (from which a goal can be scored direct against the offending side), and "Indirect" (from which a goal cannot be scored unless the ball has been played or touched by a player other than the kicker before passing through the goal).

When a player is taking a direct or an indirect free-kick inside his own penalty-area, all of the opposing players shall remain outside the area, and shall be at least ten yards from the ball whilst the kick is being taken. The ball shall be in play immediately after it has traveled the distance of its own circumference and is beyond the penalty-area. The goalkeeper shall not receive the ball into his hands, in order that he may thereafter kick it into play. If the ball is not kicked direct into play, beyond the penalty-area, the kick shall be retaken.

When a player is taking a direct or an indirect free-kick outside his own penalty-area, all of the opposing players shall be at least ten yards from the ball, until it is in play, unless they are standing on their own goal-line, between the goal-posts. The ball shall be in play when it has traveled the distance of its own circumference.

If a player of the opposing side encroaches into the penalty-area, or within ten yards of the ball, as the case may be, before a free-kick is taken, the Referee shall delay the taking of the kick, until the Law is complied with.

The ball must be stationary when a free-kick is taken, and the kicker shall not play the ball a second time, until it has been touched or played by another player.

Punishment. If the kicker, after taking the free-kick, plays the ball a second time before it has been touched or played by another player an indirect free-kick shall be taken by a player of the opposing team from the spot where the infringement occurred.

LAW XIV.—PENALTY-KICK

A penalty-kick shall be taken from the penalty-mark and, when it is being taken, all players with the exception of the player taking the kick, and the opposing goalkeeper, shall be within the field of play but outside the penalty-area, and at least 10 yards from the penalty-mark. The opposing goalkeeper must stand (without moving his feet) on his own goal-line, between the goal-posts, until the ball is kicked. The player taking the kick must kick the ball forward; he shall not play the ball a second time until it has been touched or played by another player. The ball shall be deemed in play directly after it is kicked, i.e., when it has traveled the distance of its circumference, and a goal may be scored direct from such a penalty-kick. If the ball touches the goalkeeper before passing between the posts, when a penalty-kick is being taken at or after the expiration of half-time or full-time, it does not nullify a goal. If necessary, time of play shall be extended at half-time or full-time to allow a penalty-kick to be taken.

Punishment: For any infringement of this Law:

(a) by the defending team, the kick shall be retaken if a goal has not resulted.

(b) by the attacking team other than by the player taking the kick, if a goal is scored it shall be disallowed and the kick retaken.

(c) by the player taking the penalty-kick, committed after the ball is in play, a player of the opposing team shall take an indirect free-kick from the spot where the infringement occurred.

LAW XV.—THROW-IN

When the whole of the ball passes over a touch-line, either on the ground or in the air, it shall be thrown in from the point where it crossed the line, in any direction, by a player of the team opposite to that of the player who last touched it. The thrower at the moment of delivering the ball must face the field of play and part of each foot shall be either on the touch-line or on the ground outside the touch-line. The thrower shall use both hands and shall deliver the ball from behind and over his head. The ball shall be in play immediately after it enters the field of play, but the thrower shall not again play the ball until it has been touched or played by another player. A goal shall not be scored direct from a throw-in.

Punishment:

(a) If the ball is improperly thrown in the throw-in shall be taken by a player of the opposing team.

(b) If the thrower plays the ball a second time before it has been touched or played by another player, an indirect free-kick shall be taken by a player of the opposing team from the place where the infringement occurred.

LAW XVI.—GOAL-KICK

When the whole of the ball passes over the goal-line excluding that portion between the goal-posts, either in the air or on the ground, having last been played by one of the attacking team, it shall be kicked direct into play beyond the penalty-area from a point within that half of the goal-area nearest to where it crossed the line, by a player of the defending team. A goalkeeper shall not receive the ball into his hands from a goal-kick in order that he may thereafter kick it into play. If the ball is not kicked beyond the penalty-area, i.e., direct into play, the kick shall be retaken. The kicker shall not play the ball a second time until it has touched — or been played by — another player. A goal shall not be scored direct from such a kick. Players of the team opposing that of the player taking the goal-kick shall remain outside the penalty-area whilst the kick is being taken.

Punishment: If a player taking a goal-kick plays the ball a second time after it has passed beyond the penalty-area, but before it has touched or been played by another player, an indirect free-kick shall be awarded to the opposing team, to be taken from the place where the infringement occurred.

LAW XVII.—CORNER-KICK

When the whole of the ball passes over the goal-line, excluding that portion between the goal-posts, either in the air or on the ground, having last been played by one of the defending team, a member of the attacking team shall take a corner-kick, i.e., the whole of the ball shall be placed within the quarter circle at the nearest corner-flagpost, which must not be moved, and it shall be kicked from that position. A goal may be scored direct from such a kick. Players of the team opposing that of the player taking the corner-kick shall not approach within 10 yards of the ball until it is in play, i.e., it has traveled the distance of its own circumference, nor shall the kicker play the ball a second time until it has been touched or played by another player.

Punishment:

(a) If the player who takes the kick plays the ball a second time before it has been touched or played by another player, the Referee shall award an indirect free-kick to the opposing team, to be taken from the place where the infringement occurred.

(b) For any other infringement the kick shall be retaken.

Index